T0299026

An Introduction To English Literature

Dr. Safi Mahfouz

2010

The Deposit Number at The National Library (2009/6/2612)
     Safi , Mahfkouz
     An Introduction To English Literature / Safi Mahfkouz .
     Amman : Dar Wael , 2009 .
(428) p
Deposit No. : (2009/6/2612)
Descriptors : English Literature / English Language

* تم إعداد بيانات الفهرسة والتصنيف الأولية من قبل دائرة المكتبة الوطنية

****

رقم التصنيف العشري / ديوي : 820
ISBN 978-9957-11-824-2 (ردمك)

An Introduction To English Literature
Dr. Safi Mahfouz

الطبعــة الأولى 2010
جميع الحقوق محفوظة للناشر

دار وائــل للنشر والتوزيع

* الأردن - عمان - شارع الجمعية العلمية الملكية - مبنى الجامعة الاردنية الاستثماري رقم (2) الطابق الثاني
الجبيهة)- هـاتف : 5338410-6-00962 - فاكس : 5331661-6-00962 - ص. ب (1615
* الأردن - عمان - وسط البـلد - مجمع الفحيص التجـاري- هـاتف: 4627627-6-00962
www.darwael.com
E-Mail: Wael@Darwael.Com

Dedication

To my wife, Nadia and my three sons

Nezar, Basil, and Rayan

Contents

Part I. Fiction

Part II. Drama

Part III. Poetry

Part One
Fiction

Fiction is an imaginative narrative literary genre; one of the four basic rhetorical modes : poetry, drama, fiction and nonfiction. Fiction covers a wide range of literary forms including novels, novelettes, short stories, fables, folk tales and fairy tales. Nowadays, new technologies have created a new genre of fiction; digital fiction which includes movies, televised novels, short stories, T.V series, video games, computer animated cartoons and animation pictures. The term fiction has been broadened to include all books and media that tell a story. Unlike nonfiction, fiction tells the stories of fictional characters who live in imaginary situations in imaginary or real places. Like all the other basic rhetorical modes, fiction is used to delight and instruct. All types of fiction: popular or literary fiction, book fiction or digital fiction roughly have the same elements. The elements of fiction include plot, character, point of view, setting, theme, suspense, symbol, irony allegory, emotion, humour and fantasy.

Fiction is generally classified into two broad categories: escape literature and interpretive literature. Escape literature is written primarily for entertainment and enjoyment. Such type of literature is intended to help readers enjoy their leisure time doing a purposeful activity. Literature of interpretation is intended to help us understand life better. It gives us an insight into life, human nature and human experience. However, the distinction between the two types of literature is not clear-cut; the most serious interpretative literature can delight as well as instruct its readers, and escape literature might also be purposeful and insightful. However, once escape fiction begins to illuminate some aspect of human existence, it becomes interpretive and once interpretive fiction begins to delight its readers, it becomes escape fiction. In fact, no work of literature is solely interpretative nor is any work is entirely escape. Most literary works exhibit characteristics of both types.

Every type of fiction has its own readers. Readers of escape fiction are usually immature readers who read fiction only of entertainment. Such immature readers concentrate on the events of the story and the plot summary trying to abstract a theme or a moral from the story they are reading. Whereas, mature readers read interpretive fiction to sharpen their awareness of life and human existence. Such mature readers read fiction both for entertainment and to obtain a better understanding of life and the human condition.

The Elements of Fiction
Chapter One
Plot

Plot is the sequence of related incidents or events in a story. **Plot** includes what all the characters in a story do, say and even think. However, although the plot includes what major characters say or do, it leaves out description, analysis and minor or trivial events and instead concentrates only on major happenings. For beginning readers, plot is the easiest element of fiction to understand and analyze and they equate it with the content of the literary work. Therefore, the plot for such readers is what a story is all about. These immature readers read literary works chiefly for plot and fail to go deeply into the text to analyze what it says about life and human nature. Mature readers on the other hand, use the plot of a story to understand what it says about human life. Such readers consider plot as a means towards an end. For such insightful readers, the plot is merely a means for understanding life and the human nature better.

Conflict is a clash of actions, desires, ideas, or goals in the plot of a story. Conflicts in fiction can either be external or internal. **External conflict** may exist between the main character in the story whom we consider as the hero or protagonist and some other person or persons (man against man); or between the main character and some external force mainly nature, society or malignant fate (man against environment). **Internal conflict** exists within the main character's psyche. It is a conflict between the main character and some destructive element in his own nature (man against himself). Conflict maybe physical, mental, emotional or moral.

The protagonist is the central character in the story. He can be either sympathetic or unsympathetic. The protagonist is the main character in a story whom we follow with interest and share his dreams, ambitions, fears and we even share his conflicts and the way he struggles to deal with them. **The antagonist** is any force in a story that is in conflict with the protagonist. An antagonist maybe another wicked person or it maybe the whole society. The antagonist can also be any aspect of the physical or social environment, or even a destructive element in the protagonist's own nature. All the forces arrayed against the protagonist whether persons, things, conventions of society or even traits of his own character such as anger, rash or excessive ambition and pride all can act as antagonists.

Simple Conflict and Multiple Conflict:
A simple conflict is single conflict that can be identified easily even by immature readers. The protagonist is in conflict with one antagonist at a time. However, the protagonist may be in conflict with one person or he might be in conflict with the society where he lives or he might be in conflict with environment and fate or he might be in conflict with a destructive flaw in his psyche which he seems unable to control or live with. **A multiple conflict** is a multilayered and complex conflict in which the protagonist finds himself in conflict with other many people, with society or nature, and with himself, all at the same time. Sometimes he is aware of these conflicts, but in most cases he seems to be ignorant and unaware of them.

Conflict in Great Fiction and Commercial Fiction:
Commercial fiction, however, emphasizes the conflict between man and man relying too heavily on physical conflict to provide readers with excitement. Conflict in commercial fiction takes the form of the customary conflict between good and evil or to put it plainly enough between good men and bad men. It is a conflict between morals and values; between good values respected by society and bad values which society consider as corrupt. In commercial fiction the conflict is usually clearly defined as a conflict between the hero and the villain. Whereas, great fiction makes use of all the above-mentioned types of conflict.

Suspense is a quality of a literary work that makes the reader eager to know what happens next and how it will end. This quality of a story impels readers to go on reading it to know what happens next and how things will turn out at the end. Suspense becomes quite interesting when the readers' curiosity is combined with anxiety about the fate of the central character whom they find sympathetic. Suspense is often linked with certain types of fiction that rely heavily on such an element of fiction mainly murder mysteries or detective stories in which the reader goes on reading the story to find out who committed the crime. In love stories suspense is created by the question "Will the hero marry the girl?"; "What will happen to the two lovers at the end of the story?"; "Will the lovers be reunited and how?". In great fiction suspense often raises the question "How can the hero's behaviour be explained in terms of human personality and character?". The two most common devices used to create suspense in fiction are introducing the element of **mystery** (ambiguous situations for which readers strive to find an explanation) or to place the central character in a dilemma or a serious conflict in which he must choose between two undesirable courses of action.

For immature readers suspense is the second quality that makes a good story after the conflict. Suspense is a very important element in a story and it is the element that makes readers eager to read the story to the end without losing interest. However, suspense created artificially in a story merely by simply withholding vital information from the readers makes the story artificial and makes readers less interested in what will happen next. However, ordinary suspense makes the readers eager to know what will happen next without losing interest in reading the story. This normal suspense is what makes a good story.

Surprise is an unexpected turn in the development of the plot of a story. Surprise is a very important element of fiction closely related to suspense. If readers know in advance what will happen in a story and how it will happen, then there will be no suspense. As long as readers do not know what will happen next in a story and how it will happen, whatever happens next comes with an element of surprise. Surprise becomes radical and shocking when what happens next in a story departs radically from the readers' expectations. **Surprise ending** is a completely unexpected revelation or turn of plot at the end of a story or a play. When the ending of story or a play departs radically from the readers' expectations with its shocking unexpected ending, it is said that such story has a surprise ending. Like suspense, surprise ending should be smoothly included in a story without shocking the readers. Moreover, surprise ending should not be an end in itself, but should be a means by which the writer finishes the story. Commercial fiction makes use of artificial surprise endings by withholding important information from the readers. Whereas, in great fiction surprise ending is perfectly logical and natural. As readers look back over the story, they will find that the surprise ending of the story is logical and interesting.

Stories and plays either have **happy endings or unhappy endings**. **A happy ending** is an ending in which events turn out well for the sympathetic protagonist at the end of a story or a play. In a story with a happy ending the central character whom readers like and admire fulfills his dreams, achieves his goals and solves all his problems. In a story with a happy ending, the protagonist defeats the villain and good triumphs over evil. An **unhappy ending**, on the other hand, is an ending in which events turn out unhappily for the sympathetic protagonist at the end of a story or a play. In stories with unhappy endings, the protagonist dies at the end of the story or loses his mistress or something bad happens to him.

Several writers prefer unhappy endings to happy ones for two reasons: **First**, many situations in real life have unhappy endings, therefore if fiction is to portray life as it is , it must present the two extremes of life sadness and defeat triumph and happiness. In real life success and happiness are less frequent than failure and unhappiness. Although our life is a combination of the two extremes of life; unhappiness and happiness, we experience the former more than the latter. To put it in metaphorical English, we drink more from the cup of sadness than we drink from the cup of joy. In real life we experience failure and happiness frequently, while we experience moments of happiness occasionally. **Second**, writers prefer unhappy endings because they know that they make readers ponder and contemplate life. In stories with happy endings, readers are satisfied with the world and stop thinking about the story they have read. Consequently, they feel that they do not need to ponder life. Whereas, in the case of stories with sad or unhappy endings, the readers are left with unanswered questions about the human nature and life, and therefore, they start brooding over life and the human nature, they might even think about the story in their minds to get a thorough understanding of its major themes. Some stories have indeterminate endings. An **indeterminate ending** is an ending in which the central problem or conflict is left unresolved. In stories with indeterminate endings the problems the protagonist faces remain unresolved and his conflict with the antagonist continues even at the end of the story. In real life some of our problems remain unresolved. We pass a way leaving behind us incomplete projects and unfinished stories. Such stories with indeterminate endings are left open for readers to brood over them and think of possible endings for them.

Artistic unity is very essential for a good plot. For a story to have a good plot, irrelevant material that does not contribute to the total meaning of the story should not be included in the story. Good story writers do not include in their stories any material that does not advance the central theme and intention of the story. The incidents in a story should be positioned in the most effective order which is not necessarily the chronological order. However, even the incidents which are not narrated in a chronological order as a result of using the stream of conciseness technique of narration should make a logical development once they are rearranged chronologically. In a story with artistic unity, each incident in the story's plot sprouts out of the preceding one in time and leads logically to the next. All the incidents comprising the plot in a story are linked together in a series of cause and effect.

Story writers who give their stories a turn of events so suddenly at a certain point in the story unjustified by the characters' actions and the situation they are placed in are guilty of **plot manipulation**. Any action inserted unexpectedly and unnecessarily in the story's plot causes plot manipulation. Story writers who rely too heavily on chance or coincidence to solve the protagonist's problems all of a sudden are convicted with plot manipulation. This kind of unexpected coincidental resolution is known as "**dues ex machina**". This is a Greek theatrical term which literally means "god from machine". Greek dramatists used this theatrical device in which a god descends from heaven at the last possible minute in the theatre by means of a stage machine to save the protagonist from an impossible dangerous situation.

Stages of Plot:
We can trace the development of plot in a story throughout its three stages: the rising action, the falling action and the climax. **The falling action** is that part of the plot that comes between the climax and the conclusion. **The rising action** is the development of plot in a story that proceeds and leads up to the climax. **The climax** is the highest point in a plot of a story that leads up to the resolution of the plot. The climax is the moment in a play, novel, or short story at which the crisis reaches its point of greatest intensity and is thereafter resolved. For readers and audiences in the theatre the climax constitutes the peak of emotional response and usually the turning point in the action.

Denouement is a French word which means "unknotting" of the plot in a story, novel or play. "*Denouement* is usually the result of a complex situation or sequence of events that finally end with the resolution that usually occurs near the final stages of the plot. It is the point at which all information withheld from the reader or spectator in the theatre is revealed. Moreover, at this point of the literary work all the work's complications come to an end. The Denouement comes immediately once the climax is over and after all the conflicts have been resolved shortly before the conclusion of the work of literature.

Chapter Two
The Elements of Fiction
Character

Character and plot are inseparable. Immature readers read for plot more than they read for character, while discriminating mature readers read stories for both plot and character. While the former are merely interested in what the characters do, the latter have interest in characters themselves. Reading stories for character is much more difficult than reading them for merely understanding the plot. Characters are much more complex, unpredictable and ambiguous than plot in nearly most stories. Any reader no matter how immature he or she is can retell a story and say what a story is all about, but only discriminating readers with literary appreciation can only analyze characters' personalities, motives and subjective lives.

Unlike interpretive fiction which emphasizes character more than plot and presents complex characters, escape fiction emphasizes plot and portrays characters that are simple and easy to identify and understand. Immature readers who prefer reading escape fiction to reading interpretive fiction also prefer attractive characters. Such readers enjoy reading stories in which the main character is attractive, decent, good- hearted and handsome. Readers often identify with the main character in a story; they share him his dreams, ambitions, fears and all his escapes, defeats and triumphs. Readers even overlook the hero's inadequacies and faults and keep an eye on his virtuous and noble qualities. Interpretive fiction does not reject the depiction of gorgeous and smart central characters. It simply presents a variety of central characters who are far from being totally bad or totally good. Since human nature is not entirely bad nor is it entirely good, but rather a combination of the two, interpretive fiction presents characters of neither type.

Fiction helps us understand the human nature better. Fiction acquaints us with different kinds of people; how they think, feel and behave in times of trouble as well as in times of happiness. The fictitious characters we live with while reading stories, novels and plays are quite similar to people we know in real life. The reason why we understand fictitious characters more than we understand people in real life is the way story writers and novelists depict such fictitious characters. Writers depict both external and internal reality. They depict the subjective experiences of the characters they create to make readers and spectators understand the way such fictional characters think and feel. In real life we rarely have such an opportunity. This makes us know fictional characters more than we know people in real life. In real life we do not know how real people think and feel unless they themselves are willing to speak their minds and express how they feel. However, the disclosure of their thoughts and feelings might be true or false for appearances are some times deceptive and misleading. This is not the case in fiction, since we know exactly how the fictional characters feel and think. By knowing fictional characters who are duplicates of people in real life, we understand people in real life better than we otherwise could.

Methods of Character Presentation in Fiction:

Novelists and short story writers present their fictional characters either directly or indirectly. Sometimes they use the two methods of presentation simultaneously to portray their central characters more vividly and to reveal their subjective lives in such a way to make readers see for themselves what goes in the minds and hearts of such fictional people. The direct method of character presentation is more simple, more economical and clearer than the indirect method of presentation though it is less artistic and less exciting. Using only direct presentation would make a story dull, monotonous and emotionally unconvincing. Thus, a judicious combination of the two methods of presentation makes a story more artistic and more interesting.

In **direct presentation** or **characterization** the story writer tells us directly and straight out either by revelation and exposition or by analysis what the characters are like, or he might make another character in the story tell us what they are like. Through this method of presentation the story writer not only tells us directly what the central characters look like and how they behave, but he also reveals to us quite directly how they feel and think. In **indirect presentation** or **characterization** the story writer shows us the characters in action; we infer what these fictional characters are like from what they do and say. Their behaviour reveals their personalities.

Dramatization of Characters:

Dramatization is the presentation of character; his feelings and thoughts merely through speech and action rather than through exposition, analysis, or description by the writer. A story becomes more artistic and interesting when characters are **dramatized**- shown speaking and acting for themselves, as in a play. Readers will not be convinced that a certain character is greedy until they see him behave in such a way that shows his greediness. Great writers rely entirely on indirect presentation in portraying their characters and use direct presentation occasionally.

In "The Destructors" Graham Greene uses both indirect and direct methods of presentation in presenting all the characters in the story including the kids in the gang and Old Misery though he relies more on the former than on the latter in his depiction of the characters. For example, the short story writer uses direct presentation when he tells us about Blackie: "He was just, he had no jealousy." While he uses indirect presentation to delineate the conflict between him and Trevor over who will be the leader of the gang mainly when Blackie allows the gang to vote on Trevor's new plan to destroy Old Misery's two hundred- year old shaky house .Blackie's character is also delineated indirectly when he calmly accepts to give up the leadership of the gang and follows Trevor just like the other kids. He even obeys Trevor's orders without any sign of disobedience or resentment.

Characterization in fiction should meet these three conditions. Firstly, fictional characters should be **consistent** in their behaviour: they are not supposed to behave in one way on one occasion and behave in a drastically different way on another unless this drastic change is justified. Second, fictional characters should be clearly **motivated** in whatever they do and say, particularly, when they behave in a drastically different way. Readers must understand why they behave in such a different way. Third, fictional characters should be **plausible** or lifelike. They should neither be portrayed as angles nor as devils, but should rather be portrayed as real people. Nor should such fictional characters have any improbable contradictory traits. Characters in fiction should be fully portrayed to justify their roles and make them convincing and plausible.

Fictional characters are of different types. In terms of their development, fictional characters are either flat or round. **Flat characters** are characters who are characterized by one or two traits which can be summed up in a sentence. **Round characters** are characters with complex and many-sided traits. Minor characters are always flat characters and are likely to remain so till the end of the story. Major and central characters are often round characters and are likely to remain so till the end of the story.

A **stock character** is a special kind of flat character. A stock character is a stereotyped figure who has appeared so often in a large number of stories that his character is well known and fully understood by all readers. The brilliant detective with bizarre and eccentric habits i.e. Sherlock Holmes, the handsome international spy of mysterious background, the smart courageous hero, the seductive coquettish woman , the comic English man with a monocle and an exaggerated oxford accent and the sinister wicked villain who wants to destroy the hero; all these characters are stock characters who are quite recognizable to all readers because they have read about or have seen such prototypes in various previous works of literature.

Fictional characters can also be classified as static or developing. The **static character** is the same sort of person at the end of the story as at the beginning. A static character does not change throughout the course of action. A **developing or dynamic character** is a character who undergoes a drastic and permanent change in some aspect of personality or outlook. The change might be slight or major; it may be a change for better or for worse, but it is a significant change noticeable to all readers. There are more static characters in fiction than developing characters. People in real life do not usually change drastically and fiction is supposed to be a mirror of society in this respect. To be convincing to readers the change that occurs within a developing or dynamic character should be sensible and should meet these conditions. First, the change should be within the possibilities of the character who makes it. Second, the change should be sufficiently motivated by the circumstances in which the character is placed. Third, the change must be given sufficient time to take place. A **foil character** is a minor character whose situation or actions parallel those of a major character, and thus by contrast illuminates the major character.

Chapter Three
The Elements of Fiction
Theme

The theme is simply the central idea in a literary work. The theme in a work of fiction is its dominant idea and central insight. The theme represents the writer's perception of life and human nature. It can be stated explicitly by the writer in his capacity as the narrator or through a major character in the story. It can also be implied throughout the work. More often themes are implied rather than being stated explicitly by the writer or one of the characters in the story. For readers to abstract the theme of a literary work, they must ask themselves these questions: what is the central idea in the story? What view of life does it hold? What insight into life and the human experience does it try to reveal?

Not ever story has a theme. Some stories have themes others do not. For instance, the purpose of a horror story is to scare readers; the purpose of an adventure story is to take readers to wonder lands and to carry readers through a series of escapades with the hero of the story, the purpose of a murder story is to show how create suspense and mysteries and to show how clever detectives are in solving them, and the purpose of comic stories is simply to make readers laugh. It is apparent that these kinds of works of fiction do not have a theme.

Fiction writers shed light on some major themes in their works of literature for two reasons: First, to record human experience and to stress some truth about human life and the human condition. Second, to introduce a theory of life that acts as a unifying element in the text of the story. The theme in a literary work is universal and can be generalized to include all human beings. Although a writer may be American, French, Russian, Chinese or any other nationality, the theme of his work is applicable to people in general no matter where they live. The theme of a story no matter how long or short it is can generally be summed up in one single statement. Although some literary works seem to have more than one single theme and seem to readers that they have multiple themes with complex insights into life, such stories still have one broad theme that can be summed up in a single abstracted statement. Such subthemes are still related to the main theme no matter how multiple they might seem.

Theme and Moral:
Some beginning readers mistakenly use the two terms theme and moral interchangeably. When they read a certain literary work, they search for the moral in the story – some rule of conduct they believe is applicable to their lives. Sometimes the two literary terms are interchangeable, however, in many cases they are not. Sometimes the theme of a story may be stated as a moral principle without violating the maxims of story telling. However, in many cases the term moral is too narrow to play the role of theme in a great story. Therefore, the terms message, lesson and even moral should be avoided when extracting the work's central idea and insight and the term theme should be used. Theme must not be used as an equivalent to other terms such as moral , lesson or message simply because it is not the intention of any writer to preach , but rather to instruct and please readers and present to them life and human nature undisguised. The purpose of writing stories is too make us appreciate the pleasure of reading and to give us a better awareness and greater understanding of human life and human experience.

Themes stressed in major fiction are not necessarily new. Themes might be conventional but dressed in new robes. However, some writers occasionally come up with new themes never tackled before in previous works of fiction. The themes " War is horrible" ; "Motherhood is sacred" ; "Hypocrisy is a social disease that must be combated" ; "True love always wins through" ; "Virtue and hard work are rewarded at the end" are universal traditional themes though they can be refreshed and stated differently in new and fresh works of fiction.

The ability to abstract a theme from a literary work and to state it in a single simple sentence that expresses the writer's insight into life and human experience is a literary skill which readers must master if they want to appreciate and read such literary works with enjoyment. Abstracting the story's theme and stating it nicely in a single sentence is evidence of the reader's understanding of the literary work. Beginning readers understand what a story is about simply because they exert tremendous effort to understand the events, but fail to understand the theme.

The central conflict in a story always says something about its theme. The title might also provide some clue. In discovering the theme of a story, readers should keep in mind the following principles:

1-The theme abstracted from a story should be a single statement consisting of a subject and a predicate. The subject alone does not constitute a theme. For instance, loyalty and hypocrisy are not themes but are simply subjects. In order for such subjects to become themes predicates need to be added to them since a theme must be a statement about a subject. For instance "Loyalty to one's country inspires self-sacrifice" and "Hypocrisy is a social evil that must be combated" are perfectly worded themes because each of them has a subject and a predicate.

2-The theme must be stated as a *generalization* about life, human nature and the human condition and human experience. Therefore, we should not include in a theme the names of specific people, locations, places or events. A theme must be general to include all humans regardless of their race, colour, religion or nationality. For instance, the theme of Graham Greene's "The Destructors" can not be stated as follows "A London gang of youngsters, in the aftermath of World War II, found a creative outlet in destroying a two hundred -year old shaky house designed by the famous architect Sir Christopher Wren". Rather, the story's theme must be more general to be applicable to all cultures and to all human beings no matter where they live. The theme therefore, must be something like this: "The destruction caused by a devastating war may produce among the young a conscious or unconscious rebellion against the values of society and its artistic enterprises"

3- Readers should not make the theme's generalization larger than justified by the terms of the story. Therefore, terms which are too general like all, every, always should be used cautiously and other terms such as some, sometimes or may might be used to replace them.

4-The theme is the central and unifying idea of a story. Therefore, it must be as comprehensive as possible to account for all the details of the story.

5-The theme of a story must not stand in contradiction with any detail in the story.

6-The theme must exist inside the story not outside. The theme must not rely on supposed facts that are not stated or implied clearly in the story.

7- There is no one perfect way of stating a theme. Different critics and readers may state the very same theme of a story in different ways. However, though the way a theme is stated and worded is different, the content must be the same.

8- Readers should not oversimplify the theme of a story by reducing it to a common saying or cliché that we have heard of all our lives, such as "Honesty is the best policy", or "A bird in the hand is worth two in the bush". Thus, it would be unfair to reduce the theme of Graham Greene's "The Destructors" into the common saying "When the cat is away the mice play", though it applies to the story perfectly well.

Chapter Four
The Elements of Fiction
Point of View

Point of view is the angle of vision from which a story is told. In fiction point of view or who tells the story is the related experience of the narrator rather than that of the writer. Writers rarely pop into the fictional world they create in their stories though authorial voice in some stories can be discerned especially when part of the author's autobiographical details are included in his or her story. Thus, stories whether short stories or novels encourage the reader to identify with the narrator rather than the writer. For readers to determine what point of view is used in a work of fiction, they should ask: "Who tells the story?" and "How much is this person allowed to know?" and "To what extent does the narrator have access to probe the characters' train of thoughts and feelings and thus report them to the reader?". Literary critics have discerned four major points of view in fiction: Omniscient point of view, Limited Omniscient point of view, First Person point of view and the Objective or Dramatic point of view.

In **the Omniscient point of view** the story is told by the author, using the third person singular he, she and they. In this kind of narration technique the writer's knowledge is omniscient and unlimited for he unquestionably knows and controls all the fictional characters' speech and actions, peers inside their minds and hearts thus he is knowledgeable of their feelings and train of thoughts. The omniscient narrator can shift focus from one character to another popping into their hearts and minds, commenting on their feelings, probing their thoughts and putting them in full display before readers though no single character in the story would be aware of this.

Stories that employ the Omniscient point of view differ significantly in terms of the amount of omniscience given to the narrator. For instance, in Graham Greene's " The Destructors" readers are allowed to peer inside the minds of Blackie, Mike, Old Misery and even the lorry driver, but are not given the chance to probe Trevor's thoughts and feelings though he is the protagonist of the story. The Omniscient point of view is the most flexible narration technique since it gives both the writer and the reader the widest scope for interpretation though it is also the most subject to criticism. The narrator may constantly interfere between the reader and the story. In addition, the continual shifting of the point of view from one character to another may cause a break down in the artistic unity of the story.

In the **Limited Omniscient point of view** the narrator, using the third person singular, associates himself with only one character in the story usually a major character though a minor character can also be used to achieve the purpose. This viewpoint character acts as the author's spokesperson or mouthpiece and the narrator looks at the events of the story through his eyes and his mind. The writer knows every thing about this character may be more than the character knows about himself. This kind of narration technique is limited omniscient in the sense that the writer can only report to the reader how the viewpoint character thinks and feels, but can tell them nothing about the other characters' feelings and thoughts. This characteristic makes it approximate more closely to real life than the Omniscient point of view. This narration technique is also called the "over the shoulder" perspective because it gives the writer the opportunity to stay present in the story until the end. Following and tracing the viewpoint character which is usually the protagonist allows in-depth revelation of his personality.

In the **First Person point of view** the writer, using the first person "I", narrates the story by identifying himself with a major or minor character in the story. In this narration technique, which is extremely subjective, the narrator uses the interior monologue to express the stream of consciousness and feelings of this selected character. In such a highly subjective narration technique, the narrator seems unreliable since readers are not sure whether this narrator is telling them the truth or telling lies. However, this subjective narrative technique can be best used in autobiography in which the narrator is most reliable when it comes to narrating his real past experiences or memoirs. This narration technique is also characterized by its ability to create a kind of intimacy between the storyteller and the reader by using the first person mainly because the narrator is also a character in the story. This narration technique offers readers a kind of immediacy and reality since we are told the story by a participant in the story, with the author as intermediary being eliminated. It also denies the author the opportunity to comment on the action of the story and the characters' behaviour .

In the **Objective or Dramatic point of view,** which stands in contradiction to the Unlimited Omniscient narration technique, no traces of authorial voice or narrators are left in the story. The writer engineers the plot of the story through dramatization leaving no room for authorial voice or the narrator's presence. In this kind of point of view narration completely disappears and characters are dramatized. Readers read the characters' dialogues without having any access to what goes inside their minds and hearts. This narration technique vividly displays authorial objectivity in the form of a roving sound camera. The camera takes snap shots of different locations and different characters recording only what is seen and heard. The camera can not peer inside the characters' hearts and minds and therefore can not interpret their actions and feelings. The reader is regarded here as a spectator in a cinema or a theatre. He must therefore interpret the characters' motivations and infer their feelings and thoughts. This narration technique which relies merely on dialogue and external action leaves no room for authorial voice or interpretation. Discerning what point of view is employed in a story helps the reader both understand and evaluate the story effectively and accurately.

Chapter Five
The Elements of Fiction
Symbol and Irony

Great fiction writers are always in favour of compression. **Compression** in fiction means saying as much as possible as briefly as possible. Every word jotted down in a story must be carefully chosen for maximum effectiveness on advancing the plot and revelation of character. Writers include in their stories only details that contribute to achieving the central purpose of the story. Compression in fiction can be achieved through using a variety of figures of speech mainly symbol and irony. **Symbol** is a figure of speech which means more than what it is. It has layers of meanings. Literary symbol may be used both literally and figuratively. In literature an object, a person or a name of a person, an action or even a whole situation can be used as literary symbol in the story that has both a literal meaning and another or other suggestive meanings.

In Graham Greene's "The Destructors" name symbolism permeates the entire story for most of the names in the story are used symbolically. The name of the gang "Wormsley Common Gang" which consists of a group of naughty kids is used symbolically to reflect the way the kids destroy Old Misery's two hundred-year old house. To pull down the house the kids destroy it from inside in the same way a worm eats up an apple from inside. The word common also represents the common people or lower middle class from which all the kids with the exception of Trevor come from. The name of Trevor, the new leader of the gang who put forward the destruction plan and urged the kids to accomplish it, is used symbolically. Throughout the entire story the kids call him "T" instead of his full name Trevor. It is obvious that letter T which takes the shape of a hammer is used symbolically to represent the idea of destroying and hammering. Old Misery's name symbolically reflects his desperate situation. He is a lonely old, stingy bachelor living in misery. His misery becomes worse when he is locked in his outside lavatory by the kids until they have finished destroying his house.

In addition to name symbolism, objects, items, actions and situations can be used symbolically. The success of a writer in employing symbols stems from his ability to make the symbols fit so naturally into the literal context of the story to the extent that their symbolic interpretation might only be apparent to perceptive readers. George Orwell's fable *Animal Farm* is a good representation of this success. The novel is readable with enjoyment literally and symbolically. Readers of this novel would find it interesting to read even if they have no idea what the story represents in the real world. Symbols in such a novel not only reinforce its meaning, but also help achieve the central purpose of the story.

Recognizing literary symbols in a story and interpreting them accurately in light of the context and setting of the story requires an excellent literary experience and perception on the part of the reader. This skill of recognizing and interpreting literary symbols in a text is of paramount importance for readers to fully understand and enjoy literary texts. Beginning readers with little literary experience should always bear in mind the fact that most stories even the highly symbolical ones operate almost wholly on the literal level and should be read as thus. Discovering symbols that do not exist in the story misleads rather than assists the reader in grasping its meaning. Nonetheless, recognizing and interpreting symbols is quite essential for thorough understanding of works of literature.

Here are some tips for identifying literary symbols in fiction that must be taken into account by beginning readers: First, the story itself must exhibit some hints that a person, an object or an action is to be read symbolically; writers often indicate the existence of symbols in their stories by emphasis and repetition. Second, the meaning and reference of a literary symbol must be confirmed and supported by the entire context of the story for the meaning of a symbol must be found inside not outside a story. Third, for a symbol to be called a symbol, an item must suggest a meaning different in kind from its literal meaning. Fourth, a symbol has layers of meanings that differ from a literary work to another. An item signifying a certain symbol in one literary work may represent something else in another work depending on the context in which it is used.

Irony is a literary or rhetorical device which involves a sort of discrepancy or discordance between what is said and what is meant or is generally understood. Irony entails a discrepancy between appearance and reality, between expectation and fulfillment. In most situations irony is funny, but it can also involve any kind of emotion. Some ironies make us laugh, others make us weep and feel melancholic. Irony Like symbols authors employ irony for compression.

Types of irony:
Most modern and postmodern theories of the rhetoric of fiction identify three major types of irony: verbal irony, dramatic irony, and irony of situation.

Verbal irony is a kind of irony in which what is said is opposite to what is intended. It is a disparity between verbal expression and intention. It is recorded when a character says one thing and means another or when a literal meaning stands in sharp contrast to its intended effect. Unlike the other types of irony, verbal irony is intentionally uttered by the character. **Dramatic irony** is a discrepancy between what a character says and what the reader knows to be true. Thus, the reader is knowledgeable of what the character is ignorant. Dramatic or tragic irony is recorded when there is a disparity of expression and awareness: when the readers understand and know something of which the character who is speaking is unaware of the impact and significance of what he says. The dramatic irony stems from the character's ignorance and the readers' awareness. **Irony of situation** is a kind of discrepancy between appearance and reality, or between expectation and fulfillment, or between what happens and what ought to happen. *Situational irony* is the discrepancy between intention and result or between expectations and fulfillment. In Graham Greene's "The Destructors" it is ironic that Old Misery's horoscope should read "Abstain from any dealings in first half of week. Danger of serious crash", for the horoscope is applicable to the man's situation though he is ignorant of the fact that his house will be destroyed shortly.

Chapter Six
The Elements of Fiction
Emotion and Humour

The power of fiction stems from its ability to provide readers with felt insights into life, the human nature and the human experience. The truths in fiction are stuck into our minds because they reach our minds through our feelings. The effectiveness of fiction becomes apparent when it awakens in the readers an emotional apprehension of experience that enhances their understanding of what they read. This value of fiction distinguishes imaginative literature from ordinary discourse.

For stories to be successful, they must arouse emotions in the reader. Successful stories convey their themes and achieve the purpose for which they have been written through emotions and ideas. Events void of emotion and which only address the readers' minds do not have an everlasting effect on readers and through the passage of time might be forgotten. But those events which are coated with emotions and which address both the hearts and minds of readers seem to have an everlasting effect on them and therefore, might remain in their readers' memories as long as they live. For instance, adventure thrilling stories arouse the emotions of fear, excitement, suspense, anxiety, surprise and joy. Some stories make us laugh, others make us sad and even make us even cry. Some stories fill our hearts with joy and happiness others fill our hearts with sadness and betterment. Some stories make us angry, while other stories make us relieved. Thus, we value a story because it enlightens us, enriches our imagination and diversifies our emotional experiences.

A good story does not aim at arousing the reader's emotions so directly, but it does so indirectly in the process of advancing the plot. A professional story writer loads the events of the story with emotions to help him present a sample of human experience truthfully and artistically. The emotions he arouses in his readers flow naturally and smoothly from the sample experience presented in the story. This applies to all stories that are classified as interpretive fiction. A story written for merely arousing the reader's emotions is a fake story not a genuine one. This is the case of all stories that are classified as commercial escape fiction. Events stripped off emotions, and this would not be possible in any case, tarnishes the artistic unity of a story. Events and emotions, along with all the other elements of fiction present in a story, all melt in each other to form a coherent story and contribute harmoniously to the total design of the story.

The writer must not write his story merely to arouse the emotions of his readers, but rather to instruct and please them. While he is instructing and pleasing his readers through presenting a sample human experience in the story, he has the chance to arouse his readers' emotions, not vise versa. If he does it the other way round, he will be guilty of manipulating, contriving and falsifying the plot of the story. The discriminating reader should, therefore, be able to distinguish a contrived and falsified emotion presented merely for the sake of arousing emotion from genuine emotion that runs naturally and smoothly while the writer is in the process of presenting the human experience. Emotion artistically woven into the fabric of the story is similar to a piece of background music in a movie. The background music in a movie along with the other side effects not only arouses the spectators' emotions, but they also advance the action and the plot of the movie.

The horror spectators experience in the cinema when watching the *Dracula* or the *Frankenstein* monster is far less significant than the horror they get from watching the bloody and murderous king in the televised version of Shakespeare's Macbeth whose burning ambition to stay in power drives him crazy and urges him to commit a series of horrible crimes the worst of which is the murder of innocent children. In the *Dracula* or the *Frankenstein* movies terror is an end in itself, whereas, in *Macbeth* terror is not an end but merely an accompaniment of a terrible revelation of the human nature. It shows how terrifying the human nature can be when it goes into decline to the level of an animal or even worse. The spectators watching *Macbeth* are more terrified than those watching *Dracula* or *Frankenstein* because in the former they are watching reality, whereas, in the second they are watching fictitious reality and are aware of its basic unreality.

Sentimentality and Emotion:

Writers who design their stories by contriving emotions are said to be guilty of sentimentality or even worse oversentimentality. **Sentimentality** is an unmerited or contrived tender feeling; that quality in a story that elicits or artificially seeks to elicit tears through an oversimplification or falsification of reality. Sentimentality is quite different from genuine emotion. Sentimentality is contrived or excessive or faked emotion. Whereas, emotion is genuine and is triggered by lifelike situations. A story is said to have genuine emotion when it depicts life faithfully and perceptively without falsification. The sentimentalized or oversentimentalized story oversimplifies and sweetens life to get its feeling. It mixes sorrow with joy to alleviate the hardships of life.

Like character, genuine emotion must be presented indirectly by being dramatized in lifelike situations. Characters' emotions and the emotions provoked by the situations they are placed seem real and lifelike when dramatized rather than simply identified with emotive words like angry, sad, pathetic, or passionate. Sentimental writers guilty of oversentimentality have many attributes in common. First, they often rely on words to achieve what the situation they present in the story fails to do by itself. Such writers fail to provoke dramatized emotions, therefore, resort to instructing readers how to feel through the power of words and heightened language. Second, such writers make use of irrelevant details that neither contribute to advancing the plot of the story nor contribute to the total design and purpose of the story. For sentimental writers, such trivial and unnecessary details help contrive emotions in the story which most readers demand and feel enjoyable. Third, sentimentalists often resort to using stock characters and stock themes to elicit stock responses from readers – emotions that have their source outside the facts established in the story. Stock themes such as love, death, and national patriotism produce stock responses in most readers. Finally, sentimental writers often present a sweet picture of life which most readers like. Such writers portray life favourably no matter how difficult it may be for most people. Like escapist readers, these writers are escapists themselves. For them, they dress every bad happening in a beautiful robe. For such writers, peace comes after war, the destructive storm will stop no matter how long it lasts, miserable people who die will be happy in the life after death, the villain will be defeated, true love is rewarded and good triumphs over evil.

Humour is the tendency of particular literary situations to provoke laughter and provide amusement. A story written for the sake of humour is contrived and fake. Humour, like emotion, must spring from the plot and the way the writer presents the sample comic human situation throughout the story. A story written for the sake of humour is contrived and fake. Humour, like emotion, must spring from the plot and the way the writer presents the sample comic human situation throughout the story.

Chapter Seven
The Elements of Fiction
Fantasy

It is often said that life is sometimes stranger than fiction. This is true for simple fiction, but when fiction takes the form of fantasy, it becomes far stranger than life. After all, fiction is not supposed to be real since it is the opposite of fact. Fiction is a kind of make-believe game in which the writer conjures up characters living a certain human experience, then sets what he has imagined down on paper. The fictional characters and the situations they are placed in can be pure fiction which is life like. Although the world portrayed in lifelike fiction is fictional and although the characters portrayed are the creation of the writer's mind, they are still lifelike. For we might see some people in real life who are exact copies of such fictional characters. The human experience these fictional characters live and the situations they are placed in are also lifelike and plausible. It is probable that some people somewhere in the world have gone through the same human experiences as portrayed in the fictional world of the story.

However, the dreamlike and bizarre world portrayed in a story may be far from being lifelike. The characters portrayed in the story might also be weird and do not exist in the real world because they are abnormal and do not conform to the laws of God's creation. Even the experience some fictional characters go through in the story and the situation they find themselves placed in are bizarre and improbable. When it is improbable to find such a dreamlike world, bizarre people placed in improbable situations, then we must be talking about science fiction. In science fiction some writers create fanciful creatures that possess a combination of human and animal attributes, or alien creatures from outer space like the ones that appeared in the movie *Mars Attacks*, or they might transform small harmless insects into ferocious killers by magnifying their size thousands of times like a grass hopper or a fly, or they can create a world dominated by imaginary creatures like dragons and flying wizards like those that appeared in *Lord of the Rings*.

Although the events in fiction may be entirely imaginary, they are still applicable to human life in the sense that they reveal to us some truths of human behaviour. But, in science fiction, the characters portrayed and the events narrated might be far from being real and are highly improbable. For instance, the story of the Dracula who rises from the dead to terrify all the people in the city is improbable to happen. Though fictitious characters of science fiction are placed in highly improbable situations, they still reveal some truths about human behaviour and human nature.

Fantasy is an unrealistic story that transcends all bounds of reality and all known conventions of nature. Writers of fantasy depict very bizarre and dreamlike worlds that can never resemble the real world we live in. Characters in such stories might be half humans and half monsters; they might be people with animal attributes or even animals with human characteristics. Characters in fantasy stories may possess miraculous and magical powers that no ordinary human can possess. The world portrayed in fantasy fiction is replete with characters having strange powers and occult forces.

In fantasy like in a dream every thing is probable. Animals can talk and behave just like human beings, the dead can rise from their tombs and wonder in the streets, wizards and dragons fly, people are transformed into spiders, bats and flies and a small bug can be magnified millions of times to become a ferocious creature, alien creatures from outer space may descend on earth to terrify people, creatures from other planets may attack the earth as the new invaders and misshapen bizarre creatures may appear all of a sudden to terrorize dwellers of big cities. Fantasy fiction introduces human beings into a dreamlike world where the laws of nature are suspended or violated and the boundaries of time dissolve. The landscape and the creatures are unfamiliar and are not governed by any laws. Fantasy fiction may also introduce ghosts, fairies, talking animals, murderous robots and invaders from other planets. Fables, ghost stories, and science fiction are all types of fantasy fiction.

Fantasy may be escapist or interpretive. Escapist fantasy is meant to please its readers by taking them into wonderlands and bizarre landscapes and get them acquainted with unfamiliar creatures. Such fantasy fiction widens readers' imagination and gives them the rare opportunity to see people going through weird and improbable experiences which might be true and insightful or false, genuine or fake, pleasant or terrifying. Whereas, interpretive fantasy is meant to please and instruct its readers, probe into the human psyche and interpret man's behaviour when placed in improbable situations. In interpretive fantasy dinosaurs that have now been extinct for millions of years can be resurrected and can be made to roam the planet once again to study their behaviour. The spaceship that travels at the speed of light to a distant planet like Mars in search of traces of life on the planet is meant to explore, instruct and investigate probabilities. The astronauts travelling on the spaceship may represent different stock characters and thus the writer may be interested in creating exciting and thrilling experiences in which human behaviour in outer space can be observed and studied. Like the other elements of fiction, fantasy can be employed merely for its own sake or as a means of communicating an insight about life and human experience.

It should be made clear that truth in fiction is not always identifiable with realism in method. In some cases truth can be found in fantasy more than in realistic fiction. Fantasy may convey truth through symbolism or allegory or simply by introducing bizarre experiences suitable for observing and interpreting human behaviour. Moreover, fantasy is not always a type of commercial fiction for even great fiction can be either partly or wholly fantasy. Some of the world's greatest works of literature were partly or wholly fantasy including *The Odyssey, The Divine Comedy, The Tempest, Gulliver's Travels,* and *Alice in Wonderland*. Writers of such great fiction were interested in commenting on life and the human condition.

Chapter Eight
The Elements of Fiction
The Scale of Value

Skillful reading of great interpretive fiction involves passing a judgment on the literary work and rating its value. Discriminating readers know what kind of fiction to read and how to read such fiction. Such proficient readers not only grasp the plot of the story they are reading, realize its characters' motives , abstract its major themes and sub themes, identify the conflicts in the story and even recognize all the symbols and ironies in the story, but they also evaluate the story and rate its value. Such competent readers have the ability to discriminate between commercial and great fiction, genuine and spurious fiction, serious and trivial fiction, interpretive and entertaining escape fiction. When such cultivated readers read a work of fiction, they tend to rely on their perceptivity, intelligence, and literary experience to rate the value of the literary work. The rating value of a work of fiction is measured against the scale of value that takes the shape of a rising tone with poor fiction positioned at the lowest point and great fiction at the highest point of the scale and good fiction occupying a medium position in the scale.

A first–rate story is judged as an organic whole rather than by judging its elements each in isolation. All the elements are artistically interlinked and geared towards achieving the story's central purpose. However, two basic principles should be taken into account when rating the value of a work of fiction. First, *how fully the story achieves its central purpose*. Every element of fiction present in the story such as plot, character, theme, conflict, symbol, irony, fantasy and point of view is judged by the effectiveness of its contribution to the total design and artistic unity of the story and its central purpose. In a story with a skillfully engineered plot, every element supports the other elements for the accomplishment of the central purpose of the story. Thus, no element in the story is to be evaluated in isolation from the other elements. Weakness in any element in the story and its ineffectiveness on contributing to achieving the central purpose of the story would certainly tarnish and weaken the story's artistic unity and total design. When asked to rate the value of a work of fiction, inexperienced readers often fail to rate the work against the standard scale of value simply because they often tend to dismantle the story into its individual elements and thus evaluate every element in isolation from the other elements. It is true that in some stories even the best ones a weakness in some element of the story might be discerned, but taken as a whole such stories would appear artistically woven. A story with a poor style like Sherwood Anderson's "I'm a fool" can still be a good story, because such style is used intentionally by the writer since it is essential to achieving its central purpose. By the same token, although some readers might say that John Galsworthy's "The Japanese Quince" does not have an enjoyable, fast moving plot, it is still a good story because plot can be judged only in relation to the other elements in the story and its contribution to achieving the story's central purpose. Similarly, we can not say that Graham Greene's "The Destructors" and Shirley Jackson's "The Lottery" are poor stories merely because they contain no complex round characters as those portrayed in "I'm a Fool" since in the former two stories characterization is less significant than the action performed by the characters.

Second, *a successful story is also judged by the significance of its central purpose*. Organic unity and achieving the central purpose of the story are not enough for a story to be rated as a good story. The success of a story is also judged by the extent, the range and the value of the materials woven into the fabric of the story. Thus, if the purpose of an escape story is to entertain its readers by thrilling, surprising, provoking to laughter or tears, we must judge it by the extent it succeeds in achieving this purpose. Likewise, if an interpretive story seeks to provide its readers with some revelation about life and human experience, we must measure it by the breadth and depth of this revelation and not by how much it makes its readers laugh or weep.

Applying the aforementioned two principles helps readers both understand the works of fiction they read and to pass a judgment on them by placing them on a scale of value that rises through many gradations from "poor fiction" to "good fiction" to "great fiction or the avant-garde".

The Elements of Fiction:
Test your Understanding

Choose the correct alternative A, B, C or D

1. A character with many sided- traits is known as a ....
   A) Flat character
   B) Foil character
   C) Round character
   D) Stock character

2. Any force in a story that is in conflict with the central character whether it is a wicked person, the whole society or a destructive force within his psyche is known as a /an ....
   A) Protagonist
   B) Antagonist
   C) Stock character
   D) Dynamic character

3. ....is a quality of a work of fiction which makes the reader eager to read the whole story to know what happens next.
   A) Surprise
   B) Conflict
   C) Suspense
   D) Dramatization

4. A developing or dynamic character is ....
   A) A stereotyped character that readers have seen such or similar character in a large number of stories they have read before.
   B) A character with complex and many- sided traits.
   C) A character that does not change throughout the course of action of the story. It is the same sort of person at the end of the story as at the beginning
   D) A character that undergoes a drastic change in some aspect of personality or outlook towards the end of the story. It is a change noticeable to all readers.

5. Plot in fiction can best be defined as ....
   A) A clash of actions, desires, ideas, or goals in the plot of a story
   B) An unexpected turn in the development of the plot of a story

C) The quality of a work of fiction which makes the reader eager to know what happens next in a story

D) The sequence of related incidents or events in a story

6. When a story writer or a novelist tells us directly by revelation or exposition what the characters in the story look like , how they behave, feel and think, it is said that he employs the ....

A) Indirect characterization

B) Personification

C) The direct method of character presentation

D) Inconsistent characterization

7. Which of the following is not true of theme in fiction?

A) The theme abstracted from a story should be a single statement consisting of a subject and a predicate.

B) The theme must be stated as a generalization about life, human nature, human condition and human experience.

C) There is no perfect way of stating the theme of a story but it can be stated in different ways

D) The theme of a story must exist outside the story not inside and it can be reduced to a common saying or cliché.

8. The main characteristic of the Omniscient Point of View is that ....

A) The story is told by the author using the third person

B) The writer's knowledge of the characters' actions, feelings and thoughts is omniscient and unlimited

C) The writer reports to the readers the thoughts and feelings of only one character in the story since he is not knowledgeable of how the other characters think and feel

D) (A&B)

9. Which of the following narration techniques (point of view) is the most flexible in the sense that it gives both the writer and the reader a thorough understanding of the characters' motifs, feelings and thoughts?

A) The Omniscient Point of view

B) The Limited Omniscient Point of View

C) The First Point of View

D) The Dramatic or Objective Point of View

10. In the Limited Omniscient Point of View ……………..
    A) The writer uses the first person to narrate the events of the story
    B) The story is told from the viewpoint of the central character whose thoughts, feelings and motifs are known to the readers. Readers do not have access to know how the other characters in the story think and feel.
    C) The writer's knowledge of the other characters' actions, feelings and thoughts is omniscient
    D) (A&C)

11. In the first person point of view ……………
    A) The narrator narrates the events of the story using the first person "I"
    B) The narrator uses the interior monologue to narrate his past experiences and memoirs
    C) (A&B)
    D) The writer can comment on the action of the story and the characters' feelings and thoughts

12. In which narration technique are the events of the story narrated through the roving sound camera where authorial voice disappears and characters are dramatized through acting?
    A) The Omniscient Point of View
    B) The Limited Omniscient Point of View
    C) The First Person Point of View
    D) The Dramatic or Objective Point of View

13 ………….. is an unrealistic story that transcends all bounds of reality and all conventions of nature.
    A) Fantasy
    B) Interpretive literature
    C) Escapist literature
    D) Commercial fiction

14. The scale of value involves ………….
    A) Passing a judgment on a literary work by rating its value as good or bad fiction
    B) Understanding the plot of the work of fiction only
    C) Realizing the characters' motives
    D) Abstracting the major theme and sub-themes in a story

The Destructors
By
Graham Greene

The Complete Text of the Story

It was on the eve of August Bank Holiday that the latest recruit became the leader of the Wormsley Common Gang. No one was surprised except Mike, but Mike at the age of nine was surprised by everything. 'If you don't shut your mouth,' somebody once said to him, 'you'll get a frog down it.' After that Mike kept his teeth tightly clamped except when the surprise was too great.

The new recruit had been with the gang since the beginning of the summer holidays, and there were possibilities about his brooding silence that all recognized. He never wasted a word even to tell his name until that was required of him by the rules. When he said 'Trevor' it was a statement of fact, not as it would have been with the others a statement of shame or defiance. Nor did anyone laugh except Mike, who finding himself without support and meeting the dark gaze of the newcomer opened his mouth and was quiet again. There was every reason why T., as he was afterwards referred to, should have been an object of mockery - there was his name (and they substituted the initial because otherwise they had no excuse not to laugh at it), the fact that his father, a former architect and present clerk, had 'come down in the world' and that his mother considered herself better than the neighbours. What but an odd quality of danger, of the unpredictable, established him in the gang without any ignoble ceremony of initiation?

The gang met every morning in an impromptu car-park, the site of the last bomb of the first blitz. The leader, who was known as Blackie, claimed to have heard it fall, and no one was precise enough in his dates to point out that he would have been one year old and fast asleep on the down platform of Wormsley Common Underground Station. On one side of the car-park leant the first occupied house, No. 3, of the shattered Northwood Terrace - literally leant, for it had suffered from the blast of the bomb and the side walls were supported on wooden struts. A smaller bomb and incendiaries had fallen beyond, so that the house stuck up like a jagged tooth and carried on the further wall relics of its neighbour, a dado, the remains of a fireplace. T., whose words were almost confined to voting 'Yes' or 'No' to the plan of operations proposed each day by Blackie, once startled the whole gang by saying broodingly, 'Wren built that house, father says.' 'Who's Wren?' 'The man who built St Paul's.' 'Who cares?' Blackie said. 'It's only Old Misery's.'

Old Misery - whose real name was Thomas - had once been a builder and decorator. He lived alone in the crippled house, doing for himself: once a week you could see him coming back across the common with bread and vegetables, and once as the boys played in the car-park he put his head over the smashed wall of his garden and looked at them. 'Been to the lav,' one of the boys said, for it was common knowledge that since the bombs fell something had gone wrong with the pipes of the house and Old Misery was too mean to spend money on the property. He could do the redecorating himself at cost price, but he had never learnt plumbing. The lav was a wooden shed at the bottom of the narrow garden with a star-shaped hole in the door: it had escaped the blast which had smashed the house next door and sucked out the window-frames of No. 3. The next time the gang became aware of Mr. Thomas was more surprising. Blackie, Mike and a thin yellow boy, who for some reason was called by his surname Summers, met him on the common coming back from the market. Mr. Thomas stopped them. He said glumly, 'You belong to the lot that play in the car-park?' Mike was about to answer when Blackie stopped him. As the leader he had responsibilities. 'Suppose we are?' he said ambiguously. 'I got some chocolates,' Mr Thomas said. 'Don't like 'em myself. Here you are. Not enough to go round, I don't suppose. There never is,' he added with sombre conviction. He handed over three packets of Smarties. The gang was puzzled and perturbed by this action and tried to explain it away. 'Bet someone dropped them and he picked 'em up,' somebody suggested. 'Pinched 'em and then got in a bleeding funk,' another thought aloud. 'It's a bribe,' Summers said. 'He wants us to stop bouncing balls on his wall.' 'We'll show him we don't take bribes,' Blackie said, and they sacrificed the whole morning to the game of bouncing that only Mike was young enough to enjoy. There was no sign from Mr. Thomas.

Next day T. astonished them all. He was late at the rendezvous, and the voting for that day's exploit took place without him. At Blackie's suggestion the gang was to disperse in pairs, take buses at random and see how many free rides could be snatched from unwary conductors (the operation was to be carried out in pairs to avoid cheating). They were drawing lots for their companions when T. arrived. 'Where you been, T.?' Blackie asked. 'You can't vote now. You know the rules.' 'I've been there,' T. said. He looked at the ground, as though he had thoughts to hide. 'Where?' 'At Old Misery's.' Mike's mouth opened and then hurriedly closed again with a click. He had remembered the frog. 'At Old Misery's?' Blackie said. There was nothing in the rules against it, but he had a sensation that T. was treading on dangerous ground. He asked hopefully, 'Did you break in?' 'No. I rang the bell.' 'And what did you say?' 'I said I wanted to see his house.' 'What did he do?' 'He showed it me:' 'Pinch anything?' 'No.' 'What did you do it for then?' The gang had gathered round: it was as though an impromptu court were about to form and try some case of deviation. T. said, 'It's a beautiful house,' and still watching the ground, meeting no one's eyes, he licked his lips first one way, then the other. 'What do you mean, a beautiful house?' Blackie asked with scorn. 'It's got a staircase two hundred years old like a corkscrew. Nothing holds it up.' 'What do you mean, nothing holds it up. Does it float?' 'It's to do with opposite forces, Old Misery said.' 'What else?' 'There's panelling.' 'Like in the Blue Boar?' 'Two hundred years old.' 'Is Old Misery two hundred years old?' Mike laughed suddenly and then was quiet again. The meeting was in a serious mood. For the first time since T. had strolled into the car-park on the first day of the holidays his position was in danger. It only needed a single use of his real name and the gang would be at his heels. 'What did you do it for?' Blackie asked. He was just, he had no jealousy, he was anxious to retain T. in the gang if he could. It was the word 'beautiful' that worried him - that belonged to a class world that you could still see parodied at the Wormsley Common Empire by a man wearing a top hat and a monocle, with a haw-haw accent. He was tempted to say, 'My dear Trevor, old chap,' and unleash his hell hounds. 'If you'd broken in,' he said sadly - that indeed would have been an exploit worthy of the gang. 'This was better,' T. said. 'I found out things.' He continued to stare at his feet, not meeting anybody's eye, as though he were absorbed in some dream he was unwilling - or ashamed to share. 'What things?' 'Old Misery's going to be away all tomorrow and Bank Holiday.' Blackie said with relief, 'You mean we could break in?' 'And pinch things?' somebody asked. Blackie said, 'Nobody's going to pinch things. Breaking in that's good enough, isn't it? We don't want any court stuff.' 'I don't want to pinch anything,' T. said. 'I've got a better idea.' 'What is it?' T. raised eyes, as grey and disturbed as the drab August day. 'We'll pull it down,' he said. 'We'll destroy it.' Blackie gave a single hoot of laughter and then, like Mike, fell quiet, daunted by the serious implacable gaze. 'What'd the police be doing all the time?' he said. 'They'd never know. We'd do it from inside. I've found a way in.' He said with a sort of intensity, 'We'd be like worms, don't you see, in an apple. When we came out again there'd be nothing there, no staircase, no panels, nothing but just walls, and then we'd make the walls fall down - somehow.' 'We'd go to jug,' Blackie said. 'Who's to prove? and anyway we wouldn't have pinched anything.' He added without the smallest flicker of glee, 'There wouldn't be anything to pinch after we'd finished.' 'I've never heard of going to prison for breaking things,' Summers said. 'There wouldn't be time,' Blackie said. 'I've seen housebreakers at work.' 'There are twelve of us,' T. said. 'We'd organize.! 'None of us know how...' 'I know,' T. said. He looked across at Blackie. 'Have you got a better plan?' 'Today,' Mike said tactlessly, 'we're pinching free rides. . ."' 'Free rides,' T. said. 'Kid stuff. You can stand down, Blackie, if you'd rather . . .' 'The gang's got to vote.' 'Put it up then.' Blackie said uneasily, 'It's proposed that tomorrow and Monday we destroy Old Misery's house.' 'Here, here,' said a fat boy called Joe. 'Who's in favour?' T. said, 'It's carried.' 'How do we start?' Summers asked. 'He'll tell you,' Blackie said. It was the end of his leadership. He went away to the back of the car-park and began to kick a stone, dribbling it this way and that.

There was only one old Morris in the park, for few cars were left there except lorries: without an attendant there was no safety. He took a flying kick at the car and scraped a little paint off the rear mudguard. Beyond, paying no more attention to him than to a stranger, the gang had gathered round T.; Blackie was dimly aware of the fickleness of favour. He thought of going home, of never returning, of letting them all discover the hollowness of TA leadership, but suppose after all what T. proposed was possible nothing like it had ever been done before. The fame of the Wormsley Common car-park gang would surely reach around London. There would be headlines in the papers. Even the grown-up gangs who ran the betting at the all-in wrestling and the barrow-boys would hear with respect of how Old Misery's house had been destroyed. Driven by the pure, simple and altruistic ambition of fame for the gang, Blackie came back to where T. stood in the shadow of Old Misery's wall. T. was giving his orders with decision: it was as though this plan had been with him all his life, pondered through the seasons, now in his fifteenth year crystallized with the pain of puberty. 'You,' he said to Mike, 'bring some big nails, the biggest you can find, and a hammer. Anybody who can, better bring a hammer and a screwdriver. We'll need plenty of them. Chisels too. We can't have too many chisels. Can anybody bring a saw?' 'I can,' Mike said. 'Not a child's saw,' T. said. 'A real saw.' Blackie realized he had raised his hand like any ordinary member of the gang. 'Right, you bring one, Blackie. But now there's a difficulty. We want a hacksaw.' 'What's a hacksaw?' someone asked. 'You can get 'em at Woolworth's,' Summers said. The fat boy called Joe said gloomily, 'I knew it would end in a collection.' 'I'll get one myself,' T. said. 'I don't want your money. But I can't buy a sledge-hammer.' Blackie said, 'They are working on No. 15. I know where they'll leave their stuff for Bank Holiday.' 'Then that's all,' T. said. 'We meet here at nine sharp.' 'I've got to go to church,' Mike said. 'Come over the wall and whistle. We'll let you in.'

On Sunday morning all were punctual except Blackie, even Mike. Mike had a stroke of luck. His mother felt ill, his father was tired after Saturday night, and he was told to go to church alone with many warnings of what would happen if he strayed. Blackie had difficulty in smuggling out the saw, and then in finding the sledge-hammer at the back of No. 15. He approached the house from a lane at the rear of the garden, for fear of the policeman's beat along the main road. The tired evergreens kept off a stormy sun: another wet Bank Holiday was being prepared over the Atlantic, beginning in swirls of dust under the trees. Blackie climbed the wall into Misery's garden. There was no sign of anybody anywhere. The lav stood like a tomb in a neglected graveyard. The curtains were drawn. The house slept. Blackie lumbered nearer with the saw and the sledge-hammer. Perhaps after all nobody had turned up: the plan had been a wild invention: they had woken wiser. But when he came close to the back door he could hear a confusion of sound hardly louder than a hive in swarm: a clickety-clack, a bang bang, a scraping, a creaking, a sudden painful crack. He thought: it's true; and whistled. They opened the back door to him and he came in. He had at once the impression of organization, very different from the old happy-go-lucky ways under his leadership. For a while he wandered up and down stairs looking for T. Nobody addressed him: he had a sense of great urgency, and already he could begin to see the plan. The interior of the house was being carefully demolished without touching the walls. Summers with hammer and chisel was ripping out the skirting-boards in the ground floor dining-room: he had already smashed the panels of the door. In the same room Joe was heaving up the parquet blocks, exposing the soft wood floorboards over the cellar. Coils of wire came out of the damaged skirting and Mike sat; happily on the floor clipping the wires.

On the curved stairs two of the gang were working hard with an inadequate child's saw on the banisters - when they saw Blackie's big saw they signalled for it wordlessly. When he next saw them a quarter of the banisters had been dropped into the hall. He found T. at last in the bathroom - he sat moodily in the least cared-for room in the house, listening to the sounds coming up from below. 'You've really done it,' Blackie said with awe. 'What's going to happen?' 'We've only just begun,' T. said. He looked at the sledgehammer and gave his instructions. 'You stay here and break the, bath and the wash-basin. Don't bother about the pipes. They come later.' Mike appeared at the door. 'I've finished the wires, T.,' he said. 'Good. You've just got to go wandering round now. The kitchen's in the basement. Smash all the china and glass and bottles you can lay hold of. Don't turn on the taps - we don't want a flood - yet. Then go into all the rooms and turn out the drawers. If they are locked get one of the others to break them open. Tear up any papers you find and smash all the ornaments. Better take a carving knife with you from the kitchen. The' bedroom's opposite here. Open the pillows and tear up the sheets. That's enough for the moment. And you, Blackie, when you've finished in here crack the plaster in the passage up with your sledge-hammer.' 'What are you going to do?' Blackie asked. 'I'm looking for something special,' T. said.

It was nearly lunch-time before Blackie had finished and went in search of T. Chaos had advanced. The kitchen was a shambles of broken glass and china. The dining-room was stripped of parquet, the skirting was up, the door had been taken off its hinges, and the destroyers had moved up a floor. Streaks of light came in through the closed shutters where they worked with the seriousness of creators- and destruction after all is a form of creation. A kind of imagination had seen this house as it had now become. Mike said, 'I've got to go home for dinner.' 'Who else?' T. asked, but all the others on one excuse or another had brought provisions with them. They squatted in the ruins of the room and swapped unwanted sandwiches. Half an hour for lunch and they were at work again.

By the time Mike returned they were on the top floor, and by six the superficial damage was completed. The doors were all off, all the skirtings raised, the furniture pillaged and ripped and smashed - no one could have slept in the house except on a bed of broken plaster. T. gave his orders - eight o'clock next morning, and to escape notice they climbed singly over the garden wall; into the car-park. Only Blackie and T. were left: the light had nearly gone, and when they touched a switch, nothing worked - Mike had done his job thoroughly. 'Did you find anything special?' Blackie asked. T. nodded. 'Come over here,' he said, 'and look.' Out of both pockets he drew bundles of pound notes. 'Old Misery's savings,' he said. 'Mike ripped out the mattress, but he missed them.' 'What are you going to do? Share them?' 'We aren't thieves,' T. said. 'Nobody's going to steal anything from this house. I kept these for you and me - a celebration.' He knelt down on the floor and counted them out - there were seventy in all. 'We'll burn them,' he said, 'one by one,' and taking it in turns they held a note upwards and lit the top corner, so that the flame burnt slowly towards their fingers. The grey ash floated above them and fell on their heads like age. 'I'd like to see Old Misery's face when we are through,' T. a said. 'You hate him a lot?' Blackie asked. 'Of course I don't hate him,' T. said. 'There'd be no fun if I hated him.' The last burning note illuminated his brooding face. 'All this hate and love,' he said, 'it's soft, it's hooey. There's only things, Blackie,' and he looked round the room crowded with the unfamiliar shadows of half things, broken things, former things. 'I'll race you home, Blackie,' he said.

Next morning the serious destruction started. Two were missing - Mike and another boy whose parents were off to Southend and Brighton in spite of the slow warm drops that had begun to fall and the rumble of thunder in the estuary like the first guns of the old blitz. 'We've got to hurry,' T. said. Summers was restive. 'Haven't we done enough?' he asked. -, 'I've been given a _bob for slot machines. This is like work.' 'We've hardly started,' T. said. 'Why, there's all the floors left, and the stairs. We haven't taken out a single window. You voted like the others. We are going to destroy this house. There; won't be anything left when we've finished.' They began again on the first floor picking up the top floorboards next the outer wall, leaving the joists exposed. Then they sawed through the joists and retreated into the hall, as what was left of the floor heeled and sank. They had learnt with practice, and the second floor collapsed more easily. By the evening an odd exhilaration seized them as they looked down the great hollow of the house. They ran risks and made mistakes: when they thought of the windows it was too late to reach' them. 'Cor,' Joe said, and dropped a penny down into the, dry rubble-filled well. It cracked and span amongst the broken glass. 'Why did we start this?' Summers asked with astonishment; T. was already on the ground, digging at the rubble, clearing a space along the outer wall. 'Turn on the taps,' he said. 'It's too dark for anyone to see now, and in the morning it won't matter.' The water overtook them on the stairs and fell through the floorless rooms.

It was then they heard Mike's whistle at the back. 'Something's wrong,' Blackie said. They could hear his urgent breathing as they unlocked the door. 'The bogies?' Summers asked. 'Old Misery,' Mike said. 'He's on his way,' he said with pride. 'But why?' T. said. 'He told me ...' He protested with the fury of the child he had never been, 'It isn't fair.' 'He was down at Southend,' Mike said, 'and he was on the train coming back. Said it was too cold and wet.' He paused and gazed at the water. 'My, you've had a storm here. Is the roof leaking?' 'How long will he be?' 'Five minutes. I gave Ma the slip and ran.' 'We better clear,' Summers said. 'We've done enough, anyway.' 'Oh no, we haven't. Anybody could do this - ' 'this' was the shattered hollowed house with nothing left but the walls. Yet walls could be preserved. Facades were valuable. They could build inside again more beautifully than before. This could again be a home. He said angrily, 'We've got to finish. Don't move. Let me think.' 'There's no time,' a boy said. 'There's got to be a way,' T. said. 'We couldn't have got this far...' 'We've done a lot,' Blackie said. 'No. No, we haven't. Somebody watch the front' 'We can't do any more.' 'He may come in at the back.' 'Watch the back too.' T. began to plead. 'Just give me a minute and I'll fix it. I swear I'll fix it.' But his authority had gone with his ambiguity. He was only one of the gang. 'Please,' he said. 'Please,' Summers mimicked him, and then suddenly struck home with the fatal name. 'Run along home, Trevor.' T. stood with his back to the rubble like a boxer knocked groggy against the ropes. He had no words as his dreams shook and slid. Then Blackie acted before the gang had time to laugh, pushing Summers backward. 'I'll watch the front, T.,' he said, and cautiously he opened the shutters of the hall. The grey wet common stretched ahead, and the lamps gleamed in the puddles. 'Someone's coming, T. No, it's not him. What's your plan, T.?' 'Tell Mike to go out to the lav and hide close beside it. When he hears me whistle he's got to count ten and start to shout.' 'Shout what?' 'Oh, "Help", anything.' 'You hear; Mike,' Blackie said. He was the leader again. He took a quick look between the shutters. 'He's coming, T.' 'Quick, Mike. The lav. Stay here, Blackie, all of you; till I yell.' 'Where are you going, T.?' 'Don't worry. I'll see to this. I said I would, didn't I?' Old Misery came limping off the common. He had mud on his shoes and he stopped to scrape them on the pavement's edge. He didn't want to soil his house, which stood jagged and dark between the bomb-sites, saved so narrowly, as he believed, from destruction. Even the fan-light had been left unbroken by the bomb's blast. Somewhere somebody whistled. Old Misery looked sharply round. He didn't trust whistles. A child was shouting: it seemed to come from his own garden. Then a boy ran into the road from the car-park. 'Mr. Thomas,' he called, 'Mr. Thomas.' 'What is it?' 'I'm terribly sorry, Mr. Thomas. One of us got taken short, and we thought you wouldn't mind, and now he can't get out.' 'What do you mean, boy?' 'He's got stuck in your lav.' 'He'd no business ... Haven't I seen you before?' 'You showed me your house.' 'So I did. So I did. That doesn't give you the right to... 'Do hurry, Mr. Thomas. He'll suffocate.' 'Nonsense. He can't suffocate. Wait till I put my bag in.' 'I'll carry your bag.' 'Oh no, you don't. I carry my own.' 'This way, Mr. Thomas.' 'I can't get in the garden that way. I've got to go through the house.' 'But you can get in the garden this way, Mr. Thomas. We often do.' 'You often do?' He followed the boy with a scandalized fascination. 'When? What right É?' 'Do you see É ? the wall's low.' 'I'm not going to climb walls into my own garden. It's absurd.' 'This is how we do it. One foot here, one foot there, and over.' The boy's face peered down, an arm shot out, and Mr. Thomas found his bag taken and deposited on the other side of the wall. 'Give me back my bag,' Mr. Thomas said. From the loo a boy yelled and yelled. 'I'll call the police.' 'Your bag's all right, Mr. Thomas. Look. One foot there. On your right. Now just above. To your left.' Mr. Thomas climbed over his own garden wall. 'Here's your bag, Mr. Thomas.' 'I'll have the wall built up,' Mr. Thomas said, 'I'll not have you boys coming over here, using my loo.' He stumbled on the path, but the boy caught his elbow and supported him. 'Thank you, thank you, my boy,' he murmured automatically. Somebody shouted again through the dark. 'I'm coming, I'm coming,' Mr. Thomas called. He said to the boy beside him, 'I'm not unreasonable. Been a boy myself. As long as things are done regular. I don't mind you playing round the place Saturday mornings. Sometimes I like company. Only it's got to be regular. One of you asks leave and I say Yes. Sometimes I'll say No. Won't feel like it. And you come in at the front door and out at the back. No garden walls.' 'Do get him out, Mr. Thomas.' 'He won't come to any harm in my loo,' Mr. Thomas said, stumbling slowly down the garden. 'Oh, my rheumatics,' h said. 'Always get 'em on Bank Holiday. I've got to be careful. There's loose stones here. Give me your hand. Do you know what my horoscope said yesterday? "Abstain from any dealings in first half of week. Danger of serious crash." That might be on this path,' Mr. Thomas said. 'They speak in parables and double meanings.' He paused at the door of the loo. 'What's the matter in there?' he called. There was no reply. 'Perhaps he's fainted,' the boy said. 'Not in my loo. Here, you, come out,' Mr. Thomas said, and giving a great jerk at the door he nearly fell on his back when it swung easily open. A hand first supported him and then pushed him hard. His head hit the opposite wall and he sat heavily down. His bag hit his feet. A hand whipped the key out of the lock and the door slammed. 'Let me out,' he called, and heard the key turn in the lock. 'A serious crash,' he thought, and felt dithery and confused and old.

A voice spoke to him softly through the star-shaped hole in the door. 'Don't worry, Mr. Thomas,' it said, 'we won't hurt you, not if you stay quiet.' Mr. Thomas put his head between his hands and pondered. He had noticed that there was only one lorry in the car-park, and he felt certain that the driver would not come for it before the morning. Nobody could hear him from the road in front and the lane at the back was seldom used. Anyone who passed there would be hurrying home and would not pause for what they would certainly take to be drunken cries. And if he did call 'Help', who, on a lonely Bank Holiday evening, would have the courage to investigate? Mr. Thomas sat on the loo and pondered with the wisdom of age. After a while it seemed to him that there were sounds in the silence - they were faint and came from the direction of his house. He stood up and peered through the ventilation-hole - between the cracks in one of the shutters he saw a light, not the light of a lamp, but the wavering light that a candle might give. Then he thought he heard the sound of hammering and scraping and chipping. He thought of burglars - perhaps they had employed the boy as a scout, but why should burglars engage in what sounded more and more like a stealthy form of carpentry? Mr. Thomas let out an experimental yell, but nobody answered. The noise could not even have reached his enemies. 4 Mike had gone home to bed, but the rest stayed. The question of leadership no longer concerned the gang. With nails, chisels, screwdrivers, anything that was sharp and penetrating, they moved around the inner walls worrying at the mortar between the bricks. They started too high, and it was Blackie who hit on the damp course and realized the work could be halved if they weakened the joints immediately above. It was a long, tiring, unamusing job, but at last it was finished. The gutted house stood there balanced on a few inches of mortar between the clamp course and the bricks.

There remained the most dangerous task of all, out in the open at the edge of the bomb-site. Summers was sent to watch the road for passers-by, and Mr. Thomas, sitting on the loo, heard clearly now the sound of sawing. It no longer came from the house, and that a little reassured him. He felt less concerned. Perhaps the other noises too had no significance. A voice spoke to him through the hole. 'Mr. Thomas.' 'Let me out,' Mr. Thomas said sternly. 'Here's a blanket,' the voice said, and a long grey sausage was worked through the hole and fell in swathes over Mr. Thomas's head. 'There's nothing personal,' the voice said. 'We want you to be comfortable tonight.' 'Tonight,' Mr. Thomas repeated incredulously. 'Catch,' the voice said. 'Penny buns - we've buttered them, and sausage-rolls. We don't want you to starve, Mr. Thomas.' Mr. Thomas pleaded desperately. 'A joke's a joke, boy. Let me out and I won't say a thing. I've got rheumatics. I got to sleep comfortable.' 'You wouldn't be comfortable, not in your house, you wouldn't. Not now.' 'What do you mean, boy?' But the footsteps receded. There was only the silence of night: no sound of sawing. Mr. Thomas tried one more yell, but he was daunted and rebuked by the silence - a long way off an owl hooted and made away again on its muffled flight through the soundless world. At seven next morning the driver came to fetch his lorry. He climbed into the seat and tried to start the engine. He was vaguely aware of a voice shouting, but it didn't concern him. At last the engine responded and he backed the lorry until it, touched the great wooden shore that supported Mr. Thomas's house. That way he could drive right out and down the street without reversing. The lorry moved forward, was momentarily checked as though something were pulling it from behind, and then went on to the sound of a long rumbling crash. The driver was astonished to see bricks bouncing ahead of him, while stones hit the roof of his cab. He put on his brakes. When he climbed out the whole landscape had suddenly altered. There was no house beside the car-park, only a hill of rubble. He went round and examined the back of his lorry for damage, and found a rope tied there that was still twisted at the other end round part of a wooden strut. The driver again became aware of somebody shouting. It came from the wooden erection which was the nearest thing to a house in that desolation of broken brick. The driver climbed the smashed wall and unlocked the door.

Mr. Thomas came out of the loo. He was wearing a grey blanket to which flakes of pastry adhered. He gave a sobbing cry. 'My house,' he said. 'Where's my house?' 'Search me,' the driver said. His eye lit on the remains of a bath and what had once been a dresser and he began to laugh. There wasn't anything left anywhere. 'How dare you laugh,' Mr. Thomas said. 'It was my house My house.' 'I'm sorry,' the driver said, making heroic efforts, but when he remembered the sudden check of his lorry, the crash of bricks falling, he became convulsed again. One moment the house had stood there with such dignity between the bomb-sites like a man in a top hat, and then, bang, crash, there wasn't anything left - not anything. He said, 'I'm sorry. I can't help it, Mr. Thomas. There's nothing personal, but you got to admit it's funny.

The Destructors

Summary

Graham Greene's "The Destructors" tells the story of how a group of kids who call themselves the Wormsley Common Gang destroy a very old house just for having fun. The events of the story took place in a London parking lot during the two-day August Bank Holiday shortly after World War Two. The events of the story start with the arrival of the new comer Trevor who expresses his willingness to join the gang. The gang members accepted the new member without hesitation. Trevor is very different from all the other kids and he seems incongruous to the whole parking lot where the gang used to meet. Unlike the other streetwise kids in the gang, Trevor comes from a well off family. His father was an architect before the war, but now he is a clerk. And despite the fact that his family went down in the world, his mother still clings to her phoney dreams of becoming rich once again and keeps boasting of being better than her neighbours. Although he is a social outcast amongst the gang members, he has a charismatic character that not only made all the members of the gang accept him as a member in the gang but also as their new leader in place of Blackie; the present leader of the gang . The kids euphemistically call him "T" to avoid his upper class name Trevor which for them is rather trivial and extravagant. "T" unintentionally vies with Blackie, the former leader of the gang, for the leadership of the gang. In fact, Trevor was not interested in being the new leader of the gang, but when selected by all the members of the gang, he accepted the title.

The gang meets every day in a deserted and dirty parking lot which survived the bombings of the war. Very few people park their cars there because it is deserted and fear the gang who occupy the place. Near this parking lot there still exists a two –hundred year old house that survived the bombardments of the war which completely destroyed the neighbouring house. The house is old, shabby and seems deserted though when rebuilt in the beholder's imagination seems a classic work of art. It is believed that the surviving house was built by Christopher Wren, the famous architect who built the magnificent St. Paul's Cathedral. The house is almost collapsing and is propped up with wooden struts on both sides. The kids call the house "Old Misery's House" after the man who now lives in it. Old Misery whose real name is Thomas is an aging fat and stingy man. He is an old bachelor who lives alone in a very old house that has survived the bombings of the war. Before the war Old Misery was a brick layer and a decorator. Having found the surviving house, he lived in it without making the least alterations in the house. Everything inside the house seems broken and old including the China and the lavatory. The bombings of the war destroyed nearly all the plumbings in the house including those in the lavatory. Old Misery is very stingy and opted to live in the surviving house without fixing anything. Instead of mending the plumbings in the house including those in the lavatory, he built an outdoor lavatory in the yard. However, this lavatory is made of wood and its door with the star-shaped hole is almost collapsing. Old Misery suffers from rheumatism and he rarely leaves the propped up house only once a week to buy bread and vegetables. He is an eccentric man.

The kids have no contact with Old Misery and he has rarely talked to them. He once looked over the ruined wall that separated his house and the car park where the kids used to gather and in another time when he tried to give the kids some chocolate candy as a token of good will and friendship. However, the boys refused the man's gift and considered it as a bribe so that they would not throw the ball at the walls of his house while playing in the car park. In defiance of Old Misery's bribe, Blackie made all the kids throw the ball against the walls of the house the entire day. Mike, the youngest kid in the gang, enjoyed the game very much.

The gang meets every morning in the parking lot to vote in a democratic way for the day's new activity. The kids listened to Blackie's idea to spend the whole day getting free rides on buses around the city by fooling bus conductors. Then, "T" convinced them that he had a better plan to enjoy their time. "T's top position amongst the kids becomes well-established when he comes up with the idea of destroying Old Misery's house. "T" tells the other kids that Old Misery will be a way from home throughout the two-day Bank Holiday. The kids listened attentively to "T" while explaining his plan. He tells them that he has visited Old Misery and has seen the interior of the old house. He tells them that it is a beautiful historical house especially the   amazing circular staircase and the artistic wooden paneling on the walls. Blackie becomes jealous when he senses the new comer's top position among the kids, but continued listening to the plan. Then, Blackie tells "T" that the reputation of the gang would have been tarnished unless they had broken into the house, but "T" rejects Blackie's idea and tells the kids that destroying the old house from inside would bring glory and fame to the gang not only in London, but throughout the country. "T" tells the kids that they will never be punished for destroying the house. The destruction of the house from inside, "T" explains, would not be noticeable to any outsiders and passers by and no one can prove anything against them because the whole process of dismantling and destruction will take place from inside the house before they would pull down the walls from outside at night. Above all they would not steal things from the house as some kids have thought. Having listened to Blackie's and "T's "plans, the kids unanimously voted for the destruction of the house. Blackie becomes annoyed and walks off. But having thought carefully of the plan and the glory and fame it would bring to the gang and because he is loyal to the gang, he accepts to follow "T" and join the kids in the execution of his thrilling plan.

At the start of the two-day Bank Holiday the kids meet in the car park carrying hammers , sledgehammers, chisels, saws and other tools ready to start the destruction of the house. The kids stealthily enter the old house and promptly start dismantling and destroying the interior of the house. Every one amongst the kids had a share in the destruction; some have started removing the floors, and the interior walls, while others have started cutting electric wires and sawing the staircase apart. Blackie is given orders to smash the tub and the basin in the deserted indoor lavatory. Mike is given instructions to smash all the china in the kitchen, cut open all the pillows and mattresses in the bedroom, tear up any papers and pull out all the drawers and empty their contents.

At the end of the day, the house has been damaged superficially and "T" instructs the kids to stop working, go home and come back next morning to complete the destruction of the house. Blackie and "T" are left alone in the house. While talking and searching the house "T" finds a sack stuffed with pound notes under the mattress. Blackie asks "T" if he intends to steal Old Misery's savings. "T" tells Blackie that they will steal nothing from the house even the money. Then he takes out a lighter from his pocket and starts burning the bank notes pound after the other till he burned them all. The seventy pounds have been turned into ashes. While "T" is burning the last pound, Blackie asks him if he hates Old Misery. "T" replies that he does not hate the man at all and what they are doing to the man's house has nothing to do with love and hatred, but is rather a matter of joy and having fun. He goes on to say that it would not be funny if they hated the man. Indeed "T" is a sadist destructor even the shape of letter T which the kids call him with looks like a hammer, a symbol of destruction and demolition.

The next day the real destruction of the house begins. Some of the kids become overtired and decide to quit, but "T" keeps them motivated and reminds them of the fame and the glory the destruction of the old house will bring to the gang. The kids start sawing away the joists that support the floor. At night, the kids turn on all the running water taps to flood the house. While they are destroying the house, Mike who has been ordered to stay on lookout, signals that Old Misery is walking towards the house. "T" becomes annoyed and feels betrayed by Old Misery who told him that he would be away the entire two-day Bank Holiday. Having sensed threat of spoiling his project, "T" gives decides to lock Old Misery in the outdoor lavatory while the other kids complete the destruction of the house. "T" gets out of the house to meet Old Misery. He lies to him by telling him that one of the kids is locked in the outdoor lavatory and needs his help to get him out. Old Misery is perplexed, but he accepted to help. While "T" is guiding Old Misery towards the lavatory, he begins to complain of his rheumatism and tells "T" of the big crash he read about in his horoscope in the newspaper. Ironically enough the big crash is yet to come, but the old man seems ignorant of what will happen to his house. Then, all of a sudden the old man finds himself locked inside the outdoor lavatory. While sitting in the lavatory, Old Misery shouted for help several times, but finally stayed calm as he received no response. He knows that passers by will not hear his call for help. There is only one truck in the parking lot and the driver would not come back before the morning. He knew that he would spend the whole night in the lavatory. But what made him go crazy was the sound of carpentry coming from within his house. He thought for a while that there might have been burglars in the house, but why there should be carpentry noises. However, when the hammering and sawing stop, he is relieved and falls sleep. The kids feel sorry for Old Misery and they take pity on the old man. They even give him some food and a blanket to keep himself warm through the night. He tells them he can not sleep in the lavatory because of his rheumatism, but the kids refuse his plea and tell him that he must stay in the lavatory during the night. The gang even tells Old Misery that even if he went to his house, he would not be able to sleep comfortably there, but he could not understand why.

Early next morning the driver of the truck arrives at the car park to drive his truck. As he starts the engine, he hears a voice yelling somewhere in the yard, but he takes no notice of it. Then as he backs the truck into position to drive out of the parking lot, he feels something pulling the truck from behind. As he drives on he hears the sound of bricks bouncing, then he hears a big crash behind him. He gets out of the truck to see what has happened. He becomes excited and amazed to see how the whole landscape behind him has changed. The leaning house that was standing there has disappeared and has turned into rubbles within one minute. Then he sees the rope tied to the back of the truck and realizes what really happened. While investigating and contemplating what happened and how it happened, he hears a voice coming from the outdoor lavatory. He unlocks the door of the lavatory and becomes baffled to see the old man lying motionless there huddled in a blanket and covered in crumbs. When Old Misery sees his house has disappeared, he cries out at the top of his voice and asks the driver what happened. The truck driver says he does not know and bursts into hysterical laughter. Old Misery rebukes the truck driver for laughing at his misfortune. The driver apologizes and tells him that he feels sorry for him, but when he remembers how the truck hesitated as he drove it forward and how the entire house collapsed within one minute behind his truck, he starts laughing again. He says that he feels sorry, but that Old Misery must admit that the way his house has been destroyed is very comical.

Critical Overview:

The Destructors is one of the most widely anthologized short stories in English literature. Although the setting of the story is confined to post-World War II London, it is a universal story that delineates human nature and the human condition. The story highlights man's position between free will and fate. The kids in the story have the capacity for good and evil and when they are given the choice, they choose evil. Old Misery represents fate. It is his fate to come back from a two-day Bank Holiday to find his house destroyed by a group of naughty kids. In the story evil triumphs over good, wickedness over innocence and sophistication and plotting over simplicity and naivety. The kids in the story are far from being innocent. They are cruel, sadistic, and selfish. They not only destroyed the dwelling of a poor unemployed old man who has no wife and children to take care of him in his old age, but they also destroyed a magnificent and historical building built by a famous English architect.

The Destructors is a highly symbolical story. The story is replete with symbols on multiple levels. In fact, the destruction of the old artistic house is symbolical of the destruction of civilization by the two world wars. The two world wars destroyed the infrastructure of many cities in the world, killed millions of people, left millions homeless and left millions of widows and orphans. In fact, the destruction in the story is a microcosm for the destruction in the outside world caused by the two consecutive world wars.

Major Themes:

Innocence:
The kids in "The Destructors" are teenagers except for Mike who is still a very young child. Although we expect them to be innocent, they are wicked sadists. Their childish innocence is gone and is replaced by cynicism, sadism, rebelliousness and selfishness. They have indeed become rebellious social outcasts in a society torn apart by war.

The Human Nature:
On the surface "The Destructors" is a story of action, suspense and childhood adventures, but at a deeper level, the story is about the human nature, war and delinquency. The struggle for power between Blackie and Trevor on the one hand, and the struggle for territorial dominion between the gang and Old Misery are merely microcosmic portrayal of the conflicts over power and territorial dominion that permeate the modern world.

In "The Destructors" Graham Greene depicts both sides of the human nature; the good side and the evil one. The kids represent the evil side, whereas, Old Misery represents the good side. The kids who are supposed to be portrayed as innocent are paradoxically portrayed as evil and wicked, whereas, Old Misery who represents the world of adults and grown ups is paradoxically portrayed as good and innocent. This change of roles echoes the image of the distorted world that emerged after the two global wars. The world depicted in the story is instable, distorted and gloomy. The instability of England in the aftermath of World War II is reflected in the opposing forces in the story mainly the conflicts between Blackie and Trevor and between the gang and Old Misery. These conflicts reflect a society that has survived trauma, but is still evolving and changing as a result of the consequences of the two devastating wars.

The Degradation of the Individual in the Modern World:

Characters in "The Destructors "are deeply flawed though they are still in their teens. They represent the brutality of the human nature at its worst. They destroy the old house of a helpless old man just for making fun and wasting their time. In seeking fun, they become sadists and brutes. This reflects the degradation of the individual in the modern world as a result of two devastating world wars. The story reflects man's greed for power, hegemony and sadist destruction of the world. Instead of building the world, man is recklessly destroying cities with heavy weaponry. The destruction of the historical house is symbolical of man's destruction of art and civilization in wars. During bloody wars museums, works of art and sculptures are destroyed and human civilization is wasted

Parental Negligence:

As a result of parents' negligence of their children during and in the aftermath of the war and such children tended to form destructive gangs throughout the country. Their tendency to destroy and commit criminal acts increased without schooling and without parental care. Some of these kids were orphans as their fathers were killed during the wars, others were poor and their families could not bring them up properly. The kids in the story spend most of their time in the parking lot and the streets of London. They even stay outside their homes throughout the night. They seem to have rejected the community of the adults and have established their own rebellious, destructive community. The kids have occupied the deserted parking lot and plan to make incursion into Old Misery's house just like the Nazi Germans who were trying to make incursion to England during World War II . The events in "The Destructors" parody and mimic the events of the war in the gang's microcosm.

Questions:

I. Who is the protagonist in the story- Trevor, Blackie, or the gang? Who is the antagonist? Identify the conflicts in the story.

Although he recently joined the gang, Trevor is the protagonist in the story not Blackie. His brilliant idea to destroy Old Misery's house from the interior and then bring it down attracts the attention of all the kids in the gang.

The first conflict in the story starts between Blackie, the former leader of the gang and Trevor the newcomer who vies with Blackie for the leadership among the kids on the very first day they met. The conflict becomes worse when Blackie senses that the kids did not vote for his idea to get free rides on buses and instead they voted for Trevor's idea to destroy Old Misery's shabby house which survived the bombings of the Second World War which destroyed many buildings in London among which was the house next to it. Blackie believes that breaking into the house and stealing all that the kids can find inside is a better idea than destroying the house for fun. Trevor believes that destroying Old Misery's house would certainly bring fame and glory to the gang. This becomes apparent when Trevor begins to burn the banknotes he found in Old Misery's mattress where he used to hoard his savings. Blackie wants to steal the money, but Trevor ignores his suggestion and starts burning the bank notes with enjoyment one banknote after the other till the 70 pounds turned into ashes. To show his obedience to Trevor, Blackie asks Trevor if burning the bank notes stems from his hatred for Old Misery. Trevor replies that he does not hate Old Misery at all and there would not be any enjoyment in destroying the man's house if he hated him. His remark that there isn't any love or hate in the burning of the bank notes, and that he was doing that for fun reflects his sadism and the pleasure he gets from destroying other people's properties.

At first Blackie refuses to take part in the destruction plan, but then thought that pulling off the old house would bring fame and glory to the gang. His loyalty to the gang is stronger than his love for the leadership among the kids and this devotion and loyalty to the gang made him follow T and accept him as the gang's new leader.

The second conflict in the story is an old conflict between the antagonist in the story Old Misery and the gang. Old Misery is a stingy man who instead of living in a decent house, opts to live in a deserted propped up old house. As a builder and a decorator he renovated the old house and lived there with minimal expenditures. Though the kids have little contact with the stingy man, they consider him as an eccentric man whose presence in the neighborhood is not welcome. To the gang, Old Misery poses a serious threat as his occupation of the deserted house confines their movement in their territory. To Old Misery the kids also pose a threat to his own dwelling. He looks at them with suspicion and fears that one day they will break in the house to steal his savings or even damage part of his property. On one or two occasions, he looked at them over the ruined wall of his yard as they gather in the parking lot near his house to make sure that his property is safe. To keep the kids away from his property he gives them chocolate candy which they refuse to take considering it as a bribe to make them stop bouncing the ball against the walls of his house. In defiance to the man's kindness and bribe the kids keep bouncing the ball at the walls of the man's house. The conflict between the gang and Old Misery ends with the kids' triumph when they finally lock him in the outdoor lavatory till they finish destroying the interior of the house. However, the kids did not destroy Old misery's house because they hated him, but rather to fulfill their ambitions to become the most famous destructive creative gang in the country. This becomes quite apparent when they give him food to eat and a blanket to sleep comfortably while being locked in the lavatory for the whole night.

"The Destructors"

II. Check your understanding:

1. With whom does Trevor vie to be the new leader of the Wormsley Common Gang?
   A) Mike
   B) Old Misery
   C) Blackie
   D) Summers

2. Why did the boys refuse to take the chocolate candy Old Misery offered to give to them?
   A) They realized that he was giving them the chocolate bars because he wanted them to take care of his old house while he was away buying bread and vegetables from the market
   B) They were suspicious of his offering and thought he was giving them a bribe to keep them away
      from spoiling his house
   C) None of the kids liked the chocolate candy because it was of bad quality
   D) The chocolate candy was not sufficient for the kids and they asked Old Misery to give them some money

3. Which plan did the kids vote for?
   A) Blackie's plan to get free rides on buses around the city by deceiving bus conductors
   B) Trevor's plan to destroy Old Misery's house from inside and then pulling it down with the help of a truck
   C) Mike's plan to keep bouncing the ball at Old Misery's house
   D) Trevor's plan to steal Old Misery's savings

4. Why did the gang know from the very beginning that they would not be punished for destroying Old Misery's house?
   A) They were sure that no one would see them while they were destroying the interior of the house
   B) The kids would not steal money or any thing from the house
   C) (A&B)

D) The truck driver who would unintentionally pull down the old house might be charged with destroying the house

5. For what purpose did the kids destroy Old Misery's shabby house?
   A) They hated Old Misery who continually prevented them from playing football in the nearby car park
   B) They wanted to steal Old Misery's savings
   C) They wanted to achieve fame and glory for the Wormsley Common Gang and be better off than other gangs in the city
   D) They hated the truck driver and wanted to send him to prison for destroying the house

6. Why did Blackie, the former leader of the gang, return to the gang and follow Trevor?
   A) Blackie was loyal to the gang and wanted to achieve fame and glory for the gang no matter who the leader was
   B) Blackie feared Trevor since he was stronger
   C) Blackie knew the kids hated him and would always vote for Trevor's plans
   D) Blackie thought Trevor would help him steal Old Misery's savings

7. What did Trevor do with Old Misery's savings which he found hoarded in the mattress?
   A) He gave everyone of the kids his share of the money and took nothing for himself
   B) He gave Blackie his share of the money and kept the rest for himself
   C) He did not take the money and left it in the mattress
   D) He burned the bank notes one after the other with enjoyment

8. Why did the gang lock up Old Misery in the outdoor lavatory?
   A) To keep him away from the house until they find his savings
   B) So that he would not bother them while destroying the interior of his house
   C) Because the lavatory was a comfortable place for Old Misery who suffered from rheumatism
   D) (A&C)

9. How did the truck driver react when he saw the old house destroyed completely within a second and that it was tied with a rope to his truck?

A) He couldn't stop himself from laughing

B) He felt sad and began crying

C) He apologizes to Old Misery for laughing at how his house was destroyed and how he was locked up in the lavatory, but when he remembers how the truck hesitated as he pulled it forward he starts to laugh all over again.

D) (A&C)

10. It is ironic that Old Misery's horoscope should read "Abstain from any dealings in first half of week. Danger of serious crash". The horoscope is applicable to the man's situation, but he is ignorant of the fact that his house will be destroyed shortly. **What kind of irony is used here?**

A) Irony of situation

B) Dramatic irony

C) Verbal irony

D) No irony is used here

Part Two
Drama

Tragedy and Comedy

Drama is a literary genre that includes all literary works that can be transformed into theatrical performances. A play is a dramatic work written exclusively to be performed by actors and actresses on the stage of a theatre. A play may be either written in verse or prose. Stage performances of dramatic works sharpen the audiences' awareness of life, human experience and human existence. Drama is classified into two broad categories tragedy and comedy. Generally speaking, all plays can be classified under the two broad terms: tragedy or comedy. However, it is impossible to classify all plays under the two terms tragedy and comedy since some plays combine features of tragedy and comedy. As readers we should know what type of play we are reading. Is the play a tragedy or a comedy?

The distinction between a comedy and a tragedy can be summed up as follows:
1- A comedy is funny, whereas a tragedy is sad.
2- A comedy has a happy ending, whereas a tragedy has a sad ending. The typical ending for a comedy is marriage, whereas the typical ending for tragedy is death.
3- Tragedy emphasizes human greatness, whereas comedy ridicules human weakness, his littleness, insignificance and follies. However, the distinction between tragedy and comedy is sometimes unreliable
4- Tragedy celebrates human freedom, whereas comedy points up human limitations.

5- The function of comedy is critical and corrective therefore it exposes human folly, and irrational behaviour, whereas, the function of tragedy is to show human greatness.

6- The protagonist in a tragedy is a man of noble stature, better than ourselves, whereas the protagonist in a comedy is an ordinary person with follies and inadequacies.

7- Tragedy tends to isolate the tragic hero and emphasize his uniqueness, whereas comedy places the comic hero in the midst of a group and emphasizes his commonness.

8- Where the tragic hero possesses an overpowering individuality, so that the play is often named after him (For example Othello, Macbeth, King Lear and Oedipus Rex), the comic hero tends to be a type, and his play is often named for the type (For example, The Misanthrope).

Although such differences do exist between a comedy and a tragedy, they are not true all the time. For some plays that we classify as comedies are not intended to be funny and they do not make us laugh. Great tragedies, though involve suffering and sad endings, do not leave the spectators depressed. Some funny comedies have sad endings and some tragedies do not have unhappy endings but conclude with the protagonist's triumph.

Aristotle's Definition of Tragedy:

In the *Poetics* Aristotle defined tragedy as: "The imitation in dramatic form of an action that is serious and complete, with incidents arousing pity and fear wherewith it affects a catharsis of such emotions". According to Aristotle, the language of tragedy is pleasurable and pleasing and appropriate to the situation in which it is used. The chief characters in tragedy are noble and great personages; better than ourselves. The actions these great people perform are noble and great actions. The plot in a tragedy involves a change in the protagonist's fortune, in which he falls from happiness into misery, from luxury into depression and discomfort. The protagonist is far from being perfect nor yet a bad man. The tragic hero's downfall is not caused by vice and depravity but by some error of judgment.

What are the main features of a tragic hero?

1- According to Aristotle, the tragic hero is a man of noble stature. He has a greatness about him. He is not an ordinary man but one of outstanding quality. In Greek and Shakespearean tragedy, he is usually a king or a prince. The tragic hero is great not primarily by virtue of his aristocratic birth, but also by his possession of extraordinary powers, by qualities of passion and nobility of mind. His downfall is tragic since it is a fall from a height.

2- Though the tragic hero is great, he is far from being perfect. Combined with his strength, there is a vulnerability.

3- The tragic hero suffers from a flaw in character which Aristotle calls "a tragic flaw". Aristotle describes this tragic flaw as "some error of judgment" which ultimately causes his downfall.

4- Despite all the powers he has, the tragic hero is afflicted with a tragic flaw which ultimately destroys him and brings about his downfall. The tragic flaw can be excessive pride, ambition, rash and quickness to anger, vanity or even jealousy.

5- The tragic hero's downfall is partially his own fault, the result of his own free choice, not the result of accident or villainy or some dominant malignant fate. Accident, villainy and cruel fate do contribute to the tragic hero's downfall, but only as cooperating agents.

6- Nevertheless, the hero's misfortunes are not wholly deserved. The punishment far exceeds the crime. Therefore, we are left with a sad sense for the loss and waste of a great human being.

7- The audiences are overwhelmed with a sense of sadness for the destruction and downfall of the tragic hero. Therefore, they admire his greatness, and overlook his weakness. They are filled with pity and fear as a result of what they see on stage. For they see in front of their own eyes, the collapse and destruction of a human being.

8- The tragic fall of the protagonist is not pure loss. Though it might result in the tragic hero's death, it involves some increase in self-awareness and self-knowledge- As Aristotle puts it "some discovery"- a change from ignorance to awareness and knowledge.

9- Through suffering, the tragic hero realizes his weakness and vulnerability, and thus realizes that he is not different from ordinary mortals.

10- The tragic hero does not curse his fate, but rather he accepts his defeat in life and acknowledges his ignorance and vulnerability.

11- The tragic downfall of the hero makes the audiences sad, fills their hearts with pity and fear, but doesn't leave them in a state of depression.

12- The tragic action on stage and the hero's tragic downfall make the audiences feel sad because they experience an appalling sense of human waste, a recognition of human greatness.

13- Although the tragic hero is defeated, he gains a better stature and understanding of his own limitations and vulnerability.

Comedy:

The two masks of drama; the smiling or laughing mask and the weeping mask represent the two modes of drama; comedy and tragedy respectively. The laughing mask which represents scornful or laughing comedy ridicules the absurdity of human behaviour and highlights his limitations, whereas the weeping mask which represents tragedy highlights human greatness and human waste.

Melodrama and Farce:

Melodrama is a kind of tragedy that features sensational incidents, emphasizing plot at the expense of characterization, relying on cruder conflicts. A melodrama often has a happy ending mainly the protagonist triumphs over the antagonist and good triumphs over evil. **A farce** is a type of funny comedy that emphasizes improbable situations, violent conflicts, or physical action over characterization and plot. A farce aims at making the audiences laugh, but uses cruder means than those used in a comedy. For example, characters trip over benches, insult each other, run into walls and knock each others down. Both a melodrama and a farce are escapist rather than interpretive.

The Nature of Drama

- Drama, like prose fiction, makes use of plot and characters, develops a theme and arouses a variety of human feelings and emotions.
- Like poetry, drama may draw upon all the resources of language, including verse. Great tragedies and comedies were written in verse not in prose.

- However, unlike fiction and poetry, drama is written to be performed on the stage in a theatre and not to be read.
- Drama presents its action 1) **through actors** 2) **on stage** and 3) **before an audience**.
- Through acting, the power of speech, intonation, facial expressions, gestures, and pantomime, the actor's words become more expressive than being read in a book.
- Unlike poets and novelists, playwrights can not directly comment on the action or the characters. He can not enter the actor's mind and tell us what is going on there. Though, authorial voice may be placed in the mouth of the major character in the play, but this will be at the expense of characterization.
- **Authorial voice** and entry into the hero's mind can also be achieved through certain dramatic techniques mainly the aside and the soliloquy.
- **Soliloquy** is a speech in which a character , alone on the stage, addresses himself; a soliloquy is a "thinking out aloud", a dramatic technique of letting the audience know a character's thoughts and feelings
- **Aside** is a brief speech in which a character turns from the person he is addressing to speak directly to the audience, a dramatic technique of letting the audience know what a character is really thinking and feeling as opposed to what he pretends to think or feel.(Characters speaking in soliloquies and asides are always telling the truth).

Realistic and Nonrealistic Drama
- Plays are either realistic or nonrealistic or a combination of both. **Realistic drama** depicts everyday life in both content and presentation to preserve the illusion of actual life. **Nonrealistic drama** is drama that departs from the external appearance of real life both in content and presentation. It employs nonrealistic dramatic techniques and theatrical devices to depict internal reality or the subjective experiences of the characters.
- Some plays exhibit a combination between realistic and nonrealistic dramatic techniques to depict internal and external reality or to put it straight forward to depict the characters' daily life and to depict what they think and feel.
- Drama can be realistic or nonrealistic in both content and mode of presentation. The stage performance including acting, music, sound effects, lighting, colour, make up and costuming may be used either

realistically to depict outer reality or nonrealistically to depict inner reality which includes the characters' feelings and thoughts.

- Nonrealistic drama depicts the fantasies, illusions and inner thoughts of the characters on stage by means of nonrealistic theatrical techniques and dramatic techniques, whereas realistic drama portrays only outer reality and fails to depict the characters' inner thoughts and feelings.
- The audiences in the theatre should accept all the theatrical conventions of the play's stage performance no matter how fanciful or nonrealistic they are. For example, the theatre goer should take it for granted that the missing fourth wall of the stage exists even though he knows for sure that it does not exist.
- In ordinary stage actors should face the fourth missing wall most of the time so that the audiences can see them. In an arena type theatre, the actors should not turn their backs too long to any "missing wall".
- Realistic drama utilizes real stage sets for example bookshelves with real books to perform a scene in a study, whereas in an unrealistic play the same scenery may be performed on a stage furnished with drapes and platforms.
- The language of realistic drama is quite common and realistic. Ordinary speech is used by most characters in realistic plays. Their speech is replete with inaccuracies, mistakes, slips of the tongue, hesitant speech and grammatically incorrect sentences.
- The audiences should accept all the play's dramatic conventions without questioning their reliability. For example, that a room with three walls has a fourth wall even if it does not really exist, that the actors speak the language of the audience whatever the nationality of the persons they play.
- Great plays have been written in both the realistic and nonrealistic theatrical modes.

- The chorus in Greek tragedy:
In Greek tragedy a group of actors speaking or chanting in unison, often in a chant, often while dancing with highly formalized steps. The chorus is an unrealistic theatrical device the function of which is to reveal the tragic hero's inner thoughts and feelings and to comment on the course of action he has taken or is supposed to take. In modern unrealistic drama, the chorus has been replaced with the narrator who introduces the characters, comments on their actions and reveals their inner thoughts and feelings.

Both the chorus in Greek tragedy and the narrator in modern nonrealistic plays speak the truth.

-The study of drama requires the purposeful learning of realistic and nonrealistic dramatic techniques.

-**Temporary suspension of disbelief** means that the audiences who watch a play should regard the fictional world created by the playwright as real no matter how unreal and imaginary it is.

William Shakespeare
The Tragedy of Hamlet, Prince of Denmark

Ophelia, shortly before she
drowns in the brook

Hamlet holding Yorick's skull

The Tragedy of Hamlet, Prince of Denmark

Dramatis Personæ

CLAUDIUS, King of Denmark.
HAMLET, Son to the late, and Nephew to the present King.
GERTRUDE, Queen of Denmark and Mother to Hamlet.
FORTINBRAS, Prince of Norway.
HORATIO, Friend to Hamlet.
POLONIUS, Lord Chamberlain.
LAERTES, Son to Polonius.
OPHELIA, Daughter to Polonius.
VOLTIMAND, CORNELIUS, ROSENCRANTZ, GUILDENSTERN,
OSRIC, & A Gentleman, Courtiers.
A Priest.
MARCELLUS & BERNARDO, Officers.
FRANCISCO, a Soldier.
REYNALDO, Servant to Polonius.
A Captain.
English Ambassadors.
Players. Two Clowns, Grave-diggers.
Lords, Ladies, Officers, Soldiers, Sailors, Messengers, and Attendants
Ghost of King Hamlet- Hamlet's Father.

The Complete Text

ACT I
SCENE I. Elsinore. A platform before the castle.
FRANCISCO at his post. Enter to him BERNARDO
BERNARDO
Who's there?
FRANCISCO
Nay, answer me: stand, and unfold yourself.
BERNARDO
Long live the king!
FRANCISCO
Bernardo?
BERNARDO
He.
FRANCISCO
You come most carefully upon your hour.
BERNARDO
'Tis now struck twelve; get thee to bed, Francisco.
FRANCISCO
For this relief much thanks: 'tis bitter cold,
And I am sick at heart.
BERNARDO
Have you had quiet guard?
FRANCISCO
Not a mouse stirring.
BERNARDO
Well, good night.
If you do meet Horatio and Marcellus,
The rivals of my watch, bid them make haste.
FRANCISCO
I think I hear them. Stand, ho! Who's there?
Enter HORATIO and MARCELLUS
HORATIO
Friends to this ground.
MARCELLUS
And liegemen to the Dane.

FRANCISCO
Give you good night.
MARCELLUS
O, farewell, honest soldier:
Who hath relieved you?
FRANCISCO
Bernardo has my place.
Give you good night.
Exit
MARCELLUS
Holla! Bernardo!
BERNARDO
Say,
What, is Horatio there?
HORATIO
A piece of him.
BERNARDO
Welcome, Horatio: welcome, good Marcellus.
MARCELLUS sacvbnmhgfdase
]What, has this thing appear'd again to-night?
BERNARDO
I have seen nothing.
MARCELLUS
Horatio says 'tis but our fantasy,
And will not let belief take hold of him
Touching this dreaded sight, twice seen of us:
Therefore I have entreated him along
With us to watch the minutes of this night;
That if again this apparition come,
He may approve our eyes and speak to it.
HORATIO
Tush, tush, 'twill not appear.
BERNARDO
Sit down awhile;
And let us once again assail your ears,
That are so fortified against our story
What we have two nights seen.

HORATIO
Well, sit we down,
And let us hear Bernardo speak of this.
BERNARDO
Last night of all,
When yond same star that's westward from the pole
Had made his course to illume that part of heaven
Where now it burns, Marcellus and myself,
The bell then beating one,--
Enter Ghost
MARCELLUS
Peace, break thee off; look, where it comes again!
BERNARDO
In the same figure, like the king that's dead.
MARCELLUS
Thou art a scholar; speak to it, Horatio.
BERNARDO
Looks it not like the king? mark it, Horatio.
HORATIO
Most like: it harrows me with fear and wonder.
BERNARDO
It would be spoke to.
MARCELLUS
Question it, Horatio.
HORATIO
What art thou that usurp'st this time of night,
Together with that fair and warlike form
In which the majesty of buried Denmark
Did sometimes march? by heaven I charge thee, speak!
MARCELLUS
It is offended.
BERNARDO
See, it stalks away!
HORATIO
Stay! speak, speak! I charge thee, speak!
Exit Ghost
MARCELLUS
'Tis gone, and will not answer.

BERNARDO

How now, Horatio! you tremble and look pale:
Is not this something more than fantasy?
What think you on't?

HORATIO

Before my God, I might not this believe
Without the sensible and true avouch
Of mine own eyes.

MARCELLUS

Is it not like the king?

HORATIO

As thou art to thyself:
Such was the very armour he had on
When he the ambitious Norway combated;
So frown'd he once, when, in an angry parle,
He smote the sledded Polacks on the ice.
'Tis strange.

MARCELLUS

Thus twice before, and jump at this dead hour,
With martial stalk hath he gone by our watch.

HORATIO

In what particular thought to work I know not;
But in the gross and scope of my opinion,
This bodes some strange eruption to our state.

MARCELLUS

Good now, sit down, and tell me, he that knows,
Why this same strict and most observant watch
So nightly toils the subject of the land,
And why such daily cast of brazen cannon,
And foreign mart for implements of war;
Why such impress of shipwrights, whose sore task
Does not divide the Sunday from the week;
What might be toward, that this sweaty haste
Doth make the night joint-labourer with the day:
Who is't that can inform me?

HORATIO

That can I;
At least, the whisper goes so. Our last king,
Whose image even but now appear'd to us,

Was, as you know, by Fortinbras of Norway,
Thereto prick'd on by a most emulate pride,
Dared to the combat; in which our valiant Hamlet--
For so this side of our known world esteem'd him--
Did slay this Fortinbras; who by a seal'd compact,
Well ratified by law and heraldry,
Did forfeit, with his life, all those his lands
Which he stood seized of, to the conqueror:
Against the which, a moiety competent
Was gaged by our king; which had return'd
To the inheritance of Fortinbras,
Had he been vanquisher; as, by the same covenant,
And carriage of the article design'd,
His fell to Hamlet. Now, sir, young Fortinbras,
Of unimproved mettle hot and full,
Hath in the skirts of Norway here and there
Shark'd up a list of lawless resolutes,
For food and diet, to some enterprise
That hath a stomach in't; which is no other--
As it doth well appear unto our state--
But to recover of us, by strong hand
And terms compulsatory, those foresaid lands
So by his father lost: and this, I take it,
Is the main motive of our preparations,
The source of this our watch and the chief head
Of this post-haste and romage in the land.

BERNARDO

I think it be no other but e'en so:
Well may it sort that this portentous figure
Comes armed through our watch; so like the king
That was and is the question of these wars.

HORATIO

A mote it is to trouble the mind's eye.
In the most high and palmy state of Rome,
A little ere the mightiest Julius fell,
The graves stood tenantless and the sheeted dead
Did squeak and gibber in the Roman streets:
As stars with trains of fire and dews of blood,
Disasters in the sun; and the moist star

Upon whose influence Neptune's empire stands
Was sick almost to doomsday with eclipse:
And even the like precurse of fierce events,
As harbingers preceding still the fates
And prologue to the omen coming on,
Have heaven and earth together demonstrated
Unto our climatures and countrymen.--
But soft, behold! lo, where it comes again!
Re-enter Ghost
I'll cross it, though it blast me. Stay, illusion!
If thou hast any sound, or use of voice,
Speak to me:
If there be any good thing to be done,
That may to thee do ease and grace to me,
Speak to me: (*Cock crows*)
If thou art privy to thy country's fate,
Which, happily, foreknowing may avoid, O, speak!
Or if thou hast uphoarded in thy life
Extorted treasure in the womb of earth,
For which, they say, you spirits oft walk in death,
Speak of it: stay, and speak! Stop it, Marcellus.
MARCELLUS
Shall I strike at it with my partisan?
HORATIO
Do, if it will not stand.
BERNARDO
'Tis here!
HORATIO
'Tis here!
MARCELLUS
'Tis gone!
Exit Ghost
We do it wrong, being so majestical,
To offer it the show of violence;
For it is, as the air, invulnerable,
And our vain blows malicious mockery.
BERNARDO
It was about to speak, when the cock crew.

HORATIO

And then it started like a guilty thing
Upon a fearful summons. I have heard,
The cock, that is the trumpet to the morn,
Doth with his lofty and shrill-sounding throat
Awake the god of day; and, at his warning,
Whether in sea or fire, in earth or air,
The extravagant and erring spirit hies
To his confine: and of the truth herein
This present object made probation.

MARCELLUS

It faded on the crowing of the cock.
Some say that ever 'gainst that season comes
Wherein our Saviour's birth is celebrated,
The bird of dawning singeth all night long:
And then, they say, no spirit dares stir abroad;
The nights are wholesome; then no planets strike,
No fairy takes, nor witch hath power to charm,
So hallow'd and so gracious is the time.

HORATIO

So have I heard and do in part believe it.
But, look, the morn, in russet mantle clad,
Walks o'er the dew of yon high eastward hill:
Break we our watch up; and by my advice,
Let us impart what we have seen to-night
Unto young Hamlet; for, upon my life,
This spirit, dumb to us, will speak to him.
Do you consent we shall acquaint him with it,
As needful in our loves, fitting our duty?

MARCELLUS

Let's do't, I pray; and I this morning know
Where we shall find him most conveniently.
Exeunt

SCENE II. A room of state in the castle.

Enter KING CLAUDIUS, QUEEN GERTRUDE, HAMLET, POLONIUS,
LAERTES, VOLTIMAND, CORNELIUS, Lords, and Attendants

KING CLAUDIUS

Though yet of Hamlet our dear brother's death
The memory be green, and that it us befitted

To bear our hearts in grief and our whole kingdom
To be contracted in one brow of woe,
Yet so far hath discretion fought with nature
That we with wisest sorrow think on him,
Together with remembrance of ourselves.
Therefore our sometime sister, now our queen,
The imperial jointress to this warlike state,
Have we, as 'twere with a defeated joy,--
With an auspicious and a dropping eye,
With mirth in funeral and with dirge in marriage,
In equal scale weighing delight and dole,--
Taken to wife: nor have we herein barr'd
Your better wisdoms, which have freely gone
With this affair along. For all, our thanks.
Now follows, that you know, young Fortinbras,
Holding a weak supposal of our worth,
Or thinking by our late dear brother's death
Our state to be disjoint and out of frame,
Colleagued with the dream of his advantage,
He hath not fail'd to pester us with message,
Importing the surrender of those lands
Lost by his father, with all bonds of law,
To our most valiant brother. So much for him.
Now for ourself and for this time of meeting:
Thus much the business is: we have here writ
To Norway, uncle of young Fortinbras,--
Who, impotent and bed-rid, scarcely hears
Of this his nephew's purpose,--to suppress
His further gait herein; in that the levies,
The lists and full proportions, are all made
Out of his subject: and we here dispatch
You, good Cornelius, and you, Voltimand,
For bearers of this greeting to old Norway;
Giving to you no further personal power
To business with the king, more than the scope
Of these delated articles allow.
Farewell, and let your haste commend your duty.
CORNELIUS VOLTIMAND
In that and all things will we show our duty.

KING CLAUDIUS

We doubt it nothing: heartily farewell.

Exeunt VOLTIMAND and CORNELIUS

And now, Laertes, what's the news with you?

You told us of some suit; what is't, Laertes?

You cannot speak of reason to the Dane,

And loose your voice: what wouldst thou beg, Laertes,

That shall not be my offer, not thy asking?

The head is not more native to the heart,

The hand more instrumental to the mouth,

Than is the throne of Denmark to thy father.

What wouldst thou have, Laertes?

LAERTES

My dread lord,

Your leave and favour to return to France;

From whence though willingly I came to Denmark,

To show my duty in your coronation,

Yet now, I must confess, that duty done,

My thoughts and wishes bend again toward France

And bow them to your gracious leave and pardon.

KING CLAUDIUS

Have you your father's leave? What says Polonius?

LORD POLONIUS

He hath, my lord, wrung from me my slow leave

By laboursome petition, and at last

Upon his will I seal'd my hard consent:

I do beseech you, give him leave to go.

KING CLAUDIUS

Take thy fair hour, Laertes; time be thine,

And thy best graces spend it at thy will!

But now, my cousin Hamlet, and my son,--

HAMLET

[Aside] A little more than kin, and less than kind.

KING CLAUDIUS

How is it that the clouds still hang on you?

HAMLET

Not so, my lord; I am too much i' the sun.

QUEEN GERTRUDE
Good Hamlet, cast thy nighted colour off,
And let thine eye look like a friend on Denmark.
Do not for ever with thy vailed lids
Seek for thy noble father in the dust:
Thou know'st 'tis common; all that lives must die,
Passing through nature to eternity.
HAMLET
Ay, madam, it is common.
QUEEN GERTRUDE
If it be,
Why seems it so particular with thee?
HAMLET
Seems, madam! nay it is; I know not 'seems.'
'Tis not alone my inky cloak, good mother,
Nor customary suits of solemn black,
Nor windy suspiration of forced breath,
No, nor the fruitful river in the eye,
Nor the dejected 'havior of the visage,
Together with all forms, moods, shapes of grief,
That can denote me truly: these indeed seem,
For they are actions that a man might play:
But I have that within which passeth show;
These but the trappings and the suits of woe.
KING CLAUDIUS
'Tis sweet and commendable in your nature, Hamlet,
To give these mourning duties to your father:
But, you must know, your father lost a father;
That father lost, lost his, and the survivor bound
In filial obligation for some term
To do obsequious sorrow: but to persever
In obstinate condolement is a course
Of impious stubbornness; 'tis unmanly grief;
It shows a will most incorrect to heaven,
A heart unfortified, a mind impatient,
An understanding simple and unschool'd:
For what we know must be and is as common
As any the most vulgar thing to sense,
Why should we in our peevish opposition

Take it to heart? Fie! 'tis a fault to heaven,
A fault against the dead, a fault to nature,
To reason most absurd: whose common theme
Is death of fathers, and who still hath cried,
From the first corse till he that died to-day,
'This must be so.' We pray you, throw to earth
This unprevailing woe, and think of us
As of a father: for let the world take note,
You are the most immediate to our throne;
And with no less nobility of love
Than that which dearest father bears his son,
Do I impart toward you. For your intent
In going back to school in Wittenberg,
It is most retrograde to our desire:
And we beseech you, bend you to remain
Here, in the cheer and comfort of our eye,
Our chiefest courtier, cousin, and our son.

QUEEN GERTRUDE
Let not thy mother lose her prayers, Hamlet:
I pray thee, stay with us; go not to Wittenberg.

HAMLET
I shall in all my best obey you, madam.

KING CLAUDIUS
Why, 'tis a loving and a fair reply:
Be as ourself in Denmark. Madam, come;
This gentle and unforced accord of Hamlet
Sits smiling to my heart: in grace whereof,
No jocund health that Denmark drinks to-day,
But the great cannon to the clouds shall tell,
And the king's rouse the heavens all bruit again,
Re-speaking earthly thunder. Come away.
Exeunt all but HAMLET

HAMLET
O, that this too too solid flesh would melt
Thaw and resolve itself into a dew!
Or that the Everlasting had not fix'd
His canon 'gainst self-slaughter! O God! God!
How weary, stale, flat and unprofitable,
Seem to me all the uses of this world!

Fie on't! ah fie! 'tis an unweeded garden,
That grows to seed; things rank and gross in nature
Possess it merely. That it should come to this!
But two months dead: nay, not so much, not two:
So excellent a king; that was, to this,
Hyperion to a satyr; so loving to my mother
That he might not beteem the winds of heaven
Visit her face too roughly. Heaven and earth!
Must I remember? why, she would hang on him,
As if increase of appetite had grown
By what it fed on: and yet, within a month--
Let me not think on't--Frailty, thy name is woman!--
A little month, or ere those shoes were old
With which she follow'd my poor father's body,
Like Niobe, all tears:--why she, even she--
O, God! a beast, that wants discourse of reason,
Would have mourn'd longer--married with my uncle,
My father's brother, but no more like my father
Than I to Hercules: within a month:
Ere yet the salt of most unrighteous tears
Had left the flushing in her galled eyes,
She married. O, most wicked speed, to post
With such dexterity to incestuous sheets!
It is not nor it cannot come to good:
But break, my heart; for I must hold my tongue.
Enter HORATIO, MARCELLUS, and BERNARDO

HORATIO
Hail to your lordship!

HAMLET
I am glad to see you well:
Horatio,--or I do forget myself.

HORATIO
The same, my lord, and your poor servant ever.

HAMLET
Sir, my good friend; I'll change that name with you:
And what make you from Wittenberg, Horatio? Marcellus?

MARCELLUS
My good lord—

HAMLET
I am very glad to see you. Good even, sir.
But what, in faith, make you from Wittenberg?
HORATIO
A truant disposition, good my lord.
HAMLET
I would not hear your enemy say so,
Nor shall you do mine ear that violence,
To make it truster of your own report
Against yourself: I know you are no truant.
But what is your affair in Elsinore?
We'll teach you to drink deep ere you depart.
HORATIO
My lord, I came to see your father's funeral.
HAMLET
I pray thee, do not mock me, fellow-student;
I think it was to see my mother's wedding.
HORATIO
Indeed, my lord, it follow'd hard upon.
HAMLET
Thrift, thrift, Horatio! the funeral baked meats
Did coldly furnish forth the marriage tables.
Would I had met my dearest foe in heaven
Or ever I had seen that day, Horatio!
My father!--methinks I see my father.
HORATIO
Where, my lord?
HAMLET
In my mind's eye, Horatio.
HORATIO
I saw him once; he was a goodly king.
HAMLET
He was a man, take him for all in all,
I shall not look upon his like again.
HORATIO
My lord, I think I saw him yesternight.
HAMLET
Saw? who?

HORATIO
My lord, the king your father.
HAMLET
The king my father!
HORATIO
Season your admiration for awhile
With an attent ear, till I may deliver,
Upon the witness of these gentlemen,
This marvel to you.
HAMLET
For God's love, let me hear.
HORATIO
Two nights together had these gentlemen,
Marcellus and Bernardo, on their watch,
In the dead vast and middle of the night,
Been thus encounter'd. A figure like your father,
Armed at point exactly, cap-a-pe,
Appears before them, and with solemn march
Goes slow and stately by them: thrice he walk'd
By their oppress'd and fear-surprised eyes,
Within his truncheon's length; whilst they, distilled
Almost to jelly with the act of fear,
Stand dumb and speak not to him. This to me
In dreadful secrecy impart they did;
And I with them the third night kept the watch;
Where, as they had deliver'd, both in time,
Form of the thing, each word made true and good,
The apparition comes: I knew your father;
These hands are not more like.
HAMLET
But where was this?
MARCELLUS
My lord, upon the platform where we watch'd.
HAMLET
Did you not speak to it?
HORATIO
My lord, I did;
But answer made it none: yet once methought
It lifted up its head and did address

Itself to motion, like as it would speak;
But even then the morning cock crew loud,
And at the sound it shrunk in haste away,
And vanish'd from our sight.

HAMLET

'Tis very strange.

HORATIO

As I do live, my honour'd lord, 'tis true;
And we did think it writ down in our duty
To let you know of it.

HAMLET

Indeed, indeed, sirs, but this troubles me.
Hold you the watch to-night?

MARCELLUS BERNARDO

We do, my lord.

HAMLET

Arm'd, say you?

MARCELLUS BERNARDO

Arm'd, my lord.

HAMLET

From top to toe?

MARCELLUS BERNARDO

My lord, from head to foot.

HAMLET

Then saw you not his face?

HORATIO

O, yes, my lord; he wore his beaver up.

HAMLET

What, look'd he frowningly?

HORATIO

A countenance more in sorrow than in anger.

HAMLET

Pale or red?

HORATIO

Nay, very pale.

HAMLET

And fix'd his eyes upon you?

HORATIO
Most constantly.
HAMLET
I would I had been there.
HORATIO
It would have much amazed you.
HAMLET
Very like, very like. Stay'd it long?
HORATIO
While one with moderate haste might tell a hundred.
MARCELLUS BERNARDO
Longer, longer.
HORATIO
Not when I saw't.
HAMLET
His beard was grizzled--no?
HORATIO
It was, as I have seen it in his life,
A sable silver'd.
HAMLET
I will watch to-night;
Perchance 'twill walk again.
HORATIO
I warrant it will.
HAMLET
If it assume my noble father's person,
I'll speak to it, though hell itself should gape
And bid me hold my peace. I pray you all,
If you have hitherto conceal'd this sight,
Let it be tenable in your silence still;
And whatsoever else shall hap to-night,
Give it an understanding, but no tongue:
I will requite your loves. So, fare you well:
Upon the platform, 'twixt eleven and twelve,
I'll visit you.
All
Our duty to your honour.
HAMLET
Your loves, as mine to you: farewell.

Exeunt all but HAMLET

My father's spirit in arms! all is not well;
I doubt some foul play: would the night were come!
Till then sit still, my soul: foul deeds will rise,
Though all the earth o'erwhelm them, to men's eyes.
Exit

SCENE III. A room in Polonius' house.

Enter LAERTES and OPHELIA

LAERTES

My necessaries are embark'd: farewell:
And, sister, as the winds give benefit
And convoy is assistant, do not sleep,
But let me hear from you.

OPHELIA

Do you doubt that?

LAERTES

For Hamlet and the trifling of his favour,
Hold it a fashion and a toy in blood,
A violet in the youth of primy nature,
Forward, not permanent, sweet, not lasting,
The perfume and suppliance of a minute; No more.

OPHELIA

No more but so?

LAERTES

Think it no more;
For nature, crescent, does not grow alone
In thews and bulk, but, as this temple waxes,
The inward service of the mind and soul
Grows wide withal. Perhaps he loves you now,
And now no soil nor cautel doth besmirch
The virtue of his will: but you must fear,
His greatness weigh'd, his will is not his own;
For he himself is subject to his birth:
He may not, as unvalued persons do,
Carve for himself; for on his choice depends
The safety and health of this whole state;
And therefore must his choice be circumscribed
Unto the voice and yielding of that body
Whereof he is the head. Then if he says he loves you,

It fits your wisdom so far to believe it
As he in his particular act and place
May give his saying deed; which is no further
Than the main voice of Denmark goes withal.
Then weigh what loss your honour may sustain,
If with too credent ear you list his songs,
Or lose your heart, or your chaste treasure open
To his unmaster'd importunity.
Fear it, Ophelia, fear it, my dear sister,
And keep you in the rear of your affection,
Out of the shot and danger of desire.
The chariest maid is prodigal enough,
If she unmask her beauty to the moon:
Virtue itself 'scapes not calumnious strokes:
The canker galls the infants of the spring,
Too oft before their buttons be disclosed,
And in the morn and liquid dew of youth
Contagious blastments are most imminent.
Be wary then; best safety lies in fear:
Youth to itself rebels, though none else near.

OPHELIA
I shall the effect of this good lesson keep,
As watchman to my heart. But, good my brother,
Do not, as some ungracious pastors do,
Show me the steep and thorny way to heaven;
Whiles, like a puff'd and reckless libertine,
Himself the primrose path of dalliance treads,
And recks not his own rede.

LAERTES
O, fear me not.
I stay too long: but here my father comes.
Enter POLONIUS
A double blessing is a double grace,
Occasion smiles upon a second leave.

LORD POLONIUS
Yet here, Laertes! aboard, aboard, for shame!
The wind sits in the shoulder of your sail,
And you are stay'd for. There; my blessing with thee!
And these few precepts in thy memory

See thou character. Give thy thoughts no tongue,
Nor any unproportioned thought his act.
Be thou familiar, but by no means vulgar.
Those friends thou hast, and their adoption tried,
Grapple them to thy soul with hoops of steel;
But do not dull thy palm with entertainment
Of each new-hatch'd, unfledged comrade. Beware
Of entrance to a quarrel, but being in,
Bear't that the opposed may beware of thee.
Give every man thy ear, but few thy voice;
Take each man's censure, but reserve thy judgment.
Costly thy habit as thy purse can buy,
But not express'd in fancy; rich, not gaudy;
For the apparel oft proclaims the man,
And they in France of the best rank and station
Are of a most select and generous chief in that.
Neither a borrower nor a lender be;
For loan oft loses both itself and friend,
And borrowing dulls the edge of husbandry.
This above all: to thine ownself be true,
And it must follow, as the night the day,
Thou canst not then be false to any man.
Farewell: my blessing season this in thee!

LAERTES
Most humbly do I take my leave, my lord.

LORD POLONIUS
The time invites you; go; your servants tend.

LAERTES
Farewell, Ophelia; and remember well
What I have said to you.

OPHELIA
'Tis in my memory lock'd,
And you yourself shall keep the key of it.

LAERTES
Farewell.

Exit

LORD POLONIUS
What is't, Ophelia, be hath said to you?

OPHELIA

So please you, something touching the Lord Hamlet.

LORD POLONIUS

Marry, well bethought:

'Tis told me, he hath very oft of late

Given private time to you; and you yourself

Have of your audience been most free and bounteous:

If it be so, as so 'tis put on me,

And that in way of caution, I must tell you,

You do not understand yourself so clearly

As it behoves my daughter and your honour.

What is between you? give me up the truth.

OPHELIA

He hath, my lord, of late made many tenders

Of his affection to me.

LORD POLONIUS

Affection! pooh! you speak like a green girl,

Unsifted in such perilous circumstance.

Do you believe his tenders, as you call them?

OPHELIA

I do not know, my lord, what I should think.

LORD POLONIUS

Marry, I'll teach you: think yourself a baby;

That you have ta'en these tenders for true pay,

Which are not sterling. Tender yourself more dearly;

Or--not to crack the wind of the poor phrase,

Running it thus--you'll tender me a fool.

OPHELIA

My lord, he hath importuned me with love

In honourable fashion.

LORD POLONIUS

Ay, fashion you may call it; go to, go to.

OPHELIA

And hath given countenance to his speech, my lord,

With almost all the holy vows of heaven.

LORD POLONIUS

Ay, springes to catch woodcocks. I do know,

When the blood burns, how prodigal the soul

Lends the tongue vows: these blazes, daughter,

Giving more light than heat, extinct in both,
Even in their promise, as it is a-making,
You must not take for fire. From this time
Be somewhat scanter of your maiden presence;
Set your entreatments at a higher rate
Than a command to parley. For Lord Hamlet,
Believe so much in him, that he is young
And with a larger tether may he walk
Than may be given you: in few, Ophelia,
Do not believe his vows; for they are brokers,
Not of that dye which their investments show,
But mere implorators of unholy suits,
Breathing like sanctified and pious bawds,
The better to beguile. This is for all:
I would not, in plain terms, from this time forth,
Have you so slander any moment leisure,
As to give words or talk with the Lord Hamlet.
Look to't, I charge you: come your ways.

OPHELIA
I shall obey, my lord.
Exeunt

SCENE IV. The platform.
Enter HAMLET, HORATIO, and MARCELLUS

HAMLET
The air bites shrewdly; it is very cold.

HORATIO
It is a nipping and an eager air.

HAMLET
What hour now?

HORATIO
I think it lacks of twelve.

HAMLET
No, it is struck.

HORATIO
Indeed? I heard it not: then it draws near the season
Wherein the spirit held his wont to walk.
A flourish of trumpets, and ordnance shot off, within
What does this mean, my lord?

HAMLET

The king doth wake to-night and takes his rouse,
Keeps wassail, and the swaggering up-spring reels;
And, as he drains his draughts of Rhenish down,
The kettle-drum and trumpet thus bray out
The triumph of his pledge.

HORATIO

Is it a custom?

HAMLET

Ay, marry, is't:
But to my mind, though I am native here
And to the manner born, it is a custom
More honour'd in the breach than the observance.
This heavy-headed revel east and west
Makes us traduced and tax'd of other nations:
They clepe us drunkards, and with swinish phrase
Soil our addition; and indeed it takes
From our achievements, though perform'd at height,
The pith and marrow of our attribute.
So, oft it chances in particular men,
That for some vicious mole of nature in them,
As, in their birth--wherein they are not guilty,
Since nature cannot choose his origin--
By the o'ergrowth of some complexion,
Oft breaking down the pales and forts of reason,
Or by some habit that too much o'er-leavens
The form of plausive manners, that these men,
Carrying, I say, the stamp of one defect,
Being nature's livery, or fortune's star,--
Their virtues else--be they as pure as grace,
As infinite as man may undergo--
Shall in the general censure take corruption
From that particular fault: the dram of eale
Doth all the noble substance of a doubt
To his own scandal.

HORATIO

Look, my lord, it comes!
Enter Ghost

HAMLET

Angels and ministers of grace defend us!
Be thou a spirit of health or goblin damn'd,
Bring with thee airs from heaven or blasts from hell,
Be thy intents wicked or charitable,
Thou comest in such a questionable shape
That I will speak to thee: I'll call thee Hamlet,
King, father, royal Dane: O, answer me!
Let me not burst in ignorance; but tell
Why thy canonized bones, hearsed in death,
Have burst their cerements; why the sepulchre,
Wherein we saw thee quietly inurn'd,
Hath oped his ponderous and marble jaws,
To cast thee up again. What may this mean,
That thou, dead corse, again in complete steel
Revisit'st thus the glimpses of the moon,
Making night hideous; and we fools of nature
So horridly to shake our disposition
With thoughts beyond the reaches of our souls?
Say, why is this? wherefore? what should we do?
Ghost beckons HAMLET

HORATIO

It beckons you to go away with it,
As if it some impartment did desire
To you alone.

MARCELLUS

Look, with what courteous action
It waves you to a more removed ground:
But do not go with it.

HORATIO

No, by no means.

HAMLET

It will not speak; then I will follow it.

HORATIO

Do not, my lord.

HAMLET

Why, what should be the fear?
I do not set my life in a pin's fee;
And for my soul, what can it do to that,

Being a thing immortal as itself?
It waves me forth again: I'll follow it.
HORATIO
What if it tempt you toward the flood, my lord,
Or to the dreadful summit of the cliff
That beetles o'er his base into the sea,
And there assume some other horrible form,
Which might deprive your sovereignty of reason
And draw you into madness? think of it:
The very place puts toys of desperation,
Without more motive, into every brain
That looks so many fathoms to the sea
And hears it roar beneath.
HAMLET
It waves me still.
Go on; I'll follow thee.
MARCELLUS
You shall not go, my lord.
HAMLET
Hold off your hands.
HORATIO
Be ruled; you shall not go.
HAMLET
My fate cries out,
And makes each petty artery in this body
As hardy as the Nemean lion's nerve.
Still am I call'd. Unhand me, gentlemen.
By heaven, I'll make a ghost of him that lets me!
I say, away! Go on; I'll follow thee.
Exeunt Ghost and HAMLET
HORATIO
He waxes desperate with imagination.
MARCELLUS
Let's follow; 'tis not fit thus to obey him.
HORATIO
Have after. To what issue will this come?
MARCELLUS
Something is rotten in the state of Denmark.

HORATIO
Heaven will direct it.
MARCELLUS
Nay, let's follow him.
Exeunt
SCENE V. Another part of the platform.
Enter GHOST and HAMLET
HAMLET
Where wilt thou lead me? speak; I'll go no further.
Ghost
Mark me.
HAMLET
I will.
Ghost
My hour is almost come,
When I to sulphurous and tormenting flames
Must render up myself.
HAMLET
Alas, poor ghost!
Ghost
Pity me not, but lend thy serious hearing
To what I shall unfold.
HAMLET
Speak; I am bound to hear.
Ghost
So art thou to revenge, when thou shalt hear.
HAMLET
What?
Ghost
I am thy father's spirit,
Doom'd for a certain term to walk the night,
And for the day confined to fast in fires,
Till the foul crimes done in my days of nature
Are burnt and purged away. But that I am forbid
To tell the secrets of my prison-house,
I could a tale unfold whose lightest word
Would harrow up thy soul, freeze thy young blood,
Make thy two eyes, like stars, start from their spheres,
Thy knotted and combined locks to part

And each particular hair to stand on end,
Like quills upon the fretful porpentine:
But this eternal blazon must not be
To ears of flesh and blood. List, list, O, list!
If thou didst ever thy dear father love--
HAMLET
O God!
Ghost
Revenge his foul and most unnatural murder.
HAMLET
Murder!
Ghost
Murder most foul, as in the best it is;
But this most foul, strange and unnatural.
HAMLET
Haste me to know't, that I, with wings as swift
As meditation or the thoughts of love,
May sweep to my revenge.
Ghost
I find thee apt;
And duller shouldst thou be than the fat weed
That roots itself in ease on Lethe wharf,
Wouldst thou not stir in this. Now, Hamlet, hear:
'Tis given out that, sleeping in my orchard,
A serpent stung me; so the whole ear of Denmark
Is by a forged process of my death
Rankly abused: but know, thou noble youth,
The serpent that did sting thy father's life
Now wears his crown.
HAMLET
O my prophetic soul! My uncle!
Ghost
Ay, that incestuous, that adulterate beast,
With witchcraft of his wit, with traitorous gifts,--
O wicked wit and gifts, that have the power
So to seduce!--won to his shameful lust
The will of my most seeming-virtuous queen:
O Hamlet, what a falling-off was there!
From me, whose love was of that dignity

That it went hand in hand even with the vow
I made to her in marriage, and to decline
Upon a wretch whose natural gifts were poor
To those of mine!
But virtue, as it never will be moved,
Though lewdness court it in a shape of heaven,
So lust, though to a radiant angel link'd,
Will sate itself in a celestial bed,
And prey on garbage.
But, soft! methinks I scent the morning air;
Brief let me be. Sleeping within my orchard,
My custom always of the afternoon,
Upon my secure hour thy uncle stole,
With juice of cursed hebenon in a vial,
And in the porches of my ears did pour
The leperous distilment; whose effect
Holds such an enmity with blood of man
That swift as quicksilver it courses through
The natural gates and alleys of the body,
And with a sudden vigour doth posset
And curd, like eager droppings into milk,
The thin and wholesome blood: so did it mine;
And a most instant tetter bark'd about,
Most lazar-like, with vile and loathsome crust,
All my smooth body.
Thus was I, sleeping, by a brother's hand
Of life, of crown, of queen, at once dispatch'd:
Cut off even in the blossoms of my sin,
Unhousel'd, disappointed, unanel'd,
No reckoning made, but sent to my account
With all my imperfections on my head:
O, horrible! O, horrible! most horrible!
If thou hast nature in thee, bear it not;
Let not the royal bed of Denmark be
A couch for luxury and damned incest.
But, howsoever thou pursuest this act,
Taint not thy mind, nor let thy soul contrive
Against thy mother aught: leave her to heaven
And to those thorns that in her bosom lodge,

To prick and sting her. Fare thee well at once!
The glow-worm shows the matin to be near,
And 'gins to pale his uneffectual fire:
Adieu, adieu! Hamlet, remember me.
Exit
HAMLET
O all you host of heaven! O earth! what else?
And shall I couple hell? O, fie! Hold, hold, my heart;
And you, my sinews, grow not instant old,
But bear me stiffly up. Remember thee!
Ay, thou poor ghost, while memory holds a seat
In this distracted globe. Remember thee!
Yea, from the table of my memory
I'll wipe away all trivial fond records,
All saws of books, all forms, all pressures past,
That youth and observation copied there;
And thy commandment all alone shall live
Within the book and volume of my brain,
Unmix'd with baser matter: yes, by heaven!
O most pernicious woman!
O villain, villain, smiling, damned villain!
My tables,--meet it is I set it down,
That one may smile, and smile, and be a villain;
At least I'm sure it may be so in Denmark:
Writing
So, uncle, there you are. Now to my word;
It is 'Adieu, adieu! remember me.'
I have sworn 't.
MARCELLUS HORATIO
[Within] My lord, my lord,--
MARCELLUS
[Within] Lord Hamlet,--
HORATIO
[Within] Heaven secure him!
HAMLET
So be it!
HORATIO
[Within] Hillo, ho, ho, my lord!

HAMLET

Hillo, ho, ho, boy! come, bird, come.

Enter HORATIO and MARCELLUS

MARCELLUS

How is't, my noble lord?

HORATIO

What news, my lord?

HAMLET

O, wonderful!

HORATIO

Good my lord, tell it.

HAMLET

No; you'll reveal it.

HORATIO

Not I, my lord, by heaven.

MARCELLUS

Nor I, my lord.

HAMLET

How say you, then; would heart of man once think it?
But you'll be secret?

HORATIO MARCELLUS

Ay, by heaven, my lord.

HAMLET

There's ne'er a villain dwelling in all Denmark
But he's an arrant knave.

HORATIO

There needs no ghost, my lord, come from the grave
To tell us this.

HAMLET

Why, right; you are i' the right;
And so, without more circumstance at all,
I hold it fit that we shake hands and part:
You, as your business and desire shall point you;
For every man has business and desire,
Such as it is; and for mine own poor part,
Look you, I'll go pray.

HORATIO

These are but wild and whirling words, my lord.

HAMLET
I'm sorry they offend you, heartily;
Yes, 'faith heartily.
HORATIO
There's no offence, my lord.
HAMLET
Yes, by Saint Patrick, but there is, Horatio,
And much offence too. Touching this vision here,
It is an honest ghost, that let me tell you:
For your desire to know what is between us,
O'ermaster 't as you may. And now, good friends,
As you are friends, scholars and soldiers,
Give me one poor request.
HORATIO
What is't, my lord? we will.
HAMLET
Never make known what you have seen to-night.
HORATIO MARCELLUS
My lord, we will not.
HAMLET
Nay, but swear't.
HORATIO
In faith,
My lord, not I.
MARCELLUS
Nor I, my lord, in faith.
HAMLET
Upon my sword.
MARCELLUS
We have sworn, my lord, already.
HAMLET
Indeed, upon my sword, indeed.
Ghost
[Beneath] Swear.
HAMLET
Ah, ha, boy! say'st thou so? art thou there,
truepenny?
Come on--you hear this fellow in the cellarage--
Consent to swear.

HORATIO
Propose the oath, my lord.
HAMLET
Never to speak of this that you have seen,
Swear by my sword.
Ghost
[Beneath] Swear.
HAMLET
Hic et ubique? then we'll shift our ground.
Come hither, gentlemen,
And lay your hands again upon my sword:
Never to speak of this that you have heard,
Swear by my sword.
Ghost
[Beneath] Swear.
HAMLET
Well said, old mole! canst work i' the earth so fast?
A worthy pioner! Once more remove, good friends.
HORATIO
O day and night, but this is wondrous strange!
HAMLET
And therefore as a stranger give it welcome.
There are more things in heaven and earth, Horatio,
Than are dreamt of in your philosophy. But come;
Here, as before, never, so help you mercy,
How strange or odd soe'er I bear myself,
As I perchance hereafter shall think meet
To put an antic disposition on,
That you, at such times seeing me, never shall,
With arms encumber'd thus, or this headshake,
Or by pronouncing of some doubtful phrase,
As 'Well, well, we know,' or 'We could, an if we would,'
Or 'If we list to speak,' or 'There be, an if they might,'
Or such ambiguous giving out, to note
That you know aught of me: this not to do,
So grace and mercy at your most need help you, Swear.
Ghost
[Beneath] Swear.

HAMLET

Rest, rest, perturbed spirit!

They swear

So, gentlemen,

With all my love I do commend me to you:

And what so poor a man as Hamlet is

May do, to express his love and friending to you,

God willing, shall not lack. Let us go in together;

And still your fingers on your lips, I pray.

The time is out of joint: O cursed spite,

That ever I was born to set it right!

Nay, come, let's go together.

Exeunt

ACT II

SCENE I. A room in POLONIUS' house.

Enter POLONIUS and REYNALDO

LORD POLONIUS

Give him this money and these notes, Reynaldo.

REYNALDO

I will, my lord.

LORD POLONIUS

You shall do marvellous wisely, good Reynaldo,

Before you visit him, to make inquire

Of his behavior.

REYNALDO

My lord, I did intend it.

LORD POLONIUS

Marry, well said; very well said. Look you, sir,

Inquire me first what Danskers are in Paris;

And how, and who, what means, and where they keep,

What company, at what expense; and finding

By this encompassment and drift of question

That they do know my son, come you more nearer

Than your particular demands will touch it:

Take you, as 'twere, some distant knowledge of him;

As thus, 'I know his father and his friends,

And in part him: ' do you mark this, Reynaldo?

REYNALDO

Ay, very well, my lord.

LORD POLONIUS

'And in part him; but' you may say 'not well:
But, if't be he I mean, he's very wild;
Addicted so and so:' and there put on him
What forgeries you please; marry, none so rank
As may dishonour him; take heed of that;
But, sir, such wanton, wild and usual slips
As are companions noted and most known
To youth and liberty.

REYNALDO

As gaming, my lord.

LORD POLONIUS

Ay, or drinking, fencing, swearing, quarrelling,
Drabbing: you may go so far.

REYNALDO

My lord, that would dishonour him.

LORD POLONIUS

'Faith, no; as you may season it in the charge
You must not put another scandal on him,
That he is open to incontinency;
That's not my meaning: but breathe his faults so quaintly
That they may seem the taints of liberty,
The flash and outbreak of a fiery mind,
A savageness in unreclaimed blood,
Of general assault.

REYNALDO

But, my good lord,--

LORD POLONIUS

Wherefore should you do this?

REYNALDO

Ay, my lord,
I would know that.

LORD POLONIUS

Marry, sir, here's my drift;
And I believe, it is a fetch of wit:
You laying these slight sullies on my son,
As 'twere a thing a little soil'd i' the working, Mark you,
Your party in converse, him you would sound,
Having ever seen in the prenominate crimes

The youth you breathe of guilty, be assured
He closes with you in this consequence;
'Good sir,' or so, or 'friend,' or 'gentleman,'
According to the phrase or the addition
Of man and country.

REYNALDO
Very good, my lord.

LORD POLONIUS
And then, sir, does he this--he does--what was I
about to say? By the mass, I was about to say
something: where did I leave?

REYNALDO
At 'closes in the consequence,' at 'friend or so,'
and 'gentleman.'

LORD POLONIUS
At 'closes in the consequence,' ay, marry;
He closes thus: 'I know the gentleman;
I saw him yesterday, or t' other day,
Or then, or then; with such, or such; and, as you say,
There was a' gaming; there o'ertook in's rouse;
There falling out at tennis:' or perchance,
'I saw him enter such a house of sale,'
Videlicet, a brothel, or so forth.
See you now;
Your bait of falsehood takes this carp of truth:
And thus do we of wisdom and of reach,
With windlasses and with assays of bias,
By indirections find directions out:
So by my former lecture and advice,
Shall you my son. You have me, have you not?

REYNALDO
My lord, I have.

LORD POLONIUS
God be wi' you; fare you well.

REYNALDO
Good my lord!

LORD POLONIUS
Observe his inclination in yourself.

REYNALDO
I shall, my lord.
LORD POLONIUS
And let him ply his music.
REYNALDO
Well, my lord.
LORD POLONIUS
Farewell!
Exit REYNALDO
Enter OPHELIA
How now, Ophelia! what's the matter?
OPHELIA
O, my lord, my lord, I have been so affrighted!
LORD POLONIUS
With what, i' the name of God?
OPHELIA
My lord, as I was sewing in my closet,
Lord Hamlet, with his doublet all unbraced;
No hat upon his head; his stockings foul'd,
Ungarter'd, and down-gyved to his ancle;
Pale as his shirt; his knees knocking each other;
And with a look so piteous in purport
As if he had been loosed out of hell
To speak of horrors,--he comes before me.
LORD POLONIUS
Mad for thy love?
OPHELIA
My lord, I do not know;
But truly, I do fear it.
LORD POLONIUS
What said he?
OPHELIA
He took me by the wrist and held me hard;
Then goes he to the length of all his arm;
And, with his other hand thus o'er his brow,
He falls to such perusal of my face
As he would draw it. Long stay'd he so;
At last, a little shaking of mine arm
And thrice his head thus waving up and down,

He raised a sigh so piteous and profound
As it did seem to shatter all his bulk
And end his being: that done, he lets me go:
And, with his head over his shoulder turn'd,
He seem'd to find his way without his eyes;
For out o' doors he went without their helps,
And, to the last, bended their light on me.
LORD POLONIUS
Come, go with me: I will go seek the king.
This is the very ecstasy of love,
Whose violent property fordoes itself
And leads the will to desperate undertakings
As oft as any passion under heaven
That does afflict our natures. I am sorry.
What, have you given him any hard words of late?
OPHELIA
No, my good lord, but, as you did command,
I did repel his fetters and denied
His access to me.
LORD POLONIUS
That hath made him mad.
I am sorry that with better heed and judgment
I had not quoted him: I fear'd he did but trifle,
And meant to wreck thee; but, beshrew my jealousy!
By heaven, it is as proper to our age
To cast beyond ourselves in our opinions
As it is common for the younger sort
To lack discretion. Come, go we to the king:
This must be known; which, being kept close, might
move
More grief to hide than hate to utter love.
Exeunt
SCENE II. A room in the castle.
Enter KING CLAUDIUS, QUEEN GERTRUDE, ROSENCRANTZ,
GUILDENSTERN, and Attendants
KING CLAUDIUS
Welcome, dear Rosencrantz and Guildenstern!
Moreover that we much did long to see you,
The need we have to use you did provoke

Our hasty sending. Something have you heard
Of Hamlet's transformation; so call it,
Sith nor the exterior nor the inward man
Resembles that it was. What it should be,
More than his father's death, that thus hath put him
So much from the understanding of himself,
I cannot dream of: I entreat you both,
That, being of so young days brought up with him,
And sith so neighbour'd to his youth and havior,
That you vouchsafe your rest here in our court
Some little time: so by your companies
To draw him on to pleasures, and to gather,
So much as from occasion you may glean,
Whether aught, to us unknown, afflicts him thus,
That, open'd, lies within our remedy.

QUEEN GERTRUDE

Good gentlemen, he hath much talk'd of you;
And sure I am two men there are not living
To whom he more adheres. If it will please you
To show us so much gentry and good will
As to expend your time with us awhile,
For the supply and profit of our hope,
Your visitation shall receive such thanks
As fits a king's remembrance.

ROSENCRANTZ

Both your majesties
Might, by the sovereign power you have of us,
Put your dread pleasures more into command
Than to entreaty.

GUILDENSTERN

But we both obey,
And here give up ourselves, in the full bent
To lay our service freely at your feet,
To be commanded.

KING CLAUDIUS

Thanks, Rosencrantz and gentle Guildenstern.

QUEEN GERTRUDE

Thanks, Guildenstern and gentle Rosencrantz:
And I beseech you instantly to visit

My too much changed son. Go, some of you,
And bring these gentlemen where Hamlet is.
GUILDENSTERN
Heavens make our presence and our practises
Pleasant and helpful to him!
QUEEN GERTRUDE
Ay, amen!
Exeunt ROSENCRANTZ, GUILDENSTERN, and some Attendants
Enter POLONIUS
LORD POLONIUS
The ambassadors from Norway, my good lord,
Are joyfully return'd.
KING CLAUDIUS
Thou still hast been the father of good news.
LORD POLONIUS
Have I, my lord? I assure my good liege,
I hold my duty, as I hold my soul,
Both to my God and to my gracious king:
And I do think, or else this brain of mine
Hunts not the trail of policy so sure
As it hath used to do, that I have found
The very cause of Hamlet's lunacy.
KING CLAUDIUS
O, speak of that; that do I long to hear.
LORD POLONIUS
Give first admittance to the ambassadors;
My news shall be the fruit to that great feast.
KING CLAUDIUS
Thyself do grace to them, and bring them in.
Exit POLONIUS
He tells me, my dear Gertrude, he hath found
The head and source of all your son's distemper.
QUEEN GERTRUDE
I doubt it is no other but the main;
His father's death, and our o'erhasty marriage.
KING CLAUDIUS
Well, we shall sift him.
Re-enter POLONIUS, with VOLTIMAND and CORNELIUS

Welcome, my good friends!
Say, Voltimand, what from our brother Norway?
VOLTIMAND
Most fair return of greetings and desires.
Upon our first, he sent out to suppress
His nephew's levies; which to him appear'd
To be a preparation 'gainst the Polack;
But, better look'd into, he truly found
It was against your highness: whereat grieved,
That so his sickness, age and impotence
Was falsely borne in hand, sends out arrests
On Fortinbras; which he, in brief, obeys;
Receives rebuke from Norway, and in fine
Makes vow before his uncle never more
To give the assay of arms against your majesty.
Whereon old Norway, overcome with joy,
Gives him three thousand crowns in annual fee,
And his commission to employ those soldiers,
So levied as before, against the Polack:
With an entreaty, herein further shown,
Giving a paper
That it might please you to give quiet pass
Through your dominions for this enterprise,
On such regards of safety and allowance
As therein are set down.
KING CLAUDIUS
It likes us well;
And at our more consider'd time well read,
Answer, and think upon this business.
Meantime we thank you for your well-took labour:
Go to your rest; at night we'll feast together:
Most welcome home!
Exeunt VOLTIMAND and CORNELIUS
LORD POLONIUS
This business is well ended.
My liege, and madam, to expostulate
What majesty should be, what duty is,
Why day is day, night night, and time is time,
Were nothing but to waste night, day and time.

Therefore, since brevity is the soul of wit,
And tediousness the limbs and outward flourishes,
I will be brief: your noble son is mad:
Mad call I it; for, to define true madness,
What is't but to be nothing else but mad?
But let that go.

QUEEN GERTRUDE
More matter, with less art.

LORD POLONIUS
Madam, I swear I use no art at all.
That he is mad, 'tis true: 'tis true 'tis pity;
And pity 'tis 'tis true: a foolish figure;
But farewell it, for I will use no art.
Mad let us grant him, then: and now remains
That we find out the cause of this effect,
Or rather say, the cause of this defect,
For this effect defective comes by cause:
Thus it remains, and the remainder thus. Perpend.
I have a daughter--have while she is mine--
Who, in her duty and obedience, mark,
Hath given me this: now gather, and surmise.
Reads
'To the celestial and my soul's idol, the most
beautified Ophelia,'--
That's an ill phrase, a vile phrase; 'beautified' is
a vile phrase: but you shall hear. Thus:
Reads
'In her excellent white bosom, these, & c.'

QUEEN GERTRUDE
Came this from Hamlet to her?

LORD POLONIUS
Good madam, stay awhile; I will be faithful.
Reads
'Doubt thou the stars are fire;
Doubt that the sun doth move;
Doubt truth to be a liar;
But never doubt I love.
'O dear Ophelia, I am ill at these numbers;
I have not art to reckon my groans: but that

I love thee best, O most best, believe it. Adieu.
'Thine evermore most dear lady, whilst
this machine is to him, HAMLET.'
This, in obedience, hath my daughter shown me,
And more above, hath his solicitings,
As they fell out by time, by means and place,
All given to mine ear.

KING CLAUDIUS
But how hath she
Received his love?

LORD POLONIUS
What do you think of me?

KING CLAUDIUS
As of a man faithful and honourable.

LORD POLONIUS
I would fain prove so. But what might you think,
When I had seen this hot love on the wing--
As I perceived it, I must tell you that,
Before my daughter told me--what might you,
Or my dear majesty your queen here, think,
If I had play'd the desk or table-book,
Or given my heart a winking, mute and dumb,
Or look'd upon this love with idle sight;
What might you think? No, I went round to work,
And my young mistress thus I did bespeak:
'Lord Hamlet is a prince, out of thy star;
This must not be:' and then I precepts gave her,
That she should lock herself from his resort,
Admit no messengers, receive no tokens.
Which done, she took the fruits of my advice;
And he, repulsed--a short tale to make--
Fell into a sadness, then into a fast,
Thence to a watch, thence into a weakness,
Thence to a lightness, and, by this declension,
Into the madness wherein now he raves,
And all we mourn for.

KING CLAUDIUS
Do you think 'tis this?

QUEEN GERTRUDE
It may be, very likely.
LORD POLONIUS
Hath there been such a time--I'd fain know that--
That I have positively said 'Tis so,'
When it proved otherwise?
KING CLAUDIUS
Not that I know.
LORD POLONIUS
[Pointing to his head and shoulder]
Take this from this, if this be otherwise:
If circumstances lead me, I will find
Where truth is hid, though it were hid indeed
Within the centre.
KING CLAUDIUS
How may we try it further?
LORD POLONIUS
You know, sometimes he walks four hours together
Here in the lobby.
QUEEN GERTRUDE
So he does indeed.
LORD POLONIUS
At such a time I'll loose my daughter to him:
Be you and I behind an arras then;
Mark the encounter: if he love her not
And be not from his reason fall'n thereon,
Let me be no assistant for a state,
But keep a farm and carters.
KING CLAUDIUS
We will try it.
QUEEN GERTRUDE
But, look, where sadly the poor wretch comes reading.
LORD POLONIUS
Away, I do beseech you, both away:
I'll board him presently.
Exeunt KING CLAUDIUS, QUEEN GERTRUDE, and Attendants
Enter HAMLET, reading
O, give me leave:
How does my good Lord Hamlet?

HAMLET
Well, God-a-mercy.
LORD POLONIUS
Do you know me, my lord?
HAMLET
Excellent well; you are a fishmonger.
LORD POLONIUS
Not I, my lord.
HAMLET
Then I would you were so honest a man.
LORD POLONIUS
Honest, my lord!
HAMLET
Ay, sir; to be honest, as this world goes, is to be
one man picked out of ten thousand.
LORD POLONIUS
That's very true, my lord.
HAMLET
For if the sun breed maggots in a dead dog, being a
god kissing carrion,--Have you a daughter?
LORD POLONIUS
I have, my lord.
HAMLET
Let her not walk i' the sun: conception is a
blessing: but not as your daughter may conceive.
Friend, look to 't.
LORD POLONIUS
[Aside] How say you by that? Still harping on my
daughter: yet he knew me not at first; he said I
was a fishmonger: he is far gone, far gone: and
truly in my youth I suffered much extremity for
love; very near this. I'll speak to him again.
What do you read, my lord?
HAMLET
Words, words, words.
LORD POLONIUS
What is the matter, my lord?
HAMLET
Between who?

LORD POLONIUS
I mean, the matter that you read, my lord.
HAMLET
Slanders, sir: for the satirical rogue says here
that old men have grey beards, that their faces are
wrinkled, their eyes purging thick amber and
plum-tree gum and that they have a plentiful lack of
wit, together with most weak hams: all which, sir,
though I most powerfully and potently believe, yet
I hold it not honesty to have it thus set down, for
yourself, sir, should be old as I am, if like a crab
you could go backward.
LORD POLONIUS
[Aside] Though this be madness, yet there is method
in 't. Will you walk out of the air, my lord?
HAMLET
Into my grave.
LORD POLONIUS
Indeed, that is out o' the air.
Aside
How pregnant sometimes his replies are! a happiness
that often madness hits on, which reason and sanity
could not so prosperously be delivered of. I will
leave him, and suddenly contrive the means of
meeting between him and my daughter.--My honourable
lord, I will most humbly take my leave of you.
HAMLET
You cannot, sir, take from me any thing that I will
more willingly part withal: except my life, except
my life, except my life.
LORD POLONIUS
Fare you well, my lord.
HAMLET
These tedious old fools!
Enter ROSENCRANTZ and GUILDENSTERN
LORD POLONIUS
You go to seek the Lord Hamlet; there he is.
ROSENCRANTZ
[To POLONIUS] God save you, sir!

Exit POLONIUS

GUILDENSTERN
My honoured lord!

ROSENCRANTZ
My most dear lord!

HAMLET
My excellent good friends! How dost thou,
Guildenstern? Ah, Rosencrantz! Good lads, how do ye both?

ROSENCRANTZ
As the indifferent children of the earth.

GUILDENSTERN
Happy, in that we are not over-happy;
On fortune's cap we are not the very button.

HAMLET
Nor the soles of her shoe?

ROSENCRANTZ
Neither, my lord.

HAMLET
Then you live about her waist, or in the middle of
her favours?

GUILDENSTERN
'Faith, her privates we.

HAMLET
In the secret parts of fortune? O, most true; she
is a strumpet. What's the news?

ROSENCRANTZ
None, my lord, but that the world's grown honest.

HAMLET
Then is doomsday near: but your news is not true.
Let me question more in particular: what have you,
my good friends, deserved at the hands of fortune,
that she sends you to prison hither?

GUILDENSTERN
Prison, my lord!

HAMLET
Denmark's a prison.

ROSENCRANTZ
Then is the world one.

HAMLET
A goodly one; in which there are many confines,
wards and dungeons, Denmark being one o' the worst.
ROSENCRANTZ
We think not so, my lord.
HAMLET
Why, then, 'tis none to you; for there is nothing
either good or bad, but thinking makes it so: to me
it is a prison.
ROSENCRANTZ
Why then, your ambition makes it one; 'tis too
narrow for your mind.
HAMLET
O God, I could be bounded in a nut shell and count
myself a king of infinite space, were it not that I
have bad dreams.
GUILDENSTERN
Which dreams indeed are ambition, for the very
substance of the ambitious is merely the shadow of a dream.
HAMLET
A dream itself is but a shadow.
ROSENCRANTZ
Truly, and I hold ambition of so airy and light a
quality that it is but a shadow's shadow.
HAMLET
Then are our beggars bodies, and our monarchs and
outstretched heroes the beggars' shadows. Shall we
to the court? for, by my fay, I cannot reason.
ROSENCRANTZ GUILDENSTERN
We'll wait upon you.
HAMLET
No such matter: I will not sort you with the rest
of my servants, for, to speak to you like an honest
man, I am most dreadfully attended. But, in the
beaten way of friendship, what make you at Elsinore?
ROSENCRANTZ
To visit you, my lord; no other occasion.

HAMLET

Beggar that I am, I am even poor in thanks; but I
thank you: and sure, dear friends, my thanks are
too dear a halfpenny. Were you not sent for? Is it
your own inclining? Is it a free visitation? Come,
deal justly with me: come, come; nay, speak.

GUILDENSTERN

What should we say, my lord?

HAMLET

Why, any thing, but to the purpose. You were sent
for; and there is a kind of confession in your looks
which your modesties have not craft enough to colour:
I know the good king and queen have sent for you.

ROSENCRANTZ

To what end, my lord?

HAMLET

That you must teach me. But let me conjure you, by
the rights of our fellowship, by the consonancy of
our youth, by the obligation of our ever-preserved
love, and by what more dear a better proposer could
charge you withal, be even and direct with me,
whether you were sent for, or no?

ROSENCRANTZ

[Aside to GUILDENSTERN] What say you?

HAMLET

[Aside] Nay, then, I have an eye of you.--If you
love me, hold not off.

GUILDENSTERN

My lord, we were sent for.

HAMLET

I will tell you why; so shall my anticipation
prevent your discovery, and your secrecy to the king
and queen moult no feather. I have of late--but
wherefore I know not--lost all my mirth, forgone all
custom of exercises; and indeed it goes so heavily
with my disposition that this goodly frame, the
earth, seems to me a sterile promontory, this most
excellent canopy, the air, look you, this brave
o'erhanging firmament, this majestical roof fretted

with golden fire, why, it appears no other thing to
me than a foul and pestilent congregation of vapours.
What a piece of work is a man! how noble in reason!
how infinite in faculty! in form and moving how
express and admirable! in action how like an angel!
in apprehension how like a god! the beauty of the
world! the paragon of animals! And yet, to me,
what is this quintessence of dust? man delights not
me: no, nor woman neither, though by your smiling
you seem to say so.

ROSENCRANTZ

My lord, there was no such stuff in my thoughts.

HAMLET

Why did you laugh then, when I said 'man delights not me'?

ROSENCRANTZ

To think, my lord, if you delight not in man, what
lenten entertainment the players shall receive from
you: we coted them on the way; and hither are they
coming, to offer you service.

HAMLET

He that plays the king shall be welcome; his majesty
shall have tribute of me; the adventurous knight
shall use his foil and target; the lover shall not
sigh gratis; the humourous man shall end his part
in peace; the clown shall make those laugh whose
lungs are tickled o' the sere; and the lady shall
say her mind freely, or the blank verse shall halt
for't. What players are they?

ROSENCRANTZ

Even those you were wont to take delight in, the
tragedians of the city.

HAMLET

How chances it they travel? their residence, both
in reputation and profit, was better both ways.

ROSENCRANTZ

I think their inhibition comes by the means of the
late innovation.

HAMLET

Do they hold the same estimation they did when I was
in the city? are they so followed?

ROSENCRANTZ

No, indeed, are they not.

HAMLET

How comes it? do they grow rusty?

ROSENCRANTZ

Nay, their endeavour keeps in the wonted pace: but
there is, sir, an aery of children, little eyases,
that cry out on the top of question, and are most
tyrannically clapped for't: these are now the
fashion, and so berattle the common stages--so they
call them--that many wearing rapiers are afraid of
goose-quills and dare scarce come thither.

HAMLET

What, are they children? who maintains 'em? how are
they escoted? Will they pursue the quality no
longer than they can sing? will they not say
afterwards, if they should grow themselves to common
players--as it is most like, if their means are no
better--their writers do them wrong, to make them
exclaim against their own succession?

ROSENCRANTZ

'Faith, there has been much to do on both sides; and
the nation holds it no sin to tarre them to
controversy: there was, for a while, no money bid
for argument, unless the poet and the player went to
cuffs in the question.

HAMLET

Is't possible?

GUILDENSTERN

O, there has been much throwing about of brains.

HAMLET

Do the boys carry it away?

ROSENCRANTZ

Ay, that they do, my lord; Hercules and his load too.

HAMLET

It is not very strange; for mine uncle is king of
Denmark, and those that would make mows at him while
my father lived, give twenty, forty, fifty, an
hundred ducats a-piece for his picture in little.
'Sblood, there is something in this more than
natural, if philosophy could find it out.
Flourish of trumpets within

GUILDENSTERN

There are the players.

HAMLET

Gentlemen, you are welcome to Elsinore. Your hands,
come then: the appurtenance of welcome is fashion
and ceremony: let me comply with you in this garb,
lest my extent to the players, which, I tell you,
must show fairly outward, should more appear like
entertainment than yours. You are welcome: but my
uncle-father and aunt-mother are deceived.

GUILDENSTERN

In what, my dear lord?

HAMLET

I am but mad north-north-west: when the wind is
southerly I know a hawk from a handsaw.
Enter POLONIUS

LORD POLONIUS

Well be with you, gentlemen!

HAMLET

Hark you, Guildenstern; and you too: at each ear a
hearer: that great baby you see there is not yet
out of his swaddling-clouts.

ROSENCRANTZ

Happily he's the second time come to them; for they
say an old man is twice a child.

HAMLET

I will prophesy he comes to tell me of the players;
mark it. You say right, sir: o' Monday morning;
'twas so indeed.

LORD POLONIUS

My lord, I have news to tell you.

HAMLET

My lord, I have news to tell you.

When Roscius was an actor in Rome,--

LORD POLONIUS

The actors are come hither, my lord.

HAMLET

Buz, buz!

LORD POLONIUS

Upon mine honour,--

HAMLET

Then came each actor on his ass,--

LORD POLONIUS

The best actors in the world, either for tragedy,
comedy, history, pastoral, pastoral-comical,
historical-pastoral, tragical-historical, tragical-
comical-historical-pastoral, scene individable, or
poem unlimited: Seneca cannot be too heavy, nor
Plautus too light. For the law of writ and the
liberty, these are the only men.

HAMLET

O Jephthah, judge of Israel, what a treasure hadst thou!

LORD POLONIUS

What a treasure had he, my lord?

HAMLET

Why,

'One fair daughter and no more,
The which he loved passing well.'

LORD POLONIUS

[Aside] Still on my daughter.

HAMLET

Am I not i' the right, old Jephthah?

LORD POLONIUS

If you call me Jephthah, my lord, I have a daughter
that I love passing well.

HAMLET

Nay, that follows not.

LORD POLONIUS

What follows, then, my lord?

HAMLET

Why,

'As by lot, God wot,'

and then, you know,

'It came to pass, as most like it was,'--

the first row of the pious chanson will show you

more; for look, where my abridgement comes.

Enter four or five Players

You are welcome, masters; welcome, all. I am glad

to see thee well. Welcome, good friends. O, my old

friend! thy face is valenced since I saw thee last:

comest thou to beard me in Denmark? What, my young

lady and mistress! By'r lady, your ladyship is

nearer to heaven than when I saw you last, by the

altitude of a chopine. Pray God, your voice, like

apiece of uncurrent gold, be not cracked within the

ring. Masters, you are all welcome. We'll e'en

to't like French falconers, fly at any thing we see:

we'll have a speech straight: come, give us a taste

of your quality; come, a passionate speech.

First Player

What speech, my lord?

HAMLET

I heard thee speak me a speech once, but it was

never acted; or, if it was, not above once; for the

play, I remember, pleased not the million; 'twas

caviare to the general: but it was--as I received

it, and others, whose judgments in such matters

cried in the top of mine--an excellent play, well

digested in the scenes, set down with as much

modesty as cunning. I remember, one said there

were no sallets in the lines to make the matter

savoury, nor no matter in the phrase that might

indict the author of affectation; but called it an

honest method, as wholesome as sweet, and by very

much more handsome than fine. One speech in it I

chiefly loved: 'twas Aeneas' tale to Dido; and

thereabout of it especially, where he speaks of

Priam's slaughter: if it live in your memory, begin

at this line: let me see, let me see--
'The rugged Pyrrhus, like the Hyrcanian beast,'--
it is not so:--it begins with Pyrrhus:--
'The rugged Pyrrhus, he whose sable arms,
Black as his purpose, did the night resemble
When he lay couched in the ominous horse,
Hath now this dread and black complexion smear'd
With heraldry more dismal; head to foot
Now is he total gules; horridly trick'd
With blood of fathers, mothers, daughters, sons,
Baked and impasted with the parching streets,
That lend a tyrannous and damned light
To their lord's murder: roasted in wrath and fire,
And thus o'er-sized with coagulate gore,
With eyes like carbuncles, the hellish Pyrrhus
Old grandsire Priam seeks.'
So, proceed you.

LORD POLONIUS
'Fore God, my lord, well spoken, with good accent and
good discretion.

First Player
'Anon he finds him
Striking too short at Greeks; his antique sword,
Rebellious to his arm, lies where it falls,
Repugnant to command: unequal match'd,
Pyrrhus at Priam drives; in rage strikes wide;
But with the whiff and wind of his fell sword
The unnerved father falls. Then senseless Ilium,
Seeming to feel this blow, with flaming top
Stoops to his base, and with a hideous crash
Takes prisoner Pyrrhus' ear: for, lo! his sword,
Which was declining on the milky head
Of reverend Priam, seem'd i' the air to stick:
So, as a painted tyrant, Pyrrhus stood,
And like a neutral to his will and matter,
Did nothing.
But, as we often see, against some storm,
A silence in the heavens, the rack stand still,
The bold winds speechless and the orb below

As hush as death, anon the dreadful thunder
Doth rend the region, so, after Pyrrhus' pause,
Aroused vengeance sets him new a-work;
And never did the Cyclops' hammers fall
On Mars's armour forged for proof eterne
With less remorse than Pyrrhus' bleeding sword
Now falls on Priam.
Out, out, thou strumpet, Fortune! All you gods,
In general synod 'take away her power;
Break all the spokes and fellies from her wheel,
And bowl the round nave down the hill of heaven,
As low as to the fiends!'

LORD POLONIUS
This is too long.

HAMLET
It shall to the barber's, with your beard. Prithee,
say on: he's for a jig or a tale of bawdry, or he
sleeps: say on: come to Hecuba.

First Player
'But who, O, who had seen the mobled queen--'

HAMLET
'The mobled queen?'

LORD POLONIUS
That's good; 'mobled queen' is good.

First Player
'Run barefoot up and down, threatening the flames
With bisson rheum; a clout upon that head
Where late the diadem stood, and for a robe,
About her lank and all o'er-teemed loins,
A blanket, in the alarm of fear caught up;
Who this had seen, with tongue in venom steep'd,
'Gainst Fortune's state would treason have
pronounced:
But if the gods themselves did see her then
When she saw Pyrrhus make malicious sport
In mincing with his sword her husband's limbs,
The instant burst of clamour that she made,
Unless things mortal move them not at all,

Would have made milch the burning eyes of heaven,
And passion in the gods.'

LORD POLONIUS

Look, whether he has not turned his colour and has
tears in's eyes. Pray you, no more.

HAMLET

'Tis well: I'll have thee speak out the rest soon.
Good my lord, will you see the players well
bestowed? Do you hear, let them be well used; for
they are the abstract and brief chronicles of the
time: after your death you were better have a bad
epitaph than their ill report while you live.

LORD POLONIUS

My lord, I will use them according to their desert.

HAMLET

God's bodykins, man, much better: use every man
after his desert, and who should 'scape whipping?
Use them after your own honour and dignity: the less
they deserve, the more merit is in your bounty.
Take them in.

LORD POLONIUS

Come, sirs.

HAMLET

Follow him, friends: we'll hear a play to-morrow.
Exit POLONIUS with all the Players but the First
Dost thou hear me, old friend; can you play the
Murder of Gonzago?

First Player

Ay, my lord.

HAMLET

We'll ha't to-morrow night. You could, for a need,
study a speech of some dozen or sixteen lines, which
I would set down and insert in't, could you not?

First Player

Ay, my lord.

HAMLET

Very well. Follow that lord; and look you mock him
not.
Exit First Player

My good friends, I'll leave you till night: you are
welcome to Elsinore.

ROSENCRANTZ

Good my lord!

HAMLET

Ay, so, God be wi' ye;

Exeunt ROSENCRANTZ and GUILDENSTERN

Now I am alone.
O, what a rogue and peasant slave am I!
Is it not monstrous that this player here,
But in a fiction, in a dream of passion,
Could force his soul so to his own conceit
That from her working all his visage wann'd,
Tears in his eyes, distraction in's aspect,
A broken voice, and his whole function suiting
With forms to his conceit? and all for nothing!
For Hecuba!
What's Hecuba to him, or he to Hecuba,
That he should weep for her? What would he do,
Had he the motive and the cue for passion
That I have? He would drown the stage with tears
And cleave the general ear with horrid speech,
Make mad the guilty and appal the free,
Confound the ignorant, and amaze indeed
The very faculties of eyes and ears. Yet I,
A dull and muddy-mettled rascal, peak,
Like John-a-dreams, unpregnant of my cause,
And can say nothing; no, not for a king,
Upon whose property and most dear life
A damn'd defeat was made. Am I a coward?
Who calls me villain? breaks my pate across?
Plucks off my beard, and blows it in my face?
Tweaks me by the nose? gives me the lie i' the throat,
As deep as to the lungs? who does me this?
Ha!
'Swounds, I should take it: for it cannot be
But I am pigeon-liver'd and lack gall
To make oppression bitter, or ere this
I should have fatted all the region kites

With this slave's offal: bloody, bawdy villain!
Remorseless, treacherous, lecherous, kindless villain!
O, vengeance!
Why, what an ass am I! This is most brave,
That I, the son of a dear father murder'd,
Prompted to my revenge by heaven and hell,
Must, like a whore, unpack my heart with words,
And fall a-cursing, like a very drab,
A scullion!
Fie upon't! foh! About, my brain! I have heard
That guilty creatures sitting at a play
Have by the very cunning of the scene
Been struck so to the soul that presently
They have proclaim'd their malefactions;
For murder, though it have no tongue, will speak
With most miraculous organ. I'll have these players
Play something like the murder of my father
Before mine uncle: I'll observe his looks;
I'll tent him to the quick: if he but blench,
I know my course. The spirit that I have seen
May be the devil: and the devil hath power
To assume a pleasing shape; yea, and perhaps
Out of my weakness and my melancholy,
As he is very potent with such spirits,
Abuses me to damn me: I'll have grounds
More relative than this: the play 's the thing
Wherein I'll catch the conscience of the king.
Exit
ACT III
SCENE I. A room in the castle.
Enter KING CLAUDIUS, QUEEN GERTRUDE, POLONIUS, OPHELIA,
ROSENCRANTZ, and GUILDENSTERN
KING CLAUDIUS
And can you, by no drift of circumstance,
Get from him why he puts on this confusion,
Grating so harshly all his days of quiet
With turbulent and dangerous lunacy?

ROSENCRANTZ
He does confess he feels himself distracted;
But from what cause he will by no means speak.
GUILDENSTERN
Nor do we find him forward to be sounded,
But, with a crafty madness, keeps aloof,
When we would bring him on to some confession
Of his true state.
QUEEN GERTRUDE
Did he receive you well?
ROSENCRANTZ
Most like a gentleman.
GUILDENSTERN
But with much forcing of his disposition.
ROSENCRANTZ
Niggard of question; but, of our demands,
Most free in his reply.
QUEEN GERTRUDE
Did you assay him?
To any pastime?
ROSENCRANTZ
Madam, it so fell out, that certain players
We o'er-raught on the way: of these we told him;
And there did seem in him a kind of joy
To hear of it: they are about the court,
And, as I think, they have already order
This night to play before him.
LORD POLONIUS
'Tis most true:
And he beseech'd me to entreat your majesties
To hear and see the matter.
KING CLAUDIUS
With all my heart; and it doth much content me
To hear him so inclined.
Good gentlemen, give him a further edge,
And drive his purpose on to these delights.
ROSENCRANTZ
We shall, my lord.
Exeunt ROSENCRANTZ and GUILDENSTERN

KING CLAUDIUS
Sweet Gertrude, leave us too;
For we have closely sent for Hamlet hither,
That he, as 'twere by accident, may here
Affront Ophelia:
Her father and myself, lawful espials,
Will so bestow ourselves that, seeing, unseen,
We may of their encounter frankly judge,
And gather by him, as he is behaved,
If 't be the affliction of his love or no
That thus he suffers for.

QUEEN GERTRUDE
I shall obey you.
And for your part, Ophelia, I do wish
That your good beauties be the happy cause
Of Hamlet's wildness: so shall I hope your virtues
Will bring him to his wonted way again,
To both your honours.

OPHELIA
Madam, I wish it may.
Exit QUEEN GERTRUDE

LORD POLONIUS
Ophelia, walk you here. Gracious, so please you,
We will bestow ourselves.
To OPHELIA
Read on this book;
That show of such an exercise may colour
Your loneliness. We are oft to blame in this,--
'Tis too much proved--that with devotion's visage
And pious action we do sugar o'er
The devil himself.

KING CLAUDIUS
[Aside] O, 'tis too true!
How smart a lash that speech doth give my conscience!
The harlot's cheek, beautied with plastering art,
Is not more ugly to the thing that helps it
Than is my deed to my most painted word:
O heavy burthen!

LORD POLONIUS
I hear him coming: let's withdraw, my lord.
Exeunt KING CLAUDIUS and POLONIUS
Enter HAMLET
HAMLET
To be, or not to be: that is the question:
Whether 'tis nobler in the mind to suffer
The slings and arrows of outrageous fortune,
Or to take arms against a sea of troubles,
And by opposing end them? To die: to sleep;
No more; and by a sleep to say we end
The heart-ache and the thousand natural shocks
That flesh is heir to, 'tis a consummation
Devoutly to be wish'd. To die, to sleep;
To sleep: perchance to dream: ay, there's the rub;
For in that sleep of death what dreams may come
When we have shuffled off this mortal coil,
Must give us pause: there's the respect
That makes calamity of so long life;
For who would bear the whips and scorns of time,
The oppressor's wrong, the proud man's contumely,
The pangs of despised love, the law's delay,
The insolence of office and the spurns
That patient merit of the unworthy takes,
When he himself might his quietus make
With a bare bodkin? who would fardels bear,
To grunt and sweat under a weary life,
But that the dread of something after death,
The undiscover'd country from whose bourn
No traveller returns, puzzles the will
And makes us rather bear those ills we have
Than fly to others that we know not of?
Thus conscience does make cowards of us all;
And thus the native hue of resolution
Is sicklied o'er with the pale cast of thought,
And enterprises of great pith and moment
With this regard their currents turn awry,
And lose the name of action.--Soft you now!

The fair Ophelia! Nymph, in thy orisons
Be all my sins remember'd.
OPHELIA
Good my lord,
How does your honour for this many a day?
HAMLET
I humbly thank you; well, well, well.
OPHELIA
My lord, I have remembrances of yours,
That I have longed long to re-deliver;
I pray you, now receive them.
HAMLET
No, not I;
I never gave you aught.
OPHELIA
My honour'd lord, you know right well you did;
And, with them, words of so sweet breath composed
As made the things more rich: their perfume lost,
Take these again; for to the noble mind
Rich gifts wax poor when givers prove unkind.
There, my lord.
HAMLET
Ha, ha! are you honest?
OPHELIA
My lord?
HAMLET
Are you fair?
OPHELIA
What means your lordship?
HAMLET
That if you be honest and fair, your honesty should
admit no discourse to your beauty.
OPHELIA
Could beauty, my lord, have better commerce than
with honesty?
HAMLET
Ay, truly; for the power of beauty will sooner
transform honesty from what it is to a bawd than the
force of honesty can translate beauty into his

likeness: this was sometime a paradox, but now the time gives it proof. I did love you once.

OPHELIA

Indeed, my lord, you made me believe so.

HAMLET

You should not have believed me; for virtue cannot so inoculate our old stock but we shall relish of it: I loved you not.

OPHELIA

I was the more deceived.

HAMLET

Get thee to a nunnery: why wouldst thou be a breeder of sinners? I am myself indifferent honest; but yet I could accuse me of such things that it were better my mother had not borne me: I am very proud, revengeful, ambitious, with more offences at my beck than I have thoughts to put them in, imagination to give them shape, or time to act them in. What should such fellows as I do crawling between earth and heaven? We are arrant knaves, all; believe none of us. Go thy ways to a nunnery. Where's your father?

OPHELIA

At home, my lord.

HAMLET

Let the doors be shut upon him, that he may play the fool no where but in's own house. Farewell.

OPHELIA

O, help him, you sweet heavens!

HAMLET

If thou dost marry, I'll give thee this plague for thy dowry: be thou as chaste as ice, as pure as snow, thou shalt not escape calumny. Get thee to a nunnery, go: farewell. Or, if thou wilt needs marry, marry a fool; for wise men know well enough what monsters you make of them. To a nunnery, go, and quickly too. Farewell.

OPHELIA

O heavenly powers, restore him!

HAMLET

I have heard of your paintings too, well enough; God
has given you one face, and you make yourselves
another: you jig, you amble, and you lisp, and
nick-name God's creatures, and make your wantonness
your ignorance. Go to, I'll no more on't; it hath
made me mad. I say, we will have no more marriages:
those that are married already, all but one, shall
live; the rest shall keep as they are. To a
nunnery, go.

Exit

OPHELIA

O, what a noble mind is here o'erthrown!
The courtier's, soldier's, scholar's, eye, tongue, sword;
The expectancy and rose of the fair state,
The glass of fashion and the mould of form,
The observed of all observers, quite, quite down!
And I, of ladies most deject and wretched,
That suck'd the honey of his music vows,
Now see that noble and most sovereign reason,
Like sweet bells jangled, out of tune and harsh;
That unmatch'd form and feature of blown youth
Blasted with ecstasy: O, woe is me,
To have seen what I have seen, see what I see!

Re-enter KING CLAUDIUS and POLONIUS

KING CLAUDIUS

Love! his affections do not that way tend;
Nor what he spake, though it lack'd form a little,
Was not like madness. There's something in his soul,
O'er which his melancholy sits on brood;
And I do doubt the hatch and the disclose
Will be some danger: which for to prevent,
I have in quick determination
Thus set it down: he shall with speed to England,
For the demand of our neglected tribute
Haply the seas and countries different
With variable objects shall expel
This something-settled matter in his heart,

Whereon his brains still beating puts him thus
From fashion of himself. What think you on't?
LORD POLONIUS
It shall do well: but yet do I believe
The origin and commencement of his grief
Sprung from neglected love. How now, Ophelia!
You need not tell us what Lord Hamlet said;
We heard it all. My lord, do as you please;
But, if you hold it fit, after the play
Let his queen mother all alone entreat him
To show his grief: let her be round with him;
And I'll be placed, so please you, in the ear
Of all their conference. If she find him not,
To England send him, or confine him where
Your wisdom best shall think.
KING CLAUDIUS
It shall be so:
Madness in great ones must not unwatch'd go.
Exeunt
SCENE II. A hall in the castle.
Enter HAMLET and Players
HAMLET
Speak the speech, I pray you, as I pronounced it to
you, trippingly on the tongue: but if you mouth it,
as many of your players do, I had as lief the
town-crier spoke my lines. Nor do not saw the air
too much with your hand, thus, but use all gently;
for in the very torrent, tempest, and, as I may say,
the whirlwind of passion, you must acquire and beget
a temperance that may give it smoothness. O, it
offends me to the soul to hear a robustious
periwig-pated fellow tear a passion to tatters, to
very rags, to split the ears of the groundlings, who
for the most part are capable of nothing but
inexplicable dumbshows and noise: I would have such
a fellow whipped for o'erdoing Termagant; it
out-herods Herod: pray you, avoid it.
First Player
I warrant your honour.

HAMLET

Be not too tame neither, but let your own discretion
be your tutor: suit the action to the word, the
word to the action; with this special o'erstep not
the modesty of nature: for any thing so overdone is
from the purpose of playing, whose end, both at the
first and now, was and is, to hold, as 'twere, the
mirror up to nature; to show virtue her own feature,
scorn her own image, and the very age and body of
the time his form and pressure. Now this overdone,
or come tardy off, though it make the unskilful
laugh, cannot but make the judicious grieve; the
censure of the which one must in your allowance
o'erweigh a whole theatre of others. O, there be
players that I have seen play, and heard others
praise, and that highly, not to speak it profanely,
that, neither having the accent of Christians nor
the gait of Christian, pagan, nor man, have so
strutted and bellowed that I have thought some of
nature's journeymen had made men and not made them
well, they imitated humanity so abominably.

First Player

I hope we have reformed that indifferently with us,
sir.

HAMLET

O, reform it altogether. And let those that play
your clowns speak no more than is set down for them;
for there be of them that will themselves laugh, to
set on some quantity of barren spectators to laugh
too; though, in the mean time, some necessary
question of the play be then to be considered:
that's villanous, and shows a most pitiful ambition
in the fool that uses it. Go, make you ready.

Exeunt Players

Enter POLONIUS, ROSENCRANTZ, and GUILDENSTERN

How now, my lord! I will the king hear this piece of work?

LORD POLONIUS

And the queen too, and that presently.

HAMLET

Bid the players make haste.

Exit POLONIUS

Will you two help to hasten them?

ROSENCRANTZ GUILDENSTERN

We will, my lord.

Exeunt ROSENCRANTZ and GUILDENSTERN

HAMLET

What ho! Horatio!

Enter HORATIO

HORATIO

Here, sweet lord, at your service.

HAMLET

Horatio, thou art e'en as just a man

As e'er my conversation coped withal.

HORATIO

O, my dear lord,--

HAMLET

Nay, do not think I flatter;

For what advancement may I hope from thee

That no revenue hast but thy good spirits,

To feed and clothe thee? Why should the poor be flatter'd?

No, let the candied tongue lick absurd pomp,

And crook the pregnant hinges of the knee

Where thrift may follow fawning. Dost thou hear?

Since my dear soul was mistress of her choice

And could of men distinguish, her election

Hath seal'd thee for herself; for thou hast been

As one, in suffering all, that suffers nothing,

A man that fortune's buffets and rewards

Hast ta'en with equal thanks: and blest are those

Whose blood and judgment are so well commingled,

That they are not a pipe for fortune's finger

To sound what stop she please. Give me that man

That is not passion's slave, and I will wear him

In my heart's core, ay, in my heart of heart,

As I do thee.--Something too much of this.--

There is a play to-night before the king;

One scene of it comes near the circumstance

Which I have told thee of my father's death:
I prithee, when thou seest that act afoot,
Even with the very comment of thy soul
Observe mine uncle: if his occulted guilt
Do not itself unkennel in one speech,
It is a damned ghost that we have seen,
And my imaginations are as foul
As Vulcan's stithy. Give him heedful note;
For I mine eyes will rivet to his face,
And after we will both our judgments join
In censure of his seeming.

HORATIO
Well, my lord:
If he steal aught the whilst this play is playing,
And 'scape detecting, I will pay the theft.

HAMLET
They are coming to the play; I must be idle:
Get you a place.
*Danish march. A flourish. Enter KING CLAUDIUS, QUEEN GERTRUDE,
POLONIUS, OPHELIA, ROSENCRANTZ, GUILDENSTERN, and others*

KING CLAUDIUS
How fares our cousin Hamlet?

HAMLET
Excellent, i' faith; of the chameleon's dish: I eat
the air, promise-crammed: you cannot feed capons so.

KING CLAUDIUS
I have nothing with this answer, Hamlet; these words
are not mine.

HAMLET
No, nor mine now.
To POLONIUS
My lord, you played once i' the university, you say?

LORD POLONIUS
That did I, my lord; and was accounted a good actor.

HAMLET
What did you enact?

LORD POLONIUS
I did enact Julius Caesar: I was killed i' the
Capitol; Brutus killed me.

HAMLET
It was a brute part of him to kill so capital a calf
there. Be the players ready?
ROSENCRANTZ
Ay, my lord; they stay upon your patience.
QUEEN GERTRUDE
Come hither, my dear Hamlet, sit by me.
HAMLET
No, good mother, here's metal more attractive.
LORD POLONIUS
[To KING CLAUDIUS] O, ho! do you mark that?
HAMLET
Lady, shall I lie in your lap?
Lying down at OPHELIA's feet
OPHELIA
No, my lord.
HAMLET
I mean, my head upon your lap?
OPHELIA
Ay, my lord.
HAMLET
Do you think I meant country matters?
OPHELIA
I think nothing, my lord.
HAMLET
That's a fair thought to lie between maids' legs.
OPHELIA
What is, my lord?
HAMLET
Nothing.
OPHELIA
You are merry, my lord.
HAMLET
Who, I?
OPHELIA
Ay, my lord.

HAMLET

O God, your only jig-maker. What should a man do
but be merry? for, look you, how cheerfully my
mother looks, and my father died within these two hours.

OPHELIA

Nay, 'tis twice two months, my lord.

HAMLET

So long? Nay then, let the devil wear black, for
I'll have a suit of sables. O heavens! die two
months ago, and not forgotten yet? Then there's
hope a great man's memory may outlive his life half
a year: but, by'r lady, he must build churches,
then; or else shall he suffer not thinking on, with
the hobby-horse, whose epitaph is 'For, O, for, O,
the hobby-horse is forgot.'

Hautboys play. The dumb-show enters

*Enter a King and a Queen very lovingly; the Queen embracing him, and he
her. She kneels, and makes show of protestation unto him. He takes her up,
and declines his head upon her neck: lays him down upon a bank of flowers:
she, seeing him asleep, leaves him. Anon comes in a fellow, takes off his
crown, kisses it, and pours poison in the King's ears, and exit. The Queen
returns; finds the King dead, and makes passionate action. The Poisoner,
with some two or three Mutes, comes in again, seeming to lament with her.
The dead body is carried away. The Poisoner wooes the Queen with gifts:
she seems loath and unwilling awhile, but in the end accepts his love*

Exeunt

OPHELIA

What means this, my lord?

HAMLET

Marry, this is miching mallecho; it means mischief.

OPHELIA

Belike this show imports the argument of the play.

Enter Prologue

HAMLET

We shall know by this fellow: the players cannot
keep counsel; they'll tell all.

OPHELIA

Will he tell us what this show meant?

HAMLET

Ay, or any show that you'll show him: be not you
ashamed to show, he'll not shame to tell you what it means.

OPHELIA

You are naught, you are naught: I'll mark the play.

Prologue

For us, and for our tragedy,
Here stooping to your clemency,
We beg your hearing patiently.

Exit

HAMLET

Is this a prologue, or the posy of a ring?

OPHELIA

'Tis brief, my lord.

HAMLET

As woman's love.

Enter two Players, King and Queen

Player King

Full thirty times hath Phoebus' cart gone round
Neptune's salt wash and Tellus' orbed ground,
And thirty dozen moons with borrow'd sheen
About the world have times twelve thirties been,
Since love our hearts and Hymen did our hands
Unite commutual in most sacred bands.

Player Queen

So many journeys may the sun and moon
Make us again count o'er ere love be done!
But, woe is me, you are so sick of late,
So far from cheer and from your former state,
That I distrust you. Yet, though I distrust,
Discomfort you, my lord, it nothing must:
For women's fear and love holds quantity;
In neither aught, or in extremity.
Now, what my love is, proof hath made you know;
And as my love is sized, my fear is so:
Where love is great, the littlest doubts are fear;
Where little fears grow great, great love grows there.

Player King
'Faith, I must leave thee, love, and shortly too;
My operant powers their functions leave to do:
And thou shalt live in this fair world behind,
Honour'd, beloved; and haply one as kind
For husband shalt thou--

Player Queen
O, confound the rest!
Such love must needs be treason in my breast:
In second husband let me be accurst!
None wed the second but who kill'd the first.

HAMLET
[Aside] Wormwood, wormwood.

Player Queen
The instances that second marriage move
Are base respects of thrift, but none of love:
A second time I kill my husband dead,
When second husband kisses me in bed.

Player King
I do believe you think what now you speak;
But what we do determine oft we break.
Purpose is but the slave to memory,
Of violent birth, but poor validity;
Which now, like fruit unripe, sticks on the tree;
But fall, unshaken, when they mellow be.
Most necessary 'tis that we forget
To pay ourselves what to ourselves is debt:
What to ourselves in passion we propose,
The passion ending, doth the purpose lose.
The violence of either grief or joy
Their own enactures with themselves destroy:
Where joy most revels, grief doth most lament;
Grief joys, joy grieves, on slender accident.
This world is not for aye, nor 'tis not strange
That even our loves should with our fortunes change;
For 'tis a question left us yet to prove,
Whether love lead fortune, or else fortune love.
The great man down, you mark his favourite flies;
The poor advanced makes friends of enemies.

And hitherto doth love on fortune tend;
For who not needs shall never lack a friend,
And who in want a hollow friend doth try,
Directly seasons him his enemy.
But, orderly to end where I begun,
Our wills and fates do so contrary run
That our devices still are overthrown;
Our thoughts are ours, their ends none of our own:
So think thou wilt no second husband wed;
But die thy thoughts when thy first lord is dead.
Player Queen
Nor earth to me give food, nor heaven light!
Sport and repose lock from me day and night!
To desperation turn my trust and hope!
An anchor's cheer in prison be my scope!
Each opposite that blanks the face of joy
Meet what I would have well and it destroy!
Both here and hence pursue me lasting strife,
If, once a widow, ever I be wife!
HAMLET
If she should break it now!
Player King
'Tis deeply sworn. Sweet, leave me here awhile;
My spirits grow dull, and fain I would beguile
The tedious day with sleep.
Sleeps
Player Queen
Sleep rock thy brain,
And never come mischance between us twain!
Exit
HAMLET
Madam, how like you this play?
QUEEN GERTRUDE
The lady protests too much, methinks.
HAMLET
O, but she'll keep her word.
KING CLAUDIUS
Have you heard the argument? Is there no offence in 't?

HAMLET

No, no, they do but jest, poison in jest; no offence
i' the world.

KING CLAUDIUS

What do you call the play?

HAMLET

The Mouse-trap. Marry, how? Tropically. This play
is the image of a murder done in Vienna: Gonzago is
the duke's name; his wife, Baptista: you shall see
anon; 'tis a knavish piece of work: but what o'
that? your majesty and we that have free souls, it
touches us not: let the galled jade wince, our
withers are unwrung.

Enter LUCIANUS

This is one Lucianus, nephew to the king.

OPHELIA

You are as good as a chorus, my lord.

HAMLET

I could interpret between you and your love, if I
could see the puppets dallying.

OPHELIA

You are keen, my lord, you are keen.

HAMLET

It would cost you a groaning to take off my edge.

OPHELIA

Still better, and worse.

HAMLET

So you must take your husbands. Begin, murderer;
pox, leave thy damnable faces, and begin. Come:
'the croaking raven doth bellow for revenge.'

LUCIANUS

Thoughts black, hands apt, drugs fit, and time agreeing;
Confederate season, else no creature seeing;
Thou mixture rank, of midnight weeds collected,
With Hecate's ban thrice blasted, thrice infected,
Thy natural magic and dire property,
On wholesome life usurp immediately.

Pours the poison into the sleeper's ears

HAMLET

He poisons him i' the garden for's estate. His
name's Gonzago: the story is extant, and writ in
choice Italian: you shall see anon how the murderer
gets the love of Gonzago's wife.

OPHELIA

The king rises.

HAMLET

What, frighted with false fire!

QUEEN GERTRUDE

How fares my lord?

LORD POLONIUS

Give o'er the play.

KING CLAUDIUS

Give me some light: away!

All

Lights, lights, lights!

Exeunt all but HAMLET and HORATIO

HAMLET

Why, let the stricken deer go weep,
The hart ungalled play;
For some must watch, while some must sleep:
So runs the world away.
Would not this, sir, and a forest of feathers-- if
the rest of my fortunes turn Turk with me--with two
Provincial roses on my razed shoes, get me a
fellowship in a cry of players, sir?

HORATIO

Half a share.

HAMLET

A whole one, I.
For thou dost know, O Damon dear,
This realm dismantled was
Of Jove himself; and now reigns here
A very, very--pajock.

HORATIO

You might have rhymed.

HAMLET

O good Horatio, I'll take the ghost's word for a
thousand pound. Didst perceive?

HORATIO

Very well, my lord.

HAMLET

Upon the talk of the poisoning?

HORATIO

I did very well note him.

HAMLET

Ah, ha! Come, some music! come, the recorders!
For if the king like not the comedy,
Why then, belike, he likes it not, perdy.
Come, some music!

Re-enter ROSENCRANTZ and GUILDENSTERN

GUILDENSTERN

Good my lord, vouchsafe me a word with you.

HAMLET

Sir, a whole history.

GUILDENSTERN

The king, sir,--

HAMLET

Ay, sir, what of him?

GUILDENSTERN

Is in his retirement marvellous distempered.

HAMLET

With drink, sir?

GUILDENSTERN

No, my lord, rather with choler.

HAMLET

Your wisdom should show itself more richer to
signify this to his doctor; for, for me to put him
to his purgation would perhaps plunge him into far
more choler.

GUILDENSTERN

Good my lord, put your discourse into some frame and
start not so wildly from my affair.

HAMLET

I am tame, sir: pronounce.

GUILDENSTERN
The queen, your mother, in most great affliction of
spirit, hath sent me to you.

HAMLET
You are welcome.

GUILDENSTERN
Nay, good my lord, this courtesy is not of the right
breed. If it shall please you to make me a
wholesome answer, I will do your mother's
commandment: if not, your pardon and my return
shall be the end of my business.

HAMLET
Sir, I cannot.

GUILDENSTERN
What, my lord?

HAMLET
Make you a wholesome answer; my wit's diseased: but,
sir, such answer as I can make, you shall command;
or, rather, as you say, my mother: therefore no
more, but to the matter: my mother, you say,--

ROSENCRANTZ
Then thus she says; your behavior hath struck her
into amazement and admiration.

HAMLET
O wonderful son, that can so astonish a mother! But
is there no sequel at the heels of this mother's
admiration? Impart.

ROSENCRANTZ
She desires to speak with you in her closet, ere you
go to bed.

HAMLET
We shall obey, were she ten times our mother. Have
you any further trade with us?

ROSENCRANTZ
My lord, you once did love me.

HAMLET
So I do still, by these pickers and stealers.

ROSENCRANTZ
Good my lord, what is your cause of distemper? you
do, surely, bar the door upon your own liberty, if
you deny your griefs to your friend.
HAMLET
Sir, I lack advancement.
ROSENCRANTZ
How can that be, when you have the voice of the king
himself for your succession in Denmark?
HAMLET
Ay, but sir, 'While the grass grows,'--the proverb
is something musty.
Re-enter Players with recorders
O, the recorders! let me see one. To withdraw with
you:--why do you go about to recover the wind of me,
as if you would drive me into a toil?
GUILDENSTERN
O, my lord, if my duty be too bold, my love is too
unmannerly.
HAMLET
I do not well understand that. Will you play upon
this pipe?
GUILDENSTERN
My lord, I cannot.
HAMLET
I pray you.
GUILDENSTERN
Believe me, I cannot.
HAMLET
I do beseech you.
GUILDENSTERN
I know no touch of it, my lord.
HAMLET
'Tis as easy as lying: govern these ventages with
your lingers and thumb, give it breath with your
mouth, and it will discourse most eloquent music.
Look you, these are the stops.

GUILDENSTERN

But these cannot I command to any utterance of
harmony; I have not the skill.

HAMLET

Why, look you now, how unworthy a thing you make of
me! You would play upon me; you would seem to know
my stops; you would pluck out the heart of my
mystery; you would sound me from my lowest note to
the top of my compass: and there is much music,
excellent voice, in this little organ; yet cannot
you make it speak. 'Sblood, do you think I am
easier to be played on than a pipe? Call me what
instrument you will, though you can fret me, yet you
cannot play upon me.

Enter POLONIUS

God bless you, sir!

LORD POLONIUS

My lord, the queen would speak with you, and
presently.

HAMLET

Do you see yonder cloud that's almost in shape of a camel?

LORD POLONIUS

By the mass, and 'tis like a camel, indeed.

HAMLET

Methinks it is like a weasel.

LORD POLONIUS

It is backed like a weasel.

HAMLET

Or like a whale?

LORD POLONIUS

Very like a whale.

HAMLET

Then I will come to my mother by and by. They fool
me to the top of my bent. I will come by and by.

LORD POLONIUS

I will say so.

HAMLET

By and by is easily said.

Exit POLONIUS

Leave me, friends.
Exeunt all but HAMLET
Tis now the very witching time of night,
When churchyards yawn and hell itself breathes out
Contagion to this world: now could I drink hot blood,
And do such bitter business as the day
Would quake to look on. Soft! now to my mother.
O heart, lose not thy nature; let not ever
The soul of Nero enter this firm bosom:
Let me be cruel, not unnatural:
I will speak daggers to her, but use none;
My tongue and soul in this be hypocrites;
How in my words soever she be shent,
To give them seals never, my soul, consent!
Exit

SCENE III. A room in the castle.

Enter KING CLAUDIUS, ROSENCRANTZ, and GUILDENSTERN

KING CLAUDIUS
I like him not, nor stands it safe with us
To let his madness range. Therefore prepare you;
I your commission will forthwith dispatch,
And he to England shall along with you:
The terms of our estate may not endure
Hazard so dangerous as doth hourly grow
Out of his lunacies.

GUILDENSTERN
We will ourselves provide:
Most holy and religious fear it is
To keep those many many bodies safe
That live and feed upon your majesty.

ROSENCRANTZ
The single and peculiar life is bound,
With all the strength and armour of the mind,
To keep itself from noyance; but much more
That spirit upon whose weal depend and rest
The lives of many. The cease of majesty
Dies not alone; but, like a gulf, doth draw
What's near it with it: it is a massy wheel,
Fix'd on the summit of the highest mount,

To whose huge spokes ten thousand lesser things
Are mortised and adjoin'd; which, when it falls,
Each small annexment, petty consequence,
Attends the boisterous ruin. Never alone
Did the king sigh, but with a general groan.
KING CLAUDIUS
Arm you, I pray you, to this speedy voyage;
For we will fetters put upon this fear,
Which now goes too free-footed.
ROSENCRANTZ GUILDENSTERN
We will haste us.
Exeunt ROSENCRANTZ and GUILDENSTERN
Enter POLONIUS
LORD POLONIUS
My lord, he's going to his mother's closet:
Behind the arras I'll convey myself,
To hear the process; and warrant she'll tax him home:
And, as you said, and wisely was it said,
'Tis meet that some more audience than a mother,
Since nature makes them partial, should o'erhear
The speech, of vantage. Fare you well, my liege:
I'll call upon you ere you go to bed,
And tell you what I know.
KING CLAUDIUS
Thanks, dear my lord.
Exit POLONIUS
O, my offence is rank it smells to heaven;
It hath the primal eldest curse upon't,
A brother's murder. Pray can I not,
Though inclination be as sharp as will:
My stronger guilt defeats my strong intent;
And, like a man to double business bound,
I stand in pause where I shall first begin,
And both neglect. What if this cursed hand
Were thicker than itself with brother's blood,
Is there not rain enough in the sweet heavens
To wash it white as snow? Whereto serves mercy
But to confront the visage of offence?
And what's in prayer but this two-fold force,

To be forestalled ere we come to fall,
Or pardon'd being down? Then I'll look up;
My fault is past. But, O, what form of prayer
Can serve my turn? 'Forgive me my foul murder'?
That cannot be; since I am still possess'd
Of those effects for which I did the murder,
My crown, mine own ambition and my queen.
May one be pardon'd and retain the offence?
In the corrupted currents of this world
Offence's gilded hand may shove by justice,
And oft 'tis seen the wicked prize itself
Buys out the law: but 'tis not so above;
There is no shuffling, there the action lies
In his true nature; and we ourselves compell'd,
Even to the teeth and forehead of our faults,
To give in evidence. What then? what rests?
Try what repentance can: what can it not?
Yet what can it when one can not repent?
O wretched state! O bosom black as death!
O limed soul, that, struggling to be free,
Art more engaged! Help, angels! Make assay!
Bow, stubborn knees; and, heart with strings of steel,
Be soft as sinews of the newborn babe!
All may be well.
Retires and kneels
Enter HAMLET

HAMLET
Now might I do it pat, now he is praying;
And now I'll do't. And so he goes to heaven;
And so am I revenged. That would be scann'd:
A villain kills my father; and for that,
I, his sole son, do this same villain send
To heaven.
O, this is hire and salary, not revenge.
He took my father grossly, full of bread;
With all his crimes broad blown, as flush as May;
And how his audit stands who knows save heaven?
But in our circumstance and course of thought,
'Tis heavy with him: and am I then revenged,

To take him in the purging of his soul,
When he is fit and season'd for his passage?
No!
Up, sword; and know thou a more horrid hent:
When he is drunk asleep, or in his rage,
Or in the incestuous pleasure of his bed;
At gaming, swearing, or about some act
That has no relish of salvation in't;
Then trip him, that his heels may kick at heaven,
And that his soul may be as damn'd and black
As hell, whereto it goes. My mother stays:
This physic but prolongs thy sickly days.
Exit

KING CLAUDIUS

[Rising] My words fly up, my thoughts remain below:
Words without thoughts never to heaven go.
Exit

SCENE IV. The Queen's closet.

Enter QUEEN MARGARET and POLONIUS

LORD POLONIUS

He will come straight. Look you lay home to him:
Tell him his pranks have been too broad to bear with,
And that your grace hath screen'd and stood between
Much heat and him. I'll sconce me even here.
Pray you, be round with him.

HAMLET

[Within] Mother, mother, mother!

QUEEN GERTRUDE

I'll warrant you,
Fear me not: withdraw, I hear him coming.
POLONIUS hides behind the arras
Enter HAMLET

HAMLET

Now, mother, what's the matter?

QUEEN GERTRUDE

Hamlet, thou hast thy father much offended.

HAMLET

Mother, you have my father much offended.

QUEEN GERTRUDE

Come, come, you answer with an idle tongue.

HAMLET

Go, go, you question with a wicked tongue.

QUEEN GERTRUDE

Why, how now, Hamlet!

HAMLET

What's the matter now?

QUEEN GERTRUDE

Have you forgot me?

HAMLET

No, by the rood, not so:

You are the queen, your husband's brother's wife;

And--would it were not so!--you are my mother.

QUEEN GERTRUDE

Nay, then, I'll set those to you that can speak.

HAMLET

Come, come, and sit you down; you shall not budge;

You go not till I set you up a glass

Where you may see the inmost part of you.

QUEEN GERTRUDE

What wilt thou do? thou wilt not murder me?

Help, help, ho!

LORD POLONIUS

[Behind] What, ho! help, help, help!

HAMLET

[Drawing] How now! a rat? Dead, for a ducat, dead!

Makes a pass through the arras

LORD POLONIUS

[Behind] O, I am slain!

Falls and dies

QUEEN GERTRUDE

O me, what hast thou done?

HAMLET

Nay, I know not:

Is it the king?

QUEEN GERTRUDE

O, what a rash and bloody deed is this!

HAMLET

A bloody deed! almost as bad, good mother,
As kill a king, and marry with his brother.

QUEEN GERTRUDE

As kill a king!

HAMLET

Ay, lady, 'twas my word.

Lifts up the array and discovers POLONIUS

Thou wretched, rash, intruding fool, farewell!
I took thee for thy better: take thy fortune;
Thou find'st to be too busy is some danger.
Leave wringing of your hands: peace! sit you down,
And let me wring your heart; for so I shall,
If it be made of penetrable stuff,
If damned custom have not brass'd it so
That it is proof and bulwark against sense.

QUEEN GERTRUDE

What have I done, that thou darest wag thy tongue
In noise so rude against me?

HAMLET

Such an act
That blurs the grace and blush of modesty,
Calls virtue hypocrite, takes off the rose
From the fair forehead of an innocent love
And sets a blister there, makes marriage-vows
As false as dicers' oaths: O, such a deed
As from the body of contraction plucks
The very soul, and sweet religion makes
A rhapsody of words: heaven's face doth glow:
Yea, this solidity and compound mass,
With tristful visage, as against the doom,
Is thought-sick at the act.

QUEEN GERTRUDE

Ay me, what act,
That roars so loud, and thunders in the index?

HAMLET

Look here, upon this picture, and on this,
The counterfeit presentment of two brothers.
See, what a grace was seated on this brow;

Hyperion's curls; the front of Jove himself;
An eye like Mars, to threaten and command;
A station like the herald Mercury
New-lighted on a heaven-kissing hill;
A combination and a form indeed,
Where every god did seem to set his seal,
To give the world assurance of a man:
This was your husband. Look you now, what follows:
Here is your husband; like a mildew'd ear,
Blasting his wholesome brother. Have you eyes?
Could you on this fair mountain leave to feed,
And batten on this moor? Ha! have you eyes?
You cannot call it love; for at your age
The hey-day in the blood is tame, it's humble,
And waits upon the judgment: and what judgment
Would step from this to this? Sense, sure, you have,
Else could you not have motion; but sure, that sense
Is apoplex'd; for madness would not err,
Nor sense to ecstasy was ne'er so thrall'd
But it reserved some quantity of choice,
To serve in such a difference. What devil was't
That thus hath cozen'd you at hoodman-blind?
Eyes without feeling, feeling without sight,
Ears without hands or eyes, smelling sans all,
Or but a sickly part of one true sense
Could not so mope.
O shame! where is thy blush? Rebellious hell,
If thou canst mutine in a matron's bones,
To flaming youth let virtue be as wax,
And melt in her own fire: proclaim no shame
When the compulsive ardour gives the charge,
Since frost itself as actively doth burn
And reason panders will.
QUEEN GERTRUDE
O Hamlet, speak no more:
Thou turn'st mine eyes into my very soul;
And there I see such black and grained spots
As will not leave their tinct.

HAMLET

Nay, but to live
In the rank sweat of an enseamed bed,
Stew'd in corruption, honeying and making love
Over the nasty sty,--

QUEEN GERTRUDE

O, speak to me no more;
These words, like daggers, enter in mine ears;
No more, sweet Hamlet!

HAMLET

A murderer and a villain;
A slave that is not twentieth part the tithe
Of your precedent lord; a vice of kings;
A cutpurse of the empire and the rule,
That from a shelf the precious diadem stole,
And put it in his pocket!

QUEEN GERTRUDE

No more!

HAMLET

A king of shreds and patches,--

Enter Ghost

Save me, and hover o'er me with your wings,
You heavenly guards! What would your gracious figure?

QUEEN GERTRUDE

Alas, he's mad!

HAMLET

Do you not come your tardy son to chide,
That, lapsed in time and passion, lets go by
The important acting of your dread command? O, say!

Ghost

Do not forget: this visitation
Is but to whet thy almost blunted purpose.
But, look, amazement on thy mother sits:
O, step between her and her fighting soul:
Conceit in weakest bodies strongest works:
Speak to her, Hamlet.

HAMLET

How is it with you, lady?

QUEEN GERTRUDE
Alas, how is't with you,
That you do bend your eye on vacancy
And with the incorporal air do hold discourse?
Forth at your eyes your spirits wildly peep;
And, as the sleeping soldiers in the alarm,
Your bedded hair, like life in excrements,
Starts up, and stands on end. O gentle son,
Upon the heat and flame of thy distemper
Sprinkle cool patience. Whereon do you look?
HAMLET
On him, on him! Look you, how pale he glares!
His form and cause conjoin'd, preaching to stones,
Would make them capable. Do not look upon me;
Lest with this piteous action you convert
My stern effects: then what I have to do
Will want true colour; tears perchance for blood.
QUEEN GERTRUDE
To whom do you speak this?
HAMLET
Do you see nothing there?
QUEEN GERTRUDE
Nothing at all; yet all that is I see.
HAMLET
Nor did you nothing hear?
QUEEN GERTRUDE
No, nothing but ourselves.
HAMLET
Why, look you there! look, how it steals away!
My father, in his habit as he lived!
Look, where he goes, even now, out at the portal!
Exit Ghost
QUEEN GERTRUDE
This the very coinage of your brain:
This bodiless creation ecstasy
Is very cunning in.
HAMLET
Ecstasy!
My pulse, as yours, doth temperately keep time,

And makes as healthful music: it is not madness
That I have utter'd: bring me to the test,
And I the matter will re-word; which madness
Would gambol from. Mother, for love of grace,
Lay not that mattering unction to your soul,
That not your trespass, but my madness speaks:
It will but skin and film the ulcerous place,
Whilst rank corruption, mining all within,
Infects unseen. Confess yourself to heaven;
Repent what's past; avoid what is to come;
And do not spread the compost on the weeds,
To make them ranker. Forgive me this my virtue;
For in the fatness of these pursy times
Virtue itself of vice must pardon beg,
Yea, curb and woo for leave to do him good.

QUEEN GERTRUDE
O Hamlet, thou hast cleft my heart in twain.

HAMLET
O, throw away the worser part of it,
And live the purer with the other half.
Good night: but go not to mine uncle's bed;
Assume a virtue, if you have it not.
That monster, custom, who all sense doth eat,
Of habits devil, is angel yet in this,
That to the use of actions fair and good
He likewise gives a frock or livery,
That aptly is put on. Refrain to-night,
And that shall lend a kind of easiness
To the next abstinence: the next more easy;
For use almost can change the stamp of nature,
And either [ ] the devil, or throw him out
With wondrous potency. Once more, good night:
And when you are desirous to be bless'd,
I'll blessing beg of you. For this same lord,
Pointing to POLONIUS
I do repent: but heaven hath pleased it so,
To punish me with this and this with me,
That I must be their scourge and minister.
I will bestow him, and will answer well

The death I gave him. So, again, good night.
I must be cruel, only to be kind:
Thus bad begins and worse remains behind.
One word more, good lady.

QUEEN GERTRUDE
What shall I do?

HAMLET
Not this, by no means, that I bid you do:
Let the bloat king tempt you again to bed;
Pinch wanton on your cheek; call you his mouse;
And let him, for a pair of reechy kisses,
Or paddling in your neck with his damn'd fingers,
Make you to ravel all this matter out,
That I essentially am not in madness,
But mad in craft. 'Twere good you let him know;
For who, that's but a queen, fair, sober, wise,
Would from a paddock, from a bat, a gib,
Such dear concernings hide? who would do so?
No, in despite of sense and secrecy,
Unpeg the basket on the house's top.
Let the birds fly, and, like the famous ape,
To try conclusions, in the basket creep,
And break your own neck down.

QUEEN GERTRUDE
Be thou assured, if words be made of breath,
And breath of life, I have no life to breathe
What thou hast said to me.

HAMLET
I must to England; you know that?

QUEEN GERTRUDE
Alack,
I had forgot: 'tis so concluded on.

HAMLET
There's letters seal'd: and my two schoolfellows,
Whom I will trust as I will adders fang'd,
They bear the mandate; they must sweep my way,
And marshal me to knavery. Let it work;
For 'tis the sport to have the engineer
Hoist with his own petard: and 't shall go hard

But I will delve one yard below their mines,
And blow them at the moon: O, 'tis most sweet,
When in one line two crafts directly meet.
This man shall set me packing:
I'll lug the guts into the neighbour room.
Mother, good night. Indeed this counsellor
Is now most still, most secret and most grave,
Who was in life a foolish prating knave.
Come, sir, to draw toward an end with you.
Good night, mother.
Exeunt severally; HAMLET dragging in POLONIUS

ACT IV

SCENE I. A room in the castle.

Enter KING CLAUDIUS, QUEEN GERTRUDE, ROSENCRANTZ, and GUILDENSTERN

KING CLAUDIUS

There's matter in these sighs, these profound heaves:
You must translate: 'tis fit we understand them.
Where is your son?

QUEEN GERTRUDE

Bestow this place on us a little while.
Exeunt ROSENCRANTZ and GUILDENSTERN
Ah, my good lord, what have I seen to-night!

KING CLAUDIUS

What, Gertrude? How does Hamlet?

QUEEN GERTRUDE

Mad as the sea and wind, when both contend
Which is the mightier: in his lawless fit,
Behind the arras hearing something stir,
Whips out his rapier, cries, 'A rat, a rat!'
And, in this brainish apprehension, kills
The unseen good old man.

KING CLAUDIUS

O heavy deed!
It had been so with us, had we been there:
His liberty is full of threats to all;
To you yourself, to us, to every one.
Alas, how shall this bloody deed be answer'd?
It will be laid to us, whose providence

Should have kept short, restrain'd and out of haunt,
This mad young man: but so much was our love,
We would not understand what was most fit;
But, like the owner of a foul disease,
To keep it from divulging, let it feed
Even on the pith of Life. Where is he gone?

QUEEN GERTRUDE
To draw apart the body he hath kill'd:
O'er whom his very madness, like some ore
Among a mineral of metals base,
Shows itself pure; he weeps for what is done.

KING CLAUDIUS
O Gertrude, come away!
The sun no sooner shall the mountains touch,
But we will ship him hence: and this vile deed
We must, with all our majesty and skill,
Both countenance and excuse. Ho, Guildenstern!
Re-enter ROSENCRANTZ and GUILDENSTERN
Friends both, go join you with some further aid:
Hamlet in madness hath Polonius slain,
And from his mother's closet hath he dragg'd him:
Go seek him out; speak fair, and bring the body
Into the chapel. I pray you, haste in this.
Exeunt ROSENCRANTZ and GUILDENSTERN
Come, Gertrude, we'll call up our wisest friends;
And let them know, both what we mean to do,
And what's untimely done. O, come away!
My soul is full of discord and dismay.
Exeunt

SCENE II. Another room in the castle.
Enter HAMLET

HAMLET
Safely stowed.

ROSENCRANTZ: GUILDENSTERN:
[Within] Hamlet! Lord Hamlet!

HAMLET
What noise? who calls on Hamlet?
O, here they come.
Enter ROSENCRANTZ and GUILDENSTERN

ROSENCRANTZ
What have you done, my lord, with the dead body?
HAMLET
Compounded it with dust, whereto 'tis kin.
ROSENCRANTZ
Tell us where 'tis, that we may take it thence
And bear it to the chapel.
HAMLET
Do not believe it.
ROSENCRANTZ
Believe what?
HAMLET
That I can keep your counsel and not mine own.
Besides, to be demanded of a sponge! what
replication should be made by the son of a king?
ROSENCRANTZ
Take you me for a sponge, my lord?
HAMLET
Ay, sir, that soaks up the king's countenance, his
rewards, his authorities. But such officers do the
king best service in the end: he keeps them, like
an ape, in the corner of his jaw; first mouthed, to
be last swallowed: when he needs what you have
gleaned, it is but squeezing you, and, sponge, you
shall be dry again.
ROSENCRANTZ
I understand you not, my lord.
HAMLET
I am glad of it: a knavish speech sleeps in a
foolish ear.
ROSENCRANTZ
My lord, you must tell us where the body is, and go
with us to the king.
HAMLET
The body is with the king, but the king is not with
the body. The king is a thing--
GUILDENSTERN
A thing, my lord!

HAMLET
Of nothing: bring me to him. Hide fox, and all after.
Exeunt
SCENE III. Another room in the castle.
Enter KING CLAUDIUS, attended
KING CLAUDIUS
I have sent to seek him, and to find the body.
How dangerous is it that this man goes loose!
Yet must not we put the strong law on him:
He's loved of the distracted multitude,
Who like not in their judgment, but their eyes;
And where tis so, the offender's scourge is weigh'd,
But never the offence. To bear all smooth and even,
This sudden sending him away must seem
Deliberate pause: diseases desperate grown
By desperate appliance are relieved,
Or not at all.
Enter ROSENCRANTZ
How now! what hath befall'n?
ROSENCRANTZ
Where the dead body is bestow'd, my lord,
We cannot get from him.
KING CLAUDIUS
But where is he?
ROSENCRANTZ
Without, my lord; guarded, to know your pleasure.
KING CLAUDIUS
Bring him before us.
ROSENCRANTZ
Ho, Guildenstern! bring in my lord.
Enter HAMLET and GUILDENSTERN
KING CLAUDIUS
Now, Hamlet, where's Polonius?
HAMLET
At supper.
KING CLAUDIUS
At supper! where?

HAMLET

Not where he eats, but where he is eaten: a certain
convocation of politic worms are e'en at him. Your
worm is your only emperor for diet: we fat all
creatures else to fat us, and we fat ourselves for
maggots: your fat king and your lean beggar is but
variable service, two dishes, but to one table:
that's the end.

KING CLAUDIUS

Alas, alas!

HAMLET

A man may fish with the worm that hath eat of a
king, and cat of the fish that hath fed of that worm.

KING CLAUDIUS

What dost you mean by this?

HAMLET

Nothing but to show you how a king may go a
progress through the guts of a beggar.

KING CLAUDIUS

Where is Polonius?

HAMLET

In heaven; send hither to see: if your messenger
find him not there, seek him i' the other place
yourself. But indeed, if you find him not within
this month, you shall nose him as you go up the
stairs into the lobby.

KING CLAUDIUS

Go seek him there.

To some Attendants

HAMLET

He will stay till ye come.

Exeunt Attendants

KING CLAUDIUS

Hamlet, this deed, for thine especial safety,--
Which we do tender, as we dearly grieve
For that which thou hast done,--must send thee hence
With fiery quickness: therefore prepare thyself;
The bark is ready, and the wind at help,

The associates tend, and every thing is bent
For England.
HAMLET
For England!
KING CLAUDIUS
Ay, Hamlet.
HAMLET
Good.
KING CLAUDIUS
So is it, if thou knew'st our purposes.
HAMLET
I see a cherub that sees them. But, come; for
England! Farewell, dear mother.
KING CLAUDIUS
Thy loving father, Hamlet.
HAMLET
My mother: father and mother is man and wife; man
and wife is one flesh; and so, my mother. Come, for England!
Exit
KING CLAUDIUS
Follow him at foot; tempt him with speed aboard;
Delay it not; I'll have him hence to-night:
Away! for every thing is seal'd and done
That else leans on the affair: pray you, make haste.
Exeunt ROSENCRANTZ and GUILDENSTERN
And, England, if my love thou hold'st at aught--
As my great power thereof may give thee sense,
Since yet thy cicatrice looks raw and red
After the Danish sword, and thy free awe
Pays homage to us--thou mayst not coldly set
Our sovereign process; which imports at full,
By letters congruing to that effect,
The present death of Hamlet. Do it, England;
For like the hectic in my blood he rages,
And thou must cure me: till I know 'tis done,
Howe'er my haps, my joys were ne'er begun.
Exit
SCENE IV. A plain in Denmark.
Enter FORTINBRAS, a Captain, and Soldiers, marching

PRINCE FORTINBRAS
Go, captain, from me greet the Danish king;
Tell him that, by his licence, Fortinbras
Craves the conveyance of a promised march
Over his kingdom. You know the rendezvous.
If that his majesty would aught with us,
We shall express our duty in his eye;
And let him know so.
Captain
I will do't, my lord.
PRINCE FORTINBRAS
Go softly on.
Exeunt FORTINBRAS and Soldiers
Enter HAMLET, ROSENCRANTZ, GUILDENSTERN, and others
HAMLET
Good sir, whose powers are these?
Captain
They are of Norway, sir.
HAMLET
How purposed, sir, I pray you?
Captain
Against some part of Poland.
HAMLET
Who commands them, sir?
Captain
The nephews to old Norway, Fortinbras.
HAMLET
Goes it against the main of Poland, sir,
Or for some frontier?
Captain
Truly to speak, and with no addition,
We go to gain a little patch of ground
That hath in it no profit but the name.
To pay five ducats, five, I would not farm it;
Nor will it yield to Norway or the Pole
A ranker rate, should it be sold in fee.
HAMLET
Why, then the Polack never will defend it.

Captain
Yes, it is already garrison'd.
HAMLET
Two thousand souls and twenty thousand ducats
Will not debate the question of this straw:
This is the imposthume of much wealth and peace,
That inward breaks, and shows no cause without
Why the man dies. I humbly thank you, sir.
Captain
God be wi' you, sir.
Exit
ROSENCRANTZ
Wilt please you go, my lord?
HAMLET
I'll be with you straight go a little before.
Exeunt all except HAMLET
How all occasions do inform against me,
And spur my dull revenge! What is a man,
If his chief good and market of his time
Be but to sleep and feed? a beast, no more.
Sure, he that made us with such large discourse,
Looking before and after, gave us not
That capability and god-like reason
To fust in us unused. Now, whether it be
Bestial oblivion, or some craven scruple
Of thinking too precisely on the event,
A thought which, quarter'd, hath but one part wisdom
And ever three parts coward, I do not know
Why yet I live to say 'This thing's to do;'
Sith I have cause and will and strength and means
To do't. Examples gross as earth exhort me:
Witness this army of such mass and charge
Led by a delicate and tender prince,
Whose spirit with divine ambition puff'd
Makes mouths at the invisible event,
Exposing what is mortal and unsure
To all that fortune, death and danger dare,
Even for an egg-shell. Rightly to be great
Is not to stir without great argument,

But greatly to find quarrel in a straw
When honour's at the stake. How stand I then,
That have a father kill'd, a mother stain'd,
Excitements of my reason and my blood,
And let all sleep? while, to my shame, I see
The imminent death of twenty thousand men,
That, for a fantasy and trick of fame,
Go to their graves like beds, fight for a plot
Whereon the numbers cannot try the cause,
Which is not tomb enough and continent
To hide the slain? O, from this time forth,
My thoughts be bloody, or be nothing worth!
Exit

SCENE V. Elsinore. A room in the castle.

Enter QUEEN GERTRUDE, HORATIO, and a Gentleman

QUEEN GERTRUDE

I will not speak with her.

Gentleman

She is importunate, indeed distract:
Her mood will needs be pitied.

QUEEN GERTRUDE

What would she have?

Gentleman

She speaks much of her father; says she hears
There's tricks i' the world; and hems, and beats her heart;
Spurns enviously at straws; speaks things in doubt,
That carry but half sense: her speech is nothing,
Yet the unshaped use of it doth move
The hearers to collection; they aim at it,
And botch the words up fit to their own thoughts;
Which, as her winks, and nods, and gestures
yield them,
Indeed would make one think there might be thought,
Though nothing sure, yet much unhappily.

HORATIO

'Twere good she were spoken with; for she may strew
Dangerous conjectures in ill-breeding minds.

QUEEN GERTRUDE

Let her come in.

Exit HORATIO
To my sick soul, as sin's true nature is,
Each toy seems prologue to some great amiss:
So full of artless jealousy is guilt,
It spills itself in fearing to be spilt.
Re-enter HORATIO, with OPHELIA
OPHELIA
Where is the beauteous majesty of Denmark?
QUEEN GERTRUDE
How now, Ophelia!
OPHELIA
[Sings]
How should I your true love know
From another one?
By his cockle hat and staff,
And his sandal shoon.
QUEEN GERTRUDE
Alas, sweet lady, what imports this song?
OPHELIA
Say you? nay, pray you, mark.
Sings
He is dead and gone, lady,
He is dead and gone;
At his head a grass-green turf,
At his heels a stone.
QUEEN GERTRUDE
Nay, but, Ophelia,--
OPHELIA
Pray you, mark.
Sings
White his shroud as the mountain snow,--
Enter KING CLAUDIUS
QUEEN GERTRUDE
Alas, look here, my lord.
OPHELIA
[Sings]
Larded with sweet flowers
Which bewept to the grave did go
With true-love showers.

KING CLAUDIUS
How do you, pretty lady?
OPHELIA
Well, God 'ild you! They say the owl was a baker's
daughter. Lord, we know what we are, but know not
what we may be. God be at your table!
KING CLAUDIUS
Conceit upon her father.
OPHELIA
Pray you, let's have no words of this; but when they
ask you what it means, say you this:
Sings
To-morrow is Saint Valentine's day,
All in the morning betime,
And I a maid at your window,
To be your Valentine.
Then up he rose, and donn'd his clothes,
And dupp'd the chamber-door;
Let in the maid, that out a maid
Never departed more.
KING CLAUDIUS
Pretty Ophelia!
OPHELIA
Indeed, la, without an oath, I'll make an end on't:
Sings
By Gis and by Saint Charity,
Alack, and fie for shame!
Young men will do't, if they come to't;
By cock, they are to blame.
Quoth she, before you tumbled me,
You promised me to wed.
So would I ha' done, by yonder sun,
An thou hadst not come to my bed.
KING CLAUDIUS
How long hath she been thus?
OPHELIA
I hope all will be well. We must be patient: but I
cannot choose but weep, to think they should lay him
i' the cold ground. My brother shall know of it:

and so I thank you for your good counsel. Come, my
coach! Good night, ladies; good night, sweet ladies;
good night, good night.
Exit
KING CLAUDIUS
Follow her close; give her good watch,
I pray you.
Exit HORATIO
O, this is the poison of deep grief; it springs
All from her father's death. O Gertrude, Gertrude,
When sorrows come, they come not single spies
But in battalions. First, her father slain:
Next, your son gone; and he most violent author
Of his own just remove: the people muddied,
Thick and unwholesome in their thoughts and whispers,
For good Polonius' death; and we have done but greenly,
In hugger-mugger to inter him: poor Ophelia
Divided from herself and her fair judgment,
Without the which we are pictures, or mere beasts:
Last, and as much containing as all these,
Her brother is in secret come from France;
Feeds on his wonder, keeps himself in clouds,
And wants not buzzers to infect his ear
With pestilent speeches of his father's death;
Wherein necessity, of matter beggar'd,
Will nothing stick our person to arraign
In ear and ear. O my dear Gertrude, this,
Like to a murdering-piece, in many places
Gives me superfluous death.
A noise within
QUEEN GERTRUDE
Alack, what noise is this?
KING CLAUDIUS
Where are my Switzers? Let them guard the door.
Enter another Gentleman
What is the matter?
Gentleman
Save yourself, my lord:
The ocean, overpeering of his list,

Eats not the flats with more impetuous haste
Than young Laertes, in a riotous head,
O'erbears your officers. The rabble call him lord;
And, as the world were now but to begin,
Antiquity forgot, custom not known,
The ratifiers and props of every word,
They cry 'Choose we: Laertes shall be king:'
Caps, hands, and tongues, applaud it to the clouds:
'Laertes shall be king, Laertes king!'

QUEEN GERTRUDE

How cheerfully on the false trail they cry!
O, this is counter, you false Danish dogs!

KING CLAUDIUS

The doors are broke.

Noise within

Enter LAERTES, armed; Danes following

LAERTES

Where is this king? Sirs, stand you all without.

Danes

No, let's come in.

LAERTES

I pray you, give me leave.

Danes

We will, we will.

They retire without the door

LAERTES

I thank you: keep the door. O thou vile king,
Give me my father!

QUEEN GERTRUDE

Calmly, good Laertes.

LAERTES

That drop of blood that's calm proclaims me bastard,
Cries cuckold to my father, brands the harlot
Even here, between the chaste unsmirched brow
Of my true mother.

KING CLAUDIUS

What is the cause, Laertes,
That thy rebellion looks so giant-like?
Let him go, Gertrude; do not fear our person:

There's such divinity doth hedge a king,
That treason can but peep to what it would,
Acts little of his will. Tell me, Laertes,
Why thou art thus incensed. Let him go, Gertrude.
Speak, man.
LAERTES
Where is my father?
KING CLAUDIUS
Dead.
QUEEN GERTRUDE
But not by him.
KING CLAUDIUS
Let him demand his fill.
LAERTES
How came he dead? I'll not be juggled with:
To hell, allegiance! vows, to the blackest devil!
Conscience and grace, to the profoundest pit!
I dare damnation. To this point I stand,
That both the worlds I give to negligence,
Let come what comes; only I'll be revenged
Most thoroughly for my father.
KING CLAUDIUS
Who shall stay you?
LAERTES
My will, not all the world:
And for my means, I'll husband them so well,
They shall go far with little.
KING CLAUDIUS
Good Laertes,
If you desire to know the certainty
Of your dear father's death, is't writ in your revenge,
That, swoopstake, you will draw both friend and foe,
Winner and loser?
LAERTES
None but his enemies.
KING CLAUDIUS
Will you know them then?

LAERTES

To his good friends thus wide I'll ope my arms;
And like the kind life-rendering pelican,
Repast them with my blood.

KING CLAUDIUS

Why, now you speak
Like a good child and a true gentleman.
That I am guiltless of your father's death,
And am most sensible in grief for it,
It shall as level to your judgment pierce
As day does to your eye.

Danes

[Within] Let her come in.

LAERTES

How now! what noise is that?

Re-enter OPHELIA

O heat, dry up my brains! tears seven times salt,
Burn out the sense and virtue of mine eye!
By heaven, thy madness shall be paid by weight,
Till our scale turn the beam. O rose of May!
Dear maid, kind sister, sweet Ophelia!
O heavens! is't possible, a young maid's wits
Should be as moral as an old man's life?
Nature is fine in love, and where 'tis fine,
It sends some precious instance of itself
After the thing it loves.

OPHELIA

[Sings]
They bore him barefaced on the bier;
Hey non nonny, nonny, hey nonny;
And in his grave rain'd many a tear:--
Fare you well, my dove!

LAERTES

Hadst thou thy wits, and didst persuade revenge,
It could not move thus.

OPHELIA

[Sings]
You must sing a-down a-down,
An you call him a-down-a.

O, how the wheel becomes it! It is the false
steward, that stole his master's daughter.

LAERTES

This nothing's more than matter.

OPHELIA

There's rosemary, that's for remembrance; pray,
love, remember: and there is pansies. that's for thoughts.

LAERTES

A document in madness, thoughts and remembrance fitted.

OPHELIA

There's fennel for you, and columbines: there's rue
for you; and here's some for me: we may call it
herb-grace o' Sundays: O you must wear your rue with
a difference. There's a daisy: I would give you
some violets, but they withered all when my father
died: they say he made a good end,--

Sings

For bonny sweet Robin is all my joy.

LAERTES

Thought and affliction, passion, hell itself,
She turns to favour and to prettiness.

OPHELIA

[Sings]

And will he not come again?
And will he not come again?
No, no, he is dead:
Go to thy death-bed:
He never will come again.
His beard was as white as snow,
All flaxen was his poll:
He is gone, he is gone,
And we cast away moan:
God ha' mercy on his soul!
And of all Christian souls, I pray God. God be wi' ye.

Exit

LAERTES

Do you see this, O God?

KING CLAUDIUS

Laertes, I must commune with your grief,

Or you deny me right. Go but apart,

Make choice of whom your wisest friends you will.

And they shall hear and judge 'twixt you and me:

If by direct or by collateral hand

They find us touch'd, we will our kingdom give,

Our crown, our life, and all that we can ours,

To you in satisfaction; but if not,

Be you content to lend your patience to us,

And we shall jointly labour with your soul

To give it due content.

LAERTES

Let this be so;

His means of death, his obscure funeral--

No trophy, sword, nor hatchment o'er his bones,

No noble rite nor formal ostentation--

Cry to be heard, as 'twere from heaven to earth,

That I must call't in question.

KING CLAUDIUS

So you shall;

And where the offence is let the great axe fall.

I pray you, go with me.

Exeunt

SCENE VI. Another room in the castle.

Enter HORATIO and a Servant

HORATIO

What are they that would speak with me?

Servant

Sailors, sir: they say they have letters for you.

HORATIO

Let them come in.

Exit Servant

I do not know from what part of the world

I should be greeted, if not from Lord Hamlet.

Enter Sailors

First Sailor

God bless you, sir.

HORATIO

Let him bless thee too.

First Sailor

He shall, sir, an't please him. There's a letter for
you, sir; it comes from the ambassador that was
bound for England; if your name be Horatio, as I am
let to know it is.

HORATIO

[Reads] 'Horatio, when thou shalt have overlooked
this, give these fellows some means to the king:
they have letters for him. Ere we were two days old
at sea, a pirate of very warlike appointment gave us
chase. Finding ourselves too slow of sail, we put on
a compelled valour, and in the grapple I boarded
them: on the instant they got clear of our ship; so
I alone became their prisoner. They have dealt with
me like thieves of mercy: but they knew what they
did; I am to do a good turn for them. Let the king
have the letters I have sent; and repair thou to me
with as much speed as thou wouldst fly death. I
have words to speak in thine ear will make thee
dumb; yet are they much too light for the bore of
the matter. These good fellows will bring thee
where I am. Rosencrantz and Guildenstern hold their
course for England: of them I have much to tell
thee. Farewell.

'He that thou knowest thine, HAMLET.'

Come, I will make you way for these your letters;
And do't the speedier, that you may direct me
To him from whom you brought them.

Exeunt

SCENE VII. Another room in the castle.

Enter KING CLAUDIUS and LAERTES

KING CLAUDIUS

Now must your conscience my acquaintance seal,
And you must put me in your heart for friend,
Sith you have heard, and with a knowing ear,
That he which hath your noble father slain
Pursued my life.

LAERTES

It well appears: but tell me
Why you proceeded not against these feats,
So crimeful and so capital in nature,
As by your safety, wisdom, all things else,
You mainly were stirr'd up.

KING CLAUDIUS

O, for two special reasons;
Which may to you, perhaps, seem much unsinew'd,
But yet to me they are strong. The queen his mother
Lives almost by his looks; and for myself--
My virtue or my plague, be it either which--
She's so conjunctive to my life and soul,
That, as the star moves not but in his sphere,
I could not but by her. The other motive,
Why to a public count I might not go,
Is the great love the general gender bear him;
Who, dipping all his faults in their affection,
Would, like the spring that turneth wood to stone,
Convert his gyves to graces; so that my arrows,
Too slightly timber'd for so loud a wind,
Would have reverted to my bow again,
And not where I had aim'd them.

LAERTES

And so have I a noble father lost;
A sister driven into desperate terms,
Whose worth, if praises may go back again,
Stood challenger on mount of all the age
For her perfections: but my revenge will come.

KING CLAUDIUS

Break not your sleeps for that: you must not think
That we are made of stuff so flat and dull
That we can let our beard be shook with danger
And think it pastime. You shortly shall hear more:
I loved your father, and we love ourself;
And that, I hope, will teach you to imagine--
Enter a Messenger
How now! what news?

Messenger
Letters, my lord, from Hamlet:
This to your majesty; this to the queen.
KING CLAUDIUS
From Hamlet! who brought them?
Messenger
Sailors, my lord, they say; I saw them not:
They were given me by Claudio; he received them
Of him that brought them.
KING CLAUDIUS
Laertes, you shall hear them. Leave us.
Exit Messenger
Reads
'High and mighty, You shall know I am set naked on
your kingdom. To-morrow shall I beg leave to see
your kingly eyes: when I shall, first asking your
pardon thereunto, recount the occasion of my sudden
and more strange return. 'HAMLET.'
What should this mean? Are all the rest come back?
Or is it some abuse, and no such thing?
LAERTES
Know you the hand?
KING CLAUDIUS
'Tis Hamlets character. 'Naked!
And in a postscript here, he says 'alone.'
Can you advise me?
LAERTES
I'm lost in it, my lord. But let him come;
It warms the very sickness in my heart,
That I shall live and tell him to his teeth,
'Thus didest thou.'
KING CLAUDIUS
If it be so, Laertes--
As how should it be so? how otherwise?--
Will you be ruled by me?
LAERTES
Ay, my lord;
So you will not o'errule me to a peace.

KING CLAUDIUS

To thine own peace. If he be now return'd,
As checking at his voyage, and that he means
No more to undertake it, I will work him
To an exploit, now ripe in my device,
Under the which he shall not choose but fall:
And for his death no wind of blame shall breathe,
But even his mother shall uncharge the practise
And call it accident.

LAERTES

My lord, I will be ruled;
The rather, if you could devise it so
That I might be the organ.

KING CLAUDIUS

It falls right.
You have been talk'd of since your travel much,
And that in Hamlet's hearing, for a quality
Wherein, they say, you shine: your sum of parts
Did not together pluck such envy from him
As did that one, and that, in my regard,
Of the unworthiest siege.

LAERTES

What part is that, my lord?

KING CLAUDIUS

A very riband in the cap of youth,
Yet needful too; for youth no less becomes
The light and careless livery that it wears
Than settled age his sables and his weeds,
Importing health and graveness. Two months since,
Here was a gentleman of Normandy:--
I've seen myself, and served against, the French,
And they can well on horseback: but this gallant
Had witchcraft in't; he grew unto his seat;
And to such wondrous doing brought his horse,
As he had been incorpsed and demi-natured
With the brave beast: so far he topp'd my thought,
That I, in forgery of shapes and tricks,
Come short of what he did.

LAERTES
A Norman was't?
KING CLAUDIUS
A Norman.
LAERTES
Upon my life, Lamond.
KING CLAUDIUS
The very same.
LAERTES
I know him well: he is the brooch indeed
And gem of all the nation.
KING CLAUDIUS
He made confession of you,
And gave you such a masterly report
For art and exercise in your defence
And for your rapier most especially,
That he cried out, 'twould be a sight indeed,
If one could match you: the scrimers of their nation,
He swore, had had neither motion, guard, nor eye,
If you opposed them. Sir, this report of his
Did Hamlet so envenom with his envy
That he could nothing do but wish and beg
Your sudden coming o'er, to play with him.
Now, out of this,--
LAERTES
What out of this, my lord?
KING CLAUDIUS
Laertes, was your father dear to you?
Or are you like the painting of a sorrow,
A face without a heart?
LAERTES
Why ask you this?
KING CLAUDIUS
Not that I think you did not love your father;
But that I know love is begun by time;
And that I see, in passages of proof,
Time qualifies the spark and fire of it.
There lives within the very flame of love
A kind of wick or snuff that will abate it;

And nothing is at a like goodness still;
For goodness, growing to a plurisy,
Dies in his own too much: that we would do
We should do when we would; for this 'would' changes
And hath abatements and delays as many
As there are tongues, are hands, are accidents;
And then this 'should' is like a spendthrift sigh,
That hurts by easing. But, to the quick o' the ulcer:--
Hamlet comes back: what would you undertake,
To show yourself your father's son in deed
More than in words?

LAERTES
To cut his throat i' the church.

KING CLAUDIUS
No place, indeed, should murder sanctuarize;
Revenge should have no bounds. But, good Laertes,
Will you do this, keep close within your chamber.
Hamlet return'd shall know you are come home:
We'll put on those shall praise your excellence
And set a double varnish on the fame
The Frenchman gave you, bring you in fine together
And wager on your heads: he, being remiss,
Most generous and free from all contriving,
Will not peruse the foils; so that, with ease,
Or with a little shuffling, you may choose
A sword unbated, and in a pass of practise
Requite him for your father.

LAERTES
I will do't:
And, for that purpose, I'll anoint my sword.
I bought an unction of a mountebank,
So mortal that, but dip a knife in it,
Where it draws blood no cataplasm so rare,
Collected from all simples that have virtue
Under the moon, can save the thing from death
That is but scratch'd withal: I'll touch my point
With this contagion, that, if I gall him slightly,
It may be death.

KING CLAUDIUS
Let's further think of this;
Weigh what convenience both of time and means
May fit us to our shape: if this should fail,
And that our drift look through our bad performance,
'Twere better not assay'd: therefore this project
Should have a back or second, that might hold,
If this should blast in proof. Soft! let me see:
We'll make a solemn wager on your cunnings: I ha't.
When in your motion you are hot and dry--
As make your bouts more violent to that end--
And that he calls for drink, I'll have prepared him
A chalice for the nonce, whereon but sipping,
If he by chance escape your venom'd stuck,
Our purpose may hold there.
Enter QUEEN GERTRUDE
How now, sweet queen!
QUEEN GERTRUDE
One woe doth tread upon another's heel,
So fast they follow; your sister's drown'd, Laertes.
LAERTES
Drown'd! O, where?
QUEEN GERTRUDE
There is a willow grows aslant a brook,
That shows his hoar leaves in the glassy stream;
There with fantastic garlands did she come
Of crow-flowers, nettles, daisies, and long purples
That liberal shepherds give a grosser name,
But our cold maids do dead men's fingers call them:
There, on the pendent boughs her coronet weeds
Clambering to hang, an envious sliver broke;
When down her weedy trophies and herself
Fell in the weeping brook. Her clothes spread wide;
And, mermaid-like, awhile they bore her up:
Which time she chanted snatches of old tunes;
As one incapable of her own distress,
Or like a creature native and indued
Unto that element: but long it could not be
Till that her garments, heavy with their drink,

Pull'd the poor wretch from her melodious lay
To muddy death.

LAERTES

Alas, then, she is drown'd?

QUEEN GERTRUDE

Drown'd, drown'd.

LAERTES

Too much of water hast thou, poor Ophelia,
And therefore I forbid my tears: but yet
It is our trick; nature her custom holds,
Let shame say what it will: when these are gone,
The woman will be out. Adieu, my lord:
I have a speech of fire, that fain would blaze,
But that this folly douts it.

Exit

KING CLAUDIUS

Let's follow, Gertrude:
How much I had to do to calm his rage!
Now fear I this will give it start again;
Therefore let's follow.

Exeunt

ACT V

SCENE I. A churchyard.

Enter two Clowns, with spades, & c

First Clown

Is she to be buried in Christian burial that
wilfully seeks her own salvation?

Second Clown

I tell thee she is: and therefore make her grave
straight: the crowner hath sat on her, and finds it
Christian burial.

First Clown

How can that be, unless she drowned herself in her
own defence?

Second Clown

Why, 'tis found so.

First Clown

It must be 'se offendendo;' it cannot be else. For
here lies the point: if I drown myself wittingly,

it argues an act: and an act hath three branches: it
is, to act, to do, to perform: argal, she drowned
herself wittingly.

Second Clown

Nay, but hear you, goodman delver,--

First Clown

Give me leave. Here lies the water; good: here
stands the man; good; if the man go to this water,
and drown himself, it is, will he, nill he, he
goes,--mark you that; but if the water come to him
and drown him, he drowns not himself: argal, he
that is not guilty of his own death shortens not his own life.

Second Clown

But is this law?

First Clown

Ay, marry, is't; crowner's quest law.

Second Clown

Will you ha' the truth on't? If this had not been
a gentlewoman, she should have been buried out o'
Christian burial.

First Clown

Why, there thou say'st: and the more pity that
great folk should have countenance in this world to
drown or hang themselves, more than their even
Christian. Come, my spade. There is no ancient
gentleman but gardeners, ditchers, and grave-makers:
they hold up Adam's profession.

Second Clown

Was he a gentleman?

First Clown

He was the first that ever bore arms.

Second Clown

Why, he had none.

First Clown

What, art a heathen? How dost thou understand the
Scripture? The Scripture says 'Adam digged:'
could he dig without arms? I'll put another
question to thee: if thou answerest me not to the
purpose, confess thyself--

Second Clown

Go to.

First Clown

What is he that builds stronger than either the
mason, the shipwright, or the carpenter?

Second Clown

The gallows-maker; for that frame outlives a
thousand tenants.

First Clown

I like thy wit well, in good faith: the gallows
does well; but how does it well? it does well to
those that do in: now thou dost ill to say the
gallows is built stronger than the church: argal,
the gallows may do well to thee. To't again, come.

Second Clown

'Who builds stronger than a mason, a shipwright, or
a carpenter?'

First Clown

Ay, tell me that, and unyoke.

Second Clown

Marry, now I can tell.

First Clown

To't.

Second Clown

Mass, I cannot tell.

Enter HAMLET and HORATIO, at a distance

First Clown

Cudgel thy brains no more about it, for your dull
ass will not mend his pace with beating; and, when
you are asked this question next, say 'a
grave-maker: 'the houses that he makes last till
doomsday. Go, get thee to Yaughan: fetch me a
stoup of liquor.

Exit Second Clown

He digs and sings

In youth, when I did love, did love,
Methought it was very sweet,

To contract, O, the time, for, ah, my behove,
O, methought, there was nothing meet.

HAMLET

Has this fellow no feeling of his business, that he
sings at grave-making?

HORATIO

Custom hath made it in him a property of easiness.

HAMLET

'Tis e'en so: the hand of little employment hath
the daintier sense.

First Clown

[Sings]

But age, with his stealing steps,
Hath claw'd me in his clutch,
And hath shipped me intil the land,
As if I had never been such.

Throws up a skull

HAMLET

That skull had a tongue in it, and could sing once:
how the knave jowls it to the ground, as if it were
Cain's jaw-bone, that did the first murder! It
might be the pate of a politician, which this ass
now o'er-reaches; one that would circumvent God,
might it not?

HORATIO

It might, my lord.

HAMLET

Or of a courtier; which could say 'Good morrow,
sweet lord! How dost thou, good lord?' This might
be my lord such-a-one, that praised my lord
such-a-one's horse, when he meant to beg it; might it not?

HORATIO

Ay, my lord.

HAMLET

Why, e'en so: and now my Lady Worm's; chapless, and
knocked about the mazzard with a sexton's spade:
here's fine revolution, an we had the trick to
see't. Did these bones cost no more the breeding,
but to play at loggats with 'em? mine ache to think on't.

First Clown

[Sings]

A pick-axe, and a spade, a spade,

For and a shrouding sheet:

O, a pit of clay for to be made

For such a guest is meet.

Throws up another skull

HAMLET

There's another: why may not that be the skull of a
lawyer? Where be his quiddities now, his quillets,
his cases, his tenures, and his tricks? why does he
suffer this rude knave now to knock him about the
sconce with a dirty shovel, and will not tell him of
his action of battery? Hum! This fellow might be
in's time a great buyer of land, with his statutes,
his recognizances, his fines, his double vouchers,
his recoveries: is this the fine of his fines, and
the recovery of his recoveries, to have his fine
pate full of fine dirt? will his vouchers vouch him
no more of his purchases, and double ones too, than
the length and breadth of a pair of indentures? The
very conveyances of his lands will hardly lie in
this box; and must the inheritor himself have no more, ha?

HORATIO

Not a jot more, my lord.

HAMLET

Is not parchment made of sheepskins?

HORATIO

Ay, my lord, and of calf-skins too.

HAMLET

They are sheep and calves which seek out assurance
in that. I will speak to this fellow. Whose
grave's this, sirrah?

First Clown

Mine, sir.

Sings

O, a pit of clay for to be made

For such a guest is meet.

HAMLET

I think it be thine, indeed; for thou liest in't.

First Clown

You lie out on't, sir, and therefore it is not
yours: for my part, I do not lie in't, and yet it is mine.

HAMLET

'Thou dost lie in't, to be in't and say it is thine:
'tis for the dead, not for the quick; therefore thou liest.

First Clown

'Tis a quick lie, sir; 'twill away gain, from me to
you.

HAMLET

What man dost thou dig it for?

First Clown

For no man, sir.

HAMLET

What woman, then?

First Clown

For none, neither.

HAMLET

Who is to be buried in't?

First Clown

One that was a woman, sir; but, rest her soul, she's dead.

HAMLET

How absolute the knave is! we must speak by the
card, or equivocation will undo us. By the Lord,
Horatio, these three years I have taken a note of
it; the age is grown so picked that the toe of the
peasant comes so near the heel of the courtier, he
gaffs his kibe. How long hast thou been a
grave-maker?

First Clown

Of all the days i' the year, I came to't that day
that our last king Hamlet overcame Fortinbras.

HAMLET

How long is that since?

First Clown

Cannot you tell that? every fool can tell that: it
was the very day that young Hamlet was born; he that
is mad, and sent into England.

HAMLET

Ay, marry, why was he sent into England?

First Clown

Why, because he was mad: he shall recover his wits
there; or, if he do not, it's no great matter there.

HAMLET

Why?

First Clown

'Twill, a not be seen in him there; there the men
are as mad as he.

HAMLET

How came he mad?

First Clown

Very strangely, they say.

HAMLET

How strangely?

First Clown

Faith, e'en with losing his wits.

HAMLET

Upon what ground?

First Clown

Why, here in Denmark: I have been sexton here, man
and boy, thirty years.

HAMLET

How long will a man lie i' the earth ere he rot?

First Clown

I' faith, if he be not rotten before he die--as we
have many pocky corses now-a-days, that will scarce
hold the laying in--he will last you some eight year
or nine year: a tanner will last you nine year.

HAMLET

Why he more than another?

First Clown

Why, sir, his hide is so tanned with his trade, that
he will keep out water a great while; and your water

is a sore decayer of your whoreson dead body.
Here's a skull now; this skull has lain in the earth
three and twenty years.

HAMLET
Whose was it?

First Clown
A whoreson mad fellow's it was: whose do you think it was?

HAMLET
Nay, I know not.

First Clown
A pestilence on him for a mad rogue! a' poured a
flagon of Rhenish on my head once. This same skull,
sir, was Yorick's skull, the king's jester.

HAMLET
This?

First Clown
E'en that.

HAMLET
Let me see.
Takes the skull
Alas, poor Yorick! I knew him, Horatio: a fellow
of infinite jest, of most excellent fancy: he hath
borne me on his back a thousand times; and now, how
abhorred in my imagination it is! my gorge rims at
it. Here hung those lips that I have kissed I know
not how oft. Where be your gibes now? your
gambols? your songs? your flashes of merriment,
that were wont to set the table on a roar? Not one
now, to mock your own grinning? quite chap-fallen?
Now get you to my lady's chamber, and tell her, let
her paint an inch thick, to this favour she must
come; make her laugh at that. Prithee, Horatio, tell
me one thing.

HORATIO
What's that, my lord?

HAMLET
Dost thou think Alexander looked o' this fashion i'
the earth?

HORATIO

E'en so.

HAMLET

And smelt so? pah!

Puts down the skull

HORATIO

E'en so, my lord.

HAMLET

To what base uses we may return, Horatio! Why may
not imagination trace the noble dust of Alexander,
till he find it stopping a bung-hole?

HORATIO

'Twere to consider too curiously, to consider so.

HAMLET

No, faith, not a jot; but to follow him thither with
modesty enough, and likelihood to lead it: as
thus: Alexander died, Alexander was buried,
Alexander returneth into dust; the dust is earth; of
earth we make loam; and why of that loam, whereto he
was converted, might they not stop a beer-barrel?
Imperious Caesar, dead and turn'd to clay,
Might stop a hole to keep the wind away:
O, that that earth, which kept the world in awe,
Should patch a wall to expel the winter flaw!
But soft! but soft! aside: here comes the king.

*Enter Priest, & c. in procession; the Corpse of OPHELIA, LAERTES and
Mourners following; KING CLAUDIUS, QUEEN GERTRUDE, their trains,
& c*

The queen, the courtiers: who is this they follow?
And with such maimed rites? This doth betoken
The corse they follow did with desperate hand
Fordo its own life: 'twas of some estate.
Couch we awhile, and mark.

Retiring with HORATIO

LAERTES

What ceremony else?

HAMLET

That is Laertes,
A very noble youth: mark.

LAERTES

What ceremony else?

First Priest

Her obsequies have been as far enlarged
As we have warrantise: her death was doubtful;
And, but that great command o'ersways the order,
She should in ground unsanctified have lodged
Till the last trumpet: for charitable prayers,
Shards, flints and pebbles should be thrown on her;
Yet here she is allow'd her virgin crants,
Her maiden strewments and the bringing home
Of bell and burial.

LAERTES

Must there no more be done?

First Priest

No more be done:
We should profane the service of the dead
To sing a requiem and such rest to her
As to peace-parted souls.

LAERTES

Lay her i' the earth:
And from her fair and unpolluted flesh
May violets spring! I tell thee, churlish priest,
A ministering angel shall my sister be,
When thou liest howling.

HAMLET

What, the fair Ophelia!

QUEEN GERTRUDE

Sweets to the sweet: farewell!

Scattering flowers

I hoped thou shouldst have been my Hamlet's wife;
I thought thy bride-bed to have deck'd, sweet maid,
And not have strew'd thy grave.

LAERTES

O, treble woe
Fall ten times treble on that cursed head,
Whose wicked deed thy most ingenious sense
Deprived thee of! Hold off the earth awhile,
Till I have caught her once more in mine arms:

Leaps into the grave
Now pile your dust upon the quick and dead,
Till of this flat a mountain you have made,
To o'ertop old Pelion, or the skyish head
Of blue Olympus.
HAMLET
[Advancing] What is he whose grief
Bears such an emphasis? whose phrase of sorrow
Conjures the wandering stars, and makes them stand
Like wonder-wounded hearers? This is I,
Hamlet the Dane.
Leaps into the grave
LAERTES
The devil take thy soul!
Grappling with him
HAMLET
Thou pray'st not well.
I prithee, take thy fingers from my throat;
For, though I am not splenitive and rash,
Yet have I something in me dangerous,
Which let thy wiseness fear: hold off thy hand.
KING CLAUDIUS
Pluck them asunder.
QUEEN GERTRUDE
Hamlet, Hamlet!
All
Gentlemen,--
HORATIO
Good my lord, be quiet.
The Attendants part them, and they come out of the grave
HAMLET
Why I will fight with him upon this theme
Until my eyelids will no longer wag.
QUEEN GERTRUDE
O my son, what theme?
HAMLET
I loved Ophelia: forty thousand brothers
Could not, with all their quantity of love,
Make up my sum. What wilt thou do for her?

KING CLAUDIUS
O, he is mad, Laertes.
QUEEN GERTRUDE
For love of God, forbear him.
HAMLET
'Swounds, show me what thou'lt do:
Woo't weep? woo't fight? woo't fast? woo't tear thyself?
Woo't drink up eisel? eat a crocodile?
I'll do't. Dost thou come here to whine?
To outface me with leaping in her grave?
Be buried quick with her, and so will I:
And, if thou prate of mountains, let them throw
Millions of acres on us, till our ground,
Singeing his pate against the burning zone,
Make Ossa like a wart! Nay, an thou'lt mouth,
I'll rant as well as thou.
QUEEN GERTRUDE
This is mere madness:
And thus awhile the fit will work on him;
Anon, as patient as the female dove,
When that her golden couplets are disclosed,
His silence will sit drooping.
HAMLET
Hear you, sir;
What is the reason that you use me thus?
I loved you ever: but it is no matter;
Let Hercules himself do what he may,
The cat will mew and dog will have his day.
Exit
KING CLAUDIUS
I pray you, good Horatio, wait upon him.
Exit HORATIO
To LAERTES
Strengthen your patience in our last night's speech;
We'll put the matter to the present push.
Good Gertrude, set some watch over your son.
This grave shall have a living monument:
An hour of quiet shortly shall we see;
Till then, in patience our proceeding be.

Exeunt

SCENE II. A hall in the castle.

Enter HAMLET and HORATIO

HAMLET

So much for this, sir: now shall you see the other;
You do remember all the circumstance?

HORATIO

Remember it, my lord?

HAMLET

Sir, in my heart there was a kind of fighting,
That would not let me sleep: methought I lay
Worse than the mutines in the bilboes. Rashly,
And praised be rashness for it, let us know,
Our indiscretion sometimes serves us well,
When our deep plots do pall: and that should teach us
There's a divinity that shapes our ends,
Rough-hew them how we will,--

HORATIO

That is most certain.

HAMLET

Up from my cabin,
My sea-gown scarf'd about me, in the dark
Groped I to find out them; had my desire.
Finger'd their packet, and in fine withdrew
To mine own room again; making so bold,
My fears forgetting manners, to unseal
Their grand commission; where I found, Horatio,--
O royal knavery!--an exact command,
Larded with many several sorts of reasons
Importing Denmark's health and England's too,
With, ho! such bugs and goblins in my life,
That, on the supervise, no leisure bated,
No, not to stay the grinding of the axe,
My head should be struck off.

HORATIO

Is't possible?

HAMLET

Here's the commission: read it at more leisure.
But wilt thou hear me how I did proceed?

HORATIO
I beseech you.
HAMLET
Being thus be-netted round with villanies,--
Ere I could make a prologue to my brains,
They had begun the play--I sat me down,
Devised a new commission, wrote it fair:
I once did hold it, as our statists do,
A baseness to write fair and labour'd much
How to forget that learning, but, sir, now
It did me yeoman's service: wilt thou know
The effect of what I wrote?
HORATIO
Ay, good my lord.
HAMLET
An earnest conjuration from the king,
As England was his faithful tributary,
As love between them like the palm might flourish,
As peace should stiff her wheaten garland wear
And stand a comma 'tween their amities,
And many such-like 'As'es of great charge,
That, on the view and knowing of these contents,
Without debatement further, more or less,
He should the bearers put to sudden death,
Not shriving-time allow'd.
HORATIO
How was this seal'd?
HAMLET
Why, even in that was heaven ordinant.
I had my father's signet in my purse,
Which was the model of that Danish seal;
Folded the writ up in form of the other,
Subscribed it, gave't the impression, placed it safely,
The changeling never known. Now, the next day
Was our sea-fight; and what to this was sequent
Thou know'st already.
HORATIO
So Guildenstern and Rosencrantz go to't.

HAMLET

Why, man, they did make love to this employment;
They are not near my conscience; their defeat
Does by their own insinuation grow:
'Tis dangerous when the baser nature comes
Between the pass and fell incensed points
Of mighty opposites.

HORATIO

Why, what a king is this!

HAMLET

Does it not, think'st thee, stand me now upon--
He that hath kill'd my king and whored my mother,
Popp'd in between the election and my hopes,
Thrown out his angle for my proper life,
And with such cozenage--is't not perfect conscience,
To quit him with this arm? and is't not to be damn'd,
To let this canker of our nature come
In further evil?

HORATIO

It must be shortly known to him from England
What is the issue of the business there.

HAMLET

It will be short: the interim is mine;
And a man's life's no more than to say 'One.'
But I am very sorry, good Horatio,
That to Laertes I forgot myself;
For, by the image of my cause, I see
The portraiture of his: I'll court his favours.
But, sure, the bravery of his grief did put me
Into a towering passion.

HORATIO

Peace! who comes here?

Enter OSRIC

OSRIC

Your lordship is right welcome back to Denmark.

HAMLET

I humbly thank you, sir. Dost know this water-fly?

HORATIO

No, my good lord.

HAMLET

Thy state is the more gracious; for 'tis a vice to
know him. He hath much land, and fertile: let a
beast be lord of beasts, and his crib shall stand at
the king's mess: 'tis a chough; but, as I say,
spacious in the possession of dirt.

OSRIC

Sweet lord, if your lordship were at leisure, I
should impart a thing to you from his majesty.

HAMLET

I will receive it, sir, with all diligence of
spirit. Put your bonnet to his right use; 'tis for the head.

OSRIC

I thank your lordship, it is very hot.

HAMLET

No, believe me, 'tis very cold; the wind is
northerly.

OSRIC

It is indifferent cold, my lord, indeed.

HAMLET

But yet methinks it is very sultry and hot for my
complexion.

OSRIC

Exceedingly, my lord; it is very sultry,--as
'twere,--I cannot tell how. But, my lord, his
majesty bade me signify to you that he has laid a
great wager on your head: sir, this is the matter,--

HAMLET

I beseech you, remember--

HAMLET moves him to put on his hat

OSRIC

Nay, good my lord; for mine ease, in good faith.
Sir, here is newly come to court Laertes; believe
me, an absolute gentleman, full of most excellent
differences, of very soft society and great showing:
indeed, to speak feelingly of him, he is the card or
calendar of gentry, for you shall find in him the
continent of what part a gentleman would see.

HAMLET

Sir, his definement suffers no perdition in you;
though, I know, to divide him inventorially would
dizzy the arithmetic of memory, and yet but yaw
neither, in respect of his quick sail. But, in the
verity of extolment, I take him to be a soul of
great article; and his infusion of such dearth and
rareness, as, to make true diction of him, his
semblable is his mirror; and who else would trace
him, his umbrage, nothing more.

OSRIC

Your lordship speaks most infallibly of him.

HAMLET

The concernancy, sir? why do we wrap the gentleman
in our more rawer breath?

OSRIC

Sir?

HORATIO

Is't not possible to understand in another tongue?
You will do't, sir, really.

HAMLET

What imports the nomination of this gentleman?

OSRIC

Of Laertes?

HORATIO

His purse is empty already; all's golden words are spent.

HAMLET

Of him, sir.

OSRIC

I know you are not ignorant--

HAMLET

I would you did, sir; yet, in faith, if you did,
it would not much approve me. Well, sir?

OSRIC

You are not ignorant of what excellence Laertes is--

HAMLET

I dare not confess that, lest I should compare with
him in excellence; but, to know a man well, were to
know himself.

OSRIC
I mean, sir, for his weapon; but in the imputation
laid on him by them, in his meed he's unfellowed.
HAMLET
What's his weapon?
OSRIC
Rapier and dagger.
HAMLET
That's two of his weapons: but, well.
OSRIC
The king, sir, hath wagered with him six Barbary
horses: against the which he has imponed, as I take
it, six French rapiers and poniards, with their
assigns, as girdle, hangers, and so: three of the
carriages, in faith, are very dear to fancy, very
responsive to the hilts, most delicate carriages,
and of very liberal conceit.
HAMLET
What call you the carriages?
HORATIO
I knew you must be edified by the margent ere you had done.
OSRIC
The carriages, sir, are the hangers.
HAMLET
The phrase would be more german to the matter, if we
could carry cannon by our sides: I would it might
be hangers till then. But, on: six Barbary horses
against six French swords, their assigns, and three
liberal-conceited carriages; that's the French bet
against the Danish. Why is this 'imponed,' as you call it?
OSRIC
The king, sir, hath laid, that in a dozen passes
between yourself and him, he shall not exceed you
three hits: he hath laid on twelve for nine; and it
would come to immediate trial, if your lordship
would vouchsafe the answer.
HAMLET
How if I answer 'no'?

OSRIC

I mean, my lord, the opposition of your person in trial.

HAMLET

Sir, I will walk here in the hall: if it please his
majesty, 'tis the breathing time of day with me; let
the foils be brought, the gentleman willing, and the
king hold his purpose, I will win for him an I can;
if not, I will gain nothing but my shame and the odd hits.

OSRIC

Shall I re-deliver you e'en so?

HAMLET

To this effect, sir; after what flourish your nature will.

OSRIC

I commend my duty to your lordship.

HAMLET

Yours, yours.

Exit OSRIC

He does well to commend it himself; there are no
tongues else for's turn.

HORATIO

This lapwing runs away with the shell on his head.

HAMLET

He did comply with his dug, before he sucked it.
Thus has he--and many more of the same bevy that I
know the dressy age dotes on--only got the tune of
the time and outward habit of encounter; a kind of
yesty collection, which carries them through and
through the most fond and winnowed opinions; and do
but blow them to their trial, the bubbles are out.

Enter a Lord

Lord

My lord, his majesty commended him to you by young
Osric, who brings back to him that you attend him in
the hall: he sends to know if your pleasure hold to
play with Laertes, or that you will take longer time.

HAMLET

I am constant to my purpose; they follow the king's
pleasure: if his fitness speaks, mine is ready; now
or whensoever, provided I be so able as now.

Lord
The king and queen and all are coming down.
HAMLET
In happy time.
Lord
The queen desires you to use some gentle
entertainment to Laertes before you fall to play.
HAMLET
She well instructs me.
Exit Lord
HORATIO
You will lose this wager, my lord.
HAMLET
I do not think so: since he went into France, I
have been in continual practise: I shall win at the
odds. But thou wouldst not think how ill all's here
about my heart: but it is no matter.
HORATIO
Nay, good my lord,--
HAMLET
It is but foolery; but it is such a kind of
gain-giving, as would perhaps trouble a woman.
HORATIO
If your mind dislike any thing, obey it: I will
forestall their repair hither, and say you are not
fit.
HAMLET
Not a whit, we defy augury: there's a special
providence in the fall of a sparrow. If it be now,
'tis not to come; if it be not to come, it will be
now; if it be not now, yet it will come: the
readiness is all: since no man has aught of what he
leaves, what is't to leave betimes?
*Enter KING CLAUDIUS, QUEEN GERTRUDE, LAERTES, Lords, OSRIC,
and Attendants with foils, & c*
KING CLAUDIUS
Come, Hamlet, come, and take this hand from me.
KING CLAUDIUS puts LAERTES' hand into HAMLET's

HAMLET

Give me your pardon, sir: I've done you wrong;
But pardon't, as you are a gentleman.
This presence knows,
And you must needs have heard, how I am punish'd
With sore distraction. What I have done,
That might your nature, honour and exception
Roughly awake, I here proclaim was madness.
Was't Hamlet wrong'd Laertes? Never Hamlet:
If Hamlet from himself be ta'en away,
And when he's not himself does wrong Laertes,
Then Hamlet does it not, Hamlet denies it.
Who does it, then? His madness: if't be so,
Hamlet is of the faction that is wrong'd;
His madness is poor Hamlet's enemy.
Sir, in this audience,
Let my disclaiming from a purposed evil
Free me so far in your most generous thoughts,
That I have shot mine arrow o'er the house,
And hurt my brother.

LAERTES

I am satisfied in nature,
Whose motive, in this case, should stir me most
To my revenge: but in my terms of honour
I stand aloof; and will no reconcilement,
Till by some elder masters, of known honour,
I have a voice and precedent of peace,
To keep my name ungored. But till that time,
I do receive your offer'd love like love,
And will not wrong it.

HAMLET

I embrace it freely;
And will this brother's wager frankly play.
Give us the foils. Come on.

LAERTES

Come, one for me.

HAMLET

I'll be your foil, Laertes: in mine ignorance

Your skill shall, like a star i' the darkest night,

Stick fiery off indeed.

LAERTES

You mock me, sir.

HAMLET

No, by this hand.

KING CLAUDIUS

Give them the foils, young Osric. Cousin Hamlet,

You know the wager?

HAMLET

Very well, my lord

Your grace hath laid the odds o' the weaker side.

KING CLAUDIUS

I do not fear it; I have seen you both:

But since he is better'd, we have therefore odds.

LAERTES

This is too heavy, let me see another.

HAMLET

This likes me well. These foils have all a length?

They prepare to play

OSRIC

Ay, my good lord.

KING CLAUDIUS

Set me the stoops of wine upon that table.

If Hamlet give the first or second hit,

Or quit in answer of the third exchange,

Let all the battlements their ordnance fire:

The king shall drink to Hamlet's better breath;

And in the cup an union shall he throw,

Richer than that which four successive kings

In Denmark's crown have worn. Give me the cups;

And let the kettle to the trumpet speak,

The trumpet to the cannoneer without,

The cannons to the heavens, the heavens to earth,

'Now the king dunks to Hamlet.' Come, begin:

And you, the judges, bear a wary eye.

HAMLET
Come on, sir.
LAERTES
Come, my lord.
They play
HAMLET
One.
LAERTES
No.
HAMLET
Judgment.
OSRIC
A hit, a very palpable hit.
LAERTES
Well; again.
KING CLAUDIUS
Stay; give me drink. Hamlet, this pearl is thine;
Here's to thy health.
Trumpets sound, and cannon shot off within
Give him the cup.
HAMLET
I'll play this bout first; set it by awhile. Come.
They play
Another hit; what say you?
LAERTES
A touch, a touch, I do confess.
KING CLAUDIUS
Our son shall win.
QUEEN GERTRUDE
He's fat, and scant of breath.
Here, Hamlet, take my napkin, rub thy brows;
The queen carouses to thy fortune, Hamlet.
HAMLET
Good madam!
KING CLAUDIUS
Gertrude, do not drink.
QUEEN GERTRUDE
I will, my lord; I pray you, pardon me.

KING CLAUDIUS
[Aside] It is the poison'd cup: it is too late.
HAMLET
I dare not drink yet, madam; by and by.
QUEEN GERTRUDE
Come, let me wipe thy face.
LAERTES
My lord, I'll hit him now.
KING CLAUDIUS
I do not think't.
LAERTES
[Aside] And yet 'tis almost 'gainst my conscience.
HAMLET
Come, for the third, Laertes: you but dally;
I pray you, pass with your best violence;
I am afeard you make a wanton of me.
LAERTES
Say you so? come on.
They play
OSRIC
Nothing, neither way.
LAERTES
Have at you now!
LAERTES wounds HAMLET; then in scuffling, they change rapiers, and
HAMLET wounds LAERTES
KING CLAUDIUS
Part them; they are incensed.
HAMLET
Nay, come, again.
QUEEN GERTRUDE falls
OSRIC
Look to the queen there, ho!
HORATIO
They bleed on both sides. How is it, my lord?
OSRIC
How is't, Laertes?
LAERTES
Why, as a woodcock to mine own springe, Osric;
I am justly kill'd with mine own treachery.

HAMLET

How does the queen?

KING CLAUDIUS

She swounds to see them bleed.

QUEEN GERTRUDE

No, no, the drink, the drink,--O my dear Hamlet,--
The drink, the drink! I am poison'd.

Dies

HAMLET

O villany! Ho! let the door be lock'd:
Treachery! Seek it out.

LAERTES

It is here, Hamlet: Hamlet, thou art slain;
No medicine in the world can do thee good;
In thee there is not half an hour of life;
The treacherous instrument is in thy hand,
Unbated and envenom'd: the foul practise
Hath turn'd itself on me lo, here I lie,
Never to rise again: thy mother's poison'd:
I can no more: the king, the king's to blame.

HAMLET

The point!--envenom'd too!
Then, venom, to thy work.

Stabs KING CLAUDIUS

All

Treason! treason!

KING CLAUDIUS

O, yet defend me, friends; I am but hurt.

HAMLET

Here, thou incestuous, murderous, damned Dane,
Drink off this potion. Is thy union here?
Follow my mother.

KING CLAUDIUS dies

LAERTES

He is justly served;
It is a poison temper'd by himself.
Exchange forgiveness with me, noble Hamlet:
Mine and my father's death come not upon thee,
Nor thine on me.

Dies

HAMLET

Heaven make thee free of it! I follow thee.
I am dead, Horatio. Wretched queen, adieu!
You that look pale and tremble at this chance,
That are but mutes or audience to this act,
Had I but time--as this fell sergeant, death,
Is strict in his arrest--O, I could tell you--
But let it be. Horatio, I am dead;
Thou livest; report me and my cause aright
To the unsatisfied.

HORATIO

Never believe it:
I am more an antique Roman than a Dane:
Here's yet some liquor left.

HAMLET

As thou'rt a man,
Give me the cup: let go; by heaven, I'll have't.
O good Horatio, what a wounded name,
Things standing thus unknown, shall live behind me!
If thou didst ever hold me in thy heart
Absent thee from felicity awhile,
And in this harsh world draw thy breath in pain,
To tell my story.

March afar off, and shot within

What warlike noise is this?

OSRIC

Young Fortinbras, with conquest come from Poland,
To the ambassadors of England gives
This warlike volley.

HAMLET

O, I die, Horatio;
The potent poison quite o'er-crows my spirit:
I cannot live to hear the news from England;
But I do prophesy the election lights
On Fortinbras: he has my dying voice;
So tell him, with the occurrents, more and less,
Which have solicited. The rest is silence.

Dies

HORATIO

Now cracks a noble heart. Good night sweet prince:
And flights of angels sing thee to thy rest!
Why does the drum come hither?
March within
Enter FORTINBRAS, the English Ambassadors, and others

PRINCE FORTINBRAS

Where is this sight?

HORATIO

What is it ye would see?
If aught of woe or wonder, cease your search.

PRINCE FORTINBRAS

This quarry cries on havoc. O proud death,
What feast is toward in thine eternal cell,
That thou so many princes at a shot
So bloodily hast struck?

First Ambassador

The sight is dismal;
And our affairs from England come too late:
The ears are senseless that should give us hearing,
To tell him his commandment is fulfill'd,
That Rosencrantz and Guildenstern are dead:
Where should we have our thanks?

HORATIO

Not from his mouth,
Had it the ability of life to thank you:
He never gave commandment for their death.
But since, so jump upon this bloody question,
You from the Polack wars, and you from England,
Are here arrived give order that these bodies
High on a stage be placed to the view;
And let me speak to the yet unknowing world
How these things came about: so shall you hear
Of carnal, bloody, and unnatural acts,
Of accidental judgments, casual slaughters,
Of deaths put on by cunning and forced cause,
And, in this upshot, purposes mistook
Fall'n on the inventors' reads: all this can I
Truly deliver.

PRINCE FORTINBRAS

Let us haste to hear it,
And call the noblest to the audience.
For me, with sorrow I embrace my fortune:
I have some rights of memory in this kingdom,
Which now to claim my vantage doth invite me.

HORATIO

Of that I shall have also cause to speak,
And from his mouth whose voice will draw on more;
But let this same be presently perform'd,
Even while men's minds are wild; lest more mischance
On plots and errors, happen.

PRINCE FORTINBRAS

Let four captains
Bear Hamlet, like a soldier, to the stage;
For he was likely, had he been put on,
To have proved most royally: and, for his passage,
The soldiers' music and the rites of war
Speak loudly for him.
Take up the bodies: such a sight as this
Becomes the field, but here shows much amiss.
Go, bid the soldiers shoot.
A dead march. Exeunt, bearing off the dead bodies; after which a peal of
ordnance is shot off

William Shakespeare
The Tragedy of Hamlet, Prince of Denmark

Plot Summary:
Act I.

While the two guards Bernardo and Francisco are on guard duty on the platform before Elsinore Castle in Denmark on a dark cold winter night, the ghost of the recently murdered King Hamlet walks on the ramparts of the castle. The two guards look at the ghost with excitement and horror before it finally disappears at dawn. The two watchmen wonder why the ghost of the deceased King Hamlet should appear at a time when Denmark is in a state of high alert and preparing for possible war with Prince Fortinbras of Norway. The two watchmen report to Horatio, a third guard and a scholar that they have seen the ghost of the recently deceased King Hamlet wearing his armour. When Horatio sees the ghost, he is horrified and becomes reluctant to speak to him since he says the ghost "harrows me with fear and wonder" (Line 44). Horatio tries to speak to the ghost of the deceased king, but he is irresponsive. Horatio realizes that although the ghost has refused to speak to him and the other two guards, he will certainly speak to his son Prince Hamlet. Horatio tells the other guards that the appearance of the ghost is ominous and foretells that something horrible will happen in Denmark.

At dawn and after the disappearance of the ghost, Horatio tells the other guards that King Hamlet was a great warrior. He fought King Fortinbras of Norway in a single combat and killed him. As a result of winning the fight, Denmark seized some Norwegian territory which by agreement became under the control of King Hamlet. Prince Fortinbras, the son of the late King Fortinbras and nephew to the current King of Norway, is preparing for war against Denmark to reclaim the usurped Norwegian territory his father lost to King Hamlet. Prince Fortinbras, Horatio explains, has raised a force of lawless men to help him reclaim the lands his father, King Fortinbras of Norway lost to the late King Hamlet of Denmark. Horatio describes Prince Fortinbras as unschooled, hot-blooded, bad–tempered and rash. Prince Fortinbras believes that Denmark is in a state of confusion and disarray after the murder of King Hamlet and he wants to seize the chance and invade the country. Horatio explains that the fear of possible war against Norway is the main reason for the state of high alert in Denmark and the large number of watch guards against intruders displayed before Elsinore Castle.

On the next night Hamlet, Horatio and Marcellus are all on the platform before Elsinore Castle, waiting for the ghost of King Hamlet to appear once again. While they are criticizing King Claudius's revelry celebrations and merrymaking, the apparition of the late King Hamlet appears on the platform. Horatio sees the apparition first and tells Hamlet "Look, my lord, it comes" (Line 38). When Hamlet sees the apparition he unconsciously addresses him as "Hamlet, King, father; royal Dane" (Line 45) and asks him why he has returned "Say, why is this? Wherefore? What should we do?" (Line 58).The apparition gives no satisfactory answers and makes a gesture for Hamlet to follow him. Marcellus warns Hamlet not to follow the apparition as he will take him to a deserted land where he will kill him. Hamlet pays no attention to Marcellus's warning and begins to follow the ghost. Horatio tries to stop Hamlet telling him that the ghost is ominous and will certainly lead him towards a flood or the cliff to kill him. Hamlet is inattentive to the advice of both friends and keeps following his father's spirit. Unable to stop Hamlet from following the ghost, both Marcellus and Horatio decide to follow Hamlet. Marcellus is quite cautious and feels that the appearance of the ghost is a bad omen and he remarks "Something is rotten in the state of Denmark", but Horatio trusts Hamlet and believes that God will protect him from any danger. He says to Marcellus Heaven will take care of things.

The ghost of King Hamlet informs Prince Hamlet that he is the spirit of his father "I am thy father's spirit;" (Line 9). He also tells him that he was murdered by his brother Claudius, the current king of Denmark, who inherited the throne and married his widow Queen Gertrude. The ghost tells Hamlet how his brother Claudius poured the poison in his ears while he was having a nap in the orchard. The ghost says, "Sleeping within mine orchard," (Line 60) in the afternoon, and that was his usual habit, "thy [your] uncle" (Line 64) Claudius poured poison into his ears. The Ghost laments what he has lost to his brother "Thus was I, sleeping, by a brother's hand, of life, of crown, of queen, at once dispatch'd;" (Line 74). (Thus as I was sleeping, I was murdered by my own brother who deprived me of my life, my crown and my wife, Queen Gertrude). The ghost tells Hamlet never to believe Claudius' story that his father was bitten by a snake. The ghost explains to Hamlet that Claudius lied to the citizens of Denmark when he told them that King Hamlet's death was caused by a snake bite. The ghost declares: "the whole ear of Denmark" is "Rankly abused" (Act I. Scene V. Lines 36–38).

 The Ghost orders Hamlet to take revenge on his uncle King Claudius, "Revenge his foul and most unnatural murder" (Line 25) but not to punish his mother and leave her punishment to Heaven and her conscience. What makes Hamlet more furious is when the ghost of his father tells him that he is condemned to walk in Denmark by night and burn in hell fire by day until some body avenges his death upon his murderer. The ghost says; "Doom'd (doomed) for a certain term (time) to walk the night, / And for the day confin'd (confined) to fast in fires, / Till the foul crimes done in my days of nature (life) are burnt and purg'd (purged) away" (Lines 9-13). The ghost tells Hamlet that his uncle's marriage to his mother is illegal and it is an incestuous relationship and he urges him to put an end to this marriage by killing King Claudius "Let not the royal bed of Denmark be / A couch for luxury and damned incest" (Line 84).Hamlet promises the ghost of his father that he will avenge the murder of his father. He orders both Horatio and Marcellus to keep all that they have seen tonight a secret and never tell anyone about it. From now on Hamlet will put everything aside except the ghost's commandment; to avenge his father's death. Hamlet vows to devote all his mental efforts and time to avenging his father's death. Hamlet even refuses to answer any questions from Horatio and Marcellus who have become curious to know what the ghost has said to him. Hamlet reveals his plan to pretend fake madness to both Horatio and Marcellus and gives them orders not to explain his behaviour to any one once he starts to appear mad. Having heard the ghost say "swear" (Line 181), Marcellus and Horatio swear to Hamlet to keep all that they have seen tonight a secret (Line 180).

Prince Hamlet sets forth on the mission of avenging his father's death. However, because he is so contemplative and meditative by nature, he delays completing his mission, entering into loops of acute depression and slight madness. King Claudius and Queen Gertrude do not find any justification for Hamlet's melancholy and depression and why he still mourns the death of his father although he has been dead for two months now. In Shakespeare's time the marriage of King Claudius to his sister- in-law Queen Gertrude was incestuous and illegal. When King Claudius questions Hamlet why he looks pale and sad and addresses him like his own son "But now, my cousin Hamlet, and my son/ How is it that the clouds still hang on you?", Hamlet suspiciously and ironically says in an aside "A little more than kin, and less than kind" (a little more than family and less than kind) (Line 65). Then, Hamlet addresses the king and replies that this is "Not so, my lord;" and further elaborates that he is not sad at all, but he has been in the sun too long "I am too much i' [in] the sun" (Line 67). Queen Gertrude feels that Hamlet distrusts King Claudius and deals with him suspiciously. She urges Hamlet to look cheerful and cast off his melancholy over the death of his father. She says to him "cast thy [your] nighted colour off, / And let thine [your] eye look like a friend on Denmark". Then she tells her son not to "Seek for thy noble father in the dust:" (not to look for your father in the dust). The Queen then tells Hamlet that all people are doomed to die and no one lives forever. However, after death people go to Heaven where they live eternally "all that live must die, / Passing through nature to eternity" (Lines 68-73). King Claudius tells Hamlet that he should not mourn the death of his father any longer and should live his own life as constant grief is "unmanly grief:" (Line 93).

Hamlet is so depressed to the extent that he begins to contemplate committing suicide. To him the "uses of this world" have become "weary, stale, flat, and unprofitable" (Lines 132-136). In an aside, Hamlet shares his thoughts and intentions with the audience. He praises his father King Hamlet and describes him as a kind man who was so loving to his mother. Yet within less than a month she remarries his spiteful brother Claudius. So desperate and annoyed is Hamlet that in fury he generalizes that all women, like his mother, are weak before sexual desire when he says: "Frailty, thy [your] name is woman!" (Line 146). Hamlet derides his mother and scorns her by calling her the most destructive and malicious woman on Earth "O most pernicious woman!" (Line 105). He can not understand how she dared to remarry only one month after the murder of her husband. Ironically and cynically he describes his mother as being "Like Niobe, all tears;" (Line 149), a woman who shed not a tear for the death of her husband but only for her dead children. He believes that even Niobe who did not shed a tear for the death of her husband would have mourned longer than his mother. Sarcastically, he exclaims that even a beast which lacks the faculty of reason and which can not think properly would have mourned the death of its mate longer. In excitement, Hamlet cries out "O God! a beast, that wants discourse of reason, / Would have mourn'd longer,-" (Line 151). Hamlet is so confused to the extent that he calls his mother incestuous, nymphomaniac and sensuous. He describes her speedy incestuous marriage to King Claudius as being done with the "most wicked speed, to post / With such dexterity to incestuous sheets" (Line 157). Hamlet is furious and sick at heart, but for the time being he decides that he will not speak a word about this marriage. Hamlet says: Hamlet: "It is not nor it cannot come to good; / But break, my heart, for I must hold my tongue!" (Line 158)

Hamlet's troubled nature is revealed further to the audiences when Horatio tells him that he came to attend King Hamlet's funeral and Hamlet ironically and sarcastically replies that "I think it was to see my mother's wedding"(Line 177). To Hamlet both his father's funeral and his mother's remarrying his spiteful uncle happened almost, so to speak, at the same time. Hamlet uses other sardonic and ironical statements to criticize his mother's speedy marriage to uncle Claudius. The feast which was supposed to be served at his father's funeral was used instead as a feast to be served at his mother's incestuous marriage to Claudius. Sarcastically Hamlet tells Horatio "the funeral bak'd (baked) meats / Did coldly furnish forth the marriage tables" (Line 180) (the feast prepared for his father's funeral was unemotionally served at the wedding tables. King Claudius sends ambassadors to the King of Norway who is "impotent and bed-rid"(Line 28) (sick and weak) to suppress Young Fortinbras and prevent him from invading Denmark. Laertes, son to Polonius – the Lord Chamberlain- asks for permission to leave for France to attend the coronation of King Claudius as the new king of Denmark, the predecessor of the deceased King Hamlet.

Laertes, Polonius' son, advises his sister Ophelia not to return Hamlet's affections. He warns her not to fall in love with Hamlet claiming that the man suffers from depression and melancholy and does not control himself "his will is not his own". Laertes further explains that Hamlet who is supposed to behave like a prince on whose choice "depends the safety and the health of the whole state" (Line 20) behaves just like a common man and even less than that .His behaviour , Laertes elaborates, is erratic and reckless and does not befit a prince. Laertes warns Ophelia not lose her virginity to Hamlet and urges to protect her "chaste treasure" (her virginity) (Line 32). Laertes advises his sister to be cautious when dealing with the lunatic prince and warns her not to follow her heart. He tells her that the "best safety lies in fear:" (Line 43). Ophelia promises her brother to follow his advice. Ophelia says to her brother: "I shall th'effect of this good lesson keep, / As watchman to my heart" (Lines 45-46).At this moment Polonius arrives and addresses his daughter: "Give every man thine [your] ear, but few thy [your] voice" (Line 69).Polonius warns Ophelia not to give Hamlet's affections any notice. Polonius also advises Ophelia not to be a borrower or a lender of money because the loan often loses both itself and a friend. Polonius addresses Ophelia "Neither a borrower, nor a lender be;" because "For loan oft loses both itself and friend". Then Polonius advises Ophelia to always be true to herself and never be a hypocrite. Polonius says to Ophelia: "This above all: to thine own self be true," (Line 78). Polonius tells Ophelia she must confess to him if she is indeed in love with Prince Hamlet. Before she utters a word, he tells her that he is quite sure that the young prince has very recently "Given private time to you;" and she might have returned his affections (Line 92). He tells her that he wants to make sure that his daughter still clings to her honour and that she has not lost her virginity to Prince Hamlet. Ophelia confesses to her father that Hamlet has "made many tenders / Of his affection to me" (has spoken sweet words of love to me) (Line 100), but has never asked her for more. Assured that his daughter is still virgin, Polonius says sarcastically "Affection! pooh! you speak like a green girl (innocent naive girl) (Line 101).Then he asks her if she thinks that Hamlet does indeed love her. Ophelia replies that she is not sure of his love to her. Polonius is quite sure that Hamlet does not love Ophelia and he merely wishes to seduce her. In doing so, Polonius believes that his daughter will make a fool of him. Polonius orders Ophelia not to believe Hamlet's words of affection because they are all lies. Ophelia promises her father once again to obey her father and follow his advice. She says to her father "I shall obey, my lord" (Line 136).

Act II

Polonius sends Reynaldo to Paris to spy on his son Laertes and other Danish nationals living in Paris and send him report on where they gather and how they spend their time. Polonius does not trust his son's behaviour and he is quite sure that he indulges in drinking, gambling, fencing, swearing, and quarrelling. Reynaldo tells Polonius that by inquiring about his son's behaviour in Paris he is dishonoring him with such accusations. Similarly, King Claudius sends spies to spy on Hamlet and discover his intentions and report to him the reason behind his erratic behaviour. King Claudius' spying on Hamlet and Polonius' spying on his son reflects the suspicion, mistrust, deception and espionage that permeate the entire play.

Ophelia explains to her father that Hamlet took her by the wrist, held her very hard, ogled her and studied her face before letting her go. Polonius is now certain that Hamlet is indeed in love with Ophelia. Now he knows for sure why Hamlet is acting so strangely. He believes that Hamlet is lovesick and he suffers from a shock after being rejected by Ophelia. Polonius says to Ophelia that he will take her to see King Claudius to report to him that Hamlet acts strangely because he suffers from "ecstasy of love" (Line 102) for his daughter Ophelia. Polonius asks Ophelia if she has rebuked Hamlet and rejected his affection. Ophelia replies that she did not hurt Hamlet's feelings, but rejected his love letters and did not return his affection as Polonius, her father, had demanded. Polonius is now sure that Ophelia's rejection of Hamlet's love "hath [has] made him [Hamlet] mad" (Line 111). Polonius tells Ophelia that he regrets having been so hard on Hamlet by preventing Ophelia from returning his affection.

King Claudius summons courtiers and childhood friends of Hamlet, Rosencrantz and Guildenstern and instructs them both to spy on Hamlet and find out what is causing his weird transformation and drastic change of character. Queen Gertrude informs King Claudius that the death of his father and her speedy remarriage must have caused Hamlet's drastic change of character and bizarre behavior. Claudius feels that Hamlet's transformation and change of character pose a threat to his rule of the state of Denmark and therefore decides that he must be watched very closely. He sends Hamlet's close companions and childhood friends, Rosencrantz and Guildenstern, to spy on him and find out what is causing his melancholy and change of character. Queen Gertrude tells the two courtiers that if they bring reports on the reasons for Hamlet's change of personality, they will be generously rewarded by King Claudius and shall receive the king's thanks. The two courtiers agree to spy on their close friend.

The two ambassadors Voltimand and Cornelius whom King Claudius sent to the King of Norway to restrain Prince Fortinbras and prevent him from invading Denmark have returned with good news. Polonius tells King Claudius that the two ambassadors have assured by the King of Norway that their country will never be invaded by Prince Fortinbras. King Claudius is happy to hear the news and agitatedly praises the Lord Chamberlain (Polonius) saying "Thou [you] still hast [have] been the father [source] of good news" (Line 41). Having received the King's compliment and praise Polonius becomes highly motivated to tell him the other good news. He reports to him that he has found out the cause of Hamlet's strange transformation of personality. He says: "I have found / The very cause of

Hamlet's lunacy". The King becomes excited and asks the pompous chamberlain to speak. Polonius tells King Claudius to hear first from the two ambassadors then he will give him a thrilling report about the cause of Hamlet's madness. Polonius says to King Claudius "My news shall be the fruit" (Line 52). Polonius metaphorically compares the news of discovering the cause of Hamlet's lunacy with fruit when compared to the big feast represented by the news brought by the two ambassadors that Prince Fortinbras will not invade Denmark.

Voltimand reports to King Claudius that despite his "sickness, age and impotence" (Line 66), the King of Norway persuaded his nephew not to invade Denmark. To convince him not to attack Denmark, the old King of Norway gave Prince Fortinbras "three thousand crowns in annual fee" (Lines 72) and gave him permission to use his outlaws to fight the Polacks or the Poles instead. However, the King of Norway did ask for permission to let Prince Fortinbras take his soldiers across Denmark on his way to attack the Poles. Polonius tells King Claudius and Queen Gertrude that "since brevity is the soul of wit" (Lines 92), he will be brief in explaining the cause of Hamlet's change of character. Polonius tells the King and the Queen that Hamlet is deeply in love with his daughter Ophelia. Her rejection of his love is indeed what causes his lunacy. To prove his claim, Polonius takes out a love letter Hamlet previously sent to his daughter Ophelia and starts reading it for the King and the Queen.

Hamlet's writing in the letter is distorted, confused and lacks the rhetoric we often find in love letters. Polonius reads Hamlet's letter: "To the celestial, and my soul's idol, the most beautified (beautiful) Ophelia" (Line 109) Polonius stops reading to criticize Hamlet's wording of the letter. He says that the phrase "the most beautified Ophelia-" is "a vile (terrible) phrase" (Line 110). Polonius continues reading Hamlet's letter to Ophelia "Doubt truth to be a liar; / But never doubt I love. O dear Ophelia!" Having finished reading the letter, Polonius tells the King and the Queen that his daughter is obedient to him and she informed him of all her dealings with Hamlet. Polonius further explains that he does not approve of any love affair between his daughter and Hamlet. When King Claudius asks Queen Gertrude whether she believes that Ophelia's rejection of Hamlet's affection is indeed the main cause of his lunacy, she replies doubtfully, "It may be, very likely" (Line 152).King Claudius wants to make sure that Polonius' theory about Hamlet's madness is indeed true . He asks Polonius for more evidence "How may we try it further?" (Line 159) (How can be sure of your claim?). Polonius tells King Claudius that he will arrange for a meeting between Hamlet and Ophelia in the lobby of the castle. Then they can study how Hamlet deals with Ophelia. The King agrees to act out his chamberlain's wicked plan.

Hamlet acts out his first attempt at pretending fake madness in the scene in which Queen Gertrude sees him reading a book while walking in the lobby of the castle. The second opportunity in which we see Hamlet pretend fake madness is when Polonius approaches him while walking in the lobby and asks him "Do you know me, my lord?" (Line 173), and hamlet says to him: "you are a fishmonger" (a person who sells fish) (Line 174). Hamlet paradoxically describes Polonius as a dishonest man of wicked nature "I would you were so honest a man" (I wish that you were an honest man), (Line 177). Historically fishmongers have the reputation of being dishonest. Hamlet does not respect Polonius and holds him in low esteem. Hamlet teases Polonius by telling him that Ophelia might be pregnant and advises him not to let her go wherever she wishes to go. He tells him that "conception (pregnancy) is a blessing; but not as your daughter may conceive" (Line 189). Hamlet further teases Polonius by telling him that unwanted pregnancy might drive Ophelia to lunacy. When Polonius asks Hamlet what he is reading, he vaguely replies "words, words, words" (Line 196). Polonius is so wicked and intelligent. He senses that Hamlet is pretending fake madness for some purpose. In an aside Polonius says: "Though this be madness, yet there is method in't" (though this is madness, it is done for a purpose) (Line 211). Polonius is deceived by Hamlet's fake madness and starts to think that Hamlet is really mad when he asks him if he will walk in the open and Hamlet replies that he will walk "Into my grave?" (Line 214). In fact, this line not only deceives Polonius into thinking that Hamlet is really mad, but also reveals that Hamlet is indeed contemplating the idea of committing suicide to put an end to his melancholy and depression.

Rosencrantz and Guildenstern, Hamlet's childhood friends who have been sent by King Claudius to spy on Hamlet, arrive to meet Hamlet. Hamlet greets them warmly calling them "My excellent good friends!" (Line 232). Hamlet complains to them that to him "Denmark is a prison" (Line 253). Rosencrantz tells Hamlet that he and Guildenstern view Denmark differently and believe that it is a nice country to live in. Hamlet tells them that "there is nothing either good or bad, but thinking makes it so" (what makes a thing good or bad is how we think about it) (Line 261). Hamlet's state of mind and troubled nature are changing drastically. He contemplates several possibilities to solve his dilemma that range from deserting his mother and returning to his school   in Wittenberg, to avenging his father's death to even worse committing suicide. Every scene the audiences sense a progression in his unease. Now he perceives Denmark as a rotten prison.

Hamlet speaks tenderly with the two spies Rosencrantz and Guildenstern. He is quite sure that although they have accepted to spy on him, they still like him as their childhood friend. Hamlet politely inquires why they have come to Elsinore castle. Rosencrantz replies that they have come to the castle to see him because he and Guildenstern are still his closest friends. Hamlet senses from the very beginning that they are lying and the are indeed spying on him. When Hamlet says to his two friends "I am most dreadfully attended" (Line 280), he uses an ambiguous statement with double meanings. First, he wants to say to his two friends that he knows that they are spying on him. Second, he refers to the ghost of his father who frequently visits him and directs his course of action. Hamlet asks the two men if they have been sent by King Claudius to spy on him. Hamlet says to the two spies : "there is a kind of confession in your looks which your modesties have not craft enough to colour: I know the good king and queen have sent for you" (the wish to confess that you are spying on me is written on your faces and because you are honest you do not have the skill enough to hide this confession ; I know that King Claudius and Queen Gertrude have instructed you to spy on me), (Line 293).Out of friendship, Guildenstern confesses to him that he and Rosencrantz have in deed been instructed to spy on him.

Having heard their confession to him that they are spying on him, Hamlet tells them that now he sees all the beauty of the world as filth and then declares his philosophical perception of the nature of man. He tells his two friends that the wonders of man do not interest him any more saying that man, the best of all animals "paragon of animals!" and the best of all God's creations interests him no more. Hamlet explains further that his perception of man certainly includes women. Rhetorically eloquently Hamlet says: "What a piece of work is a man! How noble in reason! how infinite in faculty (cleverness) in form (the beauty of his face), in moving, how express and admirable! (the beauty and elegance of his figure) in action how like an angel! in apprehension (understanding) how like a god! the beauty of the world (the beautiful creature)! the paragon of animals (the leader of all animals)! And yet, to me, what is this quintessence of dust? (merely created from a pile of dust- a biblical reference) man delights not me; no, nor woman neither" (Lines 321-331).

Hamlet's eloquent description of man as the peak of God's creation, the paragon of all animals, the most beautiful and most intelligent of all creations, a creature with an exciting figure and beautiful face, a creature endowed with the faculty of logic and reason and his lack of interest in such a marvelous creature reveal Hamlet's unease and disturbed state of mind. Hamlet is so sick at heart to the extent that he begins to dislike the beauty of the world and view it as filth and dust.

Rosencrantz tells Hamlet that several actors are on their way to Elsinore to perform several of their interesting plays. Hamlet suddenly becomes excited and tells Rosencrantz that he will be their host and welcome them all in particular the one who plays the role of the king. Rosencrantz further explains that these actors are "tragedians of the city" (Line 350) and they offered their services to him. Hamlet remarks that things change and nothing remain the same. During his father King Hamlet's reign people used to disrespect Claudius, now they pay a lot of money just to buy a picture of King Claudius. Hamlet trusts both Rosencrantz and Guildenstern as loyal friends and confesses to them that he is not mad but pretends fake madness for a purpose. He tells the two courtiers that "my uncle-father (King Claudius) and aunt-mother (a less affectionate and scornful name for his mother) are deceived" (have deceived him) (Line 403).

Hamlet meets the actors and discusses with them some details about acting. Hamlet shows a keen interest in acting and stage performances. He even recites some lines from Virgil's epic *Aeneid* about the Trojan war with such theatrical skill that the pompous chamberlain Polonius remarks: "well spoken" (Line 497) (well performed). Hamlet asks one of the players to recite the scene in which Phyrrus, the son of Achilles, murders King Priam and the scene in which Queen Hecuba, the wife of the murdered King Priam, grieves terribly after the assassination of her husband. Hamlet intentionally selects this scene to be performed in front of his mother who did not shed a tear for the death of her husband and hastily remarried his uncle within days after his murder. Then Hamlet tells the actors that he will arrange for them to perform the play "The Murder of Gonzago" in front of King Claudius and Queen Gertrude. Hamlet tells the actors that he has written sixteen lines and will insert them in the play.

Hamlet is tortured by feelings of guilt for not completing his mission of avenging the death of his father till now. He rebukes himself for inaction and describers himself as a coward and a villain. Hamlet believes that guilty people like Claudius watching a stage performance of a play that mimics their personal life are always moved by the play's events and often confess their sins. Hamlet firmly believes that "For murder, though it have no tongue, will speak / With most miraculous organ" (murderers often unintentionally reveal the secret of the crimes they have committed or leave traces of their crimes behind them) (Lines 625-630). Hamlet plans to arrange for the performance of a play that mimics the murder of his father in front of his uncle King Claudius to study his reactions. He says: "I'll have these players (actors) / Play something like the murder of my father / Before mine uncle". Hamlet believes that King Claudius' reactions to the play will prove that he did murder his father. Hamlet is now confident of his plan and is sure that it will work out well in providing evidence that his uncle killed his father. He believes that if Claudius reacts in a guilty manner to the scene in the play, this will provide him with proof that he is the murderer of his beloved father King Hamlet. He says: "I know my course"(Line 634). So far, Hamlet is still skeptical of the ghost's story and at times believes that the ghost is only the devil which seeks his demise and destruction. He says: "The spirit that I have seen / May be the devil" (Line 635).To him the devil might have assumed the pleasing shape of his father to destroy him. Hamlet is quite sure that in the play he will know every thing from studying his uncle's reactions to the scene in the play. He says: "the play's the thing / Wherein I'll catch the conscience of the king" (the play will help me study King Claudius' conscience and know for sure whether he was the one who assassinated my father or not. (Line 641).

Act III.

King Claudius summons both Rosencrantz and Guildenstern, the two spies whom he sent to spy on Hamlet, to Elsinore Castle and asks them to explain why Hamlet acts strangely as if he were mad. In fact, Claudius does not at all believe in Polonius' theory that lovesickness is what causes Hamlet's madness. Claudius' question to the two spies in which he inquires why Hamlet "puts on this confusion" (Act III, Line 1) reveals that he is quite aware that Hamlet is not really mad but is rather pretending to be mad. Rosencrantz lies to the King and tells him that Hamlet did indeed confess to him that he feels himself distracted" (Line 5). However, Rosencrantz further explains that Hamlet refused to reveal to him the cause of his distraction. Guildenstern backs up his friend's claim, explaining that Hamlet said nothing more than confessing to them that he is confused and distracted. Guildenstern further elaborates that Hamlet refused to reveal to them the true state of his mind. Queen Gertrude asks Rosencrantz and Guildenstern if Hamlet felt happy to see his two childhood friends. They reply that he treated them politely like gentlemen. The queen also questions them how Hamlet felt when he heard of the arrival of the actors in Elsinore Castle. Rosencrantz replies that "there did seem in him a kind of joy" (Line 18).

Polonius tells the King and the Queen that Hamlet urged him to request them to watch with him the play to be acted tonight. Claudius' heart is filled with fear of his nephew's troubled nature and distracted mental state. But, when he heard that Hamlet will watch a play, he becomes relieved and tells Polonius to inform Hamlet that he and the Queen are pleased to receive his invitation to watch the play with him tonight. King Claudius urges Rosencrantz and Guildenstern to encourage Hamlet to pursue his interest in theatrical performances if they make him content and cheerful "give him (Hamlet) a further edge, / And drive his purpose on to these delights" (Line 25). Left alone on the stage, King Claudius tells Queen Gertrude that she must go to her chamber now because he and Polonius have arranged for the meeting between Hamlet and Ophelia during which they will hide so that they can eavesdrop on their conversation to prove Polonius' theory that "the affliction of his love" (lovesickness) (Line 36) is the cause of Hamlet's lunacy. Before Queen Gertrude leaves she tells the beautiful Ophelia that she wishes that her "good beauties be (are) the happy cause / Of Hamlet's wildness (lunacy) and that she wishes that she will return her son's affection so that he becomes normal once again. The Queen says: "I hope your virtues / Will bring him to his wonted (normal) way again" (Line 39). Ophelia's shyness and her love for Hamlet are quite apparent in her reply to the Queen "Madam, I wish it may" (Line 41).

Polonius urges Ophelia to walk in the lobby pretending to be reading a book while he and the King will hide behind the tapestry wall so that they can hear Hamlet's conversation with her. Sensing that Ophelia might be offended to realize that she is spying on the man she loves, Polonius comforts her that she is doing this out of her devotion and love for Hamlet. King Claudius backs up Polonius' comforting words to Ophelia telling her that sometimes people do wrong things or even lie for a good and noble purpose. In an aside King Claudius utters the words that reveal his regret for killing his brother King Hamlet. "O heavy burden!" (I am tortured by the burden of my guilt).

When Polonius sees Hamlet approaching, he tells King Claudius that they must hide behind the arras before he senses their presence. Hamlet and Ophelia cordially greet each other. Ophelia tells Hamlet that she has come to return to him his "remembrances" or love letters. Hamlet denies having sent Ophelia any love letters, but she insists on saying that he did send her those letters. Ophelia reminds Hamlet of the content of the letters saying that they are all love letters beautifully worded. Ophelia demands that Hamlet confesses that he sent her those love letters which were once sweet but he turned to be unkind to her. Ophelia rebukes Hamlet for being unkind to her and she tells him that all the gifts including the love letters he gave to her mean nothing to her. Ophelia says: "Rich gifts wax poor (lose value) when givers (like Hamlet) prove unkind" (Lines 100-101). Hamlet senses that Ophelia is treating him more warmly than her usual habit and begins to sense that she has been sent to spy on him. He distrusts her and begins to deal with her cautiously. Hamlet becomes very rude and implies that Ophelia is a prostitute when he says to her: "Ha, ha! are you honest?" (Line 103), and then asks her "Are you fair?" (Line 105).

Hamlet distrusts Ophelia and even senses that somebody hiding somewhere in the lobby of the castle is eavesdropping on their conversation. Cautiously but wittily Hamlet tells Ophelia that he used to love her, but he does not love her any more "I did love thee once" (Line 117). Ophelia tells Hamlet that he made her think that he loves her. Hamlet becomes annoyed and replies that he was merely telling her lies. He even denies having ever loved her "I loved you not" (Line 122). Ophelia feels that Hamlet has indeed deceived her and he is not that man to be trusted. In fury, Hamlet tells Ophelia to go to a nunnery and declares his wish that marriage must be banned. Hamlet calls all women breeders of sinners and Ophelia is one of those women. Hamlet tells Ophelia that he himself is a sinner who has committed many sins so far and wishes that his mother had not given birth to him. Hamlet tells Ophelia that he is now revengeful and ambitious and gives her a very distorted image of men. He says: "We (men) are all arrant (homeless) knaves (fools or dishonest barbarians), all (without exception)" (Line 132). He gives her a good advice not to believe any man because all men are liars "believe none of us" (Line 133).and tells her that it would be better for her if she goes to a nunnery and never gets married. Then, suddenly he wittily asks Ophelia "Where's your father?" (Line 135). She lies to him and replies that her father is at home. Hamlet is now sure that Ophelia has betrayed him and is spying on him for Claudius and Polonius. Before Hamlet departs he senses the presence of the two villains and implicitly insults both King Claudius and Polonius when he says to Ophelia: " Let the doors be shut upon him, that he may play the fool nowhere but in's (in his) own house"(Lines 136-139).This indicates that Hamlet wants both Claudius and Polonius in their hide to know that he feels their presence.

Having lost his temper Hamlet openly insults Ophelia telling her that if he should ever marry her, and this is impossible, he would offer her plague as her dowry. Hamlet repeatedly advises Ophelia never to marry and go to a nunnery. If she should ever marry, he tells her, she must marry a fool because decent men will never ask for hand in marriage "for wise men know well enough what monsters you make of them" (Line 145). Ophelia now realizes that Hamlet is indeed mad and prays for God to return him to normal. Hamlet rebukes Ophelia and all women telling her that "god hath (has) given you one face, and you make yourselves another (God has given you a face and you painted it with make up and deception). Hamlet tells Ophelia to get out of his sight at once because she "hath made me (Hamlet) mad" (Line 155) and that he wishes he would never see her again. Having insulted her and all women on Earth and having denounced all marriages, Hamlet departs leaving Ophelia in a state of incomprehension and amazement. She begins to cry over the loss of her love. She becomes shocked to see Hamlet in such a confused state of mind and she mourns "what a noble mind is here o'er-thrown (overthrown)" (Line 159)

King Claudius and Polonius appear from behind the arras. Having heard the conversation King Claudius is now sure that the cause of Hamlet's lunacy is not lovesickness as Polonius claimed. King Claudius further explains to Polonius that what Hamlet said "Was not like madness" (Line 173).King Claudius further elaborates that Hamlet's madness is fake not real since he says "There's something in his soul / O'er (over) which his melancholy (lunacy , depression or bad mood) sits on brood" (Lines 174-175). From now on Claudius' fear of Hamlet increases to the extent that it turns into a phobia. Since King Claudius is now certain that Hamlet poses a real threat to his reign of Denmark, he decides to send him to England. King Claudius says to Polonius: "I have in quick determination / Thus set it down: he shall with speed to England". Polonius tells King Claudius that he still believes that the cause of Hamlet's madness is neglected love and asks for his permission to eavesdrop on Hamlet's conversation with his mother Queen Gertrude. Permission is granted and Polonius starts looking for a plan to help him spy on Hamlet and his mother. In an aside King Claudius reveals his fear of Hamlet's fake madness "madness in great ones (Hamlet) must not unwatch'd go (madness in great people like Hamlet should not go unwatched)" (Lines 195-196).

Hamlet meets the actors who will perform the play "The Murder of Gonzago" in the evening in the presence of King Claudius and Queen Gertrude. Hamlet gives the actors some instructions that pertain to theatrical performances which reveal that he has a keen interest and a good skill in stage performances. He advises the actors to be natural and realistic in their acting and not to overact. He further explains to them that their actions on stage must match their words. In giving his instructions to the actors to make the play subtle and not overdone and inserting some lines in the play, Hamlet wants to flush out his uncle's guilt quite naturally. Hamlet asks Polonius "will the king (Claudius) hear this piece of work (watch the play) (Line 52). Polonius tells Hamlet that both King Claudius and Queen Gertrude have told him that they would like to watch the play.

Hamlet praises his trusted friend Horatio as a loyal friend of sound judgment and asks him to study King Claudius' reactions to the play. Hamlets tells Horatio "Observe mine uncle;" (watch my uncle's reactions), (Line 85). Hamlet urges Horatio to pay close attention to King Claudius' reactions mainly in the scene that re-enacts the murder of his father with poison. Hamlet says: "One scene of it comes near the circumstance / Which I have told thee of my father's death" (Lines 80-82).Hamlet tells Horatio that if his uncle's guilt is not revealed in one specific speech, then the ghost they have seen on the platform of Elsinore Castle must have been the devil in disguise of the pleasing shape of his father. Hamlet says: "if his occulted guilt / Do not unkennel in one speech, / It is a damned ghost that we have seen" (Lines 86-88). Hamlet tells Horatio that he will also be studying King

Claudius' facial expressions throughout the whole play and once the play is finished both will determine whether King Claudius killed his father or not. Before the play begins Hamlet orders Horatio to take his seat and tells him that he will pretend to be idle.

King Claudius, Queen Gertrude, Polonius the Lord Chamberlain, Ophelia, Rosencrantz and Guildenstern and other lords and ladies now enter to watch the play. Hamlet asks Polonius if it is true that he acted in a play at university and Polonius replies that he acted in *Julius Caesar*. Ironically, Polonius says: in the play "I was kill'd (killed) i' (in) the Capitol; Brutus killed me" (Line 109-110).In fact, Polonius' words ironically foreshadow his murder at the hand of Hamlet. When Queen Gertrude asks Hamlet to sit beside her during the play, he declines. Hamlet distrusts his mother and thinks that she is sensuous and disloyal to her former husband King Hamlet. Hamlet even insults his mother when he sarcastically says to her: "No, good mother, here's metal more attractive" (I will sit beside any body, but not you) (Line 117). Having noticed Hamlet's hostility towards his mother, Polonius asks King Claudius to see for himself how badly Hamlet treats his own mother. Then Hamlet approaches Ophelia and sarcastically asks her if he can sit in her lap "Lady, shall I lie in your lap? (Line 120). Ophelia feels offended taking into account Hamlet's perception of her as a destructive prostitute. Ophelia declines and replies "No, my lord" (Line 121). Having sensed that he has insulted Ophelia more than she can bear, Hamlet pretends that what he meant was putting his head upon her lap. Hamlet says to Ophelia: "I mean, my head upon your lap?" (Line 122). Then Hamlet continues his verbal attack against Ophelia and he even dares to ask her "Do you think I meant country matters?" (Did you think I was talking about sex?) (Line 124).Ophelia becomes very shy and to keep her virtue and good reputation, she respectfully replies "I think nothing, my lord" (Line 125).Hamlet directly insults Ophelia when he says that he likes to lie between women's legs "That's a fair thought to lie between maids' legs" (I like to lie between women's legs). Hamlet's vulgar language is so insulting to shy Ophelia and shows no respect for her.

In fact, Hamlet has a much distorted image of women in general. He believes that they are all; including his mother, nymphomaniac, lusty, deceptive and disloyal and Ophelia is no exception. Ophelia tells Hamlet that he looks merry and he tells her that why he should not look cheerful when his mother looks so happy only two hours after the death of her husband. Ophelia remarks that King Hamlet died two months ago. Hamlet tells Ophelia that the memory of good people, like that of his beloved father, long lives beyond their death.

In the dumb show or short play that is performed shortly before the main play the Queen kneels with respect before the King who lovingly lifts her up, places his head on her neck and kisses her forehead. The King and the Queen have great affection for each other. They embrace and the King goes to the orchard to have a nap. While asleep one of the lords in the castle approaches the sleeping King, strips him of his crown, kisses the crown and pours a large amount of poison in the King's ears. Having made sure that the King is motionless, the poisoner hastily leaves the orchard. When the Queen returns and finds her husband dead, she declares her grief for only two minutes. The poisoner returns and starts courting the queen and embracing her expressing his love for her. At first, she rejects his affection then being nymphomaniac and lusty submits to her lust and accepts the new suitor's warm kisses.

Despite the fact that this dumb show mimics the murder of King Hamlet at the hands of his brother Claudius, neither King Claudius nor his wife Gertrude shows any familiarity with the story and none of them gives the wanted reactions. Although King Claudius realized that the events in the dumb show imitate those of his crime, he was able to control himself and showed no reactions. Queen Gertrude has given no response to the events of the dumb show because she does not know that Claudius murdered her former husband with poison to usurp his throne and marry her. When Ophelia asks Hamlet "What means this, my lord?" (What is the play about, my lord?), Hamlet replies that it is about scandalous deeds committed by the devil. When Ophelia says to Hamlet that the dumb show is brief, he replies "As woman's love" (Line 166) referring at once to both Ophelia and Queen Gertrude whom he thinks are a pair of disloyal women. He meant to insult both his mother who quickly remarried shortly after the death of her husband and Ophelia who shifted her loyalty from Hamlet to King Claudius. Having performed the dumb show, the actors start acting the main play "The Murder of Gonzago".

The plot of the main play mimics the plot of the dumb show. The play starts with the player King and the player Queen declaring their love to each other. The player Queen promises the King that she would never remarry after his death. These lines which might have been added to the play by Hamlet reveal his wish that his mother remained a widow after his father's death.

Hamlet interrupts the play and asks his mother if she likes thee play "Madam, how like you this play?" (Line 241). Queen Gertrude unknowingly replies that the player Queen swears too much "The lady doth (does) protest too much, me-thinks (I think)" (Line 242). Queen Gertrude begins to feel that the player Queen's behaviour stands in sharp contrast to her behaviour when she immediately remarried after the death of her husband. To tease his mother, Hamlet praises the player Queen saying that she is worthy of respect because she will certainly keep her promise to her husband and she will never remarry after his death .Hamlet says to his mother: "O! but she'll keep her word" (she will keep her promise and remain a widow) (Line 244).

King Claudius asks Hamlet if he intended in some way or another to make the play insulting or offensive to him and his mother. Hamlet replies that the play is not offensive at all but seems realistic. Having received an acceptable explanation, Claudius asks Hamlet what the title of the play is. Ironically Hamlet tells King Claudius that the title of the play is "The Mouse-trap" which really reveals Hamlet's purpose of performing the play that is to catch his uncle's conscience and reveal his guilt. To elicit a confession from his uncle that he did murder his brother, Hamlet explains the plot of the play. He tells him that the whole play is a description of the murder of Duke Gonzago of Vienna. Hamlet remarks that the play is a "knavish piece of work" (malicious work of art), but it should not bother people who have free and incorruptible souls. In the play Lucianus, the Duke's nephew approaches Duke Gonzago as he is asleep in the orchard and pours poison in his ears. Hamlet provides constant commentary on the events of the play. Hamlet explains to the audiences watching the play that Lucianus having murdered the Duke, he will attempt to win the love of his wife. Hamlet says: "the murderer gets the love of Gonzago's wife" (Line 280).

Having realized that the play mimics the crime he once committed, King Claudius furiously rises from his seat saying "Give me some light: away!" (Line 285). King Claudius feels threatened and alarmed by the events of the play and leaves the theatre immediately. Hamlet enjoys studying Claudius facial expressions and reactions, but pretends to have noticed nothing and feigns innocence. Hamlet asks King Claudius "What! frighted with false fire?" (Was King Claudius frightened by a fabricated story?) (Line 282).Having noticed that the King is upset and displeased Polonius demands that the performance of the play end at once. All members of the audiences leave except for Hamlet and Horatio who left alone, start discussing Claudius' reactions to the play. Hamlet tells Horatio that he is now certain that his uncle was the murderer who poured the poison in his father's ears while asleep in the orchard and tells him that all that the ghost said to him was true. Hamlet says to Horatio "I'll take the ghost's word for a thousand pound" (Line 302). Horatio confirms Hamlet's theory saying that there is no shadow of a doubt that King Claudius was the one who killed King Hamlet.

Rosencrantz and Guildenstern enter and tell Hamlet that King Claudius is sitting in his chamber totally distempered. Hamlet pretends to know nothing and asks the two courtiers why the King is upset. Guildenstern replies that King Claudius is afflicted "with choler", excessive and uncontrollable anger (Line 320).Hamlet tells him that King Claudius should consult his doctor. Guildenstern also tells Hamlet that Queen Gertrude would like to have a word with him in private in her chamber. Rosencrantz feels that Hamlet still distrusts him. When he says to Hamlet "you once did love me" (Line 355), Hamlet replies that he is no more his loyal friend and he no longer trusts him. When the musicians with musical instruments arrive at Elsinore Castle, Hamlet seizes the chance to humiliate Guildenstern. Hamlet asks Guildenstern to play any musical instrument and then asks him to play upon the pipe. Guildenstern replies that he can not play any musical instrument. In fury Hamlet spitefully tells Guildenstern that playing a musical instrument is "as easy as lying" indicating that the man is professional at lying (Line 379). Hamlet becomes outraged and he directly accuses his fake friend of disloyalty and espionage "You would play upon me; (spy on me for the King) you would seem to know my stops; you would pluck out the heart of my mystery (you wish to know all my secrets) ; you would sound me from my lowest note to the top of my compass (you wish to trace all my moves); and there is much music, ex-cellent voice, in this little organ, yet cannot you make it speak (you will never learn my secrets)" (Lines 386-395).Then Hamlet sarcastically asks Guildenstern if he thought that he was an easy instrument to play upon. Hamlet threateningly says to Guildenstern: "Call me what instrument you will, though you can fret (annoy) me, you cannot play upon me (spy on me and find out my plans)" (Line 396).At this moment Polonius approaches Hamlet telling him that his mother wants to speak to him in her chamber and that he has to go to her chamber at once.

Left alone Hamlet contemplates what he has achieved so far and in soliloquy urges himself to continue with his plan until he achieves his mission of avenging the death of his father as the his ghost demanded. Hamlet urges himself to be firm in his purpose and never let mercy or kindness ever invade his heart. Hamlet says: "O heart! lose not thy nature; let not ever / The soul of Nero enter this firm bosom; / Let me be cruel, not unnatural;. He must punish both his mother and his uncle without taking mercy upon them. Remembering the words of his father's ghost Hamlet declares that he will not harm his mother physically. Hamlet says: "I will speak daggers to her (I will hurt her feelings, but use none (but I will not hurt her physically) (Lines 417-419).

King Claudius reveals his amounting fear of Hamlet to both Rosencrantz and Guildenstern and he even tells them that he does not like him at all. King Claudius says " I like him (Hamlet) not," (Line 1).He further explains that his madness is becoming very dangerous for all those around him including Ophelia and his mother and decides to put an end to his lunacy by sending him to England accompanied by both Rosencrantz and Guildenstern. King Claudius tells the two spies that he will not " let his madness range (continue)" (Line 2).King Claudius fears Hamlet's lunacy and perceives him as a serious threat to his reign of Denmark. King Claudius expresses his fear of Hamlet's madness saying: "The terms of our estate may not endure / Hazard so dangerous as doth hourly grow / Out of his lunacies" (Lines 4-6). Rosencrantz and Guildenstern promise the King that they are ready to do whatever they can to ensure his safety and the continuation of his reign of the country. The comfort of the citizens depends on the comfort of the King. They both pledge loyalty to the King and leave for England.

Polonius tells King Claudius that he will go to the Queen's chamber to hide behind the arras to eavesdrop on Hamlet's conversation with his mother. Polonius tells King Claudius that hearing what is said inside the Queen's chamber is quite necessary since Hamlet might reveal some of his secrets and plans to his mother. Left alone King Claudius reveals his stream of consciousness to the audiences in soliloquy. King Claudius says: "O! my offence is rank, it smells to heaven; / It hath the primal eldest curse upon't (upon it); / A brother's murder!" (Line 36) In his soliloquy King Claudius confesses having committed one of man's greatest sins; fratricide or the killing of one's own brother and reveals to us that his heart is filled with remorse. King Claudius tells us that his crime is wicked and its awful smell reaches Heaven. King Claudius resembles his crime to man's first crime, when Cain killed Abel; a brother killing his brother- a biblical reference to the first two sons of Adam and Eve immediately after being tossed out of the heavenly paradise. King Claudius views himself as Cain in the sense that both are cursed by God for murdering their brothers.

To express his repentance King Claudius reveals his intent to spend some time praying believing that only praying can redeem him for God does not deny forgiveness to those who pray asking for it. King Claudius believes that God will not accept his repentance because he still possesses the effects for which he committed the crime and still enjoys the fruits of his sin "My crown, mine own ambition and my queen" (His reign of Denmark, his ambition and his victim's wife Queen Gertrude) (Lines 55). King Claudius wants to repent but without giving up the joyful fruits of his sin. However, King Claudius' soliloquy does indeed reveal that remorse and repentance have transformed the fruits of his sin mainly his reign of Denmark and the Queen's sensuality into agony and filth. King Claudius desperately cries out: "O wretched state (reign of Denmark)! O bosom (the Queen's breasts) black as death!". Then, in fear and desperation he asks for mercy from angels "Help, angels!" then, filled with fear, he requests his "stubborn knees" to kneel down so that he can pray (Lines 65-67).

While saying his prayers Hamlet enters King Claudius' chamber with the bloody intention to kill him. Having seen the King kneel down in prayer, Hamlet becomes hesitant to kill his uncle. In an aside Hamlet reveals his thoughts to the audiences:
"Now might I do it pat, now he is praying;
And now I'll do't. And so he goes to heaven;
And so am I revenged. That would be scann'd:
A villain kills my father; and for that,
I, his sole son, do this same villain send
To heaven.
O, this is hire and salary, not revenge.
He took my father grossly, full of bread;
With all his crimes broad blown, as flush as May;
And how his audit stands who knows save heaven?"
Hamlet says that he can kill King Claudius now if he likes "Now might I do it pat", but he would not kill him while he is praying. Hamlet knows that if he kills Claudius while he is praying, he would certainly go to Heaven unlike his father who was murdered while he was asleep and was not given the chance to repent his sins. Hamlet wants to make sure that once Claudius

is killed, he will be sent to Hell. Hamlet gets out of King Claudius' chamber and goes to his mother's private chamber.

Inside the Queen's private chamber, Polonius tells Queen Gertrude that he has been ordered by King Claudius to hide behind the arras to eavesdrop on Hamlet's conversation with her. Before Hamlet enters his mother's chamber, Polonius takes his hiding position behind the arras. Hamlet asks his mother why she has sent for him. Queen Gertrude scolds Hamlet telling him that he has offended his father with his lunacy. Queen Gertrude says: "Hamlet, thou hast thy father much offended". Hamlet starts launching his verbal attack against his mother telling her "Mother, you have my father much offended" (You have offended my dead father by remarrying his murderer) (Line 11). Queen Gertrude rebukes Hamlet further telling him "you answer with an idle tongue" (Line 12). Hamlet scolds his mother telling her "Go, go, you question with a wicked tongue" (Line 13).Queen Gertrude tells Hamlet that he is speaking rudely with her and reminds him that she is his mother. Hamlet tells Queen Gertrude that he knows for sure that she is the Queen and "your husband's brother's wife" (Line 16). Hamlet insults his mother when he tells her that he wishes that she were not his mother because he is ashamed of what she did. Hamlet says to his mother: "And,-would it were not so!-you are my mother" (Line 16). As Queen Gertrude intends to leave her chamber, Hamlet prevents her from leaving telling her to look in the mirror to see the wicked reflection of her soul. Hamlet tells his mother "set you up a glass / Where you may see the inmost part of you" (Line 20).Having sensed that Hamlet is becoming more aggressive in dealing with her, Queen Gertrude asks him : "thou wilt not murder me?" (You will not murder your mother me, will you?) (Line 21).Having received no reply from her Hamlet except for his aggressive eyes burning with revenge, the Queen cries out for help "Help, help, ho!" (Line 22).

Polonius , forgetting that he is hiding behind the arras, echoes the Queen's cry yelling at the top of his voice "What, ho! help! help! help!" (Line 23). Having heard the sound coming from behind the arras and thinking that it is the voice of King Claudius, Hamlet shouts "How now! a rat? and draws out his sword and stabs Polonius through the hanging tapestry. Before Polonius dies he shouts "O! I am slain"(Line 24).Queen Gertrude asks Hamlet why he has stabbed the man. Hamlet still believing that he has stabbed King Claudius inquires : "is it the king?" that he has slain (Line 26).Hamlet remarks that stabbing somebody with a sword is indeed a bloody crime similar to somebody pouring poison in his brother's ears while he is asleep and marrying his wife. So far Queen Gertrude does not know that her former husband King Hamlet was murdered. When Hamlet lifts up the arras, he becomes surprised to find that it was Polonius whom he killed not his target King Claudius. But, he does not regret having killed the rascal since he believes that the man did deserve some kind of punishment. Hamlet addresses Polonius' corpse lying behind the arras: "Thou wretched, rash, intruding fool" (Line 31).

Queen Gertrude asks Hamlet why he hates her though she is his mother. Hamlet scolds his mother for remarrying after the death of his father. Hamlet chides his mother for marrying her former husband's brother and describes their marriage as incestuous. Hamlet tells his mother that Claudius did not marry her because he loved her but to usurp the throne from his father King Hamlet. Hamlet even accuses his mother of being nymphomaniac, lusty and sensuous. Hamlet says to his mother: "Nay, but to live / In the rank sweat of an enseamed bed, / Stew'd in corruption, honeying and making love / Over the nasty sty,-" (Line 91). Queen Gertrude begs Hamlet to stop insulting her since his words are as harsh as daggers "These words like daggers enter in mine ears;" (Line 94). Hamlet directly and frankly reveals King Claudius' crime. Hamlet tells his mother that King Claudius is "A murderer, and a villain;" (Line 96).

At this moment the ghost of King Hamlet reappears. Hamlet believes that the ghost has reappeared to chide him for his delay in not avenging the death of his father till now. The ghost tells Hamlet that he has reappeared to prevent him from mercilessly insulting his mother and to remind him of his mission; to avenge the death of his father by killing Claudius. The ghost then urges Hamlet to speak tenderly and affectionately to his mother. The ghost says to Hamlet: "Upon the heat and flame of thy [your] distemper (lunacy) / Sprinkle cool patience" (Line 122).Queen Gertrude thinks that Hamlet is mad and is talking to himself. Hamlet tells his mother if she can see King Hamlet in the chamber. Queen Gertrude tells him that the ghost is the creation of his exhausted mind and hallucinations. But Hamlet tells her that it is not madness, the ghost is real. Hamlet begs his mother never to sleep with King Claudius "go not to mine uncle's bed" (Line 159) and to become virtuous again. Before he leaves his mother's chamber, Hamlet utters his famous saying "I must be cruel only to be kind" (Line 178).

Hamlet tells his mother not to tell King Claudius that she knows everything about the murder of King Hamlet and urges her to tell him that he is pretending to be mad on purpose "not in madness, /But mad in craft". Queen Gertrude assures Hamlet that she will keep all that he said to her confidential and that she will not sleep with Claudius in the same bed at all. Hamlet surprises his mother when he tells her that he will leave for England to meet his two school fellows Rosencrantz and Guildenstern whom King Claudius has ordered to spy on him. Hamlet compares the two spies with two fanged snakes ready to strike. Hamlet assures his mother that he will punish them both for their spying on him. Before he leaves he drags Polonius' corpse out of his mother's chamber and hides it in the neighbouring room.

Act IV

King Claudius senses that Queen Gertrude's mind is not at ease and he hears her sighs. He asks her "There's matter in these sighs" (What worries you?) (Line 1). King Claudius then asks the Queen "How does Hamlet?" (What's wrong with Hamlet? (Line 6).Queen Gertrude tells King Claudius that her son is indeed mad. Metaphorically speaking, Queen Gertrude says: Hamlet is "Mad as the sea and wind, when both contend / Which is the mightier" (Line 7). (Hamlet is as mad as the rough sea and the wind when they fight each other to know which is stronger). Queen Gertrude then tells King Claudius that having heard a noise behind the arras, Hamlet drew his sword out and stabbed the fabric killing the Lord Chamberlain Polonius who was hiding behind the arras eavesdropping on our conversation as you ordered him to do. Queen Gertrude tells Claudius: "In his lawless fit (furiously mad)," Hamlet shouted "A rat! a rat!' / And, in his brainish apprehension, kills / The unseen good old man (Polonius)" (Lines 8-11). Having heard how Hamlet killed Polonius, fear creeps into King Claudius' heart and guilty conscience and he begins to shake with fear believing that Hamlet could have killed him if he had been the one hiding behind the arras.

King Claudius tells Queen Gertrude that Hamlet poses a serious threat to their safety and must be banished to England for his own good. King Claudius says: "His liberty (irresponsible behaviour) is full of threats to all; / To you yourself (Queen Gertrude), to us, to every one" (Line 14). King Claudius reveals his intent that he will not tell anyone that Hamlet killed Polonius, but he wonders how he can explain his murder to the lords and subjects of Denmark. King Claudius tells Gertrude: "how shall this bloody deed (murder) be answer'd?" (Line 16). King Claudius tells Queen Gertrude that he should have suppressed Hamlet's bizarre actions earlier before "This mad young man (Hamlet)" (Line 19) committed his terrible crime. King Claudius asks the Queen where Hamlet has gone and the Queen replies that he has dragged Polonius' body off her chamber to hide it somewhere where it will not be found by anybody. Queen Gertrude also tells King Claudius that he did not think that it was a man hiding behind the arras, but thought it was a big rat and he regretted having killed the old man. The Queen says: "he weeps for what is done" (Line 27).

King Claudius summons both Rosencrantz and Guildenstern and informs them that Hamlet has murdered Polonius and has dragged his body out of his mother's chamber. He urges both spies to look for Hamlet and once they find him they should "speak fair" (Line 36) or kindly and gently to him without provoking his anger. He tells them that they must not return without bringing Polonius' body to the chapel as the man deserves the rituals of a good funeral before being buried. King Claudius tells Queen Gertrude that his soul is heavily burdened with guilt, remorse and panic "My soul is full of discord and dismay" (Line 44).

Hamlet has just finished hiding Polonius' body. The two courtiers Rosencrantz and Guildenstern approach Hamlet and ask him where he has hidden Polonius' body. Hamlet replies that he buried the rotten corpse. Rosencrantz insists that Hamlet show him Polonius' body so that they can take it to the chapel to receive its funeral rituals. Hamlet refuses to tell them where he has hidden the body and tells both courtiers that he no longer trusts them. He describes them both as lapdogs or even worse sponges that soak up the Kings' rewards. However, Hamlet agrees to go with them to see King Claudius.

King Claudius expresses his fear of Hamlet telling the two courtiers Rosencrantz and Guildenstern that Hamlet is a dangerous man and must be restrained. King Claudius says: "How dangerous is it that this man goes loose (is free)!" (Line 2).King Claudius also reveals to both courtiers that he can not send Hamlet to prison for killing Polonius because the public love him so much. Claudius says: "He's loved of the distracted multitude (the public love him)"(Line 4). King Claudius believes that sending the psychopath to England is the safest and wisest decision. Rosencrantz enters and tells King Claudius that Hamlet refused to tell him where he has hidden

Polonius' body. King Claudius is upset and demands the presence of Hamlet at once. At this moment Hamlet and Guildenstern enter. King Claudius asks Hamlet where he has hidden Polonius' body Hamlet ironically and defiantly replies: "At supper" (Line 18) referring at once that he is being eaten by grave worms. Then , Hamlet tells King Claudius frankly that he has already buried Polonius' body and the worms are eating him now. Hamlet sarcastically says to Claudius: "a certain convocation of politic (wise) worms are e'en [eating] at him" (Line 20).

When King Claudius persists with questioning Hamlet demanding to know where he has hidden Polonius' body, Hamlet tells him that Polonius is now in Heaven and suggests that he can send his two lapdogs Rosencrantz and Guildenstern as messengers to Heaven to find out whether what he said is true or not. Hamlet then reveals to King Claudius where he left Polonius' body telling him that "if you find him not within this month, you shall nose him as you go up the stairs into the lobby" (Line 40). Hamlet wants to say that if nobody finds Polonius' body within one month, the smell of his corpse will spread throughout the lobby of the castle. King Claudius sends the guards upstairs to check this out. King Claudius tells Hamlet that for his own safety, he must be sent to England and leave the country at once. King Claudius assures Hamlet that everything has been arranged for his departure to England by sea. The boat is ready to sail and the attendants are waiting for him on the boat. Hamlet replies that he will leave for England as requested by his uncle. King Claudius lies to Hamlet telling him that he is doing all this for his sake and he tells him not to forget his father Claudius: "Thy loving father, Hamlet" (Line 53). Having seen Hamlet leave the lobby, King Claudius tells both courtiers Rosencrantz and Guildenstern to follow Hamlet and make sure he boards the boat sailing to England. Left alone King Claudius reveals to the audiences his plan to arrange for killing Hamlet in England.

Prince Fortinbras, who is leading his army of outlaws across Danish territories to fight against Poland, sends an ambassador to King Claudius to make sure that he still has the King's permission to go across Danish lands on his way to Poland. When Hamlet asks the Norwegian ambassador what land they are fighting for, he replies that it is merely a small piece of land. He also explains that they are not seeking the worthless land, but are seeking the glory and honour of liberating Norwegian usurped lands. Hamlet reveals his admiration and envy of Prince Fortinbras whom he believes is a great warrior. Hamlet wishes that he had the courage of Prince

Fortinbras and rebukes himself for the delay in completing his mission and not killing King Claudius till now. Hamlet further reveals his envy of Prince Fortinbras who is fighting just for his honour, whereas his father was killed and the bed of his mother has become the bed of incestuous pleasures and he can do nothing to avenge the death of his father and restore his mother's stained honour. Realizing that he does not have the courage and determination Prince Fortinbras has Hamlet is determined more than ever to be firm of purpose and make his thoughts bloody until he fulfills his mission. Hamlet says: "from this time forth, / My thoughts be bloody, or be nothing worth!" (Line 66).

A gentleman tells Queen Gertrude that Ophelia would like to have a word with her in private. At first the Queen refuses to meet Ophelia, but when the gentleman tells her that the girl is no longer normal after the death of her father "She is importunate, indeed distract" (Line 2). , the Queen agrees to see her. The gentleman further explains that Ophelia "speaks much of her father" (Line 4) though what she says is senseless and meaningless. Queen Gertrude reveals to Horatio that she is conscience-stricken and her soul is sick. The Queen says: "To my sick soul, as sin's true nature is" (Line 17). Queen Gertrude wants to say that she might have unintentionally committed a sin and stained her son's honour by remarrying after the death of his father. When Ophelia enters the Queen's chamber, she inquires "Where is the beauteous majesty of Denmark?" (Line 22) and immediately starts to sing a song containing three verses the first of which is about true love, the second and the third are about the death of her father Polonius. When King Claudius sees Ophelia in such a state, he asks "How long hath she been thus?" (How long has she been behaving strangely like this? (Line 67). Ophelia tells King Claudius that she can do nothing but to mourn her father's death. She also tells him that her tears might warm her father in his cold grave. She thanks everyone for speaking words of condolences to her and tells everybody that her brother Laertes will be shocked to know that his beloved father is now dead. Before leaving she begins to say some hallucinations. King Claudius asks his aides to follow Ophelia and take care of her in the absence of her brother. King Claudius remarks that when sorrows come, they do not come in spies but in battalions (Misfortunes or troubles seldom come singly). King Polonius refers to recent dreadful events mainly the murder of Polonius, Hamlet's madness, the people's gossiping, the confusion and fear that have penetrated his heart and now Ophelia's madness.

A noise is heard outside the door of Elsinore Castle. Frightened of Hamlet though he is now in England, King Claudius gives orders to his switzers or bodyguards to stay close to him to protect him from any possible danger and guard the gate of the castle. A gentleman enters and informs the King that Laertes, Polonius' son, has come back from France and demands to see his father's body. He also reports to the King that the mobs have broken into the castle crying out "'Laertes shall be king, Laertes king!'" (Line 108).King Claudius is frightened as this is a clear threat to his reign of Denmark. Laertes breaks into the castle and demands to see King Claudius. With his men standing outside the King's chamber, Laertes says to King Claudius "Give me my father" (Line 115). Having calmed down, Laertes dismisses his supporters and asks the King to speak to him in private. King Claudius tells Laertes that his father was slain by Hamlet and he mourned his loss as if he were his brother. At this moment Ophelia enters singing an incomprehensible song, mourning the death of her father. Realizing that his sister has become mad after the death of her father, Laertes declares that his sister is mad. Ophelia, now carrying bunch of flowers, remarks that all the roses in the world withered with the death of her father. The flowers that represent Ophelia's hopes of love and happiness have all withered. Laertes feels sorry for noticing that his sister has lost her sanity. King Claudius tells Laertes that he was not involved in the murder of his father and if he can prove his involvement in the crime, he will give up his rule of Denmark. Otherwise, he continues, Laertes should help him discover the identity of his father's murderer and give him the punishment he deserves. Laertes swears that he will avenge the death of his father and kill the man who murdered his father and denied him a decent burial. King Claudius encourages Laertes to take revenge upon the murderer saying "where the offence is let the great axe fall"(Line 218).

Horatio, Hamlet's closest friend, receives some letters from Hamlet sent to him buy a sailor. In the letter Hamlet tells Horatio that the ship Hamlet was sailing to England was attacked by bloody pirates killing all the passengers on board the ship. Hamlet was taken as a prisoner. However, the pirates agreed to take Hamlet back to Denmark in return for Hamlet doing them a favour when needed in the future. Hamlet demands that Horatio send the other letters to King Claudius and to meet him without delay telling him that he needs to talk to him to discuss his plans with him. In the letter Hamlet writes to Horatio: "I have words to speak in thine (your) ear (that) will make thee dumb (shocked with amazement) (Line 26). Hamlet tells Horatio that the sailor will show him his hiding place. Horatio leaves with the sailor to meet Hamlet.

King Claudius persuades Laertes to take revenge upon Hamlet; the man who killed his father and attempted to kill him. Laertes asks King Claudius why he did not send Hamlet to prison for killing his father. King Claudius replies that he did not send Hamlet to prison for two reasons namely "The queen his mother lives almost by his looks" (Queen Gertrude loves Hamlet and if he is sent to prison , she will be heartbroken) (Line 12) and he can not bear living without Queen Gertrude as he loves her very much. Secondly, King Claudius explains, the "great love the general gender (the Danish people) bear him;" (Line 18). If Hamlet was sent to prison, the public would not tolerate seeing their idol being punished and would certainly start raising opposition against his reign of Denmark. Laertes declares that he will take revenge upon Hamlet who killed his father and caused his sister's madness. Satisfied with what he has heard, King Claudius tells Laertes that he will tell him later how he plans to help him kill Hamlet. A messenger enters and declares that he has two letters; one for King Claudius and the other for Her Majesty the Queen. King Claudius reads his letter and announces that Hamlet will return to Denmark.

King Claudius discusses with Laertes his plan to kill Hamlet in a fencing match. King Claudius praises Laertes' skill in fighting with the rapier (sword). To arouse his vengeance King Claudius wittily asks Laertes: (was your father) "dear to you?" (Line 107). King Claudius tells Laertes that he can kill Hamlet in the fencing match and he will help him do this by giving him a foil with a sharp blade. Laertes explains that he has also planned to dab his sword in a deadly poison. Excited, King Claudius explains that if Hamlet does not die of the wound, he will certainly die of the poison on the foil. Laertes elaborates further that a slight wound would certainly kill him. Inspired by Laertes' idea of poisoning his foil, King Claudius has a back up plan to kill Hamlet in case he does not die of the poisoned sword. He will pour some poison in a goblet of wine and give it to thirsty Hamlet to drink should he ask for a drink.

Queen Gertrude enters to announce Ophelia's death b y drowning. Weeping, Queen Gertrude tells Laertes: "One woe doth (does) tread upon another's heel / So fast they follow: your sister's drown'd, Laertes" (Moments of sadness follow one another so quickly- your sister Ophelia has drowned in the river) (Line 164). She further explains a branch of a tree fell on her dragging her into the river. Queen Gertrude eloquently and metaphorically describes Ophelia's death:

"Fell in the weeping brook. Her clothes spread wide;
And, mermaid-like, awhile they bore her up:
Which time she chanted snatches of old tunes;
As one incapable of her own distress,
Or like a creature native and indued
Unto that element: but long it could not be
Till that her garments, heavy with their drink,
Pull'd the poor wretch from her melodious lay
To muddy death"

While singing by a brook holding a bunch of roses in her hands, a bough from a tree fell on her dragging her into the brook. She floats on the surface of the water for some time before she sinks to the bottom of the brook. Laertes is heart broken for the loss of his sister saying "Too much of water hast thou, poor Ophelia," (you have drunk too much water while drowning) (Line 186). Having mourned the death of his sister, Laertes bids farewell to the King and the Queen telling them that he is burning with the desire to avenge the death of both his father and sister. King Claudius asks Queen Gertrude to follow Laertes to calm his rage.

Act V

The two grave diggers who are digging Ophelia's grave are joking while digging the grave as if they were not digging a grave but rather enjoying their time. The first clown (grave digger) believes that people who commit suicide like Ophelia should not be honoured with a Christian burial. He asks the second grave digger "Is she (Ophelia) to be buried in Christian burial that willfully seeks her own salvation?" (Line 1). In fact, it is a Christian belief that committing suicide is a sinful act and that is what has made the first grave digger inquire if Ophelia who willfully committed suicide deservers a proper and decent Christian burial with all the necessary rituals. The second clown (grave digger) tells his fellow worker that the poor girl shall get a proper Christian burial and tells him to "make her grave straight" (her grave should look like all the other decent graves, no more no less) (Line 4).The first grave digger is not convinced an remarks that she does not deserve a proper Christian burial unless "she drowned herself in her own defence (unless she drowned herself to protect her chastity and virginity from rape) (Line 6).The two clowns or grave diggers continue their argument whether Ophelia deserves a proper Christian burial or not. Realizing the fact that both are not sure whether she drowned herself deliberately or she drowned in the water by accident, they decide to honour her with a decent and proper burial that befits a Christian girl. The first digger describes himself and his fellow worker as "ancient gentlemen" (Line 33) like "gardeners, ditchers and grave-makers;" who have all practised "Adam's profession" (Line 34).

Hamlet and Horatio arrive at the burial in the churchyard. The first grave digger send the second grave digger to a bottle of alcohol to drink. To amuse himself while digging the grave the first digger begins to sing. Hamlet becomes excited to see the grave digger singing merrily while digging graves for the dead. Hamlet asks Horatio "Has this fellow no feeling of his business, that he sings at grave-making?" (Line 72). Horatio replies that "Custom" has made this grave digger accustomed to his job to the extent that he can eat and drink while digging the holes for the dead. Routine, Horatio explains, has desensitized him to feeling gloomy about his work. The grave digger continues singing throwing up an old skull he has unearthed from the grave. This very act makes Hamlet contemplate and wonder whose skull that was. Then, Hamlet remarks that to whom the skull belongs is insignificant. The skull is now merely food for grave worms. Amazingly, the grave digger unearths another skull and throws it up out of the grave. Hamlet again wonders whom that second skull once belonged to. Hamlet wonders if it was a lawyer's skull. Hamlet remarks that the poor lawyer with all his wit and prestige could not prevent "this rude knave" (the grave digger) from unearthing his skull with a dirty shovel. Hamlet continues guessing whose skull the grave digger has just unearthed. Then he says that it might have belonged to a landlord "a great buyer of land"; a rich man who has been reduced to a pile of dust and a skull. Hamlet explains that death is the great leveler and equalizer of life which treats people equally the same regardless of their status, reputation, fame, wealth, poverty, health, sickness, race, colour, and power. Death the leveler reduces all people to the same fate; from dust to dust.

Hamlet and the first grave digger converse with each other exchanging their witticisms. The grave differ informs Hamlet that he has been working as a grave digger for thirty years. Ignorant of the fact that he is speaking with Prince Hamlet, the grave digger says that he has started working as a grave digger since the birth of Prince Hamlet, a man whom King Claudius sent to England because of his madness. While digging the grave and conversing with Hamlet, the first grave digger unearths a skull and says it belongs to Yorick ; King Hamlet's jester (comedian or clown). Hamlet takes the skull and contemplates it for a moment then says: "Alas! poor Yorick" (Line 202). Hamlet explains to the first grave digger that he used to be very fond of the comedian Yorick when he was a child. Hamlet still holding the skull in his hand and contemplating it asks his friend Horatio "Dost thou think Alexander looked o' this fashion i' the earth?" (Do you think that even Alexander the Great has been reduced to a skull in his grave?) (Line 217). Horatio replies that even Alexander the Great looks like Yorick in the dirt in his grave. Hamlets makes further inquiries about the skull and tells Horatio that he would like to know if the smell of Alexander the Great is as bad as Yorick's skull.

Hamlet satirically comments on the meaninglessness and insignificance of man's existence revealing that after death all people without exception and regardless of their power, wealth, poverty, race and social status will be reduced to dust; the basic substance of their creation .Hamlet satirically shows the insignificance of political power and political authority I the face of death the leveler. Death shows no respect for political power and people with high ranking titles and posts. Death treats people equally the same no matter how wealthy or poor they are. Holding Yorick's skull but talking about Alexander the Great, Hamlet says to Horatio: "To what base uses we may return, Horatio! Why may not imagination trace the noble dust of Alexander, till he find it stopping a bung-hole?" (Line 225). Hamlet says that once people die, they turn to dust, the basic substance of their creation. Even Alexander the Great who has been dead for ages now has been turned into dust. Hamlet says that Alexander the Great was not only turned into dust after his death, but his dust was mixed with water and was turned into clay which was in turn used by a poor man to cover a hole in a beer barrel. Hamlet tells Horatio that "Alexander died, Alexander was buried, Alexander returneth (returned) into dust; the dust is earth; of earth we make loam (clay or mud), and why of that loam, whereto he was converted, might they not stop a beer-barrel?" (Lines 230-234).Hamlet also satirically speaks of Julius Caesar who, dead for ages now, was turned into clay. A poor man unknowingly mixed the remains of the Caesar's body with water to make clay which he later used to cover a hole in the wall of his house to keep the wind away. Hamlet says: "Imperious Caesar, dead and turn'd (turned) to clay, / Might stop a hole to keep the wind away" (Line 235).Hamlet further remarks that even people who have been great in their life can neither control their fate after death nor prevent other people who are alive now from using what remains of their bodies in trivial and humiliating uses such as making clay to cover holes in their houses. A funeral procession enters the churchyard carrying Ophelia's corpse to be buried. Priests, Laertes, King Claudius, Queen Gertrude and other mourners walk in the funeral procession mourning the dead youth. Having noticed the procession approaching the grave, Hamlet and Horatio walk away so that they would not be seen.

The priest doubts that Ophelia died a natural death. He suspects that she committed suicide by drowning herself in the brook and therefore, does not deserve the rites of a Christian burial. Queen Gertrude is heartbroken for the untimely death of Ophelia. Queen Gertrude bids farewell to Ophelia and scatters white flowers over her coffin saying that she hoped that Ophelia would have been her son's wife. Laertes bitterly mourns the loss of his sister and leaps into her grave. Hamlet tells Laertes that nobody in this world has loved Ophelia more than he has. Hamlet too leaps into Ophelia's grave and fights with Laertes. Horatio and the other mourners part the two men, forcing them to get out of the grave. With tears flooding his eyes Hamlet confesses that "I lov'd (loved) Ophelia", then he elaborates "forty thousand brothers / Could not, with all their quantity of love, / Make up my sum"(the love of forty thousand men does not match my deep love for Ophelia), (Line 292).King Claudius remarks that Hamlet is indeed mad, and Queen Gertrude to defend her son agrees. Hamlet continues to pretend fake madness to deceive King Claudius until he fulfills his mission.

Hamlet reveals to Horatio how King Claudius planned to kill him while boarding the ship to England. Hamlet explains that luckily he found out the plan to put him to death shortly before the two spies Rosencrantz and Guildenstern could carry out the plan. Hamlet tells Horatio that he stealthily entered the two spies' cabin and opened the grand commission or the King's orders to them to put Hamlet to death in England. The King's order was to cut off Hamlet's head by an axe in England. Hamlet gives the commission to Horatio to read for himself. Hamlet deceived King Claudius by writing a new commission in the King's own writing telling the King of England that Denmark would like to maintain good political ties with England and to put the two bearers of the commission to sudden death. Hamlet explains that he sealed the commission with King Hamlet's official seal or signet to make it look authentic. Horatio is not surprised by King Claudius' evil actions and he comments "Why, what a king is this!" (Why did King Claudius plan to kill you? What kind of king is he?). Hamlet tells Horatio that he has the right to kill King Claudius as he was the one who "hath kill'd my king and whor'd my mother" (he killed my father King Hamlet and made my mother a whore) (Line 64). Hamlet tells Horatio that it is fair to kill King Claudius before he commits further evil acts.

Osric enters and salutes Hamlet. Hamlet asks Horatio if he has ever met this water fly (insignificant man – mosquito) before. Horatio tells Hamlet that he has never seen him before, but he might be one of the King's lords or attendants. Osric tells Hamlet that the King has sent him to inform Hamlet that he and Laertes will fight each other in a friendly fencing match to please the audiences. Osric explains that King Claudius, Queen Gertrude and many lords will watch the fencing match. Osric tells both Hamlet and Horatio that King Claudius has betted "six horses" on Hamlet losing by no more than three hits out of twelve passes and Laertes has betted six French swords that he will beat Hamlet by more than three hits. Hamlet tells Osric that he accepts to challenge Laertes in the fencing match and he will win the match for King Claudius. Not realizing that Laertes' sword will have a poisoned sharp blade, Hamlet explains that if he loses the fencing match, he will only get the shame of a few blunt hits from Laertes' blunted sword. With Osric leaving, a Lord enters and tells Hamlet that the King wants to know how much time he needs to prepare himself for fighting Laertes in the friendly fencing match. Hamlet replies that he will "follow the king's pleasure" and will be ready to challenge his opponent any time the King wishes. Horatio warns Hamlet that he will lose the fencing fight and he fears the consequences of that loss. Hamlet ignores Horatio's warning assuring him that he is certain that he will win the match. Hamlet adds that while he was in France he used to practise his fencing skill very often. Horatio is still skeptical and urges Hamlet that if his mind is not at eases about the duel, he should postpone the fight or even cancel it for his safety. Horatio even suggests that Hamlet should apologize to the King for not being fit for the fight or pretend that he is sick and can not accept the challenge. Horatio says to Hamlet: "say you are not fit" (Line 230). Hamlet tells his friend that he is determined to challenge Laertes in the fencing match.

King Claudius, Queen Gertrude, Osric and Lords enter, occupying their seats to watch the friendly fencing match. King Claudius begins the duel by wickedly placing Laertes' hand on Hamlet's. Hamlet feels that Laertes is indeed a decent man worthy of respect. He apologizes to him for fighting him near Ophelia's grave and asks for his forgiveness. Hamlet tells Laertes that he must excuse his insane conduct at Ophelia's grave for he is "punish'd / With sore distraction" (Line 244) (his madness made him behave foolishly at Ophelia's funeral). Laertes does not accept Hamlet's apology though he tells him that he knows that Hamlet has never meant to harm him. Laertes tells Hamlet that he seeks to restore his honour and reveals to him that he will not live in peace till he takes revenge upon the man who killed has father and drove his sister to the brink of madness and caused her untimely death. Laertes tells Hamlet that he will remain outraged until he receives assurances from "elder masters," (Line 262) respectful Danish citizens that his sister's honour (chastity and virginity) was not spoiled by any man. Till that time, Laertes explains, he will treat Hamlet as a friend and will not reject his goodwill. Before the fight begins both Hamlet and Laertes hold their blunt swords. Hamlet tells Laertes that as a gesture of goodwill he will help him show off his fencing skill in front of the King and the Queen. Laertes regards Hamlet's words as an insult, believing that he is mocking him. Hamlet denies such an accusation telling Laertes that he indeed meant what he said.

Osric, the referee of the fencing match, gives Hamlet and Laertes their foils and asks them if they both know the rules of the match. To chide his uncle , Hamlet says to King Claudius that he must have betted on "the weaker side" (Hamlet) , but wickedly King Claudius assures Hamlet that he has betted on the right side and he is certain that Hamlet will win the match and beat Laertes. Both Hamlet and Laertes complain about their foils and demand new ones. While the two opponents prepare themselves for the duel, King Claudius pours some poison in a goblet of wine for Hamlet to drink when he becomes thirsty. King Claudius wittily places the poisoned wine on a table for Hamlet to see. King Claudius announces that if his nephew Hamlet wins the first three hits or rounds, he will drink to "Hamlet's better breath" (Line 285) and he will put a pearl which he calls an "onion" in a glass for the winner. The duel begins and Hamlet hits Laertes who claims that it was not a hit. Osric, the referee, judges that Hamlet did in fact hit Laertes and score the first hit. King Claudius holds the pearl and says to Hamlet: "this pearl is thine" (this pearl is yours now) (Line 296)

To tease Hamlet and make him drink the poisoned wine , King Claudius takes a sip from his glass of wine saying to Hamlet: "Here's to thy health" (cheers, to your health) (Line 297). Though thirsty and in need of a drink,

Hamlet puts the goblet aside and does not drink from it saying that he will win the match first then drink to celebrate his victory. The fight starts again and Hamlet hits Laertes another hit asking Laertes what he thinks of this hit. Laertes replies that he hardly touched him. King Claudius hypocritically says: "Our son shall win" (Our son Hamlet is about to win the fencing match) (Line 301). Although Queen Gertrude doubts that her son will win the match, she supports him and gives him her napkin to rub his face of sweat. Having noticed Queen Gertrude pick up the poisoned goblet to drink some wine, King Claudius warns her "Gertrude, do not drink" (Line 304). Queen Gertrude gives no attention to Claudius' warning and replies "I will, my lord". King Claudius is completely distracted to see his beloved wife drink from the poisoned wine which he himself has prepared for Hamlet. In an aside King Claudius reveals his worries about his beloved wife whom he could not prevent from drinking the poisoned liquor saying: "It is the poison'd (poisoned) cup!" Noticing that Queen Gertrude has drunk from the poisoned goblet to the last sip, King Claudius shouts out "it is too late"(Line 306).

Laertes approaches King Claudius telling him that now he will wound Hamlet with his poisoned sword. Deeply touched by the approaching death of his beloved wife, King Claudius tells Laertes "I do not think't " (I doubt that you can do this) (Line 310).As Hamlet and Laertes continue fighting Laertes finally wounds Hamlet with the poisoned foil. Hamlet snatches the poisoned sword from Laertes and wounds him. Noticing that Queen Gertrude is dying Osric says to King Claudius: "Look to the queen there, ho!" (Line 317). Horatio notices that Hamlet and Laertes are bleeding and wonders why they are bleeding when the two foils are supposed to be blunt not sharp. Before he dies Laertes says "I am justly kill'd with mine own treachery" (I deserve to be killed because of my disloyalty to the Prince of Denmark) (Line 321).Before she dies Queen Gertrude warns Hamlet not to drink wine from the poisoned goblet from which she has drunk. Queen Gertrude tells Hamlet that it was Claudius who poured the poison in the wine for her to drink. In his fury Hamlet shouts "villainy" and orders the guards to lock the doors of the courtyard so that Claudius will not escape. Before Laertes dies he says to Hamlet "thou art slain" (you will die of poison just like your father) (Line 327).Laertes tells Hamlet that he will die within half an hour urging him to kill King Claudius with the poisoned sword which he still holds in his hand. Laertes says to Hamlet: "The treacherous instrument is in thy hand, / Unbated and envenom'd" (the very same poisoned foil that killed you is still in your hand. It is still tipped with poison. Use it to kill King Claudius) (Line 330).Laertes also tells Hamlet that King Claudius killed your mother with the poisoned.

Outraged and filled with the burning desire to take revenge upon the man who killed his father and whored and killed his mother, Hamlet, shouting "venom, to thy (your) work" (Lines 336) stabs King Claudius with the poisoned sword. Noticing that King Claudius is breathing his last breath, Hamlet says to the dying villain "incestuous, murderous, damned Dane, Follow my mother" (die with my mother) (Line 340).Laertes, who is still alive, remarks that the villain has been "justly serv'd" (justly killed) telling Hamlet that they should forgive each other as they will both die of poison soon. Before Laertes dies he says to Hamlet "Mine and my father's (Polonius') death come not upon thee (you), / Nor thine (yours) on me!" (Hamlet is not to blame for his death and his father's death and Laertes is not to blame for Hamlet's death) (Line 344).

While breathing his last breath, Hamlet tells his loyal friend "I am dead, Horatio". He bids farewell to his mother saying "Wretched queen, adieu! (shameful and miserable queen, goodbye) (Line 348). Noticing Horatio is totally depressed and realizing that he might commit suicide after his death, Hamlet begs Horatio never to take his own life after his death. Hamlet tells Horatio that he must live to tell his story otherwise he will have "a wounded name," or bad reputation amongst the public who has always loved and admired him. Hamlet also tells Horatio that Prince Fortinbras must be crowned as the new King of Denmark since he is a great warrior worthy of respect. Hamlet further explains that Prince Fortinbras will be a kind and just King and the Danish people will certainly like him. Horatio promises Hamlet to tell his story to Prince Fortinbras and all the citizens of Denmark. Noticing that Hamlet has died, Horatio remarks "Now cracks a noble heart" (Line 372) (the noble prince finally died and made his heart break). With his eyes flooding with tears, Horatio bids farewell to his dear prince saying "Good-night, sweet prince, / And flights of angels sing thee (you) to thy (your) rest!" (Farewell good prince. The angels will take you to Heaven) (Line 374).

Prince Fortinbras, escorted by his soldiers and the English ambassadors, enters. Having achieved victory in Poland, he has come to Denmark to reclaim the Norwegian lands his father lost to King Hamlet. Prince Fortinbras and the ambassadors are shocked to see the bloodshed. Prince

Fortinbras remarks that he has never seen in his entire life the waste of such royal blood. Horatio approaches Prince Fortinbras addressing him as the new King of Denmark as Hamlet demanded and tells him Hamlet's story. Horatio tells Prince Fortinbras that upon dying Hamlet has requested him to tell his story to "the yet unknowing world" (Line 393), the story "Of carnal (lustful), bloody, and unnatural acts, / Of accidental judgments, casual slaughters; / Of deaths put on by cunning and forc'd (forced) cause". (the story of fratricide, incestuous marriage, bloody massacres of royal blood, and wicked espionage).In admiration of Hamlet, Prince Fortinbras gives orders to four captains to bury Hamlet with the full honours and rites of a grand funeral that befits a true Prince of royal blood. The play ends with the four captains carrying Hamlet's corpse in a royal funeral procession heading towards the cemetery where Prince Hamlet is to be buried.

The Tragedy of Hamlet, Prince of Denmark

Commentary:

The Tragedy of Hamlet is no doubt Shakespeare's most philosophical play and is one of his greatest tragedies. The play is replete with philosophical speculations to the extent that it can be said that all the characters in the play whether they are major characters or minor characters who do not make their own philosophical speculations. Hamlet, the young Prince of Denmark, is the most eloquent philosophical speculator in the play. Hamlet's persuasive philosophical speculations cover the main themes of the play namely death as the leveler and equalizer, the frailty of women, the corruption of political power, the meaninglessness of man's existence, love, lust, incest, fratricide and revenge.

Francisco's famous two lines "'tis (it is) bitter cold, / And I am sick at heart" and Marcellus' line "Something is rotten in the state of Denmark" and the ghost's commandment to Hamlet to avenge the death of his father all establish the ominous tone of play and foreshadow the killings and trappings that take place throughout the entire course of the drama. Though Hamlet has been instructed by the ghost of his father to take revenge upon his uncle who killed his father and whored his mother, he remains dilatory and spends a lot of time reflecting upon the enormity of the crime. Instead of putting his plan to avenge the death of his father into immediate practice, he spends most of his time feigning madness and indulges in philosophical speculations. Even Hamlet chides himself for being dilatory and infirm of purpose.

Hamlet is arguably the most intricate dramatic character Shakespeare ever created. Hamlet is a crestfallen prince of extreme contradictions. He is reckless and cautious, mad and wise, gentle and furious, affectionate and vengeful, a coward and a stubborn killer. He is deeply in love with Ophelia but wittily hides his love for her and mercilessly drives her to the brink of insanity with his verbal assault against her. He seems inattentive, but all of a sudden reveals his vengeful thoughts and highly sophisticated plans. He feigns madness for a purpose, but occasionally appears mad beyond doubt. He treats Ophelia gently and sends her love letters, but all of a sudden he insults her using words that make a whore blush. He is so loving to his mother though at times he insults her and looks down upon her perceiving her as a prostitute. He is indecisive though he does not hesitate at all to stab Polonius while hiding behind the curtains in his mother's chamber and mercilessly drags his corpse upstairs. To take revenge upon the man who murdered his father, Hamlet kills or causes the death of many innocent people namely Polonius, Ophelia, and his former school mates Rosencrantz and Guildenstern. As Hamlet becomes more obsessed with the ghost's commandment, his tragic flaws amount to the extent that he turns into a wild beast or a vengeful social outcast. Dressed in a black cloak, the grief-stricken Hamlet vows that he will take revenge upon his father's assassin. Being so dilatory, indecisive, thoughtful and contemplative, he decides to plan for what course of action he must pursue to achieve his mission.

Shakespeare portrays Queen Gertrude as a passive sensuous woman who seems to be ignorant of her new husband's criminality. Two months after the death of her husband King Hamlet she hastily marries her brother-in-law Claudius and proclaims him as the new King of Denmark. Queen Gertrude's advice to Hamlet "Thou know'st tis common, all that lives must die/Passing through nature to eternity" (You know it is natural that people die to live eternally in the other life) (Act I. Scene II. Lines 71-2), makes Hamlet more scornful of her. He believes that she has betrayed his father by marrying his murderer. Hamlet despises King Claudius and listens derisively to him while calling him "our son". In particular, Hamlet becomes more contemptuous of King Claudius when he asks him to stop mourning his father's death, to take off the black cloak and to consider him as his father. King Claudius says to Hamlet: "We pray you to throw to earth/This unprevailing woe, and think of us/As of a father" (Lines 106-8, Act I. Scene II.).Hamlet is so devoted to the memories of his father and still can not believe that his beastly uncle Claudius is whoring his mother in his father's own bedroom. When King Claudius asks Hamlet to treat him as his own father "think of us/As of a father" (Line 108, Act I. Scene II), Hamlet becomes outraged and compares his tender and kind father to Hyperion, a Titan or a super human being in Greek mythology, while he compares his wicked and murderous uncle to Satyr, a distorted creature half-goat and half-man, known for its sadist sensuality and nymphomania. Hamlet recalls his father's kindness saying:

"So excellent a king, that was to this
Hyperion to a satyr, so loving to my mother,
That he might not beteem the winds of heaven
Visit her face too roughly; heaven and earth,
Must I remember?" (Lines 141-45, Act I. Scene II)

Throughout the play Hamlet develops his disgust for and contempt of his incestuous uncle calling him names that befit a beast or a sub- human. He likens him to Satyr, who is portrayed in classical mythology as a misshapen creature half beast and half man known for its brutality, excessive alcoholism and abnormal sensuality. Shortly before Hamlet forces King Claudius to drink from the poisoned goblet he calls him "incestuous, murderous, damned Dane". Throughout the play Hamlet keeps referring to his uncle as the "adulterate beast".

Queen Gertrude's incestuous marriage and her excessive sensuality have formed a very distorted image of all women in Hamlet's mind. After his mother's remarriage, Hamlet begins to develop a disgust for all women. He perceives all women including his mother as sensuous, lusty, adulterous, passive, and naïve. In fact, this distorted stereotypical image of women is what makes Hamlet mistreat Ophelia despite his love for her. His distrust of his mother has also made him distrust Ophelia. But, without any shadow of a doubt Hamlet has a good reason for distrusting both women. Both have spied on him for the murderer of his father and both have accused him of insanity without ever trying to find out what causes his depression and melancholy and offer their help. Both Gertrude and Ophelia are passive indeed and seem dominated and controlled by the males in their families. Much of Queen Gertrude's behaviour seems to be affected by her sensuality and love for Claudius. She spies on her son for her husband and does not hesitate to let her son slip into insanity without ever trying to help or understand what causes his morbid mood. Similarly, Ophelia spies on Hamlet for the sake of her father and King Claudius and lies to him. In obedience of her father she takes part in the conspiracy against Hamlet to reveal to her father and the King that lovesickness or her rejection of Hamlet's love is what causes his madness.

Ophelia fails to realize that Hamlet indeed loves her. The love letters he once has sent her and the many gifts he has given to her all indicate that Hamlet is in love with Ophelia. Realizing that all women are traitorous and lusty, Hamlet feigns madness, lashes out at her with vulgar words and drives her crazy till at the end she commits suicide. Hamlet's cruelty towards Ophelia is sadistic and brutal. He both insults her describing her as a prostitute like his mother and seduces her by telling her while watching the play that he wishes he could lay his head between her legs. Hamlet is no doubt fueled by rage as a result of his mother's incestuous marriage. Her behaviour has destroyed in him his faith in humanity in general and in women in particular.

From the moment Hamlet speaks to the ghost of his father, his life is turned upside-down and he goes through a cycle of mental unrest. The ghost's commandment to Hamlet to commit murder by taking revenge upon the man who assassinated his father and whored his mother constitutes a heavy burden on Hamlet's shoulders. From that moment Hamlet's life becomes chaotic and his mind becomes distracted. The ghost's commandment has placed Hamlet in unnatural circumstances. Although several months have passed since the appearance of the ghost to Hamlet, he is still determined to fulfill his mission by avenging the death of his father. Being a pensive and contemplative scholar, Hamlet puts the ghost's commandment into test. Hamlet does not take revenge upon King Claudius until he has gathered sufficient evidence that he was the man who murdered his father. Though he once has the opportunity to kill his uncle while saying his prayers in his chamber, he delays killing the man till he finds a better opportunity. Hamlet delays killing Claudius because he knew that if he killed the murderer of his father while praying, he would certainly go to heaven.

When Hamlet returns from his exile in England, his character seems to have developed drastically. He has become less fearful of death, more courageous and more determined than ever to avenge the death of his father. To avenge the death of his father, Hamlet must commit the very same act for which he seeks revenge. In his pursuit of taking revenge upon the man who murdered his father, Hamlet becomes a professional killer. So far, he has killed one man and caused the death of two others. He killed Polonius by stabbing him while hiding behind the arras to eavesdrop on his conversation with his mother and has arranged for the death of his two school mates in England. At the end of the play the massacre is complete. By the end of the play Hamlet will have killed three people: Polonius, King Claudius and Laertes and caused the death of three others: Ophelia, and the two courtiers Rosencrantz and Guildenstern.

Claudius is a ruthless king who is ready to do anything he can to protect his rule of the state. He is a murderer who kills his own brother to usurp the throne and marry his sister-in-law. The two crimes he committed are quite unnatural: fratricide or regicide and incest. Both crimes cause the state to become rotten and to be under the curse of ghosts and spirits. As a ruthless king he knows that a change of government usually creates civil unrest, rebellions, oppositions and even worse military coups. He uses all tactics no matter how deadly they are to enjoy both his incestuous marriage and kingship. Having poured the poison into the ears of his brother King Hamlet and thus killed him, Claudius courts and seduces his sister–in–law and within less than two months he marries her. Having married the Queen and usurped the throne, Claudius wittily assumes the role of the chief mourner of the death of his brother King Hamlet so that the Danish people would unite behind him in a collective mourning. Claudius is the cause of all Hamlet's suffering and the suffering of all the Danish people. The ghost of the former King describes him as "that incestuous, that adulterate beast" (Line 42, Act I. Scene V) and his crimes of fratricide and incest constitute what is "rotten in the state of Denmark. Hamlet likens him to Satyr, a creature half goat and half man with excessive sensual behaviour. King Claudius clearly represents the worst in the human nature. He represents sensuality, lust, greed for power, wickedness, brutality, and political corruption. His crime of fratricide echoes the primal fratricide when Cain killed Abel.

More than any other character in the play the character of Gertrude stands in sharp contrast to that of her son Hamlet. Their attributes form binary oppositions. Hamlet is a pensive and contemplative scholar who is always seen involved in philosophical speculations searching for logical answers to the many puzzling questions about man's existence. Hamlet has no interest in humanity and believes that man has been a sinner since the very first day of his creation. He likens the murder of his father at the hands of his brother to the primal fratricide when Cain killed Abel. In contrast, Gertrude is shallow, sensuous and thoughtless. Her nymphomania is what makes Hamlet despise her and look down upon her as a whore. In fact, Gertrude's excessive lust is the pivotal point around which all the events of the play turn. She might have seduced her brother-in-law even during her former husband's lifetime. Her coquettish seduction might have motivated Claudius to murder his brother to usurp the throne and marry her. Although she might not have taken part in the murder of her husband, she could have unintentionally and indirectly spurred her lover to commit the crime. Even the ghost of Hamlets father reveals to Hamlet that his wife might have betrayed him in his lifetime with his brother Claudius. The ghost reveals to Hamlet how sensuous Claudius, the "incestuous, that adulterate beast" has wittily seduced his traitorous wife with his gifts. The ghost indirectly says that his wife had betrayed him and lied to him as she pretended to be virtuous when she was in fact betraying him with his brother. The ghost cynically says:

"Ay, that incestuous, that adulterate beast,
With witchcraft of his wit, with traitorous gifts,
O wicked wit, and gifts that have the power
So to seduce!--won to his shameful lust
The will of my most seeming-virtuous queen" (Lines 42-5, Act I. Scene V)

It is clear that Queen Gertrude influences the male characters in the play mainly her former husband King Hamlet, her son Prince Hamlet and her current husband Claudius. These characters have great devotion to her and much of their actions are motivated by her influence. Much of Hamlet's bizarre behaviour is caused by his mother's incestuous marriage and Claudius' love for Gertrude seems to have been the impetus behind killing his brother .Though we do not see much of King Hamlet's behaviour on stage except for the appearance of his ghost who gives a commandment to Hamlet to avenge the death of his father, the way he tells Hamlet not to harm his mother and leave her punishment to divine justice indicates that the former King had deep devotion to Gertrude.

Though Queen Gertrude seems naive and simple to most readers and audiences, she is in fact witty and has a sharp mind. She might have wittily seduced her brother-in-law and unintentionally motivated him to kill her husband. Although she does not know that Claudius killed her former husband to court her and usurp the throne, she did indeed give a motif to her brother-in-law to murder her husband. Queen Gertrude's hasty remarriage without ever mourning the death of her former husband reveals that she might not have loved King Hamlet. However, when Hamlet tells her about the truth of the murder of his father and the wicked intentions and deeds of her current husband, Queen Gertrude feels ashamed of her actions. Conscience–stricken, Queen Gertrude says to Hamlet:
"O Hamlet, speak no more:
Thou turn'st my very eyes into my soul,
And there I see such black and grained spots
As will not leave their tinct" (Lines 88-91, Act III. Scene IV.)

In the lines quoted above, Queen Gertrude confesses to Hamlet that she has been blind to what she and her husband Claudius have done. Hamlet's

scornful words have made her see her true wicked and sinful nature which she dares not to look at. Deep in her soul she can see her sins referring at once to her incestuous marriage, and betrayal of her former husband. She goes on to say that Hamlet's contemptuous words to her are like daggers entering her ears referring unintentionally to Claudius' pouring the poison into her former husband's ears. She tells Hamlet to speak no more because she can not look back at her wrong and sinful actions. Gertrude says:
"O speak to me no more;
these words like daggers enter my ears;
No more, sweet Hamlet!" (Lines 94-6, Act III. Scene IV.)

Queen Gertrude has the potential for great love for all the people around her. Despite the fact that Hamlet lashes out at her the most disrespectful words, she still loves him and tries to protect him from King Claudius. To find an excuse for her son's bizarre behaviour, she tries to convince King Claudius that her son is indeed mad. Queen Gertrude has great love for Claudius. She is much concerned about his safety and the continuation of his rule of Denmark. She even spies on Hamlet in order to please him.

Horatio acts as a foil to the character of Prince Hamlet. Although his role in the play is minor, his influence on Hamlet is great and his personality is very memorable to readers of Shakespeare's drama. Horatio's role in the play serves two purposes that are very crucial for the development of the play's plot. Shakespeare intended to make Horatio the harbinger of truth. He says nothing wrong and he is devoted and loyal to his friend Hamlet despite his feigned madness and mental distraction. He is the only friend who does not leave Hamlet in moments of grief. He understands Hamlet's thoughts and tolerates his madness. When Hamlet lies dying, Horatio is ready to take his own life and die with his friend. Horatio has seen the ghost of Hamlet's father and despite the fact that Hamlet does not reveal to him what the ghost said to him, Horatio does not hesitate to support Hamlet in fulfilling his mission. Horatio is Hamlet's confidant to who he reveals his inner thoughts and feelings. Throughout the play Hamlet reveals his thoughts and feelings only in his famous soliloquies and in his conversations with his confidant Horatio. Horatio is indeed Hamlet's foil character whose actions mirror and illuminate those of the great mentally disturbed prince. Both Hamlet and Horatio are rational, pensive and philosophical. However, as a foil character Horatio illuminates Hamlet's character either by similarity or by discrepancies. To shed light on Hamlet's unrest, Horatio is presented as a calm scholar. Horatio seems to be more courageous than Hamlet. When

Horatio sees the ghost, he boldly confronts it and demands it speak to him. Horatio bravely asks the ghost if he has a confession to make about the state of Denmark:

"If thou art privy to thy country's fate...
O, speak!
Or if thou hast uphoarded in thy life
Extorted treasure in the womb of earth...
Speak of it, stay and speak!" (Lines 133-9, Act I. Scene I.)

In the lines quoted above, Horatio asks the ghost if it has any prophecy about the future of the state of Denmark or it has appeared to show them that during its life time it hoarded treasure in the earth and has come to unearth it. Having sensed that the ghost is ominous and might be the devil in the disguise of the pleasant shape of Hamlet's father, he warns Hamlet not to follow the ghost because it might be fatal.

Ophelia, the epitome of innocence, virginity and goodness, is not exempted from Hamlet's perception of women as fragile whores. In obedience of her father she spies on Hamlet and rejects his romantic overtures. She silently slips into insanity as a result of grief over the death of her father and the loss of her love. Unable to endure the adversities inflicted upon her, Ophelia crumbles into insanity and finally commits suicide by drowning herself in a brook. Hamlet's rage against his sensuous mother has made Hamlet despise all women and look down upon them as sex objects. His derision of his mother is directed towards poor Ophelia. Realizing that Ophelia is spying on him for her father and King Claudius, Hamlet lashes out at her the most vulgar words. During the performance of the play within the play Hamlet treats her awfully as if she were a whore. In fact, Ophelia's innocence and virginity defies Hamlet's distorted image of women as insensitive sensuous beasts. Despite the fact that Hamlet loves Ophelia and is quite sure that she is innocent and virtuous, he describes her as a prostitute. However, in the cemetery where Ophelia is to be buried, Hamlet declares his deep love for Ophelia. While quarrelling with Laertes on top of Ophelia's grave, Hamlet declares to all the mourners that he loved Ophelia.

Hamlet's perception of Ophelia as a disrespectful woman though deep inside he is sure that she is pure and virtuous reflects his hatred of all women and his distorted image of women as harlots. For Hamlet even those women who seem pure and honest like Ophelia are black from inside. They pretend to be innocent and virtuous while they are all morally degenerate and controlled by nymphomania and sexual desire. Hamlet wants to say that all women are whores even his mother. Like Queen Gertrude, Ophelia is naïve and shallow and both seem obedient to their males. Both Ophelia and Gertrude never take decisions pertaining to their welfare. They let the males think on behalf of them and decide what course of action they must follow. Both are content to be inferior to the males in their families and find pleasure in such blind obedience. Ophelia's death is both tragic and gorgeous at the same time though the priest was about to deny her the rites of a Christian burial on the assumption that she committed suicide. She commits suicide by drowning herself in a brook. She dies of lovesickness and grief over the death of her beloved father. Shortly before she dies Ophelia crumbles into insanity and spends most of her time singing bawdy songs even in front of King Claudius, Queen Gertrude and Laertes. Singing such bawdy songs reveals the fact that corruption and vulgarity have tarnished even the most innocent and most virtuous of all women.

The Tragedy of Hamlet is a revenge play. The structure of the play is similar to the structure of all revenge plays that were very popular during the Elizabethan and Jacobean eras. All revenge tragedies share the same structure and the same characteristics which include: First, a tragic hero is doomed to avenge the death of someone dear to him. The apparition of the victim often appears to urge the tragic hero to take revenge upon his murderer. Second, to fulfill his mission of taking revenge upon the murderer, the hero feigns insanity and in some cases he indeed becomes mad. Third, in pursuit of his goal, the hero commits murder and kills many people. Fourth, the hero takes revenge upon the killer and finally dies violently. Hamlet himself goes through this structure in pursuit of avenging the death of his father. The plot of the revenge play starts with the appearance of the apparition that urges Hamlet to avenge the death of his father "So art thou to revenge, when thou shalt hear" (Do you promise to avenge the death of your father when you hear the story?) and then the ghost orders Hamlet to take revenge upon his uncle Claudius who committed two unnatural crimes: fratricide and incest. The ghost says to Hamlet: "Revenge his foul and most unnatural murder" (25). The ghost's commandment weighs heavily on Hamlet's shoulder and constitutes for him a mission hindered by paralysis and disablement.

After the appearance of the ghost, Hamlet becomes a new man and undergoes drastic changes in his personality. The good and kind scholar transforms into an instrument of evil in the state of Denmark. The ghost, a hallucinatory creature from the supernatural world, represents evil for he is the devil in the disguise of the pleasant shape of King Hamlet. The ghost corrupts Hamlet with his desire for vengeance and his commandment to him to commit murder. When Hamlet says that he is compelled to his revenge by Heaven and Hell, he means that he is not sure whether vengeance is something right or wrong or whether it is a commandment from an angel from Heaven or a commandment from the devil from Hell.

On more than one occasion throughout the course of the play Claudius' crime of fratricide is likened to the story of Cain and Abel. In an aside King Claudius reveals his guilt and confesses that he has committed the worst crimes in the history of the humankind "the primal eldest curse upon't, A brother's murder". King Claudius likens his crime of fratricide to the first murder in the history of humanity when Cain killed his brother Abel and buried the corpse. Conscience-stricken and remorseful King Claudius says:

"O, my offence is rank it smells to heaven;
It hath the primal eldest curse upon't,
A brother's murder"

Claudius' murder of his brother echoes the primordial fratricide; the first crime to be committed in the history of humanity. The crime resulted in the disintegration and degeneration of humanity. Since then greed, lust, crime, brutality, hatred, territorial conflicts, discrimination and many other sins have become part of the human behaviour.

Hamlets' mission to avenge the death of his father is far from being divine, but is rather satanic. To fulfill his mission, he kills three people and causes the death of three others. Hamlet's insanity is less than madness, but more than feigned. Hamlet's behaviour is irrational and bizarre. His mind is distracted and his soul is sick with vengeance. Having learned from the ghost of his father that his uncle Claudius murdered his father to marry the Queen and usurp the throne, Hamlet becomes mentally disturbed and goes through a cycle of solitary confinement and melancholy.

Themes, Motifs & Symbols

The Tragedy of Hamlet is a highly philosophical and thematic play that was intended to shed light on the mysteries of life and the daunting questions and man's existence. In particular, the tragedy tackles the following main themes:

Death the Leveler:

Death is a major theme in the play to the extent that it runs throughout the entire course of the drama. After the ghost had revealed to Hamlet how his uncle Claudius murdered his father by pouring poison into his ears, Hamlet became obsessed with the concept of death and he keeps contemplating it and even thinking seriously of committing suicide. Hamlet philosophically speculates about the spirituality of death and the life after death. For Hamlet death is a form of sleep in which one finds comfort and rest after a long journey in the world of pain and suffering. The apparition of Hamlet's father, a visitant from the underworld, the skull of the former King's jester Yorick and the decayed corpses in the cemetery all acquaint Hamlet with death. Death, the leveler, treats people equally the same regardless of their socioeconomic status, political power, race, faith or colour. Death treats kings and beggars equally the same taking their lives at any moment without prior notification.

While addressing Yorick's skull unearthed by the grave digger, Hamlet reveals all the mysteries of death. He stresses the inevitability of death and the decay of the corpses after death and how they turn into dust; the original substance of their creation "from dust to dust". He urges the skull to go to his mother's chamber to remind her that all those who are alive now will die one day and all that will remain of them is the skull and some bones. Mockingly Hamlet addresses the skull: "get you to my lady's chamber, and tell her, let her paint an inch thick, to this favor she must come" (death is inevitable and inescapable) (Lines 178–179, Act V. Scene I.). Hamlet explains that all people are eaten by worms within days after their death. All kings and emperors have gone through the same experience. Hamlet says that once the human body is discarded in the grave, it is devoured by worms and nothing remains of the body except for the skull and the bones of the hip. Once the human flesh is eaten by worms, the bones are turned into dust; the same substance of man's original creation. Even great emperors like Alexander the Great were transformed into dust and even worse a poor man might have used the dust that remained of the emperor's corpse by mixing it with water to make clay to cover a hole in his house or to cover a hole in a beer barrel.

The Legitimacy of Suicide:

Throughout the course of the play Hamlet contemplates the legitimacy of suicide to put an end to one's pain and suffering in a world that is unbearably painful. In Christianity committing suicide is prohibited and those who take their own lives are not given a respectful Christian burial. On Ophelia's grave, the priest wants to make sure that Ophelia did not commit suicide by drowning herself in the brook so that he can start with the rites of a decent and proper Christian burial. Had the priest found proof that Ophelia did in fact commit suicide, he would not have certainly denied her the rites of a decent Christian burial. On more than one occasion Hamlet has revealed his intention to commit suicide to put an end to his misfortunes and miseries in life. Hamlet also contemplates the idea of committing suicide to put an end to his indecisiveness and inactivity in taking the final decision to fulfill his mission. He finds himself unable to commit murder, but at the same time believes that he must avenge the death of his father so that the spirit of his father can rest in peace in the grave and stop wandering at night seeking vengeance. Hamlet wishes to commit suicide, but as believer in the Christian faith, he can not do this because he knows that if he takes his own life, he will be punished with eternal suffering in Hell. In his well-known soliloquy "To be or not to be" Hamlet seems torn apart between the two choices; to commit suicide or go on living and endure his suffering and pain. Hamlet has to choose one of the two painful alternatives ; to commit suicide to put an end to the dreadful circumstances in which he has found himself entrapped or to go on living and endure the pain of seeing the murderer of his father unavenged and his incestuous mother still enjoying the pleasures of her incestuous marriage. Hamlet believes that no one would wish to endure the suffering of his living if he can put an end to his miseries in life with one stroke of a sharp knife. Hamlet wants to say that many people wish to commit suicide to put an end to their unbearable pain. But what prevents them from taking their own lives is their fear of the punishment awaiting them in Hell for taking this course of action.

The Meaninglessness of Life and Man's Insignificance, Littleness and Nothingness:

The Tragedy of Hamlet highlights the meaninglessness of man's existence in a painful world. During his feigned insanity Hamlet philosophically dwells upon the absurdity of man's life. Hamlet's satirical remarks about man's existence appear in the scene in which he holds Yorick's skull in his hand and contemplates the meaninglessness of man's existence. Hamlet sarcastically comments on the meaninglessness of life and man's insignificance in a gigantic world when compared with the forces of nature namely death and time. Hamlet remarks that after death all people without exception from kings to beggars are reduced to dust; the basic substance of their creation. Hamlet cites an example from history to sarcastically comment on man's insignificance and the meaninglessness of his existence. Hamlet remarks that even Alexander the Great who was once a great emperor died and was turned into dust. The dust that remained of his corpse and bones was later mixed with water by a poor man to make clay to cover a hole in his house.

Political Corruption and the Illegitimacy of King Claudius' Reign

The Tragedy of Hamlet sheds light on the fact that the welfare of the whole state depends on the sound judgment and moral legitimacy of the royal family. Corruption of the entire royal family is responsible for the corruption of the whole sate. Claudius murders his brother King Hamlet to usurp the throne and court his wife. King Claudius fears the civil unrest that usually accompanies the transfer of power from one king to another. Hamlet realizes that the legitimacy of the ruler's reign of the state reflects favourably on the whole state and the welfare of its citizens. All the killings that we see on the stage at the end of the play and the blood of the royal family that is spilled on the stage after the massacre mirror the corruption of the ruler and the illegitimacy of his reign. As a result of the illegitimacy of King Claudius' rule and the crimes he committed, Denmark becomes a rotten state where killing is the norm and stability is the exception. Under the legitimate reign of King Hamlet, the state of Denmark was strong and the citizens used to live in peace and stability. At the end of the play when the righteous Prince Fortinbras usurps the throne without bloodshed and without resistance, power, peace and stability will be restored to the sate of Denmark once again.

Misogyny, Hatred of Women:

Queen Gertrude's hasty incestuous remarriage and her spying on him for the sake of her husband and Ophelia's spying on him for her father and the King make Hamlet detest women in general. Hamlet begins to develop a kind of hatred of all women perceiving them as morally degenerate. Hamlet views women as sexual predators whose behaviour is much controlled by their nymphomania and sexual ecstasy. This motif of misogyny, or hatred of women dominates much of Hamlet's thoughts and he treats his mother and Ophelia accordingly. He accuses his mother of nymphomania when he indirectly tells her that lust is her weakness "Frailty, thy name is woman"(Line 146, Act I. Scene II) and breaks Ophelia's heart when he urges her to go to a nunnery and protect her virginity and chastity. While watching the play within the play Hamlet indirectly accuses Ophelia of being sensuous like his mother when he asks her to put his head in her lap

Memorable Quotations:
1-To be, or not to be: that is the question:
Whether 'tis nobler in the mind to suffer
The slings and arrows of outrageous fortune,
Or to take arms against a sea of troubles,
And by opposing end them? To die: to sleep;
No more; and by a sleep to say we end
The heart-ache and the thousand natural shocks
That flesh is heir to, 'tis a consummation
Devoutly to be wish'd. To die, to sleep;
....
For who would bear the whips and scorns of time,
The oppressor's wrong, the proud man's contumely,
The pangs of despised love, the law's delay,
The insolence of office and the spurns
That patient merit of the unworthy takes,
When he himself might his quietus make
With a bare bodkin? who would fardels bear,
To grunt and sweat under a weary life,
But that the dread of something after death,
The undiscover'd country from whose bourn
No traveller returns, puzzles the will
And makes us rather bear those ills we have
Than fly to others that we know not of?
Thus conscience does make cowards of us all;
And thus the native hue of resolution
Is sicklied o'er with the pale cast of thought,
And enterprises of great pith and moment
With this regard their currents turn awry,
And lose the name of action.--Soft you now!
The fair Ophelia! Nymph, in thy orisons
Be all my sins remember'd.

This is Hamlet's most interesting soliloquy in the play and perhaps the most memorable soliloquy in English literature. In this soliloquy Hamlet logically investigates the legitimacy of committing suicide to put an end to one's suffering in a painful world. The soliloquy starts with Hamlet's famous line "To be, or not to be: that is the question "which roughly means to live or not to live. The soliloquy crowned with the famous line "to be or not to be" has several interpretations in the play. Hamlet wonders:

"Whether 'tis nobler in the mind to suffer
The slings and arrows of outrageous fortune
Or to take arms against a sea of troubles"

Hamlet does not know what course of action to take; to endure suffering passively or to take his own life to put an end to his suffering. Hamlet thinks of committing suicide as the first alternative, but then rules it out remembering that in Christianity it is prohibited and those who commit suicide go to Hell. The phrase also indicates that Hamlet is not determined yet to take revenge upon King Claudius for killing his father or to spare his life and leave his punishment for divine justice. Hamlet also uses the phrase in reference to the ghost of his father. Hamlet is not certain whether the ghost he has seen on the platform of Elsinore castle is the Devil in the disguise of the pleasant shape of his father or the good spirit of his father. In this soliloquy Hamlet appears to be totally distracted for he can not determine what course of action he must follow. He can not decide whether to remain silent and suffer from melancholy and depression or to take action and avenge the death of his father and thus put an end to his worries. Hamlet asks the question whether it is better for him to sleep or die and then he contemplates the difference between the two concepts; sleep and death. Hamlet compares death to sleep since in both man finds comfort and rest. Hamlet believes that man's pains only stop when he sleeps or dies. In both sleep and death man is relieved of the pain of living "The heart-ache and the thousand natural shocks/ That flesh is heir to". Having contemplated both sleep and death Hamlet concludes that suicide is the right course of action "a consummation / Devoutly to be wished". Hamlet yearns to commit suicide to end his suffering, but because he knows that such an act is condemned by his creed, he becomes hesitant to take action. The word devoutly quoted above indicates that Hamlet fears the consequences of committing suicide and the punishment awaiting him in Hell if he opts for such an act.

Hamlet's soliloquy also sheds light on man's fear of the afterlife and what awaits him there. In Christianity it is commonly believed that those who take their lives to put an end to the pain of their living will certainly go to Hell. The soliloquy also stresses the fact that the afterlife is spiritually vague. Hamlet believes that what prevents many people from committing suicide to put an end to the pain of their living is their fear of the punishment awaiting them in the afterlife. Hamlet mentions some of man's miseries and worries in life that range from lovesickness to hard labour and political oppression and asks who would prefer to endure these miseries passively when he can end them with a knife "[w]hen he himself might his quietus make / With a bare bodkin (knife)?" Hamlet answers the question saying that fear of the afterlife is what makes people passively endure the pain of living. Hamlet explains that people prefer to submit to the pains of life to experiencing another kind of existence which might be even more miserable. This fear, Hamlet says, makes people cowards when it comes to committing suicide "conscience does make cowards of us all". Hamlet says: "who would fardels bear,
To grunt and sweat under a weary life,
But that the dread of something after death"

2- O that this too too solid flesh would melt,
Thaw, and resolve itself into a dew!
Or that the Everlasting had not fix'd
His canon 'gainst self-slaughter! O God! O God!
How weary, stale, flat, and unprofitable
Seem to me all the uses of this world!
Fie on't! O fie! 'tis an unweeded garden,
That grows to seed; things rank and gross in nature
Possess it merely. That it should come to this!
But two months dead!—nay, not so much, not two:
So excellent a king; that was, to this,
Hyperion to a satyr; so loving to my mother,
That he might not beteem the winds of heaven
Visit her face too roughly. Heaven and earth!
Must I remember? Why, she would hang on him
As if increase of appetite had grown
By what it fed on: and yet, within a month,—
Let me not think on't,—Frailty, thy name is woman!—
A little month; or ere those shoes were old

With which she followed my poor father's body
Like Niobe, all tears;—why she, even she,—
O God! a beast that wants discourse of reason,
Would have mourn'd longer,—married with mine uncle,
My father's brother; but no more like my father
Than I to Hercules: within a month;
Ere yet the salt of most unrighteous tears
Had left the flushing in her galled eyes,
She married:— O, most wicked speed, to post
With such dexterity to incestuous sheets!
It is not, nor it cannot come to good;
But break my heart,—for I must hold my tongue (129–158, Act I , Scene II)

Having been requested by King Claudius and Queen Gertrude not to go back to school at Wittenberg and stay in Denmark, Hamlet is enraged and his disgust of his mother's incestuous marriage increases. Hamlet recites this soliloquy to show his resentment of his mother who hastily married his uncle shortly after the death of his beloved father. In the first four lines of this soliloquy Hamlet directly and for the first time reveals his wish to commit suicide. He wishes that his flesh would melt from his bones and turns into dew. Then Hamlet inquires why God has prohibited self-slaughter or suicide and made it a sin.

> "O that this too too solid flesh would melt,
> Thaw, and resolve itself into a dew!
> Or that the Everlasting had not fix'd
> His canon 'gainst self-slaughter! O God! O God!"

Then Hamlet reveals his resentment of the world we live in which now teems with misery, suffering and sins. For Hamlet the world we live in is exhausted, sinful, rotten, and is not worthy of living in. Hamlet shows his resentment and damnation of the world we live by verbally abusing it "Fie on't! O fie!" and by comparing it with an unweeded garden teeming with unwanted grass , thorns and insects.

> "How weary, stale, flat, and unprofitable
> Seem to me all the uses of this world!
> Fie on't! O fie! 'tis an unweeded garden"

Hamlet then reveals the causes of his melancholy and pain specifically his mother's incestuous marriage to Claudius; the very same man who murdered his father and whored his mother with incest. He metaphorically describes how his mother hastily married his uncle shortly after the death of his beloved father saying that her shoes that she wore while going to his father's grave were not worn out before she remarried. Hamlet resents his mother for hastily remarrying after the death of his beloved father and what makes her remarriage worse is that it is incestuous and unnatural. Hamlet says that his mother hastily went to the incestuous bed of her brother-in-law "[w]ith such dexterity to incestuous sheets" .Hamlet then makes a comparison between his father and his uncle resembling his father to Hyperion, a kind and fair king, while resembling his uncle to a satyr, a creature half goat and half human of sensuous behaviour. Hamlet says:

> "So excellent a king; that was, to this,
> Hyperion to a satyr; so loving to my mother,
> That he might not beteem the winds of heaven
> Visit her face too roughly. Heaven and earth!"

Queen Gertrude's nymphomania and incestuous marriage have developed in Hamlet a disgust at all women in general. His hatred of women or misogyny includes all women even those whom he once loved including his mother and Ophelia. His mother's incestuous marriage also made Hamlet form a distorted image of all women whom he perceives as sexual predators and harlots. According to Hamlet, sex is the weakness of all women including his mother and Ophelia. Hamlet says: "Frailty, thy name is woman".

3. "Something is rotten in the state of Denmark"
This famous line is said by Marcellus, a guard on duty at the gate of Elsinore Castle. Having seen the ghost of Hamlet's father and having seen Hamlet follow the ghost into the dark night, Marcellus senses that the ghost is ominous and tells Horatio that it will certainly bring about miseries to Denmark. This line though said by a minor character who rarely appears in the play except at the outset establishes the ominous tone of the play and foreshadows the many killings that will take place in the state of Denmark. The statement also is intended to link between the legitimacy of the rule of the state and the welfare of the state and its citizens. The three crimes committed by King Claudius; fratricide, incest and usurping the throne have transformed the state of Denmark into a rotten state of civil unrest and rebellion.

4. I have of late--but
wherefore I know not--lost all my mirth, forgone all

custom of exercises; and indeed it goes so heavily
with my disposition that this goodly frame, the
earth, seems to me a sterile promontory, this most
excellent canopy, the air, look you, this brave
o'erhanging firmament, this majestical roof fretted
with golden fire, why, it appears no other thing to
me than a foul and pestilent congregation of vapours.
What a piece of work is a man! how noble in reason!
how infinite in faculty! in form and moving how
express and admirable! in action how like an angel!
in apprehension how like a god! the beauty of the
world! the paragon of animals! And yet, to me,
what is this quintessence of dust? man delights not
me: no, nor woman neither, though by your smiling
you seem to say so. (Lines 287–298, Act II, Scene II)

In the lines quoted above, Hamlet addresses his two university fellows
Rosencrantz and Guildenstern whom King Claudius has sent to spy on him
to find out the cause of his insanity. Hamlet reveals to his two university
companions the misery and melancholy he has been afflicted with since the
death of his father. As a learned scholar of philosophical meditations
Hamlet rhetorically glorifies the earth and the human race before he starts
lashing out his accusations at them declaring that humanity is merely
"quintessence of dust". Hamlet rejects the earth, the sun and the air
describing them as "a sterile promontory" and "a foul and pestilent
congregation of vapors". He praises the creation of the human race and
describes man as a noble creature of infinite mental faculties "What a piece
of work is a man! how noble in reason!/ how infinite in faculty!". Humans,
Hamlet goes on to say, have a beautiful physique and they admirably move
fast "in form and moving how express and admirable!", humans' actions are
angelic "in action how like an angel!" and their understanding is godlike "in
apprehension how like a god!". Hamlet further praises the beauty of the
creation of the human race and describes humans as the best of God's
creation and the leader of all animals "the beauty of the world! the paragon
of animals!". All of a sudden Hamlet's thoughts shift drastically when he
says that despite the fact that humans are the most beautiful and the most
intelligent animals, he has no interest in them since they are merely dust "
man delights not me: no, nor woman neither". In fact, Hamlet says that both
men and women do not delight him because they are merely dust.

Part Three
Poetry

Chapter One
What is Poetry?

Homer   **Aristotle**   **Shakespeare**

Poetry is a supreme form of expression used by poets to express thoughts, feelings and intellect through meaning, sound, and rhythmic language and to evoke an emotional response in the reader or listener. It is an ancient imaginative art form which is mostly metrical, but it can also be prose. Poetry, as a mode of expression, can be either written or spoken or both. Poetry is a form of art in which language is used for its aesthetic and evocative qualities in addition to its ostensible meaning. Poetry employs meter and rhyme, but this is by no means necessary. The language of poetry, which is mostly metaphorical and lyrical, is pleasurable as it employs figures of speech, poetic and musical devices. Poetry is a language from that says more and says it more intensely than does ordinary language. Poetry is meant to increase our understanding and awareness of life and the human condition, and to sharpen our perception of nature and existence .In fact; there are as many definitions of poetry as there are poets and it seems very hard to give poetry an absolute definition. For instance, Wordsworth defined poetry as "the spontaneous overflow of powerful feelings".

Poetry is the most compressed art form and leaves little space on the page for the poet to say much. Given little space on the page the poet has to communicate his information to the reader so intensely making use of all the rhetorical and poetic devices he masters. The poet's concern is not only the beauty of his language and philosophical truth, but also the beauty of the poetic devices he uses to convey the poetic experience to his readers. The poet has to say most using few words. As a condensed and concentrated art form, poetry relies on shades of meanings and unexpected connotations of his words. Denotations and connotations are mingled to convey the poetic experience to the reader in a very compressed and concentrated way. This would make poetry seem dull and ambiguous to the incompetent poor reader, but a treasure for the competent reader. Unlike ordinary language which is one dimensional and straightforward in the sense that it addresses one part of the listener- his understanding, poetry which communicates experience is multidimensional since it addresses the listener's mind, heart and soul. Poetry has four dimensions: the intellectual dimension, the sensuous dimension, the emotional dimension and the imagination dimension. It involves the listener's intelligence, his senses, emotions and imagination.

The Elements of Poetry

Chapter Two
How to Read a Poem

Reading a poem is exciting though quite demanding. It needs concentration and attention. The task is a little bit difficult, but is worth doing for better understanding of the poem and literary appreciation. Some poor readers find poetry dull and difficult to understand and are reluctant to exert any effort when reading a poem taking it for granted that they would not be able to understand it. They find poetry ambiguous, and replete with difficult, ambiguous and archaic words. They fail to understand the figurative language of the poem and as a result fail to understand the whole poem. However, once a reader becomes acquainted with the language of poetry and its poetic devices, he will find it easy to understand and appreciate.

The following suggestions can certainly develop poor readers' understanding and literary appreciation of poetry:
1- Read the poem more than once slowly and attentively. The meaning of a poem does not usually become clear to the reader from first reading. In the first reading the reader should concentrate on reading rather than analysis. It will be sufficient at this stage if the reader grasps the general idea of the poem from first reading. In the second reading, the reader should understand the main idea in the poem, grasp all the images, metaphorical and poetic devices used in the poem and abstract the main theme in the poem. The third reading will be necessary for identifying the musical devices in the poem and its metrical form.

2-Use a good dictionary to look up unfamiliar words. This should be done in the second reading of the poem not the first one. Other reference books might be helpful mainly the Bible, and a good book on Greek mythology. The reader can use these secondary reference books when needed since not all poems include references to the Bible or Greek mythology. However, there presence is a must and very much recommended.

3-Keep reciting the poem aloud mainly in the third reading paying close attention to the poem's musical devices, rhyme scheme and rhythm.

4- While reading the poem keep both form and content in mind. Reading the poem affectionately, naturally and sensitively will make the poem express itself. This can be done by paying careful attention to the rhythmical pattern of the poem and stopping precisely on grammatical pauses.

5-You should not distort the natural pronunciation of the words in the poem or the normal syllabification and accentuation of the poetic sentence.

6- Maintain mental alertness while reading the poem looking for figures of speech and any poetic devices.

7- To understand any poem keep asking the following questions:
-Who is the speaker in the poem? Is it the poet or a fictional character? What kind of person is he?
-Who are the poet's audience? Does he address a particular audience? If so, what kind of audience is he addressing?
- What is the occasion of the poem?
-What is the setting in the poem – in time (century, year, historical era, season of the year, and so on)
- What is the setting in the poem – place (country, city, province, region, and so on)
-What is the central purpose of the poem?
-What is the central idea in the poem and what is its theme?
-What is the tone of the poem?
-How is the main structure of the poem developed?
- What are the main events in the story of the poem?
-Paraphrase the poem.
-What kind of imagery is used in the poem?
-What figures of speech does the poet use in the poem?
-What musical devices does the poet use in the poem?
-Identify examples of metaphor, simile, personification, metonymy and any other figures of speech used throughout the poem.
- Explain the symbols in the poem. Is the poem allegorical? If so, explain.
-Are there any examples of allusion in the poem? Explain.
- Point out examples of paradox, overstatement, understatement and irony?
-Point out examples of musical devices mainly assonance, consonance and alliteration
-What is the metrical form of the poem and the number of feet in every line?
-Is there a remarkable rhythmical pattern in the poem? Explain.

-Mark the scansion of the poem.
-What is the rhyme scheme of the poem?
-Write a critical analysis and evaluation of the poem

Paraphrasing a poem:
What does it mean to paraphrase a poem?

Paraphrasing a poem means restating it in different language. A poem written in verse is paraphrased using prose to make it as clear as possible. The paraphrase may be longer or shorter than the original poem, but certainly clearer and easier. The paraphrase should include all the ideas stated in the poem. It also contains illustration of all the figures of speech used in the poem. Figurative language is simplified and reduced to its literal level and implied metaphors are turned into similes.

The Elements of Poetry

Chapter Three
The Victorian Poets

Alfred Tennyson (1809-1892)   **Queen Victoria (1837-1901)**

Victorian Poetry

Victorian Poetry refers to all the poetry written during the reign of Queen Victoria and constitutes the major part of the literature of the Victorian Era. The Victorian Era constitutes a transitional link between the Romantic age and the modern literature that appeared in the twentieth century. Alfred Tennyson was a British poet often viewed as the chief representative of the poetry of the Victorian Age. Victorian Poetry was a remarkable period in the history of English literature and provided a bridge between the Romantic Movement and the Modernist Movement of the twentieth Century.

Victorian Poetry describes and reflects the events and social customs of the British society during the reign of Queen Victoria (1837-1901). Social conformity with the customs and traditions of the British society constituted the main subject matter and central themes of much of the poetry in this era. During the Victorian era new poetic forms and ideals developed such as the sonnet which was used extensively to express the ideals and customs of the

Victorian society. Victorian poets were influenced by their predecessors the Romantic poets mainly Keats, William Blake, Shelley and William Wordsworth. Lord Tennyson succeeded Wordsworth as the Poet Laureate of the Victorian period. In fact, Lord Tennyson was Queen Victoria's favourite poet.

The Eagle
Alfred, Lord Tennyson (1809-1892)

The Eagle

He clasps the crag with crooked hands;
Close to the sun in lonely lands,
Ringed with the azure world, he stands.

The wrinkled sea beneath him crawls;
He watches from his mountain walls,
And like a thunderbolt he falls.

Commentary

In "The Eagle" Alfred, Lord Tennyson describes the eagle with extravagant terms. The poet describes the eagle as a bird of prey and a ferocious predator, a bird with keen vision; a powerful, strong and graceful bird that lives lonely in the mountains. The poet admires the bird because it soars high in the sky. Unlike other predators the eagle, a sea-fishing predator, soars high in the sky and all of a sudden falls down to the land or sea to scoop up its prey. The poet uses many expressions that indicate that the eagle is a symbol of freedom from the bonds of gravity and show how the bird soars high in the sky such as "close to the sun", "Ringed with the azure world" and "The wrinkled sea beneath him crawls". The eagle soars high in the sky close to the sun and he is surrounded by the blue sky and beneath him he can see the sea. The eagle is also a swift and fast bird of prey. While soaring high in the sky he keeps looking down searching for a prey. He uses his keen vision to see the prey no matter where it is on land or under the surface of the sea that crawls beneath him. The poet uses many images to show how swift or fast this predator dives to scoop up his prey from the water or the land. While sitting in his abode he watches all that moves on land or sea "He watches from his mountain walls" and "Like a thunderbolt he falls" to capture his prey whether it is a fish in the sea or a rabbit on land.

In "The Eagle", the poet's description of the eagle as a bird soaring high in the sky in lonely lands is used to show that the eagle is a symbol of freedom. The eagle is customarily associated with freedom for it soars high in the sky without limits. The poet uses many expressions to show that the eagle is a symbol of freedom such as "Ringed with the azure world" and "close to the sun".

Some critics have claimed that the eagle in Alfred, Lord Tennyson's poem "The Eagle" tumbles hopelessly into the sea and eventually dies perhaps of old age and infirmity. Such critics refer to some expressions in the poem in justifying such an interpretation of the poem mainly "And like a thunderbolt he falls". Actually this interpretation is possible. The poet wants to say that even the eagle which is a mighty creature becomes weak and eventually dies. Having reached the peak of his life span, the bird becomes weak and eventually deserts his abode and flies for some time before he finally tumbles into the sea and dies. This symbolizes the destructibility of even the mightiest of creatures. The poet wants us to see the eagle as both a swift predator and a powerful bird that is nonetheless susceptible to defeat by other forces mainly nature, death and humans. On the other hand, the expression "And like a thunderbolt he falls" is used figuratively to show how fast and swift this bird of prey dives into the sea to scoop up his prey then rises up towards the sky once again.

In "The Eagle" the poet uses the two expressions "close to the sun" and "Like a thunderbolt he falls" to make an allusion the Myth of Icarus who after getting too close to the sun, falls to the earth and dies. Although the poet portrays a picture of the eagle as a powerful and majestic bird, he surrounds the bird's abode with the walls of mountains to show the bird's littleness and smallness compared to the huge mountains that surround him. It also shows the frailty of the mightiest of birds and the limitations imposed on them. This resonates man's littleness and insignificance when compared to the huge universe in which he lives. Although the author paints a portrait of the eagle as majestic and strong, standing high above "the azure world", he makes an allusion to the myth of Icarus, who after getting too close to the sun, falls to the earth and dies.

The Eagle

Test your understanding of the poem:

1. In his poem "The Eagle" which of the following expressions does Alfred, Lord Tennyson use to show that the bird soars high in the sky?
   A) "Close to the sun"
   B) "Ringed with the azure world"
   C) "The wrinkled sea beneath him crawls"
   D) (A, B&C)

2. In "The Eagle" which expression does Alfred, Lord Tennyson use to show how swift or fast the eagle as a bird of prey dives to scoop up his prey from the water?
   A) "He watches from his mountain walls"
   B) "He clasps the crag with crooked hands"
   C) "The wrinkled sea beneath him crawls"
   D) "And like a thunderbolt he falls"

3. Which phrases in "The Eagle" show that the eagle is a symbol of freedom?
   A) "Ringed with the azure world"
   B) "Close to the sun"
   C) (A&B)
   D) "And like a thunderbolt he falls"

4. Some critics have claimed that the eagle in Alfred, Lord Tennyson's poem "The Eagle" tumbles hopelessly into the sea and eventually dies perhaps of old age. What expression in the poem do such critics refer to in justifying such an interpretation of the poem?
   A) "He clasps the crag with crooked hands"
   B) "He watches from his mountain walls"
   C) "And like a thunderbolt he falls"
   D) (A& B)

5. In "The Eagle" Alfred, Lord Tennyson uses the two expressions "close to the sun" and "Like a thunderbolt he falls" to make an allusion to.........
   A) The Myth of Icarus who after getting too close to the sun, falls to the earth and dies

B) The Myth of Prince Narcissus who drowned in the lake while contemplating the reflection of his exceptional manly beauty in the water

C) The Myth of Cupid

D) The Myth of Venus

6. Although the poet portrays a picture of the eagle as a powerful and majestic bird, he surrounds the bird's abode with the walls of mountains to show ....

A) The destructibility of even the mightiest of creatures

B) The frailty of the mightiest of creatures and the limitations imposed on them

C) The bird's littleness and smallness compared to the huge mountains that surround him resonates man's littleness and insignificance when compared to the huge universe in which he lives.

D) (A, B&C)

7. In "The Eagle" Alfred, Lord Tennyson describes the eagle as..........

A) A bird of prey and a ferocious predator

B) A bird with keen vision

C) A powerful, strong and graceful bird that lives lonely in the mountains

D) (A,B&C)

8. In "The Eagle", the poet's description of the eagle as a bird soaring high in the sky in lonely lands is used to show that the eagle is a symbol of ....

A) Freedom

B) Limitations and imprisonment

C) Frailty and infirmity in old age

D) Destructibility of mighty creatures

8- In "The Eagle" the poet describes the eagle as a strong predator. He says, "He clasps the crag with crooked hands". What kind of imagery does the poet use in the aforementioned line?

A) Tactile imagery

B) Auditory imagery

C) Organic imagery
D) Olfactory imagery

9- What figure of speech does the poet use in "The Eagle" in the line which reads "Ringed with the azure world"?
A) Understatement
B) Overstatement
C) Personification
D) Apostrophe

10- In "The Eagle" what figure of speech does Alfred, Lord Tennyson use when he describes the eagle as a bird of prey that soars high in the sky in the line "Close to the sun in lonely lands"
A) Understatement
B) Paradox
C) Overstatement
D) Synecdoche

The Elements of Poetry

Chapter Four
Denotation and Connotation

A word consists of three components: sound, denotation and connotations. **Denotation** is the basic meaning or dictionary meaning or meanings of a word. **Connotation** is what a word suggests beyond its denotative meaning. Connotations of a word are its shades of meanings and overtones of meaning. In addition to its denotative meaning a word might have shades of meanings that might be or might not be related to its basic meaning. Words acquire connotations by their past history and the circumstances in which they were used. Connotative meanings are quite essential in poetry for they enrich the poet's language and make it metaphorically pleasurable. Connotations also help the poet compress his poem, thus say much in very few words. Compression which is achieved mainly through connotations and figurative language makes reading poetry a pleasurable activity.

Good poetry not only makes use of denotations, but it also utilizes multiple denotations. A word might have more than one denotative meaning, but rather several denotations and connotations. For instance, the word spring has several denotations. The noun spring means a season of the year, a natural source of water, or a coiled elastic wire. As a verb the word spring means to leap. Apart from these denotations, the word might also have several connotations. Poets use multidimensional vocabulary in which they use the dimensions of connotation to coat the dimensions of denotations. This multidimensionality of poetic vocabulary is considered as a generous resource for the poet, but a resource of difficulty to readers of poetry especially beginners. Therefore, readers of poetry should develop a sense for understanding connotations. This can be achieved through the frequent use of a dictionary and the extensive reading of poetry.

There Is No Frigate Like A Book

Emily Dickinson

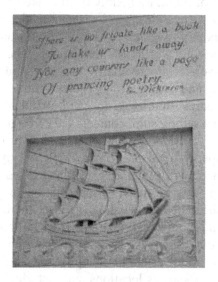

There is no frigate like a book
To take us lands away,
Nor any coursers like a page
Of prancing poetry.
This traverse may the poorest take
Without oppress of toll;
How frugal is the chariot
That bears a human soul!

Critical Analysis:
In "There is no Frigate Like a Book" Emily Dickinson celebrates the power of books mainly literature books in carrying us away to exotic ancient and modern lands. Books of literature mainly poetry take our souls to wonderful adventurous lands, ancient cities, virgin islands and rough and calm seas. Through reading poetry we can escape from our immediate dull surroundings into fanciful worlds of imagination where we feel free and unbound by earthly worries. Poetry elates us to the status of angels who live happily in Heaven and who do not have any worries. The poet metaphorically compares the book to various means of transportation mainly a frigate- a fast sailing ship, coursers – a carriage driven by a team of swift horses, and a chariot- a two- horse drawn carriage. The poet metaphorically compares a poem from a book of joyful love poetry to a swift horse that runs swiftly and elegantly and takes its rider to fanciful fairy lands. Although this means of transportation or poetry so to speak takes travelers to different exotic lands, it costs them nothing. Even the poorest of all men and women can take this traverse free of charge without having to worry about travel expenses "without oppress of toll". While sitting in one's study room drinking a cup of tea, the reader of poetry is metaphorically taken to various locations and historical eras thus travelling through time and space without any constraints. The poem ends with stressing the fact that poetry is a very economical means of transportation and it not only bears the traveller's body, but it bears his soul as well taking them both to ancient and modern lands.

In this poem Dickinson has paid much attention to her diction or choice of words. All the means of transportation mentioned in the poem such as the frigate, the coursers and the chariot are grandiose terms and have romantic connotations. Thus, she used the word "frigate" instead of the word ship, the word "coursers" instead of a team of swift horses and the word "chariot" instead of a carriage drawn by two horses. Unlike the word ship, a frigate suggests exploration and adventure, the word "coursers" suggests beauty, spirit and speed, and the word "chariot" reflects a sense of speed as this vehicle can travel both on land and in the air. If we replace these romantic connotative words with the ordinary words steamship for frigate, horses for coursers and streetcar for chariot, the poem would appear dull and would certainly lose its poetic effect. In fact, Dickinson's words in the poem are all poetic and metaphorical. She uses the word "frugal" instead of the word cheap, the word "lands" instead of miles and "prancing" to mean dance and leap joyfully and gaily.

The poem highlights the excitement and joy one gets from reading books mainly literature books and in particular poetry. The poet says that there is no means of transportation, either ancient or modern, that can take the human soul into fanciful worlds like poetry. Unlike other means of transportations which cost a lot of money, travelling through books of poetry is cheap and costs nothing. The poet implies that reading is a gift that one should treasure most than any wealth.

The theme that can be abstracted from this poem is that fantasy and imagination one finds when reading poetry or any other work of literature are much better than any real trip to the same place because in fantasy and imagination everything is probable. Through literature and in particular through poetry the reader can travel ages back in time, and ages ahead in the future and thus can see exotic and adventurous lands that he would never have the same opportunity to see in real life due to the limitations of space and time in real life compared to imagination.

There Is No Frigate Like a Book

Test your understanding:

1- In "There is no Frigate Like a Book" Emily Dickinson................

    A) Celebrates the power of books mainly literature books in carrying us away to exotic ancient and modern lands

    B) Praises several means of transportation mainly the frigate, the coursers and the chariot

    C) Highlights the power of imagination

    D) (B&C)

2- The expression "without oppress of toll" means............

    A) Reading poetry , which is metaphorically compared to various means of transportation, is inexpensive and costs nothing

    B) Reading poetry is expensive

    C) The poor can not read poetry

    D) The poor can ride chariots and the coursers because they are cheap

3- The word "prancing" means ....

    A) Joyful

    B) Sad

    C) Boring

    D) Gloomy

4- The word "frugal" means ....

    A) Expensive

    B) Cheap and economical

    C) Interesting

    D) Pessimistic

The Elements of Poetry

Chapter Five

Figurative Language

Metaphor and Simile,
Personification and Apostrophe
Metonymy and Synecdoche

Figurative language is poetic language that employs figures of speech such as metaphor, simile or any other figure of speech. Figurative language is not to be taken literally but should be understood figuratively in the context of the poem. **A figure of Speech** is any way of saying something other than the ordinary way. It is a way of saying one thing and meaning another. Through figures of speech the poet can say less or more than what he means, he can say the opposite of what he means, and he can say something other than what he means.

What makes a figurative statement more expressive and more effective than a direct ordinary statement is the fact that apart from its denotative meaning or multiple denotative meanings, a figurative statement is loaded with many connotative meanings. Why is a figurative statement more expressive and more effective than a direct ordinary statement?

First, a figurative statement is quite pleasurable and aesthetic as it provides us with imaginative pleasure. The reader's mind finds delight in comparisons between things that are essentially different and distinct. Second, a figurative statement is highly metaphorical and is replete with imagery, thus through imagery it is made more concrete and more sensuous than an ordinary concrete statement. Third, a figurative statement shows the speaker's attitudes and is more emotionally intense than an ordinary statement which is only informative and void of any emotions. Fourth, a figurative statement is highly compressed and concentrated. It says much in very few words. For instance, in *Macbeth* Shakespeare compares life to a brief candle when he says "out, out. Life is a brief candle". To Shakespeare, both life and the candle are quite very similar in that both begin and end in darkness. While the candle is burning, it gives off light, then it gradually consumes itself, becomes shorter and shorter. Like the candle which can be snuffed out at any moment, life may end at any moment through fate or accident. Life is very short just like the candle which burns only for a short period of time. Macbeth's metaphorical description of life as a brief candle is highly poetic and very compressed. In a very short statement Macbeth said many truths about human life. Literal language would fail to express such philosophical truths in very few words. Macbeth's soliloquy is highly poetic, extremely metaphorical, connotative and above all bears emotional intensity.

Figurative language is perplexing to the incompetent reader who does not have enough literary knowledge to interpret and understand figures of speech. This not only leads to lack of literary appreciation, but also to misinterpretation of such figurative language. However, once the reader becomes acquainted with figurative language, his understanding and literary appreciation of poetry will develop. Figures of speech are interlinked and sometimes they blend into each other to the extent that it becomes very difficult to identify and classify a certain figure of speech. Sometimes a certain figure of speech can be a symbol or a metaphor, or an allegory, understatement, or irony, or even a paradox. The choice largely depends on the context of the poem and the reader's literary appreciation.

Metaphor is a figure of speech in which an implicit comparison is made between two things essentially unlike. There are four forms of metaphor. (1) A metaphor in which the literal term and the figurative term are named; (2) A metaphor in which the literal term is named and the figurative term is implied; (3) A metaphor in which the literal term is implied and the figurative term is named; (4) A metaphor in which both the literal term and the figurative term are implied. For instance, in the lines quoted below from Macbeth's soliloquy, Macbeth metaphorically compares life with a brief candle that gives light for a short period of time before the light finally vanishes and is snuffed out. Then, he metaphorically compares life with a walking shadow and man is merely a player performing his role on the stage of a theatre. Finally, he metaphorically resembles life to a tale told by an idiot.

Out, out, brief candle!
Life's but a walking shadow, a poor player,
That struts and frets his hour upon the stage,
And then is heard no more, it is a tale
Told by an idiot, full of sound and fury
Signifying nothing (Act V , Scene V, lines 20 – 26)

Simile is a figure of speech in which an explicit comparison is made between two things essentially unlike. The comparison is made explicit by the use of some word or phrase as *like, as, than, similar to, resembles,* or *seems.* For instance, in "There Is No Frigate Like A Book" Emily Dickinson uses a simile when she compares a book of literature to a sailing ship.

Personification is a figure of speech in which human attributes are given to an animal, an object, or a concept. For instance, in "Mirror" Sylvia Plath personifies the mirror by giving it human attributes to empower it to speak for itself. The mirror addresses women of fading beauty worldwide telling them that, it is not cruel, but is merely faithful. It tells them the truth and nothing else but the truth unaffected by feelings of love or hatred. The mirror says:

"I am silver and exact. I have no preconceptions.
Whatever I see, I swallow immediately.
Just as it is, unmisted by love or dislike
I am not cruel, only truthful"

Apostrophe is a figure of speech in which someone absent or dead or something nonhuman is addressed as if it were alive and present and could reply. For instance, the whole poem "Death, Be Not Proud" is an apostrophe in which John Donne rhetorically mocks and rebukes mighty death. Death is something abstract, but is given human attributes. The poet addresses death as an embodiment of fake pride:
"Death be not proud, though some have called thee
  Mighty and dreadful, for, thou art not so"

Synecdoche is a figure of speech in which a part is used for the whole. Whereas, **metonymy** is a figure of speech in which some significant aspect or detail of an experience is used to represent the whole experience. Metonymy (the use of something closely related for the thing actually meant) is to be distinguished from synecdoche (the use of the part for the whole). In "Out, Out" Robert Frost uses metonymy when he describes how the injured boy who cut his hand with the electric saw is holding his cut hand "as if to keep the life from spilling". Instead of using the phrase to keep the blood from spilling, the poet uses the word life in replace of the word blood. Like many figures of speech metonymies and synecdoches are even used in ordinary speech. For instance, the expression "redhead" is a metonymy used for a person with red hair, "hands" constitute a synecdoche for manual workers, and "tongue" is used to refer to language. Synecdoche and metonymy are very much alike that sometimes it is very difficult to recognize which is which. Some literary critics even use metonymy for both figures of speech.

The Elements of Poetry

Chapter Six
Figurative Language: Symbol and Allegory

Symbol can be defined as something that means more than what it is. Besides its literal meaning, an object has a figurative or symbolical meaning. Thus, a symbol is a figure of speech which may be read both literally and figuratively. The literal meaning in Robert Frost's poem "the Road Not Taken" is that of a man walking in the woods and passes through a fork of two roads. The walker has to make a choice which road he must explore and he knows that if he explores one road, he will not be able to explore the other. Despite this fact, he convinces himself that he will explore the road not taken later in life. By the time we reach the last stanza, we realize that the poem is not only concerned with the choice between merely two roads in the wood, for such a choice is insignificant when taken literally. Figuratively, the two roads symbolize the choice between any two alternatives in life especially when the choice made makes a big difference later in life. The choice not taken will be remembered with a sigh, remorse and regret. Therefore, the fork of the two roads in the wood symbolize any choice in life between two alternatives which are equally attractive but will result through the years in a big difference in the experience one passes through.

Symbol is the most difficult figure of speech to understand and interpret because it might represent a variety of meanings. The two roads in Robert Frost's "The Road Not Taken" symbolize the choice between two alternatives that are equally attractive. It can stand for any choice in life; a choice of profession, a choice of residence, a choice of spouse or any kind of choice in life. Robert Frost wants to say that possibilities and choices in one's life are many, but one can not experience them all due to the limitations of time and place. The speaker in the poem would have liked to explore both roads, but could explore only one, and thus leaves the other unexplored. Later in life, he regrets not having explored the other road which might have been better than the one he has taken. The poem highlights man's position between free will and determinism.

Allegory:

Allegory is a narrative or description having a second meaning beneath the surface one. Although the surface description or narrative is applicable and has its own interest, the poet's main interest is in the second or hidden meaning. Allegory is applicable to all genres of literature: poetry, fiction and drama. Allegory is often used to disguise the meaning of a poem from certain people and reveal it to others. The story of the Pharaoh's dream as narrated in the Bible is a good example of allegory. The Pharaoh has a dream in which seven fat kine (cows) are devoured by seven lean kine, the story does not become significant until Prophet Josef interprets the allegorical meaning of the dream for the Pharaoh: that Egypt is to witness seven years of wealth and good harvest followed by seven years of famine and misfortune.

The Difference between Allegory, Extended Metaphor and symbolism:

Allegory is sometimes mistakenly equated with extended metaphor and a series of related symbols. It is different from both figures of speech. Allegory is distinguishable from an extended metaphor which is sustained through a number of lines in a poem or through the whole poem. Unlike an extended metaphor which comprises only one comparison, allegory includes a set of related comparisons. Allegory is also to be distinguished from symbolism in the sense that it lays less emphasis than symbolism on images for their own sake and sheds more light on the hidden meaning in a poem.

"The Road Not Taken"
Robert Frost

Two roads diverged in a yellow wood
And sorry I could not travel both
And be one traveler, long I stood
And looked down one as far as I could
To where it bent in the undergrowth;

Then took the other, as just as fair
And having perhaps the better claim,
Because it was grassy and wanted wear;
Though as for that, the passing there
Had worn them really about the same,

And both that morning equally lay
In leaves no step had trodden black.
Oh, I kept the first for another day!
Yet knowing how way leads on to way,
I doubted if I should ever come back.

I shall be telling this with a sigh
Somewhere ages and ages hence:
Two roads diverged in a wood and I--
I took the one less traveled by,
And that has made all the difference.

Summary

The poem draws a pictorial landscape of a walker in the woods who reaches a crossroad where the two roads look exactly the same. He contemplates the two roads one after the other before he finally makes the choice to travel through one of them. For the walker the two roads in the wood were equally the same. Both roads were virgin and untrodden by any passers by. The persona prefers to travel through one road and convinces himself that he will come back to the fork of the two roads later and travel through the road not taken. He knew that it was impossible for him to travel through both roads and he had to make his choice. The speaker chooses one and convinces himself that he will take the other another day. But, he seems to be ignorant of the fact that having taken one road entailed that he would not be able to travel through the other. He confesses that in the future he might regret not having taken the other road. Later in his life, when he has become an old man, he would regret not having taken the other road for he is still eager to know what he might have seen on the road not taken.

Commentary

It is apparent that the fork in the two roads is symbolical of man's position between fate and free will. It also represents the decision everyone makes in times of crises and perplexing situations that require taking a decision and making a choice or preference. Identical forks, in particular, symbolize for us the nexus of free will and fate: people have the free will to choose what to do, but they are never sure whether they have made the right choice or not. Years later, their choice might be evaluated and the person will realize whether he made the right or wrong decision. When people get old and look back at what they did in their, youth and manhood, they reflect on their experiences on life and contemplate the decisions they have made. They will come to realize that some of the decisions they have made were right, while others were wrong and led to serious consequences. This kind of realization is ironical and in some cases pathetic. Regret and remorse seem to be the central theme of the poem. When old, people look back in anger at some of their past experiences and the mistakes they have committed in their youth and they even fail to find a justification why they committed such serious mistakes and why they have taken such wrong decisions.

The Road Not Taken

Test your understanding:

1-The two roads in Robert Frost's "The Road Not Taken" symbolize.........
   A) The choice between two alternatives that are equally attractive.
   B) The choice between any two alternatives in life especially when the choice made makes a big difference later in life such as a choice of profession, a choice of residence, a choice of spouse or any kind of choice in life.
   C) The choice between life and death
   D) D.(A&B)

2-The persona in Robert Frost's "The Road Not Taken" would have liked to explore both roads, but could explore only one, and thus left the other unexplored. Later in life, he regrets not having explored the other road which might have been better than the one he has taken. The poem highlights...................
   A) Man's position between free will and determinism or fate
   B) Man's dissatisfaction with what he owns
   C) Man's inability to explore all possibilities and choices due to the limitations of time , space and potential abilities
   D) (A,B&C)

3- Robert Frost's "The Road Not Taken" draws a pictorial landscape of a walker in the woods who reaches a crossroad where the two roads look exactly the same. He contemplates the two roads one after the other before he finally makes the choice to travel through one of them. What kind of imagery does the poet use to convey this experience to the reader?
   A) Auditory imagery
   B) Tactile imagery
   C) Gustatory imagery
   D) Visual imagery

The Elements of Poetry

Chapter Seven
Figurative Language: Imagery

Unlike ordinary language, poetic language is sensuous, metaphorical and figurative. It is a language replete with figures of speech and sense impressions. What distinguishes ordinary language from poetic language is that while the former is straight forward and denotative, the latter is metaphorical, connotative and is full of imagery of all types. Imagery is one of the most important elements of poetry that the poet uses to evoke vivid experience in the reader or listener. **Imagery** is the personification of some experience through language. Through imagery the poet not only conveys emotions, desires, wishes, and thoughts, but also creates mental reproduction of sensations in the readers' mind.

Types of Images in Poetry

Poets generally use the following types of imagery:

1- Visual imagery: (Associated with seeing)
Images or poetic mental pictures seen in the mind's eye. The reader of poetry can discern such visual images through seeing or forming an imaginary mental picture of the poetic experience. Most images in poetry belong to this kind of imagery for it occurs most frequently and heavily in most poetry. For instance, Tennyson's poem "The Eagle" is replete with visual images. The reader who reads the poem can see for himself all the visual images that the poet depicts. While reading the poem he can draw a mental picture of all the images of the poem .He will form a mental image of an eagle clasping the rock "He clasps the crag with crooked hands", the visual image of a bird soaring high in the sky "Close to the sun in lonely lands", a visual image of the eagle surrounded by the blue sky in lonely lands "Ringed with the azure world", and finally an image of the eagle flying above the sea while attempting to scoop up its prey from the water "The wrinkled sea beneath him crawls"

Robert Frost's "After Apple Picking" is also replete with visual images. The poem starts with a pictorial landscape in which the reader can draw mental images of the apple tree with the ladder sticking through it toward heaven. The barrel that was half-filled with apples and the old man crouching on the grass. The poet says "My long two-pointed ladder's sticking through a tree toward heaven still. And there's a barrel that I didn't fill"

2- **Auditory imagery:** (Associated with hearing)

An image that represents a sound that can be heard. For instance, in "After Apple Picking" Robert Frost conveys so vividly the old farmer's experience of apple picking. The poem is replete with auditory imagery. While in a trance, the old farmer hears the sound of loading and unloading of apples in the cellar. He exclaims; "The rumbling sound of load on load of apples coming in".

3- **Olfactory imagery:** (Associated with smelling)

An image that represents a smell that can be sniffed or smelt. There are many examples of olfactory imagery in "After Apple Picking". While in his sleep-wake condition the old farmer smells the scent of apples and the cider or apple drink. The old man says, "The scent of apples: I am drowsing off"

4- **Gustatory imagery:** (Associated with tasting)

An image that represents a taste of something. Gustatory or tasting images can be found throughout Robert Frost's "After Apple Picking". For instance, the taste of apple and the taste of the cider or apple drink.

5- **Tactile imagery:** (Associated with touching)

An image that represents touching such as hardness, softness, wetness, or heat or cold. Tactile images can be found in Tennyson's poem "The Eagle" "He clasps the crag with crooked hands". In this tactile imagery, the eagle clasps the hard rock which is a fragment of the mountain with his strong claws. Tactile images are also plentiful in "After Apple Picking". In his visionary dream, the old farmer sees thousands of apples and starts touching them to classify them into spiked or bruised apples. He says, "There were ten thousand thousand fruit to touch, Cherish in hand, lift down, and not let fall, for all that struck the earth, no matter if not bruised, or spiked with stubble, went surely to the cider-apple heap as of no worth"

6- **Organic imagery**: (Associated with internal sensation)

An image that represents an internal organic sensation such as hunger, thirst, fatigue, or nausea.

An example of organic imagery can be found in Sylvia Plath's poem "Mirror" in which she compares the mirror to a monster that swallows all that it sees. The mirror says, "I am silver and exact. I have no preconceptions. Whatever I see, I swallow immediately. Just as it is, unmisted by love or dislike". Another example of organic imagery is found in Robert Frost's "After Apple Picking". Having worked all the day picking the apples, the old farmer becomes exhausted and fed up with apple picking. He says, "For I have had too much of apple-picking; I am overtired of the great harvest I myself desired".

7- Kinesthetic imagery: (Associated with movement or tension in the muscles or joints)

A kinesthetic image is an image that represents movement of people, animals and objects through poetic imagery. The falling of the eagle from its mountain abode like a thunderbolt into the sea in Tennyson's "The Eagle", the old farmer picking the apples in the orchard and filling them in the barrel in Robert Frost's poem "After Apple Picking", the woman bending over the lake to see her reflection in Sylvia Plath's poem "Mirror" are all examples of kinesthetic imagery because they all involve a kind of movement.

After Apple Picking
Robert Frost

My long two-pointed ladder's sticking through a tree
Toward heaven still.
And there's a barrel that I didn't fill
Beside it, and there may be two or three
Apples I didn't pick upon some bough.
But I am done with apple-picking now.
Essence of winter sleep is on the night,
The scent of apples; I am drowsing off.
I cannot shake the shimmer from my sight
I got from looking through a pane of glass
I skimmed this morning from the water-trough,
And held against the world of hoary grass.
It melted, and I let it fall and break.
But I was well
Upon my way to sleep before it fell,

And I could tell
What form my dreaming was about to take.
Magnified apples appear and reappear,
Stem end and blossom end,
And every fleck of russet showing clear.
My instep arch not only keeps the ache,
It keeps the pressure of a ladder-round.
And I keep hearing from the cellar-bin
That rumbling sound
Of load on load of apples coming in.
For I have had too much
Of apple-picking; I am overtired
Of the great harvest I myself desired.
There were ten thousand thousand fruit to touch,
Cherish in hand, lift down, and not let fall,
For all
That struck the earth,
No matter if not bruised, or spiked with stubble,
Went surely to the cider-apple heap
As of no worth.
One can see what will trouble
This sleep of mine, whatever sleep it is.
Were he not gone,
The woodchuck could say whether it's like his
Long sleep, as I describe its coming on,
Or just some human sleep.

Summary

The poem tells the story of an old farmer who experiences a very strange feeling shortly before he dies. The aging man has been planting and picking apples in his orchard for so many years; maybe since he was a small kid. Today, like all the other days of his long life, he has been picking apples from the early morning till the evening. By the end of the day, the old man becomes completely exhausted and fed up with the routine work of apple picking and sits down under the apple tree to have a short rest. During this short rest he feels drowsy and falls into a trance; a strange state between sleep and awakening. The old man is neither awake nor asleep. He is even not sure whether it is an ordinary human sleep for a short time or an everlasting sleep or death.

Commentary

The poem starts with depicting a rural landscape in which we see an apple tree and a ladder sticking through it with nobody standing on the ladder. Beside the apple tree and the ladder we see a barrel half-filled with apples. Close to this scene we see a motionless old farmer crouching on the grass. Then the poet takes us directly from this rural landscape into the mind of the old farmer to trace his stream of consciousness and the way he feels towards life and death.

In "After Apple Picking" Robert Frost uses many symbols and images of all types to convey his message to his readers. The first two lines of the poem portray a ladder sticking through the apple tree and heading toward heaven. The apple tree is symbolical of the Garden of Eden and the ladder represents man's life which the poet describes merely as a path to heaven and eternal life. The ladder sticking through the apple tree could also symbolize the different stages of man's life: childhood, manhood and old age with death being the end of this long cycle. The barrel that the old farmer did not fill with apples and the three apples that he did not mange to pick up from the tree and remained on the bough of the tree could possibly represent the man's unfulfilled dreams, desires, and ambitions which he could not achieve while he was still alive. The three apples might also symbolize the missed life experiences which we all regret not living.

The old farmer seems very exhausted after along day of apple picking and is fed up with the drudgery and routine of daily living. Apple picking should not be taken literally, but should rather be read figuratively. Apple picking is symbolical of life itself and what comes after life is death and heaven. The old farmer firmly believes that he has been a pious person who nearly did all his duties in life those for God and people.

The poem is not merely about apple picking, but rather about what comes after apple picking which is everlasting sleep or death. This interpretation justifies the poem's title "After Apple Picking". The old farmer is fed up with life and yearns for death and the eternal life after death. He yearns to see the Garden of Eden of eternal happiness and everlasting carefree life. The image of the ladder sticking through the apple tree toward heaven represents the old man's willingness to die and go to heaven. Having got tired of life and life's troubles and cares, the old man expresses his desire to die and rest in peace. He says "I am done with apple picking". Then he expresses his desire to sleep, but we are not sure whether he desires the normal human sleep or death. While the old man is reflecting back on his life, he smells the scent of apples and consequently becomes drowsy and falls in a slumber. At this moment of strangeness, he sways between sleep and awakening, between life and death. Entrapped in a wake- sleep condition, the old man has a dream. In that dream he sees many apples of enormous size rolling and rolling on the grass. He saw the huge apples appear and disappear. Some of those huge apples were ripe, while others were not. The apple picker even knew what kind of dream he would have even before he fell in the trance for he says "And I could tell what form my dreaming was about to take".

While in the trance, the aging man sees the ladder sticking through the apple tree sway and the boughs of the tree bend. He also hears the sound of the loading and unloading of apple boxes in the cellar. Although the old man is entrapped in a wake- sleep condition, his senses are still quite vivid for he can see the apple tree and the ladder sticking through it; he can see the barrel that was half-filled with apples; he can smell the scent of apple and winter; and he can hear the sound of the loading and unloading of the apples in the cellar. He even touches some of the apples for he says "There were ten thousand thousand fruit to touch- cherish in hand, lift down, and not let fall". He even could tell which apples were bruised or spiked and which were not. He tells us that all apples whether bruised, spiked or not were all gathered on a heap to be made into cider or apple drink.

Throughout the poem the old man frequently and repetitively expresses his exhaustion in life and the tediousness of apple picking and how he has become fed up with apple picking. In line 6 he says "I am done with apple picking now" and in lines 27 and 28 he says "For I have had too much of apple picking" then in the same lines he elaborates "I am overtired". He tells us that he is very tired of apple picking. Although the apple harvest was great and the quality of apples was excellent, he became very tired of picking the apples, loading them and unloading them in the cellar.

The final lines of the poem stress the old man's inability to distinguish between dream and reality; between sleep and awakening; and even between life and death. While in the trance, the old man does not know what kind of sleep he has fallen in. Was it a short normal human sleep or a long sleep similar to that of the woodchuck or marmot which hibernates during winter? Or was he breathing his last breath and will die shortly? The woodchuck or the marmot hibernates underground for a long period of time in winter. This kind of sleep is sepulchral, long-lasting and underground, and is often used in poetry as a metaphor for death.

Having reflected back on his past experiences, the speaker comes to realize how significant some of the experiences he had had and how trivial other experiences were. But at the time of living the experiences, he was ignorant of their significance. Having looked at his past experiences through the pane of glass to magnify them and reflect back on them, he sees through the mistakes he committed in his life and now regrets having made such mistakes. Thus, it is clear that the "russet" parts of the skin or the wrinkles or bruises on the apples" symbolize the man's mistakes in life. The speaker's words "I cannot rub the strangeness from my sight I got from looking through a pane of glass I skimmed this morning from the drinking trough and held against the world of hoary grass" indicate the man's dissatisfaction with old age. When he saw the reflection of his aging and wrinkled face in the drinking trough and realized how old he turned, he became perplexed. He saw that his face was wrinkled and his hair was hoary and grey.

The poem is replete with references to incomplete and unfinished projects "a barrel that I didn't fill.", "two or three apples I didn't pick upon some bough". Although the speaker has done his utmost in picking the apples, he could not pick the apples that were out of his reach. This is indicative of humans' incompleteness and the imperfection of their work no matter how hard they work. Taken literally the melting of the ice in the poem would mean nothing and would not be related to apple picking. But read figuratively, it would go smoothly into the fabric of the poem. The melting of the ice represents how experiences become comprehensible when looked at through the pane of glass or through contemplation and reflection. While people are living certain experiences, they might neither understand them nor realize their significance in their life, but when they reflect back on them, they become clearer and more understandable. Then, they can see what lies below the melting snow. The glasslike sheet of ice which the old man saw in the drinking trough early in the morning represents the transparent glass wall that separates the dreamlike world and the real world. The glassy wall was shattered and the two worlds mingled thus allowing the drowsy old man to live in both. Thus, the melting of ice could also represent the breaking of the boundaries between the world of reality and the world of illusion. Having stepped out of the hallucinatory world of daydreaming, the old man becomes baffled, and could not tell whether his sleep was normal, hibernation or even encroaching death.

"After Apple Picking"

Test your understanding:

1- In "After Apple Picking" Robert Frost starts the poem with depicting a rural landscape in which we see an apple tree and a ladder sticking through it with nobody standing on the ladder. Beside the apple tree and the ladder we see a barrel half-filled with apples. Close to this scene we see a motionless old farmer crouching on the grass. What figure of speech does the poet start his poem with?
A) Visual imagery
B) Understatement
C) Personification
D) Verbal irony

2- While the old farmer in Robert Frost's "After Apple Picking" is entrapped in a wake-sleep trance he hears the sound of the loading and unloading of the apples in the cellar. He says "And I keep hearing from the cellar-bin that rumbling sound of load on load of apples coming in". What kind of imagery does the poet use here?
A) Kinesthetic imagery
B) Auditory imagery
C) Tactile imagery
D) Olfactory imagery

3- What do the persona's words in Robert Frost's "After Apple Picking" mentioned underneath highlight?
"The woodchuck could say whether it's like his
Long sleep, as I describe its coming on,
Or just some human sleep"
A) The old man's inability to distinguish between dream and reality since he is in a deep trance after a long day of apple picking in the orchard.
B) The old man's inability to distinguish between sleep and awakening; and even between life and death.
C) The old man's ignorance of the kind of sleep he has fallen in. He does not know whether it was a short normal human sleep or a long sleep similar to that of the woodchuck or marmot which hibernates during winter.
D) (A, B&C)

4-"After Apple Picking" is replete with several symbolical references to incomplete and unfinished projects or unfulfilled desires in the old man's life. Such as, ……….
A) "a barrel that I didn't fill."
B) "two or three apples I didn't pick upon some bough"
C) "I am overtired of the great harvest I myself desired"
D) (A&C)

5- In "After Apple picking" , what kind of imagery does Robert Frost use in the line that reads "The scent of apples: I am drowsing off"
A) Olfactory imagery
B) Gustatory imagery
C) Tactile imagery
D) Organic imagery

6- In "After Apple picking", what kind of imagery does Robert Frost use in the line in which the old farmer says that he is tired of and fed up with apple picking. The farmer says, "For I have had too much of apple-picking; I am overtired of the great harvest I myself desired".
A) Olfactory imagery
B) Organic imagery
C) Tactile imagery
D) Gustatory imagery

The Guitarist Tunes Up

Frances Cornford (1886-1960)

With what attentive courtesy he bent
Over his instrument;
Not as a lordly conqueror who could
Command both wire and wood,
But as a man with a loved woman might,
Inquiring with delight
What slight essential things she had to say
Before they started, he and she, to play.

Critical Analysis:

In "The Guitarist Tunes Up" the guitar is personified to be a sexy woman and the guitarist is a man in love. The poet metaphorically compares the way the guitarist plays the guitar with the way a man makes love with a woman. Both processes; playing the guitar and making love are gentle and need careful attention. While playing the guitar, the guitarist pays extraordinary attention to his instrument; to both wire and wood. By personifying the guitar as a coquettish, lusty woman, the poet highlights the mutual love affair that exists between a man and a woman, which is quite similar to the relationship between the musician and his guitar.

The whole poem constitutes one long statement that begins with the word "with" which is also the first word in the poem, and ends with the word "play" which is also the last word in the poem. The guitarist who is a professional musician pays close attention to the instrument he plays. Like a man and a woman making love, the guitarist bends over his guitar with courtesy and attention. The poet says that the way the guitarist bends over his guitar before he plays the instrument is quite different from the way a warrior conquers foreign lands using heavy weaponry, but he is like a gentle lover who gently and tenderly speaks to his mistress before he and she initiate the sexual intercourse.

"The Guitarist Tunes Up"

Test Your Understanding:
1- In "The Guitarist Tunes Up" Frances Cornford ....
   A) Metaphorically compares the guitar to a coquettish sexy woman and the guitarist to a man making love with a woman.
   B) Metaphorically compares the guitar to an old woman and the guitarist to a military commander toughly giving orders to soldiers.
   C) Metaphorically states that both love making and playing music are the same in the sense that they are both gentle processes that need attention and concentration.
   D) (A&C)

2- In "The Guitarist Tunes Up" the poet says that the way the guitarist bends over his guitar before he plays the instrument is ....
   A) Similar to the way a warrior conquers foreign lands using heavy weaponry.
   B) Similar to a gentle lover who gently and tenderly speaks to his mistress before he and she initiate the sexual intercourse.
   C) Similar to love making since before playing the guitar, it must be tuned up and its strings need to be adjusted and in the same way love making needs warming up.
   D) (B&C)

Elements of Poetry
Chapter Eight

Figurative Language
Paradox, Tone
Overstatement and Understatement

Paradox is a statement or situation containing apparently contradictory elements. A **Paradoxical statement** is a figure of speech in which an apparently self-contradictory statement is nevertheless found to be true and does indeed make sense. For example, in "Death, Be Not Proud" John Donne ends the poem with a paradoxical statement "And death shall be no more; death, thou shalt die". Though on the surface the statement seems contradictory, but when one contemplates it, it appears true for there will be no death in Heaven and people will live eternally.

Tone is the writer's or poet's attitude toward his persona, his subject, his audience, or himself; the emotional colouring, or emotional meaning of a poem or a story. For instance, Christopher Marlowe's "The Passionate Shepherd to His Love" which celebrates simple rural life and sensuous love has an optimistic and blissful tone. Whereas, the tone of Shakespeare's *Hamlet* is ominous and gloomy; a tone suitable for foreshadowing the many crimes committed in the play.

Overstatement (Also known as hyperbole) is a figure of speech in which exaggeration is used in the service of truth. For instance, in "The Eagle" Alfred, Lord Tennyson uses an overstatement when he describes the eagle as a bird of prey that soars high in the sky close to the sun in the line "Close to the sun in lonely lands".

Understatement is a figure of speech that consists of saying less than one means, or saying what one means with less force than the occasion warrants. For instance, someone who says that "**Anthony** Quinn was a pretty good actor" is certainly using an understatement to show his admiration of the movie star.

Elements of Poetry

Chapter Nine
Figurative Language: Allusion

"OUT, OUT"
By Robert Frost
(1874-1963)

The buzz saw snarled and rattled in the yard
And made dust and dropped stove-length sticks of wood,
Sweet-scented stuff when the breeze drew across it.
And from there those that lifted eyes could count
Five mountain ranges one behind the other
Under the sunset far into Vermont.
And the saw snarled and rattled, snarled and rattled,
As it ran light, or had to bear a load.
And nothing happened: day was all but done.
Call it a day, I wish they might have said
To please the boy by giving him the half hour
That a boy counts so much when saved from work.
His sister stood beside him in her apron
To tell them "Supper." At the word, the saw,
As if it meant to prove saws know what supper meant,
Leaped out at the boy's hand, or seemed to leap -
He must have given the hand. However it was,
Neither refused the meeting. But the hand!
The boy's first outcry was a rueful laugh,

As he swung toward them holding up the hand
Half in appeal, but half as if to keep
The life from spilling. Then the boy saw all -
Since he was old enough to know, big boy
Doing a man's work, though a child at heart -
He saw all was spoiled. "Don't let him cut my hand off -
The doctor, when he comes. Don't let him, sister!"
So. The hand was gone already.
The doctor put him in the dark of ether.
He lay and puffed his lips out with his breath.
And then - the watcher at his pulse took a fright.
No one believed. They listened to his heart.
Little - less - nothing! - and that ended it.
No more to build on there. And they, since they
Were not the one dead, turned to their affairs.

Summary and Critical Analysis:
In "Out, Out" Robert Frost recounts the shocking and violent death of
a young boy while chopping wood on the family farm. While the boy is
sawing the wood with an electric saw to make sticks of wood for the winter
stove, he accidentally cuts his head with the saw. **Allusion** is a reference,
explicit or implicit, to something in previous literature or history. The title
of the poem is an allusion to a quotation from Shakespeare's *Macbeth*; the
most famous quotation in English literature. Having been informed of his
wife's death, Macbeth says a very shattering and shocking soliloquy in
which he mourns the premature death of his wife and spells out his
perception of life and death. Macbeth's soliloquy reads:

> *Out, out, brief candle!*
> *Life's but a walking shadow, a poor player,*
> *That struts and frets his hour upon the stage,*
> *And then is heard no more, it is a tale*
> *Told by an idiot, full of sound and fury*
> *Signifying nothing (Act V , Scene V, lines 20 – 26)*

Macbeth metaphorically compares life with a brief candle that gives light
for a short period of time before the light finally vanishes and is snuffed out.
Then, he metaphorically likens life to a walking shadow or something

abstract rather than something concrete. He believes that man is merely a player or a performer in a theatre who plays his part on the stage for an hour, then he leaves the stage and then is heard no more. In his soliloquy Macbeth stresses the brevity of man's life and its meaninglessness. For Macbeth life is cruel, uncertain, unpredictable, signifies nothing and it may be accidentally ended at any moment. The soliloquy also reveals man's insignificance, littleness and nothingness in the huge universe. Frost uses allusion to reinforce the emotion in his poem and to help state its main theme. The title of the poem which is an allusion to Macbeth's soliloquy stresses the shortness of the boy's life in Frost's poem "Out, Out". The boy's life is untimely snatched away from him by an electric buzz saw. What makes the boy's death sentimental is the fact that it is premature and untimely. However, the poem lacks any rational justification for the accident and the death of the boy.

"Out, Out" reveals the harsh living conditions of American farmers in the early twentieth century. All family members including women and children worked hard on their farms to make enough money to cope financially. Certainly all the family members in the poem are hard at work and everyone is doing a certain farm task. The boy is in charge of chopping the wood sticks for the winter stove with an electric buzz saw which "snarled and rattled in the yard" in a menacing way. The scent of chopped wood can be smelt from a distance and the dust of the chopped wood covers the yard. The result of the laborious work of the boy who is "Doing a man's work, though a child at heart" is five heaps of sticks of wood piled one after the other.

Although the farm, which is located in the beautiful countryside of Vermont, is a pretty one, the workers on the farm have no time to contemplate the beauty of the place since they are all busy at work. The scenery around the farm is a beautiful and pictorial one, but the farm workers seem to have no time to admire and appreciate the beauty of the scenery around their farm. They are busy working on the farm and seem to have no time to enjoy the beauty of the scenery and vegetation around them. While the boy is chopping the wood into small sticks with the buzz saw, his sister called him to have supper. Having heard his sister calling for him to have a rest for half an hour to have supper, the boy becomes happy to have such a short rest from work and therefore, he momentarily loses control over the buzz saw which cuts his hand within a second. Like a hungry monster, the buzz saw leaped at the boy's hand, and devoured it with its sharp metal teeth. Unaware of the injury, the boy cries at the top of his voice with a loud hilarious laugh. As he is running toward his parents, brothers and sisters holding his chopped blood-stained hand as if to prevent the blood from spilling, he does not even know that his hand has been cut. The boy seems to realize the hard fact that even if he recovers from this accident he will be unable to work once again on the farm to help his family, and will therefore become a burden to them.

When the doctor arrives, the boy appeals to his sister not to let the doctor cut off his hand, *"Don't let him cut my hand off-- The doctor, when he comes. Don't let him, sister!"* (Lines 25 – 26). He seems to be unaware of the fact that his hand has already been cut off by the buzz saw. When the doctor puts the boy on the table to check his heart beat and pulse, he listens to his heart beat .At first, the doctor hears the boy's slow heart beat, then the heart beats gradually become slower and finally the heart stops beating. That is the end of the boy's story. He is dead. The boy seems to have died as a result of the shock he has undergone.

The way the family members reacted to the tragic and sudden death of their son is shocking. They seemed coldhearted and uncaring on first reading. *"And they, since they were not the one dead, turned to their affairs".* (Lines 33 – 34). Being not the one who died, all the family members went back to work as if nothing serious happened. However, this is not the case. The family members felt sad for the tragic and sudden death of their son, mourned his death for sometime, but unable to do anything, they accepted to let life go on. They all know that they could not mourn the lost child forever, for that reason every one went back to work as if nothing happened. The situation described in the poem is not exceptional, but can rather be generalized to all human beings. The end of the poem seems realistic rather than callous for after the death of one family member, the rest must go on living. Life goes on despite the death of a family member.

"OUT, OUT"

Test Your Understanding:

1-Robert Frost's "Out, Out" is ....

    A) A narrative poem in which the poet narrates the story of the premature death of a boy who accidentally cuts his hand with the electric saw while chopping wood for the winter stove in the family farm.

    B) An allusion to Macbeth's soliloquy from Shakespeare's *Macbeth* "*Out, out, brief* candle*!*" in which Macbeth says a very shattering and shocking soliloquy mourning the *premature* death of his wife.

    C) A specimen poem from rural poetry that celebrates the beauty of the countryside and the serenity of the farmers' life there.

    D) (A, B&C)

2- What figure of speech does the poet use in the quotation quoted below?
"The buzz saw snarled and rattled in the yard
 And made dust and dropped stove-length sticks of wood"

    A) Auditory imagery

    B) Organic imagery

    C) Gustatory imagery

    D) Simile

3- In the quotation quoted below, what does the word neither in the last line of the quotation refer to?
   "His sister stood beside him in her apron
   To tell them "Supper." At the word, the saw,
   As if it meant to prove saws know what supper meant, Leaped out at the boy's hand, or seemed to leap
   He must have given the hand. However it was,
   Neither refused the meeting"

    A) The boy's hand

    B) The electric saw

    C) The boy's hand and the electric saw

    D) Supper

4- In "Out, Out" Robert Frost ……………..
   A) Reiterates Macbeth's perception of life in the sense that both believe that life is cruel, uncertain, unpredictable, signifies nothing and it may be accidentally ended at any moment.
   B) Echoes Macbeth's perception of the brevity and meaninglessness of life.
   C) Uses allusion to reinforce the emotion in his poem and to help state its main theme which stresses the shortness of man's life and how it might end accidentally at any moment.
   D) (A, B &C)

5- **Which statement is incorrect in light of reading the last two lines of the poem quoted below?**
   "No more to build on there. And they, since they
   Were not the one dead, turned to their affairs"
   A) The boy was unimportant to the family and his death meant nothing to them.
   B) They all loved the boy, but being not the one who died, all the family members went back to work as if nothing serious happened.
   C) The family members felt sad for the premature death of their son, mourned his death for sometime, but unable to do anything, they accepted to let life go on.
   D) The end of the poem seems realistic rather than callous for after the death of one family member, the rest must go on living. Life goes on despite the death of a family member.

Elements of Poetry

Chapter Ten

Musical Devices

Unlike ordinary language, poetic language is musical. The language of poetry makes greater use of music than prose. Words in poetry do not only convey meanings, but they also have a sound effect on the listener's ears. The words in a poem are coated with musical devices so that they can reinforce the meaning of the entire poem. Good poets use many musical devices to make their poetry musical namely alliteration, assonance and consonance. Good poetry also makes use of other music resources to make their poetry musical. In fact, the poet's music repertoire also includes rhyme scheme, rhythm, rhetorical devices and figures of speech. Poets generally achieve musical quality in their poetry by both the arrangement of the sounds in the poem through the use of musical devices and by the arrangement of accented and unaccented syllables to form the meter and dominant foot in the poem. Musical quality in poetry can also be achieved through the use of repetition or refrain; which means repeating certain words, phrases, lines or even a complete stanza throughout the poem.

Alliteration is the repetition at close intervals of the initial consonant sounds of accented syllables or important words (for example cat- camel, man-moon). Important words and accented syllables beginning with vowels can also alliterate with each other when they all lack the initial consonant sound.

Assonance is the repetition at close intervals of the vowel sounds of accented syllables or important words (for example hat- ran- cat- apple, vein –made).

Consonance is the repetition at close intervals of the final consonant sounds of accented syllables or important words (for example book-back-block-thick)

Rhyme is the repetition of the accented vowel sound and all succeeding sounds in important words (for example old-cold- fold-hold, cat-fat-sat)

Rhyme scheme is any fixed pattern of rhymes characterizing a whole poem or its stanzas.

Masculine Rhyme (Also known as single Rhyme) is a rhyme in which the repeated accented vowel sound is in the final syllable of the words involved (for example dance- starts, scald- recalled)

Feminine Rhyme is a rhyme in which the repeated accented vowel is in either the second or third last syllable of the words involved (for example ceiling-appealing)

Internal Rhyme is a rhyme in which one or both of the rhyming words occur within the same line.

End Rhyme is a rhyme in which rhyming words occur at the ends of consecutive lines.

Approximate Rhymes (Also known as imperfect rhyme, near rhyme, slant rhyme or oblique rhyme) is a term used for words in a rhyming pattern that seem to have some kind of sound correspondence but are not perfect rhymes (for example arrayed-said)

Single Rhyme (Also known as Masculine Rhyme) is a rhyme in which the repeated accented vowel sound is in the final syllable of the words involved (for example dance- starts, scald- recalled)

Double Rhyme is a rhyme in which the repeated vowel is in the second last syllable of the words involved (for example politely-rightly)

Triple Rhyme is a rhyme in which the repeated accented vowel sound is in the third last syllable of the words involved (for example painfully, disdainfully)

Elements of Poetry
Chapter Eleven

The Scansion of Poetry

Rhythm, Meter and Foot

Scanning a poem to identify its dominant meter, its rhyme scheme and its stanzaic form is used to analyze the rhythm of the poem. **Scansion** is the analysis of the metrical pattern or metrical structure of a poem; the process of measuring verse, that is, of marking accented and unaccented syllables, breaking the lines into feet, identifying the metrical pattern of a poem, and identifying significant variations from that metrical structure. **Rhythm** is any wavelike recurrence of motion and sound. **Meter** is the basic rhythmic structure in poetry. **Meter** is regularized rhythm, an arrangement of the poetic language in which the accents occur at apparently equal intervals in time.

Types of Meter in English Poetry:
(1)- Iambic Meter is a meter in which the majority of feet are iambs. This is the most frequently used meter in English poetry.
Iamb is a metrical foot consisting of one unaccented syllable followed by one accented syllable. (for example, the sun ⌣ — **and** refer ⌣ —)

"When I / consi/der how/ my light / is spent" John Milton "On His Blindness"
⌣ — / ⌣ —/⌣ — / ⌣ — / ⌣ —
iamb   iamb   iamb   iamb   iamb

Iambic Pentameter

(2)- Trochaic Meter is a meter in which the majority of feet are trochees
Trochee is a metrical foot consisting of one accented syllable followed by one unaccented syllable (for example doctor — ⌣)

"There they/ are, my/ fifty / men and/ women" Robert Browning
— ⌣ / — ⌣ / — ⌣ / — ⌣ / — ⌣
trochee   trochee trochee trochee   trochee

Trochaic Pentameter

(3)- Anapestic Meter is a meter in which the majority of feet are anapests **Anapest** is a metrical foot consisting of two unaccented syllables followed by one accented syllable (for example understand ⌣ ⌣ —)

"For the moon /never beams /without bring/ing me dreams

⌣ ⌣ —   / ⌣ ⌣ —   / ⌣ ⌣ —   / ⌣ ⌣ —

anapest   anapest   anapest   anapest

of the beau/tiful A/nnabel Lee"   Alexander Pope

⌣ ⌣ — / ⌣ ⌣ —/ ⌣ ⌣ —

anapest anapest anapest

Anapestic Heptameter

(4)- Dactylic Meter is a meter in which the majority of feet are dactyls. **dactyl** is a metrical foot consisting of one accented syllable followed by two unaccented syllables (for example merrily — ⌣ ⌣)

Take her up / ten.der.ly

— ⌣ ⌣ / — ⌣ ⌣

dactyl   dactyl

Dactylic Dimeter

(5)- Spondaic Meter is a meter in which the majority of feet are spondees **spondee** is a metrical foot consisting of two equally accented syllables (for example true blue — —)

Monosyllabic foot is a foot consisting of a single accented syllable (for example shine —)

Name of Meter	Name of Foot	Form	Example
Iambic Meter	**iamb**	⌣ —	**the sun** ⌣ — **, refer** ⌣ —
Trochaic Meter	**trochee**	— ⌣	**Doct-or** — ⌣
Anapestic Meter	**anapest**	⌣ ⌣ —	**Un-der-stand** ⌣ ⌣ —
Dactylic Meter	**dactyl**	— ⌣ ⌣	**Mer-ri-ly** — ⌣ ⌣
Spondaic Meter	**spondee**	— —	**true blue** — —
	Monosyllabic foot	—	**shine** —

Foot is the basic unit used in the scansion of verse. A foot usually contains one accented syllable and one or two unaccented syllables.

Metrical lines in a poem might contain the following variations or number of feet:

Monometer	One foot		Pentameter	Five feet
Dimeter	Two feet		Hexameter	Six feet
Trimeter	Three feet		Heptameter	Seven feet
Tetrameter	Four feet		Octameter	Eight feet

Stanza is a group of lines in a poem. The metrical pattern of a stanza or its rhyme scheme is repeated throughout the poem.

Free Verse is non-metrical verse. Poetry written in free verse is arranged in lines, may be more or less rhythmical, but does not have a fixed metrical pattern. Whereas, **Blank Verse** is unrhymed iambic pentameter.

Scansion : Practice

Scan the meter of the following extracts from various poems. Mark the accented and unaccented syllables. Name the foot, count the number of feet and name the meter.

1- "In Memory of W.B. Yeats"
   by W. H. Auden

   Earth, receive an honoured guest;

   William Yeats is laid to rest:

   Let this Irish vessel lie

   Emptied of its poetry. (Trochaic meter)

2- "There was a young lady from York

   Who had a great fondness for pork"   (Anapestic Trimeter)

3- "And the white breast of the dim sea" Spondee

4- "Down in the valleys the shadows are thickening;

   Stars coming on and the lights of the houses" (Dactylic tetrameter)

5- When as in silks my Julia goes,

   Then, then, me thinks, how sweetly flows

   That liquefaction of her clothes!   Iambic Tetrameter:

Check your Understanding of the Elements of Poetry

1-The basic meaning or dictionary meaning a word is called ....
  A) Denotation
  B) Connotation
  C) Personification
  D) Metonymy

2-.............. is what a word suggests beyond its denotative meaning. A word in poetry has shades of meanings and overtones of meaning.
  A) Connotation
  B) Denotation
  C) Organic imagery
  D) Apostrophe

3- A .... is a figure of speech in which an implicit comparison is made between two things essentially unlike.
  A) Simile
  B) Synecdoche
  C) Paradox
  D) Metaphor

4- A/an.............. is a figure of speech in which an explicit comparison is made between two things essentially unlike. The comparison is made explicit by the use of some word or phrase as *like, as, than, similar to, resembles,* or *seems.*
  A) Metaphor
  B) Simile
  C) Alliteration
  D) Paradox

5-...........is a figure of speech in which human attributes are given to an animal, an object, or a concept.
  A) Personification
  B) Apostrophe
  C) Metonymy
  D) Synecdoche

6- .... is a figure of speech in which a part is used for the whole.
  A) Assonance
  B) Apostrophe
  C) Consonance
  D) Synecdoche

7-................. is a statement or situation containing apparently contradictory elements, nevertheless found to be true and does indeed make sense.
A) Irony of situation
B) Dramatic irony
C) Paradox
D) Apostrophe

8- ....is a musical device in which the initial consonant sounds of accented syllables or important words (for example cat- camel, man-moon) are repeated at close intervals in a line of poetry.
A) Assonance
B) Consonance
C) Alliteration
D) Apostrophe

9-................. is the repetition at close intervals of the final consonant sounds of accented syllables or important words in a line of poetry (for example book-back-block- thick)
A) Assonance
B) metonymy
C) Alliteration
D) Consonance

10- A/ an.............. is a rhyme in which the repeated accented vowel sound is in the final syllable of the words involved (for example dance- starts, scald- recalled)
A) Masculine Rhyme
B) Feminine Rhyme
C) Internal Rhyme
D) End Rhyme

11-A/an ....is a rhyme in which rhyming words occur at the ends of consecutive lines in a poem.
A) Single Rhyme
B) Feminine Rhyme
C) End Rhyme
D) Double Rhyme

12- The .... consists of one unaccented syllable followed by one accented syllable.(For example, the sun ⌣ — and refer ⌣ —)
A) Trochaic Meter
B) Iambic Meter
C) Dactylic Meter
D) Spondaic Meter

13-The Anapest is a metrical foot consisting of ....
A) Two unaccented syllables followed by one accented syllable (for example understand ⌣ ⌣ —)
B) One accented syllable followed by two unaccented syllables (for example merrily — ⌣ ⌣)
C) Two equally accented syllables (for example true blue — —)
D) A single accented syllable (for example shine —)

14- Tetrameter is a metrical line containing ....
A) Four feet
B) One foot
C) Seven feet
D) Six feet

15- Hexameter is a metrical line containing ....
A) Six feet
B) eight feet
C) Three feet
D) Five feet

16- ....is the process of measuring verse, that is, of marking accented and unaccented syllables, dividing the lines into feet and identifying the metrical pattern of a poem.
A) Personification
B) Scansion
C) Assonance
D) Alliteration

17- This figure of speech can be defined as something that means more than what it is. Besides its literal meaning, an object, a person or a place has a figurative meaning. This figure of speech may be read both literally and figuratively. Which figure of speech are we talking about?
A) Dramatic irony
B) Personification
C) Metaphor
D) Symbol

The Elements of Poetry

Chapter Twelve

Confessional Poetry

Confessional poetry is that kind of lyric poetry that portrays the poets' domestic life and personal relationships. This genre of American poetry dominated the new mainstream American poetry throughout the 1950s and 1960s. American Confessional poets like Robert Lowell, Sylvia Plath and Anne Sexton made their poetry highly personal, autobiographical and confessional. American confessional poets found an escape route in their poetry thus rendering it as a confessional box like that we find in a church. However, unlike the confessional box in the church in which sinners confess their sins to the priest, confessional poets used poetry as a vehicle to reveal their stream of consciousness, fears, wishes and desires to their readers. Confessional poetry is the personal poetry of the poet's "I". The confessional poet considers the poem as a personal account of his domestic life and the wishes, desires and fears that roam his or her psyche or inner self.

The American confessional poetry of the mid and late twentieth century tackled daring themes and subject matters that had not been openly tackled before in any kind of poetry. Confessional poets frankly and autobiographically revealed their subjective experiences mainly their depression, sex mania, abnormal sexuality, alcoholism, suicidal attempts and death. Confessional poets were particularly interested in the psychological aspect of poetry and the poetic self. To them the poet was a psycho making a confession to his readers in the same way a sinner makes a confession in the church. Although some poets' confessions were quite shocking to readers, the poetic form in which they coated these horrible subjective experiences was pioneering, interesting and revealed their mastery of poetry as a craftsmanship.

Mirror

Sylvia Plath (1932-1963)

I am silver and exact. I have no preconceptions.
Whatever I see, I swallow immediately.
Just as it is, unmisted by love or dislike
I am not cruel, only truthful –
The eye of a little god, four-cornered.
Most of the time I meditate on the opposite wall.
It is pink, with speckles. I have looked at it so long
I think it is a part of my heart. But it flickers.
Faces and darkness separate us over and over.

Now I am a lake. A woman bends over me.
Searching my reaches for what she really is.
Then she turns to those liars, the candles or the moon.
I see her back, and reflect it faithfully
She rewards me with tears and an agitation of hands.
I am important to her. She comes and goes.
Each morning it is her face that replaces the darkness.
In me she has drowned a young girl, and in me an old woman
Rises toward her day after day, like a terrible fish.

The Poet's life and background:

Sylvia Plath was a very famous confessional American poet with suicidal tendencies. Her short life was marked with stress and depression which made her commit suicide at a very early age. Her unhappy marriage and the acute depression she suffered from were the reasons behind her suicide attempts. Her first attempt to commit suicide occurred when she was only twenty years old, but it was a fiasco. Ten years later after producing the most notable poems in American poetry, she made her second attempt to commit suicide and it finally worked out. She killed herself by the inhalation of natural gas. Her melancholy and depression affected her writing and thus her poems tended to have a depressing and dark tone.

Mirror: In-depth Analysis

Mirror highlights the strong and everlasting relationship between women and mirrors. It is a relationship marked with obsession and contemplation. Women spend more time in front of mirrors than men do. Unlike men, women are obsessed with the concepts of glamorous beauty and elegance. Women keep looking into the mirror for comfort and assurance that they are still beautiful and attractive. But, some women become depressed when they notice that their beauty has started to decline and fade and they have started to age. For a woman the decline and fading of her beauty makes her depressed and melancholic. This holds true for all women, but it might be more depressing for aging women who once had superb beauty in their youth. In particular, pretty middle-aged women become depressed when their beauty begins to fade and wrinkles start to appear under their eyes and on their necks.

Although the poem consists of two stanzas, the story in the poem is told from two conflicting points of view; that of the mirror and that of the woman or the poet herself. In the first stanza, the poet uses personification by giving the mirror human attributes to empower it to speak for itself. The mirror addresses the readers worldwide telling them that for such women of fading beauty, it is not cruel, but is merely faithful. It tells them the truth and nothing else but the truth whether they like it or not. Whether such pretty women of declining beauty accept the harsh fact that their glamorous beauty is fading and they are losing their attractivity or not is their own choice. Their youth being lost away through the passing of time is nonstopable and beyond the mirror's control. The mirror boasts of being silver and a faithful reflection of reality. It is fair and unbiased and therefore reflects reality without making any preconceptions. The mirror goes on to say that it only reflects reality without passing any judgment on the beauty or ugliness of the person who looks into it. Like the lake which swallows whatever we throw in it, the mirror swallows whatever and whoever it sees unaffected by love or hatred. The mirror is fair and senseless as it is void of the emotions of love and hatred. It sees its viewers with impartial eyes unaffected by feelings of love and hatred and without favouring one over another.

In line four the mirror stops talking and the poet starts talking. The poet says that very often while sitting in her room she keeps contemplating the mirror fixed to the opposite wall. For her, the mirror is an idol whom she worships and to whom she turns for comfort, assurance and consolation. To her the mirror is a little goddess taking the shape of a square with four corners. The poet feels that the mirror is a part of her and she identifies with it as if they were one. She has been looking in the mirror for so long. When she was young and beautiful, every time she peered into the mirror, it used to assure her that she had superb beauty. As a middle-aged woman of fading beauty, the mirror can not but tell the truth. It reflects the poet's fading beauty without passing a judgment. The poet does not accept the mirror's truth that she is aging and her beauty is fading gradually. The poet still believes that the mirror flickers beauty and fading beauty thus making her swing between hope and despair. For when she looks in the mirror, she sometimes sees herself beautiful and is still attractive and sometimes she realizes that she is no more beautiful and her beauty has indeed started to fade a way. The poet seems in the habit of constantly looking in the mirror because she says that she looks in the mirror every day, over and over again. The poet is not sure whether to see herself from the real perspective of the mirror or the distorted one of her own thoughts and the compliments of those hypocrite people around her who lie to her by telling her that she is still beautiful and attractive.

In the second stanza the mirror starts talking once again. It compares itself to a lake "Now I am a lake" in which a woman of fading beauty keeps looking for assurance that she is still beautiful and attractive. The mirror even realizes that it is a goddess for whom women kneel down to worship. The woman of fading beauty peers into the surface of the water and realizes that she is no more beautiful and her beauty is fading away. She turns her back to the lake and she damns the candles and the moon whom she describes as liars. The moon and the candle are symbols of love and romance. She calls them liars because she seems to have been deceived by emotions of love and romance. The poet might be making a confession here by referring to her unhappy marriage and her dreams of love and romance which she might have lost long time ago. Unlike the moon and the candles which falsify facts by turning black into white and white into black, the mirror faithfully reflects reality no matter how harsh it is. The poet ridicules the hypocrisy of her acquaintances who flatter with her and tell her that she is still as beautiful as the moon and is still as romantic as candlelight. Having realized that her beauty is fading, the woman starts crying and trembling with agitation.

The mirror goes on to say that it is important not only for the poet but for every woman. Women come and go to look in the mirror as if kneeling down before their idol. The poet is a constant beholder of the mirror. Every day she looks in the mirror several times to contemplate her fading beauty and the wrinkles that have started to appear on different parts of it. In the last two lines of the poem, the mirror speaks of the poet with ridicule and sarcasm. It says that it has known the poet for so long. It knew her when she was a young girl, and still knows her now in her middle age while her beauty is fading and soon she will become old. The mirror's words "In me she has drowned a young girl, and in me an old woman" reveals the long relationship between the mirror and the woman. They have been acquaintances for so long. The mirror is the woman's little god. She bends to look in it like a worshipper kneeling down before a god. But like a ferocious monster the mirror, swallowed the beautiful girl and is now witnessing the decline of her beauty in middle age and will even witness her when she becomes old and weak. The mirror's words "And in me an old woman rises towards her day after day, like a terrible fish" reveals the poet's fear of the approaching old age which is even worse than middle age. It also reveals that the poet becomes older and older day after day and for her this fact is terrifying. It is exciting that the poet chose a fish instead of any other animal to represent her fading beauty. When the poet used the surface of the lake as a mirror to see her reflection, she may have needed a creature that lives in water to show that a woman depends on the mirror in the same way a fish depends on water for its survival.

In *Mirror* Sylvia Plath makes use of several poetic devices and figures of speech mainly personification and metaphors to highlight the theme and characters of the poem. Through personification the mirror which is a senseless object is made to speak and contemplate the woman who looks in it. The poet also makes use of rhetorical devices such as binary oppositions to show the difference between human beings and the mirror. While humans are subjective in their judgment, the mirror is objective and reflects reality as it is without distortions. The mirror not only reflects the physical appearance of the poet, but also mirrors her inner turmoil and self-hatred that resulted from losing her beauty and passing through the aging process. Moreover, when we look in a mirror, we not only see the reflection of our faces, but we also retrieve our conscious and unconscious memories of our life. The poem also makes a comparison between the mirror, on one hand, and the moon and the stars, on the other. The mirror is faithful to reality, while the stars and the moon provide us with the suggestive side of reality.

The lake metaphor in which the mirror compares itself to the lake echoes the Mythology of Narcissus. Prince Narcissus was exceptionally beautiful and one day whilst drinking from a lake he started contemplating his reflection in the water. With admiration and vanity the young handsome prince looked at the reflection of his face in water for so long until he fell in the lake and drowned.

Several theme statements can be abstracted from the story of the woman and the mirror. But the central theme is the contrast between truth and dishonesty or reality and negation of reality. Mirror is very much an existentialist poem about the human condition and his inability to cope with time and old age. The poet highlights the pain associated with the aging process. The poem also ridicules women who are deceived by men's flattery and compliment especially those who keep telling them that they are still pretty and attractive though they are aging. The woman in the poem is deceived by the flattery of the hypocrites around her who lie to her when they tell her that she is still beautiful. This unjustified flattery makes the woman feel that the mirror is cruel, unfaithful and unsympathetic when it has reflected her fading beauty. But the mirror defends itself by telling the woman that it is only reflecting her real physical appearance without compliments and that she has to accept reality no matter how ugly it is. In this sense, the woman symbolizes all those women who refuse to face up to reality and keep taking shelters in illusions and deceptive flattery of hypocrites.

Another interpretation of the poem comes to surface when we think of the woman who constantly looks into the mirror as some one searching for his or her true identity. The search for one's identity is interesting in this poem especially when we realize that the story of the woman and the mirror is told mostly from the point of view of a mirror.

Themes in the Poem:
Several themes can be abstracted from Sylvia Plath's poem "Mirror". Here are some of these themes:

1- People's fear of old age when they turn weak and ugly.
2- The poem makes a contrast between reality and the negation of reality, and between truth and hypocrisy or dishonesty.
3- Passing through the aging process mainly the final stage which is old age is a terrifying experience particularly for women of fading beauty.
4- Mirror is an existentialist poem about man's inability to cope with time and old age.
5- The poem highlights the pain and agony associated with the aging process which all people must pass through.
6- The poem ridicules middle-aged women of fading beauty who are always deceived by the flattery and compliment of men who keep flattering with them and telling them that they are still pretty and attractive.

"Mirror"

Test your understanding of the poem:

1. The central idea in Sylvia Plath's poem "Mirror" is that ....
   A) The mirror is not cruel to women of fading beauty, but it merely gives a faithful reflection of their appearance
   B) The mirror is truthful since it reflects reality without making any judgment on the beauty or ugliness of the person who looks into it.
   C) (A&B)
   D) The mirror is unfair and distorts reality. It does not reflect reality faithfully.

2. In "Mirror" the expression "I am important to her. She comes and goes" highlights ....
   A) The importance of the mirror to women
   B) Women's obsession with mirrors and how frequent they look into them every day
   C) Women are not obsessed with their beauty and elegance and therefore do not look into mirrors so often
   D) (A&B)

3. In "Mirror" the poet says, "Then she turns to those liars, the candles or the moon". This phrase means that.............
   A) The woman is not sure whether to judge her fading beauty from the view point of the mirror or from the view point of her hypocrite acquaintances who flatter with her by telling her that she is still pretty and attractive
   B) The moon and candles which are symbols of love and romance make lovers blind to the truth and thus make them falsify facts by turning black into white and vice versa.
   C) She calls the moon and the candles, liars because she might have been deceived by emotions of love and romance
   D) (A,B&C)

4. In "Mirror" the two liars referred to in the expression "Then she turns to those liars" are ....
   A) The lake and the candles
   B) The candles and the moon
   C) Faces and darkness
   D) Young girls and old women

5. In "Mirror" what does the mirror want to reveal in saying, "And in me she has drowned a young   girl, and in me an old woman rises toward her day after day"?

   A) The woman is now in her middle age and is aging very quickly. Soon she will become an old woman

   B) The mirror has known the woman since she was a young girl, knows her now in her middle age and will witness her when she turns into an old woman

   C) The aging process and how fast people get old

   D) (A,B &C)

6. In "Mirror" the mirror's words "And in me an old woman rises toward her day after day like a terrible fish" reveal................

   A) The poet's fear of the approaching old age and the complete loss of her fading beauty

   B) The poet is happy to become old

   C) The poet does not fear the aging process and thinks it is a natural phenomenon

   D) The poet has been attacked by an old woman while looking in the mirror

7. In light of reading the poem "Mirror" which of the following statements is incorrect in the context of the poem?

   A) The poet personifies the mirror which is a senseless object, thus allows it to speak and contemplate the woman who looks in it

   B) The poet makes a contrast between the mirror whose reflection of people is faithful and truthful and humans whose judgment of the external appearance of other people is subjective and might be distorted

   C) The mirror not only truthfully reflects the external appearance of the poet, but it also reveals her inner turmoil and self-hatred that resulted from seeing her fading beauty in the mirror and starting to pass through the aging process

   D) Unlike the mirror which does not reflect reality truthfully, the candles and the moon, the   symbols of love and romance, provide us with truthful and objective reflections of the people   we love and admire.

8. The middle-aged woman of fading beauty in the poem believes that.............
   A) The mirror is cruel, unfaithful and unsympathetic
   B) The mirror is truthful since it is only reflecting her physical appearance and fading beauty without compliments and she has to accept this reality no matter how hard it is
   C) The moon and the candles reflect reality more truthfully and faithfully than the mirror
   D) Both candles and the moon are not liars

9- What figure of speech does the poetess use when she gives human attributes to the mirror , a senseless object, and makes it speak to and contemplate the woman who looks in it   as if it were a human being?
   A) Understatement
   B) Metaphor
   C) Simile
   D) Personification

10- The best theme or themes that can be abstracted from Sylvia Plath's poem "Mirror" are ....
   A) The poem makes a contrast between reality and the negation of reality, and between truth and hypocrisy or dishonesty
   B) Passing through the aging process mainly the final stage which is old age is a terrifying experience particularly for women of fading beauty
   C) The poem highlights the pain and agony associated with the aging process which all people must pass through
   D) (A, B &C)

11. In "Mirror", what kind of imagery does the Sylvia Plath use when she compares the mirror to a monster that swallows all that it sees? The mirror says, "I am silver and exact. I have no preconceptions. Whatever I see, I swallow immediately. Just as it is, unmisted by love or dislike"
   A) Organic imagery
   B) Gustatory imagery
   C) Tactile imagery
   D) Kinesthetic imagery

12. In "Mirror", what kind of imagery does Sylvia Plath use when she portrays how the woman bends over the lake to see her reflection in the water? The mirror says, "Now I am a lake. A woman bends over me"
   A) Kinesthetic imagery
   B) Organic imagery
   C) Gustatory imagery
   D) Tactile imagery

13. In "Mirror", what figure of speech does Sylvia Plath use when the mirror says, "Now I am a lake"
   A) Metaphor
   B) Simile
   C) Understatement
   D) Apostrophe

Elements of Poetry

Chapter Thirteen
Romanticism and Romantic Poetry

Romanticism as a literary movement that stressed the "spontaneous overflow of emotions" from the poet's heart to the reader's soul and heart. Romanticists addressed their readers' hearts rather than their minds. Romantic poetry gave priority to intuition and romance over reason and logic and the rural landscape over the urban landscape. Romantic poets used new poetic forms and used the vernacular language to express their thoughts and feelings. The "Big Six" of English romantic poetry who formed the Romantic movement of the late Eighteenth and early Nineteenth century England were William Wordsworth, William Blake, Samuel Taylor Coleridge , George Gordon, Percy Bysshe Shelley and John Keats.

The main tenets of Romanticism in poetry can be summed up as follows:

1) Romanticism is synonymous with optimism. Romantic poets strived hard to change the individual and society in a period full of overwhelming social problems. The Romantic poets hoped to elevate the individual's soul and to create a spiritual community despite the hardships of life.
2) Romantic poets explore the neglected side of the individual and probe deeply inside his psyche and subjective feelings and thoughts.
3) Romantic poets seek infinite perfection in both nature and the human beauty.
4) Romantic poetry relies on individual expression and does not adhere to formal rules or decorum in art.
5) Romantic poetry is sensuous and concrete.
6) The Romantics are absolutely nature poets. Romantic poetry encourages readers to return to nature and the serene and simple life of the countryside. For the Romantic poets nature is a regenerator of imagination and an escape refuge from technology, industrialism and urbanization.
7) Romantic poets view poetry as a source of creative imagination.
8) Romantic poets give much attention to the emotional or "passionate" element in human beings.

9) Romantic poets lay much emphasis on the mutual relationship between the art form and its content.

10) For the Romantics the lyric poem is their favorite poetic form which they found capable of conveying their passions and ideas.

11) Romantic Poetry does not delight and teach, but rather helps the reader undergo a poetic and spiritual experience.

12) Romantic poetry is highly sensuous and defies all moral codes of the society.

The Romantic Poets

Percy Bysshe Shelley
1792-1822
online-literature.com

Ozymandias

I met a traveller from an antique land
Who said: "Two vast and trunkless legs of stone
Stand in the desert. Near them on the sand,
Half sunk, a shattered visage lies, whose frown
And wrinkled lip and sneer of cold command
Tell that its sculptor well those passions read
Which yet survive, stamped on these lifeless things,
The hand that mocked them and the heart that fed.
And on the pedestal these words appear:
`My name is Ozymandias, King of Kings:
Look on my works, ye mighty, and despair!'
Nothing beside remains. Round the decay
Of that colossal wreck, boundless and bare,
The lone and level sands stretch far away.

"Ozymandias"

Summary:

In *Ozymandias* the speaker recalls having met a traveller from ancient Egypt "an antique land" who told him that while traveling in the Egyptian desert he came across the ruins of a huge statue of Ozymandias, the Greek name for the Egyptian king Rameses II (1304-1237 BC). The statue, the strange traveller thus tells the speaker, was completely destroyed. All that remained of the statue were two huge legs without a body standing in the desert "Two vast and trunkless legs of stone". Close to these two bare legs of stone, lies a massive crumbling and frowning face of stone that was half sunk in the desert's sand. The visage is cracked and ruined with a noticeable frown as if to reveal the misery and anger of the subject of the statue. The statue is a masterpiece of sculpture of a great ancient king. The sculptor who sculpted the statue was a great artist who understood the passions of his subject and showed them on the statue. Ozymandias was a tyrant; he oppressed his people and treated them as slaves. Ozymandias was an arrogant king who looked down upon his people and enslaved them. This is quite clear from the inscriptions on the pedestal of the statue which read "My name is Ozymandias, king of kings: Look on my works, ye Mighty, and despair!" Although Ozymandias was a great and powerful king, nothing is left of his power except for two trunkless legs of stone and a frowning face half sunk in the desert sand. Around the statue of the ancient king, the traveller could see nothing except for the sand that stretched far away in the desert.

Commentary and Critical Analysis:

Ozymandias is Shelley's most celebrated and most anthologized sonnet. The whole poem constitutes only one metaphor: the ruined statue of the ancient king Ozymandias shattered in the desert. All that remains of the statue are the two legs of stones standing on a cracked pedestal with the inscription of the name of the king and his boastful remark "king of kings" and a frowning cracked face that lies a distance from the two legs. Ironically, through the passage of time the powerful arrogant king has become no more than a ruined statue barely visible to the traveller. The poem ridicules the ancient king's proud boast of being the king of all kings. Ironically, the ancient king's civilization disappeared long time ago and he himself had been turned into dust and stone. Ozymandias's works and civilization which he had been proud of had vanished throughout the destructive power of history. The poem stresses man's insignificance, littleness and nothingness when compared to time and history. Time is depicted as a ravisher of beauty and art. The beautiful statue has been ruined and turned into dust and scattered pieces of stones. The poem does not only shed light on the insignificance of political power and the equality of people in front of death the leveler, but it also stresses the futility of man's hubris and vanity which is crushed by time; the destroyer and ravisher of all civilizations. All that remains of the great king is a work of art; a piece of sculpture half sunk in the desert sand. This demonstrates the fact that language and works of art are everlasting and certainly long outlast the other legacies of power mainly political power and kingship. The ancient tyrant has been rendered less commanding "sneer of cold command" and less powerful through the passage of time. He had been distanced into history and his power had ended through the passage of time. The poet spoils the mental image we have of the great king and distances him further into centuries of ruin and decay. For the people of his time, Ozymandias was a powerful and great king, but for people of the modern age he is no more than a shattered statue or a ruined work of art.

Ozymandias

Test your Understanding:

1-In the following lines quoted from "Ozymandias" Shelley.............

> *I met a traveller from an antique land*
> *Who said: "Two vast and trunkless legs of stone*
> *Stand in the desert. Near them on the sand,*
> *Half sunk, a shattered visage lies, whose frown*
> *And wrinkled lip and sneer of cold command*
> *Tell that its sculptor well those passions read*
> *Which yet survive, stamped on these lifeless things*

    A. Depicts a visual imagery of the ruined statue of king Ozymandias of ancient Egypt. All that remained of the statue are two legs of stone without a body and a cracked frowning face.

    B. Stresses the fact that time is an inescapable destructor even of political power and great tyrannical kings.

    C. Stresses the fact that works of art mainly sculpture are everlasting, but political power does not last for long.

    D. (A, B & C)

2-The inscriptions on the pedestal of the ruined statue which read :

> *"My name is Ozymandias, King of Kings:*
> *Look on my works, ye mighty, and despair!'*
> *Nothing beside remains. Round the decay*
> *Of that colossal wreck, boundless and bare,*
> *The lone and level sands stretch far away".*

    A. Are meant to be an irony which reveals the fact that the great ancient king was defeated and destroyed by time and nothing remains of the legacy of his power.

    B. Are meant to praise the ancient king for his greatness

    C. Are meant to ridicule the sculptor who sculpted the statue of the ancient king

    D. Are meant to express the traveller's admiration of the ancient Egyptian civilization and the ancient Egyptian king Ozymandias.

The Romantic Poets
William Blake

The Chimney Sweeper

When my mother died I was very young,
And my father sold me while yet my tongue
Could scarcely cry 'weep! 'weep! 'weep! 'weep!
So your chimneys I sweep, and in soot I sleep.

There's little Tom Dacre, who cried when his head,
That curled like a lamb's back, was shaved: so I said,
"Hush, Tom! never mind it, for when your head's bare,
You know that the soot cannot spoil your white hair."

And so he was quiet; and that very night,
As Tom was a-sleeping, he had such a sight, -
That thousands of sweepers, Dick, Joe, Ned, and Jack,
Were all of them locked up in coffins of black.

And by came an angel who had a bright key,
And he opened the coffins and set them all free;
Then down a green plain leaping, laughing, they run,
And wash in a river, and shine in the sun.

Then naked and white, all their bags left behind,
They rise upon clouds and sport in the wind;
And the angel told Tom, if he'd be a good boy,
He'd have God for his father, and never want joy.

And so Tom awoke; and we rose in the dark,
And got with our bags and our brushes to work.
Though the morning was cold, Tom was happy and warm;
So if all do their duty they need not fear harm.

A Critical Analysis of "The Chimney Sweeper"

In *The Chimney Sweeper*, a young chimney sweeper named Tom Dacre recounts a dream he had in which he saw all his fellow chimney sweepers who were all children locked up in black coffins. Then an angel with a bright key rescued the kids from the coffins, set them free and took them to a sunny meadow where they played joyfully and washed their bodies in the river. The boy recounting the dream is completely ignorant of the bad living conditions he and his fellow chimney sweepers live in. The kids in the poem are innocent and do not have enough experience in life to understand the social injustice they suffer from. In *The Chimney Sweeper* William Blake protests against the living and working conditions of innocent chimney sweepers during the industrial revolution in eighteenth century England. The poet wants to draw society's attention to the misery and unbearable lives of such innocent kids who were sold by their poor parents to sweep chimneys in London. Blake was indirectly calling upon the British government to pass a law to prevent such kids from working as chimney sweepers and improve their life conditions.

Chimney sweepers in eighteenth century England lived and worked in very harsh and hostile conditions. For instance, they slept in cellars on bags of the soot that they had swept, and the less fortunate kids had to sleep in the streets. Children chimney sweepers were underfed and as a result suffered from malnutrition and many diseases mainly cancer of the scrotum and had several respiratory problems. Such very young chimney sweepers received no care from society. They were not clothed properly and had to sweep the chimneys naked so that their masters would not bother themselves with buying them clothes or washing them. Such kids were rarely bathed and they were always dirty and covered with soot. Some of them suffocated to death while sweeping chimneys, while others were burnt alive. The more fortunate kids had difficulty breathing, while others were left with diseases of the ankles and spines. Chimney sweeping left a large number of kids with many deformities of the knees, spine and kneecaps from climbing up chimneys. Such soot covered chimney sweepers were considered subhuman creatures and not a part of any human society.

The speaker in the poem is a very young chimney sweeper whose father sold him to the chimney sweeper master shortly after the death of his mother while he was still a child. It was customary during the industrial revolution for many poor British families to sell their children into labour. In the last stanza of the poem William Blake criticizes the church and society for not stopping this kind of child abuse and not providing those needy children with food, shelter and education. Although the poet does not blame reckless fathers for not taking care of their children and for selling them into labour to the chimney sweeping masters, he indirectly criticizes the church and the state for letting this happen. His criticism of the church and the state is quite apparent in the last stanza of the poem. Instead of putting an end to the desperate lives of the young chimney sweepers, both society and the church expected them to perform their duties without complaint. It is ironical that the angel in the dream who set the boys free from the black coffins with the bright key and took them to a green meadow where they played joyfully made fuss of the boys and deceived them when he told them that if they did their duties without complaint, they would live happily and God would love them more.

In *The Chimney Sweeper* the poet highlights the harsh work and living conditions of the young chimney sweepers. When Tom Dacre cried because his hair was shaved , the speaker comforted him by telling him that now it would be better for him to sweep the chimneys with the brush bare headed then he would not need to have to wash his hair every day to remove the soot from it. Throughout the poem the poet keeps using the two colors white and black to highlight the images in the poem. The boys are white, but their naked bodies and faces are covered with soot which is black. White stands for the innocence and purity of the young chimney sweepers, whereas, the soot which spoils the chimney sweepers' clean white faces stands for the industrial revolution which enslaved young children .

"The Chimney Sweeper"

Test Your Understanding:

1. In light of reading William Blake's "The Chimney Sweeper", circle the incorrect statement:

A) In "The Chimney Sweeper" William Blake implicitly protests against the living and work conditions of innocent young chimney sweepers during the industrial revolution in England.

B) The poet wants to draw society's attention to the bad living conditions of such innocent homeless kids who were sold into labour at a very early age to sweep the chimneys of London.

C) Blake was indirectly criticizing both the church and society for allowing such young children to   work as chimney sweepers.

D) The young chimney sweepers in the poem seem very happy in their lives because on every Sunday, the chimney sweeper masters take them for a journey beside the river to wash and play joyfully.

2. The lines quoted below from "The Chimney Sweeper", reveal that.........
   "When my mother died I was very young,
   And my father sold me while yet my tongue
   Could scarcely cry 'weep! 'weep! 'weep! 'weep!
   So your chimneys I sweep, and in soot I sleep"

A) The boy was happy to go into labour as he liked to work as a chimney sweeper.

B) The orphan boy, like all the other young chimney sweepers portrayed in the poem, was unaware and ignorant of the social injustice he suffered from because he was still very young.

C) The boy does not blame his reckless father for selling him to the chimney sweeper master.

D) The boy had difficulty pronouncing the word "sweep" and instead used to say "weep" while calling "chimney sweeping" for people to hear him in the streets of London because his tongue was cut.

3. In the lines quoted below from "The Chimney Sweeper", the poet ....
   "And the angel told Tom, if he'd be a good boy,
   He'd have God for his father, and never want joy"

A) The poet is praising the church for helping such young chimney sweepers find a good job that would make them earn money to feed their poor families.

B) The poet is ironically criticizing the church for letting such children go into labour at a very early age and for convincing them to work without any complaint.

C) The poet believes that the angel, who opened the black coffins, set the boys free and took them to a sunny meadow where they played joyfully and washed their bodies in the river was doing that for their own good.

D) The young chimney sweepers always hated playing because they considered themselves not young anymore and they only needed work

The Romantic Poets

William Wordsworth
Composed upon Westminster Bridge

Earth has not anything to show more fair:
Dull would he be of soul who could pass by
A sight so touching in its majesty:
This City now doth, like a garment, wear
The beauty of the morning; silent, bare,
Ships, towers, domes, theatres, and temples lie
Open unto the fields, and to the sky;
All bright and glittering in the smokeless air.
Never did the sun more beautifully steep
In his first splendour, valley, rock, or hill;
Ne'er saw I, never felt, a calm so deep!
The river glideth at his own sweet will:
Dear God! The very houses seem asleep;
And all that mighty heart is lying still!

Composed upon Westminster Bridge

Summary:

In *Composed Upon Westminster Bridge* William Wordsworth celebrates the beauty of London and in particular Westminster Bridge; one of London's marvelous sights. The persona in the sonnet who seems to be the poet himself is standing on Westminster Bridge early in the morning and is contemplating the beauty of the scenery from over the bridge. While standing on the bridge in the early morning, he starts contemplating the beauty of the city of London and the scenery evokes in him a stream of emotions and arouses his poetic faculties. Thrilled with the beauty of the scenery and with all his poetic faculties boosted, he composes his poem while standing on the bridge. His description of the city of London is so dazzling and impressive and leaves the reader who has not seen the bridge with exceptional yearning to see it. The visual imagery the poet paints for the bridge and the natural landscape that surrounds it harmoniously combines city and nature in a very astonishing way. In such a narrative poem, the poet narrates the story of the bridge and how majestic and impressive it looks like in the early morning.

The poet admires the calmness and peacefulness of the city of London in the early morning when viewed from over Westminster Bridge. The poet compares the city of London in the early morning with a beautiful lady wearing a fanciful dress "This City now doth, like a garment, wear". In the early morning the city of London is quiet and peaceful and no noises could be heard. Everything in the city is calm and noiseless and the city dwellers are still asleep. In fact, the poet says the whole city is asleep including people, animals, theatres, churches, and temples. The only thing that is wakeful in the poem is the rising sun which shines so tenderly on the city. In the early morning everything is silent, whereas at night and during the day time the city becomes bustling and full of life again; at night people go to restaurants, cafes and theatres and during the day people go to work, farmers go to their fields, school boys go to their schools, ships start to move in the river and life in the city is revived once again. But, in the early morning, everything is standstill except for the rising sun, the smokeless fresh air and the stunning scenery of the city of London viewed from the bridge. The poet admires the glamorous beauty of the city in the silence of the early morning when everything is silent and people are still asleep "The beauty of the morning; silent, bare. Ships, towers, domes, theaters, and temples lie open unto fields, and to the sky." The poet also admires the beauty of the River Thames early in the morning when it flows so gently and sweetly in the smokeless air "The river glideth at his own sweet will". The only thriving image in the poem is that of the sun which warms the place with its rays so tenderly and without any obstacles. The calmness of the city makes the sun shine freely on every corner of the city and on the valleys, the hills and the fields. The poet praises the sunshine and says "Never did the sun more beautifully steep, in his first splendour, valley, rock, or hill".

The poet is thrilled with joy and happiness to the extent that his heart momentarily and metaphorically stopped beating then started to beat with joy to see the River Thames flow so gently through the smokeless air of the city of London. The poet says he felt the peacefulness and calmness of the city deep in his heart; a feeling he experiences for the first time as he seems to have never stood on the bridge in the early morning "Ne'er saw I, never felt, a calm so deep!"

Commentary:
The sonnet creates a visual imagery of a calm and peaceful city in the early morning with the rising shining sun warming the place and the river flowing gently through the clear sky and the fresh air of the early morning. The poet not only admires the beauty and calmness of the city in such an early hour, but also admires the natural landscape surrounding the city. To the poet, the city of London is exceptionally beautiful in the early morning, the most beautiful city on earth. The poet asserts that the city of London is the queen of all the cities of the world with all its majestic beauty, peacefulness and calmness "Earth has not anything to show more fair". The poet claims that anybody who passes by such a majestic sight and is not moved emotionally is certainly dull, without any emotions and is spiritually barren "Dull would he be of soul who could pass by. A sight so touching in its majesty" especially when the city is silent after long bustling hours during the day and throughout the night. In astonishment and baffled by the beauty of the sight the poet makes an appeal to God to protect the city from calamities so that it will remain thus forever.

Composed upon Westminster Bridge

Test your understanding:

1-The persona in William Wordsworth's sonnet *Composed Upon Westminster Bridge* ....

   A) Celebrates the beauty of Westminster Bridge; one of London's splendid sights.

   B) Glorifies the poem he composed upon Westminster Bridge.

   C) Celebrates the beauty of the city of London in the early morning especially when viewed from over the Westminster Bridge.

   D) (A&B)

2-Which river is the poet talking about in the line quoted below?
"The river glideth at his own sweet will".

   A) The River Thames

   B) The Amazon River

   C) All rivers in the world

   D) The Nile

3- What sight is the poet talking about in the line quoted below?

     Earth has not anything to show more fair:

     Dull would he be of soul who could pass by

     A sight so touching in its majesty:

   A) Westminster Bridge only

   B) Only the natural landscape that surrounds the city of London

   C) The city of London in the early morning, the ships in the river and the natural landscape that surrounds the whole city.

   D) (A &B)

Elements of Poetry

Chapter Fourteen
Pastoral Poetry

Pastoral Poetry is that type of poetry which portrays rural life in the village and the serenity of the lives of shepherds in the countryside. Pastoral poetry is a form of rural poetry and a genre of Romantic poetry that highlights the serenity and innocence of life in the countryside in comparison with the corruption and misery of life in the city with all its modern life problems mainly pollution, overcrowdedness and crime. Pastoral and rural poets express their wish to live in the countryside to enjoy seeing the beautiful scenery and flocks of animals. They frequently draw contrast between life in the city and life in the countryside. Pastoral poets use simple rustic characters in their poetry as a means to express their moral, social, or literary views. Some pastoral poets employ the device of "singing matches" between two or more shepherds. Themes in pastoral poetry are numerous, but the most notable themes are those that deal with the simplicity of life in the village, the serenity of the lives of the shepherds, the beauty of the countryside and the melodious sound of flocks of animals such as sheep and cows and the major themes of love and death. Many poets can be considered as pastoral poets, but some poets have written more pastoral poetry than others. The most outstanding pastoral poets are Sir Phillip Sidney, Thomas Nash, Christopher Marlowe, John Donne, Sir Walter Raleigh, Andrew Marvell, and Thomas Campion.

Pastoral poetry is characterized by a state of happiness and of innocent and romantic love. Rural country folk are portrayed in an idealized rural setting, while they are tending to their flocks and contemplating the perfect beauties of nature and the peaceful world that is absent in the city. For pastoral poets city life is wicked, impure, noisy, polluted and overcrowded, whereas, country life is simple, quiet and peaceful.

Pastoral Poets
Christopher Marlowe

The Passionate Shepherd to His Love

COME live with me and be my Love,
And we will all the pleasures prove
That hills and valleys, dale and field,
And all the craggy mountains yield.

There will we sit upon the rocks
And see the shepherds feed their flocks,
By shallow rivers, to whose falls
Melodious birds sing madrigals.

There will I make thee beds of roses
And a thousand fragrant posies,
A cap of flowers, and a kirtle
Embroider'd all with leaves of myrtle.

A gown made of the finest wool
Which from our pretty lambs we pull,
Fair linèd slippers for the cold,
With buckles of the purest gold.
A belt of straw and ivy buds

With coral clasps and amber studs:
And if these pleasures may thee move,
Come live with me and be my Love.

Thy silver dishes for thy meat
As precious as the gods do eat,
Shall on an ivory table be
Prepared each day for thee and me.

The shepherd swains shall dance and sing
For thy delight each May-morning:
If these delights thy mind may move,
Then live with me and be my Love.

Summary:

Christopher Marlowe's "The Passionate Shepherd to His Love" is the most widely anthologized pastoral poem. In a tone that is optimistic and blissful the poem celebrates simple rural life and pure love. The poem is highly sensuous and extremely romantic. The poet sets the poem in a rural locale where shepherds tend their flocks. The passionate shepherd is courting a young city girl of superb beauty and invites her to seize the chance and be his sweetheart and enjoy with him the beauties and pleasures of life in nature. The poet praises country life and yearns to enjoy its beauties and pleasures. The poet appeals to the girl to be his love and join him in seeing the beauties and pleasures of country life. He is trying to convince her to leave the city and live with him in the country far a way from all the city's complicated problems.

Critical Analysis:

The persona in "The Passionate Shepherd to His Love" is a shepherd who promises to offer the girl, the female object of his desires, the beauties of nature if she accepts to be his sweetheart and submit to his sexual desires. The shepherd is very sensuous and invites the girl for sensuous pleasures. Time in the poem is static as it is ignorant of both the future and the past. What matters for the shepherd is the present moment neither the past nor the future. The shepherd does not ask the girl for a long-term love affair or marriage, but rather he asks her to join him in momentary pleasures. The shepherd has a fervent sexual desire for the woman. The shepherd gives the girl many improbable promises and the woman's response to his offers is never heard. She remains silent and nonresponsive. She is not present in the poem except as the shepherd's sex object and ardent sensuality. As a suitor seeking refuge in country life, the shepherd asks the girl for his "carpe diem" and seize the chance and be his amour.

The shepherd is courting the girl and is trying to convince her to live with him the life of a shepherd. The poem is highly sensuous and is replete with images of all types. Visual imagery is abundant in the poem such as the image of the two lovers sitting on the rock to see the shepherds feed their flocks. Auditory imagery can also be found in the image in which the melodious birds sing madrigals by the river. Olfactory imagery is also present throughout the poem mainly in the line in which the poet promises to make the girl beds of roses and fragrant posies and a cap and a long dress made of flowers. The poem also contains tactile imagery mainly in the line in which the poet he and his beloved will "sit upon the rocks" to see the shepherds tending their flocks. The various images the poet uses throughout the poem and which nearly appeal to all the senses of the reader make the poem look like a painting of a rural landscape full of melodious sounds and evoke the feeling that nature depicted in the poem is pure and booming. The poet also uses many musical devices mainly alliteration to make the poem look like a lyric. For instance, the poet uses alliteration by repeating the "l" sound as the initial sound of the words "live" and "love", and the "f"" sound in the words flocks", "falls" and the "m" sound in the words "myrtle" "mountain", "madrigals", "myrtle".

Line by line commentary:
"The Passionate Shepherd to His Love" consists of seven stanzas each of which constitutes a quatrain. In the first stanza the shepherd addresses his beloved and makes a plea to her to live with him in the countryside. He promises her to make her happy and that she will enjoy country life. He offers her all the beauties of nature and promises her that she will enjoy the scenery and the rural landscape. There she will enjoy the beauty of the valleys, the pastures and the high mountains. In the second stanza the poet continues giving promises to his mistress. He promises her that they will enjoy sitting on the rocks while looking at the shepherds tending their flocks in the green pastures. They will sit by the river and listen to the birds singing madrigals and other melodious songs. In the third stanza the shepherd offers the girl different pleasures not those of nature, but those of

his sensuous body. Here the shepherd becomes very sensuous and promises the girl with sexual ecstasy. He promises her that he will make her beds, rather than one bed, of roses with nice fragrance. He will make her a cap and a dress embroidered with leaves of myrtle which has lovely smell. In the fourth stanza the poet goes on with his promises to the girl. He promises to make her a gown made of the finest wool woven from his own lambs. He will also make her a pair of slippers with buckles of gold which she can wear in winter. In the fifth stanza the poet promises his beloved to make her a belt of straw embroidered with flowers of different colours. They will also ride amber horses. The poet tells the girl that once she is convinced that these pleasures will make her happy, she can come to the countryside and live with him. In the sixth stanza the shepherd promises the young girl to make her eat delicious food in silver dishes placed on a table made of ivory.

In the final stanza the shepherd tells the girl that he will make her march like a queen amidst his swains or very handsome young country fellows who will merrily sing and dance for them both every morning. In the refrain of the poem the shepherd reminds the girl once again if she likes all that he has offered her, then she can come to the countryside and live with him as his mistress.

Theme:
The poem is a merry celebration of youth, sensuous love, simplicity of country life and man's happy return to nature. The poem is also a celebration of the ecstasy and delight of springtime love in a simple, rural locale. The motif of *carpe diem*–Latin for "seize the day." seems to be the central theme in the poem for the shepherd urges the girl to enjoy the moment without worrying about the future.

"The Passionate Shepherd to His Love"

Test your understanding:

1- In "The Passionate Shepherd to His Love", what kind of imagery does Christopher Marlowe use in the line that reads "Melodious birds sing madrigals"?
   A).Tactile imagery
   B). Olfactory imagery
   C). Auditory imagery
   D). Gustatory imagery

2- What figure of speech does Christopher Marlowe use in the lines quoted underneath from "The Passionate Shepherd to His Love"?
   "There will I make thee beds of roses
   And a thousand fragrant posies,
   A cap of flowers, and a kirtle
   Embroider'd all with leaves of myrtle"
   A). Apostrophe
   B). Hyperbole
   C). Metonymy
   D).Understatement

3-The tone of the poem is ....
   A). Pessimistic
   B). Gloomy
   C). Depressing
   D).Optimistic and cheerful

4- In "The Passionate Shepherd to His Love" ....
   A). The shepherd is courting a young city girl of superb beauty. He invites her to seize the chance, be his sweetheart and enjoy with him the beauties and pleasures of country life.
   B). The shepherd seeks momentary pleasures with the girl and does not give her any promises of a long-term relationship.
   C) The shepherd is making a marriage proposal to the girl and is trying to convince her that once they get married, they will live in the countryside.
   D) (A&B)

Pastoral Poetry
THERE IS A GARDEN IN HER FACE.

A Classic Love Poem

By Thomas Campion. (1567-1620)

There is a garden in her face
Where roses and white lilies grow;
A heavenly paradise is that place
Wherein all pleasant fruits do flow.
There cherries grow which none may buy,
Till "Cherry ripe" themselves do cry.

Those cherries fairly do enclose
Of orient pearl a double row,
Which when her lovely laughter shows,
They look like rose-buds filled with snow;
Yet them nor peer nor prince can buy,
Till "Cherry ripe" themselves do cry.

Her eyes like angels watch them still,
Her brows like bended bows do stand,
Threatening with piercing frowns to kill
All that attempt with eye or hand
Those sacred cherries to come nigh,
Till "Cherry ripe" themselves do cry.

Summary

Thomas Campion's "There is a Garden in Her Face" is a classic love poem in which the speaker praises the beauty of a virgin girl who is still in her teens. "Cherry ripe" was a London street cry; street vendors used to cry "cherry ripe" while selling cherries in the streets of London. In the context of the poem the virgin girl crying "Cherry ripe" means that she is ready to be kissed and to have sex with her lover. The poet compares the beauty of the girl's face to the Garden of Eden where flowers and roses of all colours grow. The poet believes that the virgin innocent girl of angelic beauty is similar to the sacred Garden of Eden which is still unspoiled by human touch. The girl is still a virgin teenager and is still not suitable for suitors who will ask for her hand in marriage. The girl is guarding her virginity and will not let it go to any man, until she decides to choose her marriage partner.

The poem is replete with all kinds of imagery mainly colour imagery. The white lilies symbolize purity and virginity for the girl is still virgin, but soon will grow up into a fair lady and will be courted by her lover- the man she chooses herself to be the one who will spoil her virginity. However, the girl will not remain virgin forever. But, she knows for sure that an unmarried woman who is not virgin is spoiled and dirty. For her virginity is something sacred and sanctified. Nonetheless, the red colour stands in sharp contrast to the white colour. It is a symbol of sex and crimson joy. Once she loses her virginity and chastity which are associated with the white colour, she will be associated with the red colour; the symbol of love and passion. But, the virgin girl will not allow any man even if he was a prince or a noble man to give him her cherries till they are ripe. And she herself, and nobody else, will decide when these cherries are ripe.

The last stanza of the poem makes it clear what the poet means by the girl's cherries. Obviously the girl's cherries are her cheeks which are almost ready to be kissed. Her cheeks are well guarded by her eyes in the same way angles guard the Garden of Eden from humans after Adam and Eve were tossed out of the heavenly garden. The poet says, "Her eyes like angels watch them still" and her eyebrows become like bows that will kill anybody who dares to look or touch these sacred cheeks. The poet says, " Her brows like bended bows do stand, threatening with piercing frowns to kill all that attempt with eye or hand those sacred cherries to come nigh". Nobody can kiss the girl or spoil her virginity without her consent. When she becomes ready to be kissed and make love with the man she chooses, she will give him her cherries willingly. This explains the poet's words "Till Cherry ripe themselves do cry". The girl guards her chastity and virginity or her paradise in the same way angles guard the Garden of Eden.

In the second stanza the poet compares the girl's teeth with oriental pearls. Her teeth are as white as pearls of the orient. The poet compares the girl's cheeks with cherries that enclose pearls or her white teeth. When she laughs, the two rows of pearls inside her mouth are turned into red rose buds which yearn to be kissed.

The girl is on the threshold of womanhood and soon her rose bud which is still not in full bloom will blossom and become ready for sex. Until she grows into a fair lady who can make love with her lover, the girl should cling to her virginity and innocence and guard her forbidden fruit from men.

Commentary

In "There is a Garden in her Face" the poet compliments the beauty of a virgin teenager in the most extravagant terms. In such description, the poet uses similes, metaphors and images of all kinds. The poet warns her suitors, himself included, that the girl will not allow anyone to kiss her or have sex with her until she agrees to do so. The poem contains an extended metaphor in which the woman's face is likened to a garden with a variety of fruits, and flowers of all colours and smells.

In the first stanza the poet uses a metaphor to praise the girl's beauty for he says, "there is a garden in her face". This means she is like a garden. The girl's cheeks are rosy and soon will be ready to be kissed by lovers. The poet describes the girl as if she were an unattainable angle that descended from paradise. She is as virgin as an angel and will not be spoiled by lovers until she is ready to do so. The poet emphasizes the fact that the girl will cling to her chastity and virginity until she grows up into a fair, marriageable lady through the repetition of the line "Till "Cherry ripe" themselves do cry" which he positions at the end of every stanza.

All the girl's stunning beauty lies in her cheeks. Her cheeks are rosy and will soon be ready for kisses. Inside her cheeks are two rows of pearls which represent her white teeth. She has a lovely smile with those lovely white teeth. When she smiles her white teeth become like rosebuds filled with snow.

"There is a Garden in Her Face"

Test your Understanding

1-Thomas Campion's "There is a Garden in Her Face" is a classic love poem in which the speaker praises the beauty of a virgin girl who is still in her teens. What does the poet mean by the girl's cherries which seems to be the central image in the poem?
A) Her teeth
B) Her lips
C) Her eyes
D) Her cheeks

2- In the two lines quoted below he poet compares the beauty of the girl's face to a garden where red   roses and white lilies grow. What figure of speech does the poet use to make the comparison?
"There is a garden in her face
Where roses and white lilies grow"
A) Simile
B) Metaphor
C) Synecdoche
D) Understatement

3- The expression "Till "Cherry ripe" themselves do cry"................
A) Indicates that the girl is still a virgin teenager and is still not suitable for suitors who will ask for her hand in marriage.
B) Stresses the fact that the girl is guarding her virginity and will not let it go to any man, until she   decides to choose her marriage partner.
C) Echoes the London street vendors who used to call "cherry ripe" while selling ripe red cherries.
D) (A,B&C)

4- "Those cherries fairly do enclose
Of orient pearl a double row,
Which when her lovely laughter shows,
They look like rose-buds filled with snow"
In the lines quoted above, the poet says................
A) He will buy the girl orient pearls
B) He will bring the girl roses from wonderlands
C) He metaphorically compares the girl's white teeth with two rows of orient pearls
D) He metaphorically compares the girl's hair with red roses

5- "Her eyes like angels watch them still"
   In the line quoted above, the poet says...................
   A) The girl's cheeks are metaphorically well guarded by her eyes in the same way angles guard the Garden of Eden from humans after Adam and Eve were tossed out of the heavenly garden.
   B) The girl hides her cheeks with a veil
   C) The girl is looking at the sky to see the angles descending from Heaven
   D) The angles are protecting the girl from lustful lovers.

6- "Her brows like bended bows do stand,
   Threatening with piercing frowns to kill
   All that attempt with eye or hand
   Those sacred cherries to come nigh,
   Till "Cherry ripe" themselves do cry"
   In the lines quoted above, ...
   A) The poet compares the girl's eyebrows with two bows aimed at those lusty lovers who dare to approach to kiss her lovely cheeks or even dare to ogle her cheeks
   B) The poet says that the girl is always carrying a bow and arrows to shoot all those who dare to ask her for a kiss.
   C) The poet declares that the virgin girl is more than willing to be kissed by lusty men.
   D) The girl confesses that she is not virgin any more

7- "Those sacred cherries to come nigh,
   Till "Cherry ripe" themselves do cry"
   In the lines quoted above, the expression "sacred cherries" refers to......
   A) The girl is still virgin
   B) The girl has not even been kissed before by any man
   C) Virginity is something sacred to all unmarried girls and should be protected until they get married
   D) (A,B &C)

8- The poet emphasizes the fact that the girl will cling to her chastity and virginity until she grows up into a fair marriageable lady through.........
  A) The repetition of the line "Till "Cherry ripe" themselves do cry" which he positions at the end of every stanza.
  B) The different metaphors in which he compares the girl's sacred cherries or cheeks with the sacred heavenly paradise.
  C) The different metaphors which convey the sense of protecting the girl's cheeks from the lovers' unwanted kisses such as "Her eyes like angels watch them still" and "Her brows like bended bows"
  D) (A,B&C)

The Poetry of William Shakespeare
Sonnet 18

Statue of Shakespeare Outside Carnegie Museum, Pittsburgh

"Self-glorification and Immortality of Poetry"

Shall I compare thee to a summer's day?
Shall I compare thee to a summer's day?
Thou art more lovely and more temperate:
Rough winds do shake the darling buds of May,
And summer's lease hath all too short a date:
Sometime too hot the eye of heaven shines,
And often is his gold complexion dimm'd,
And every fair from fair sometime declines,
By chance, or nature's changing course untrimm'd:
But thy eternal summer shall not fade,
Nor lose possession of that fair thou ow'st,
Nor shall death brag thou wander'st in his shade,
When in eternal lines to time thou grow'st,
So long as men can breathe, or eyes can see,
So long lives this, and this gives life to thee.

Sonnet is a poem with a fixed form of fourteen lines, normally iambic pentameter, with a rhyme scheme conforming to or approximating one of the two main types –the Italian sonnet or the Shakespearean or English sonnet. **Couplet** – two successive lines, usually in the same meter, linked by rhyme and usually situated at the end of a sonnet.

Critical Analysis:
A Shakespearean sonnet consists of fourteen lines mostly written in iambic pentameter. The fourteen lines are divided into three quatrains and a couplet. The quatrain is a four-line stanza and the couplet is the last two lines in a sonnet. Shakespearean sonnets have intricate sentence structure and sophisticated pattern of sounds and imagery. Of all the 154 Shakespearean sonnets, Sonnet 18 is perhaps Shakespeare's loveliest sonnet. It is straightforward in both language and intent. Sonnet 18 is a classical love poem in which the persona compares his mistress to a calm lovely Summer's day. The poet wittily immortalizes both poetry and his beloved.

In the first quatrain of the sonnet the poet wonders if he can compare his beautiful mistress to a calm and lovely summer's day. Then, he answers the question himself. He states that he will not compare his beloved to a summer's day because she is lovelier, more romantic and more pleasant than a summer's day "Thou art more lovely and more temperate". For the speaker his mistress is perfect and more pleasant than a summer day for not all the days of summer are calm and cool. Some days in May are windy and a little bit cold and the wind roughly shakes the flowers and roses "Rough winds do shake the darling buds of May" , and above all summer and all its beauties pass a way very quickly "And summer's lease hath all too short a date".

In the second quatrain the speaker says that unlike the beauties of summer which do not last for a long period of time, the beauty of his mistress is everlasting and eternal. And unlike summer days in which the sun "the eye of heaven" is sometimes unbearably hot and sometimes clouds dim the "gold complexion" of the sun make some summer days a little bit cold. "And often is his gold complexion dimm'd", the beauty of his mistress is perpetual and everlasting. Although summer may seem like a time of paradise, it can be so hot and makes people sweat all over. The poem takes a twist in line 7 in which the poet states that beauty fades a way and vanishes "every fair from fair sometime declines" either by accident "by chance" through the passage of time "nature's changing course untrimm'd". A woman might lose her beauty in an accident such as burning or any other kind of accident or she loses her beauty when she becomes old and the wrinkles start to appear on her face.

In the third quatrain the poet praises his mistress's beauty which he compares to an eternal summer. Unlike real summer, her beauty is eternal and will not fade away "But thy eternal summer shall not fade". His mistress will never lose her glamorous beauty and she will remain pretty forever. The poet even immortalizes his mistress and challenges death that it will never boast of having her soul "Nor shall death brag thou wander'st in his shade". In fact, the poet immortalizes his mistress in his poetry. Both his poetry and his beloved will be immortalized because they both live in each other. The more readers will read this sonnet, the more they will remember the poet's mistress because she has been immortalized in his poetry. Her fame and her glamorous beauty will grow in size as more and more readers read the sonnet "When in eternal lines to time thou grow'st". In the couplet the poet glorifies his poetry and boastfully claims that it has immortalized him and his mistress because as long as people live in this world and as long as this sonnet is read by readers, his mistress will live forever. His verse will continue giving life to his mistress and thus she will lead eternal life. The poet believes that his mistress will never be forgotten and she will never fall prey to decay, death and oblivion as long as she lives in his verse. The poet glorifies his verse and boastfully claims that it is the fountain of youth. He challenges other poets, biographers, critics and historians across all the centuries of time and bets them on the greatness and eternity of his poetry and the immortality of his amour or beloved.

The poem can be analyzed from two perspectives. On the one hand, it can be read as praise of the poet's mistress. On the other hand, it can be read as glorification of the poet's verse which to him is eternal and will always have everlasting influence on readers and other poets. Upon first reading, the poem looks like a love poem, but upon second reading and elaborate analysis and contemplation, it becomes crystal clear that it is written in praise of itself rather than in praise of the mistress. Some critics refer to the beloved as "he"; a paragon of youth with whom, they believe, the poet had some kind of sexual intimacy. This view is almost universally accepted by critics who believe that Shakespeare's love interest is a young man rather than a woman. However, Shakespeare's homosexuality is still controversial and doubtful and the poem should be read as praise of the beauty of a woman and as glorification of the immortality and eternity of the poet's verse.

The sonneteer uses enjambments throughout the poem. Lines 7 and 8 form an enjambment in which the two lines are read as one run on statement without any grammatical pauses "every fair from fair sometimes declines/ By chance or nature's changing course untrimmed" which mean that the cycle of life and death and the cycles of seasons go on nonstop forever.

"Shall I compare thee to a summer's day?"

Test your understanding:

1- What does the persona state in the lines quoted below?

"Shall I compare thee to a summer's day?
Thou art more lovely and more temperate"

A) He will not compare his beloved to a summer's day because she is lovelier, more romantic and more pleasant than a summer's day.

B) He asserts that both a summer's day and his mistress are equally the same in terms of beauty and fairness.

C) He claims that his mistress is perfect and more pleasant than a summer day for not all the days of summer are calm and cool. Some Summer days are either too hot or a little bit cold.

D) He sates that his mistress can not be compared to a summer's day because unlike summer, the beauty of his mistress will vanish very soon either by accident or when she gets old.

2- What does the speaker mean by "the eye of heaven" in the lines quoted underneath?

"Sometime too hot the eye of heaven shines,
And often is his gold complexion dimm'd"

A) Life after death

B) The moon

C) Immortalized Poetry

D) The sun

3- In the third quatrain of the sonnet quoted below the poet states explicitly the purpose of writing the poem. For what purpose did he write it?

"Nor shall death brag thou wander'st in his shade,
When in eternal lines to time thou grow'st,
So long as men can breathe, or eyes can see,
So long lives this, and this gives life to thee"

A) The poet is glorifying and immortalizing his verse which he claims is eternal and will certainly influence other poets.

B) The poet is immortalizing his beloved in his eternal poetry. As long as she lives in his poetry which is eternal, she will be immortalized and remembered long after his death.

C) Death will not have the chance to boast of snatching his beloved's soul because it has already been immortalized in the poet's eternal lines of poetry.

D) (A, B&C)

William Shakespeare

"Good friend for Jesus sake forbeare,
To dig the dust enclosed here.
Blessed be the man that spares these stones,
And cursed be he that moves my bones"

Words written on Shakespeare's tombstone

Sonnet 138

When my love swears that she is made of truth,
I do believe her, though I know she lies,
That she might think me some untutor'd youth,
Unskilful in the world's false forgeries.
Thus vainly thinking that she thinks me young,
Although I know my years be past the best,
I smiling credit her false-speaking tongue,
Outfacing faults in love with love's ill rest.
But wherefore says my love that she is young?
And wherefore say not I that I am old?
O, love's best habit is a soothing tongue,
And age, in love, loves not to have years told.
Therefore I'll lie with love, and love with me,
Since that our faults in love thus smother'd be.

Summary:

Shakespeare's Sonnet 138 "When My Love Swears that she is Made of Truth" portrays a middle life crisis. The persona is a middle-aged man in his mid-forties who has fallen in love with a twenty-year old young dark woman. The poet reveals to his readers the nature of his love affair with the dark lady and his fear of the approaching old age and the fading out of his youth. In this sonnet the middle-aged poet stresses the fact that he is still sexually active and assures himself that he is still attractive and worthy of being loved despite his age. The sonnet sheds light on the fact that time and the aging process are man's greatest nemesis or opponent after death. Time is the ravager and waster of youth and beauty in the same way death is the destroyer of life itself. The poet is happy that he is in love once again at such an advanced age. To him this love affair gives him both sexual gratification and assurance that he is still worthy of love. To him, it is a middle-life love story that seems to have escaped the ravages of time. The poet fears the approaching old age because then he will lose his sexual activity completely. But for the time being he wants to make use of all that remains of this sexual strength.

The poem is contradictory and shows conflicting views of love. On the one hand, the poem seems to be skeptical about love and portrays it as a deceptive and ephemeral bond that involves pretense and deception from both lovers. On the other hand, the poem celebrates the power of love which knows no boundaries and is not restricted to a certain age group. A middle-aged man might fall in love with a young woman at any moment. Love does not fade away with age but rather becomes more powerful and more pleasurable. The middle-aged speaker in the poem knows that his mistress lies to him when she tells him that he is still attractive and young, because he knows that his youth is about to fade away and the best of his years are gone. Although he is quite sure that his mistress is unfaithful and that she has another love affair with another guy, he pretends to know nothing and finds joy in making such pretense. Although the speaker has realized that his mistress is telling him lies, he finds consolation in her lies and finds them quite interesting.

Line by line analysis:

In the first line the poet states that he is quite sure that his mistress is unfaithful even if she swears to him that she is faithful to him. He knows for sure that she loves another man "When my love swears that she is made of truth." Although he is quite sure that the woman is unfaithful and is lying to him, he finds pleasure in pretending that he believes her lies. In the third line, the poet says that his mistress might think that he is inexperienced in love and sex "Unlearned in the world's false subtleties" and that he is ignorant of the deception involved in love and sex. The speaker himself is a liar and pretends to be young though deep in his heart he knows that he is not young any more and that his youth is about to fade away. But, in vain he tries to deceive his mistress and convince her that he is still young "Thus vainly thinking that she thinks me young". However, both lovers find no comfort in the truth and finds comfort only in deception and telling lies to each other. The woman is also sure that her lover is not young and he is lying to her when he claims that he is still young and attractive "Although she knows my days are past the best". The poet enjoys listening to his woman's lies when she tells him that he is still attractive and young "Simply I credit her false speaking tongue" , though he knows that she lies to him. Both lovers are liars and hide the truth to enjoy love, romance and sex "On both sides thus is simple truth suppress'd." He knows that she is unfaithful and a liar, but prefers to suppress this truth and she knows that he is not young and she pretends not to know his true age.

In lines 9 and 10 the poet inquires why his mistress does not confess to him that she is unfaithful "But wherefore says she not she is unjust?" and why he does not confess to her that he is not young any more "And wherefore say not I that I am old?" The poet believes that love is blind and that lovers; all lovers without exception are liars and disguise the truth and favour the pretence of truth "love's best habit is in seeming trust". In line 12 the poet says that older lovers do not like to reveal their true age. In the couplet of the sonnet the speaker uses word play. The word lie has double meaning. In one sense, the poet uses the word lie to mean tell a lie and hide the truth. In another sense, it means lie on the bed to get ready for the sexual intercourse. Actually, both senses of the word are applicable to the interpretation of the poem for the two lovers are both telling lies and are making love in bed. The two lovers find both comfort and sexual gratification in lying to each other. The lies they tell each other help them forget their faults; nymphomania of the woman and old age of the male lover.

Commentary:

William Shakespeare's Sonnet 138 portrays a middle-aged male lover's rationalization of deceit in a love affair with a young promiscuous woman. The two lovers are both liars and deceive one another for the sake of enjoying love, romance and sex. The dark young woman is nymphomaniac and unfaithful whereas the man tells her that he is much younger than he actually is. The speaker portrays his middle-life crisis. He is involved in a deceitful love affair with a promiscuous and lusty young girl at a rather advanced age. Three main ideas permeate the entire sonnet: dishonesty, deception, aging and lust. Both lovers are convinced that mutual deceit is important for perpetuating their love affair. The speaker finds lame excuses for his deception. He claims that he is younger than he actually is and he knows that his mistress is unfaithful and promiscuous. He has to suppress this fact to gain sexual gratification and to assure himself that he is still young and worthy of being loved. Fear of aging makes is the man's underlying cause behind his love affair with a degenerate woman, and lust is the woman's motive in being involved in a love affair with a much older man than she really is and dishonesty is the means through which both gain sexual gratification. For both lovers honesty is unimportant in their love affair. Their love affair is based on lust rather than pure love. Sexual gratification seems to be the target for both lovers.

The speaker knows that his mistress is fooling him and he enjoys playing the role of the simpleton or naive. The speaker uses "lie with," which implies sexual intercourse rather than lie to which implies hiding the truth. Dishonesty and making love become one: to lie is to lie with. Their lies help them both achieve sexual gratification. To keep his love affair with the young woman the aging lover metaphorically puts on the masque of a young immature man and plays the role of the fool and simpleton. Similarly, the unfaithful woman plays the role of the faithful woman to win the affection of the aging lover and achieve her sexual gratification. Although she knows that the aging lover is acting the role of the fool, she accepts his acting. For both lovers deception and dishonesty seem to be the only way to make their love affair survive and thus achieve sexual gratification. For the speaker sexual pleasure can diminish the effects of aging. The very fact that his mistress is promiscuous makes the speaker sexually excited. The two bumbling lovers are sexually attracted to each other. Their love affair is entirely based on sex without love. The speaker explicitly reveals the lust bond that unites him and his young woman in the couplet of the sonnet when he says, "Therefore I'll lie with love, and love with me, Since that our faults in love thus smother'd be."

The middle-life crisis the speaker suffers from is very universal. Middle-aged men become sexually agitated and they do everything that young people do to assert their youthfulness. They want to prove to every one else around them that they are still young, attractive and worthy of love. Such men get involved in new love affairs with younger women even outside marriage life, buy new sport cars, some of them even divorce their wives and start looking for young sex partners.

"When my Love Swears that she is Made of Truth"

Test your understanding:

1- In sonnet 138 "When my Love Swears that she is Made of Truth"
William Shakespeare is addressing ....
A) A dark woman
B) A fair woman
C) Another gay
D) (B&C)

2- In the lines quoted underneath , the speaker believes the young woman
although he knows that she lies to him because.......
"When my love swears that she is made of truth
I do believe her, though I know she lies"
A) The love affair with the young woman is very important to him since
this relationship gives him both sexual gratification and assurance
that he is still young and worthy of love
B) He is not sure that she lies to him
C) She is faithful to him
D) He is inexperienced in matters related to love and sex

3- In the lines quoted underneath , what are "the world's false forgeries"?
"That she might think me some untutor'd youth,
Unskilful in the world's false forgeries"
A) Love and sex
B) Money and work
C) Education and marriage
D) Age and death

4- In the lines quoted underneath , in what sense is the speaker lying to his
mistress?
"Thus vainly thinking that she thinks me young,
Although I know my years be past the best"
A) He pretends to be much younger than he actually is
B) He pretends that he is faithful to her though he has another love affair
with another woman
C) He keeps telling her that he is rich
D) He keeps telling her that she is pretty though he knows that she is
dark and not beautiful

5- In the lines quoted underneath, in what sense is the woman lying to her male lover?
   "When my love swears that she is made of truth
   I do believe her, though I know she lies"
   A) She pretends that she is faithful to him though she is promiscuous and nymphomaniac
   B) She lies to him about his age when she tells him that he is still young and attractive
   C) She lies to him about her own age when she tells him that she is much younger than she actually is.
   D) (A&B)

6- What do the lines quoted underneath reveal?
   "I smiling credit her false-speaking tongue,
   Outfacing faults in love with love's ill rest"
   A) The man finds joy in the woman's lies as knowing that she is unfaithful and promiscuous arouses his sexual desire towards her.
   B) The man detests the woman because she is unfaithful
   C) The man has never questioned the woman about her infidelity and nymphomania
   D) The woman does not lie to her lover and she is indeed faithful to him

7- In the lines quoted underneath , what does the speaker want to say?
   "But wherefore says my love that she is young?
    And wherefore say not I that I am old?
    O, love's best habit is a soothing tongue,
    And age, in love, loves not to have years told"
   A) He wonders why his mistress is concerned about their true age
   B) Lying is the habit of lovers and that's what makes love blind and exciting
   C) Love is not restricted to a certain age in the sense that it knows no boundaries
   D) (A, B &C)

8- In the lines quoted below , the speaker employs word play in the word lie in the sense that ....
   "Therefore I'll lie with love, and love with me,
    Since that our faults in love thus smother'd be"
   A) They both lie to each other
   B) They lie on bed to make love
   C) They tell the truth to one another
   D) (A&B)

Elements of Poetry
Chapter Fifteen

Metaphysical Poetry

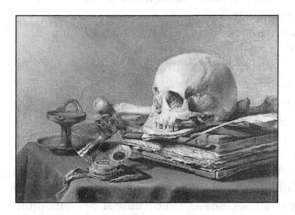

What is metaphysical poetry?

Metaphysical poetry refers to that poetry written by a group of seventeen century poets whose verse was distinguished from other poetry for its intellectual and philosophical style. Metaphysical poetry was highly scientific and philosophical and employed extended metaphors to compare very dissimilar objects. Metaphysical poets included John Donne, George Herbert, Richard Crashaw, Andrew Marvell, Henry Vaughn and Abraham Cowley.

Main Characteristics of Metaphysical Poetry:

1) Metaphysical poets were not hesitant to use ordinary language replete with puns, paradoxes, extended metaphors, irony, word play and conceits. Their paradoxical statements were quite shocking to readers as the objects compared were very dissimilar. For instance comparing love to a compass.

2) Metaphysical poetry is very witty, intellectual and scientific. The figures of speech employed by metaphysical posts were very original in the sense that they made the readers think critically and creatively to understand them. Metaphysical poetry is replete with references to alchemy, sea-voyages, mythology and religion. Some metaphysical images recur so frequently in metaphysical poems to the extent that they have become typical archetypes.

For instance, kingship and rule; subjectivism, elixir of life, cosmology, microcosm, and macrocosm.

3) Metaphysical poetry uses puzzling terminology drawn from science, alchemy, astrology and the other sciences.

4) Metaphysical poetry is highly argumentative. Metaphysical poems are presented in the form of an argument. Sometimes there may be two or more arguments in a poem.

5) Metaphysical love poetry often reflects ideas from Renaissance Neo-Platonism to reveal the harmony between the soul and the body, and that between the mind and the heart. The two lovers' souls and bodies are united in a very strange way. Neo-Platonism is the doctrines of Plato who argues that since the physical world is merely an imperfect imitation of the divine archetype, the poet depicting the world is imitating an imitation, and thus creating something that stands at least two removes from the truth.

6) The metaphysical poets portrayed the two lovers' internal reality and psychological realism and created for them love microcosms superior to the outside world.

7) Metaphysical poetry portrays platonic love in its hedonic and sensuous sense. Metaphysical poets equated absolute beauty with the divine beauty of God. The metaphysical Platonic lover moves in stages through the desire for his mistress, whose beauty he views as an imitation of God's beauty. This resemblance between God and the lover makes both worthy of worship. However, in some metaphysical poems Platonic love transcends crude sexuality and attains a form of spirituality.

Metaphysical Poetry

THE SUN RISING
by John Donne

Busy old fool, unruly Sun,
Why dost thou thus,
Through windows, and through curtains, call on us ?
Must to thy motions lovers' seasons run?
Saucy pedantic wretch, go chide
Late school-boys and sour prentices,
Go tell court-huntsmen that the king will ride,
Call country ants to harvest offices;
Love, all alike, no season knows nor clime,
Nor hours, days, months, which are the rags of time.

Thy beams so reverend, and strong
Why shouldst thou think?
I could eclipse and cloud them with a wink,
But that I would not lose her sight so long.
If her eyes have not blinded thine,
Look, and to-morrow late tell me,
Whether both th' Indias of spice and mine
Be where thou left'st them, or lie here with me.
Ask for those kings whom thou saw'st yesterday,
And thou shalt hear, "All here in one bed lay."

She's all states, and all princes I;
Nothing else is;
Princes do but play us; compared to this,
All honour's mimic, all wealth alchemy.
Thou, Sun, art half as happy as we,
In that the world's contracted thus;
Thine age asks ease, and since thy duties be
To warm the world, that's done in warming us.
Shine here to us, and thou art everywhere;
This bed thy center is, these walls thy sphere.

"The Sun Rising"

Summary

The persona and his mistress are lying naked in bed in the early morning. They have been busy making love. The man addresses the rising sun of the early morning and rebukes it for stealthily entering the bedroom without permission and bothering them with its suspicious looks. The word busy in the first line of the poem has two underlying meanings. On the one hand, it refers to the two lovers who are busy making love. In this context, the speaker scolds the rising sun for impudently entering the bedroom and ogling the two lovers' naked bodies. On the other hand, the word busy refers to the rising sun which the speaker rebukes and describes as the "busy old fool". To the speaker, the sun is as old as the universe and it is a foolish old heavenly body.

The speaker rebukes the sun, the intruder, for being impolite as it sneakily entered the bedroom through the window and the curtains. The speaker inquires why the sun behaves thus and whether it does have a magic spell over lovers. Then the speaker gives the miserable, boring and impudent sun an order to leave the bedroom and go somewhere else. Instead of staying in the two lovers' bedroom, she should go and rebuke late school boys and unskillful workers "sour prentices". The speaker believes that he and his mistress have done nothing wrong and do not deserve to be rebuked. To him love making is neither a sin nor a crime, but rather instinctive and natural behavior. He wonders why the sun is ogling their naked bodies and is rebuking them. They have done nothing to be ashamed of. He believes that the sun must go somewhere else to rebuke wrong doers such as lazy apprentices and late school boys. The sun could also go and remind the court-huntsmen to escort the king in his early morning horse ride or awaken farmers to harvest their crops in the fields. The speaker asserts that love making is not restricted to specific time, season or climate; it can be done anywhere and any time. When the two lovers are caught in a love trance and sexual ecstasy, they become unaware of time and place.

In the second stanza the speaker ridicules the sun and inquires why she must think that her sun rays are strong. He challenges the sun and tells her that he could eclipse her sunshine simply by winking his eye "I could eclipse and cloud them with a wink". But he would not close his eyes because he can not bear not looking at his beloved while lying beside him in bed even for an instant. Then, he praises his mistress's eyes which outshine the sun. The speaker then addresses the sun and tells her that the two Indias are in bed with him. The speaker metaphorically compares his mistress to India in the sense that both are hot and burning with sexual desire. The speaker wants to say that the woman lying in his bed whom he considers to be his sex object is so spicy. The speaker feels that he is richer than all kings because he is caught in sexual ecstasy with his lover.

In the third stanza the speaker reveals his intentions toward his beloved. He considers her as his territory and he is the prince and owner of that territory. To him she is merely a sex object; an embodiment of all the beauties of the world. Sex becomes too commercial here, and the mistress herself is looked upon as being inferior to the male lover; a symbol of the market place. She is every country in the world and he is the king of all kings "She's all states, and all princes I" and he desires nothing more. He believes that he is a real prince not a fraud because his beloved is in bed with him. All the princes in the world are not real princes and they merely imitate him in being a prince "Princes do but play us; compared to this". Being a prince with a territory is merely an imitation compared to what the two lovers are doing in bed. The speaker claims that love making is a kind of honour for him; the best honour one can yearn to have. Other honours are imitations of his honour "All honour's mimic". He then compares his beloved to a wealth; more valuable than any wealth in the world. For him making love with the woman he loves is a wealth and all other wealth is false alchemy through which scientists tried in vain to change cheap metals into gold. For him his mistress is pure gold not false alchemy.

The speaker takes pity on the old sun and decides to ease the burdens of her old age, he declares "Shine here to us, and thou art everywhere". He addresses the sun and tells her that she is not as happy as he and his beloved are "Thou, Sun, art half as happy as we". The speaker dwells upon the idea of contraction in love. When caught in a love trance the two lovers feel that the world around them has contracted to the place where they are. They even become unaware of time and place. For them time becomes static and they become the center of the world "In that the world's contracted thus". The speaker then tells the sun to shine on the bed where he and his mistress are lying and warm them because if it shines on their bed and warms them, it will warm the whole universe. This would make the sun's job much easier in her old age "To warm the world, that's done in warming us".

In the final two lines of the poem the speaker tells the sun that the bed where he and his beloved make love is the center of the universe around which the sun turns and the walls of the bedroom is the sun's orbit. The speaker believes that if the sun shines on the two lovers' bed, it will be shining on the whole universe "Shine here to us, and thou art everywhere" because their bed is its center and the walls of their bedroom are its orbit "This bed thy center is, these walls thy sphere"

Commentary:
"The Sun Rising" is a metaphysical love poem based on hyperbolic assertions. The poem consists of three stanzas each of which contains ten lines where lines one, five and six are metered in iambic tetrameter, line two is metered in iambic dimeter and lines three , four and seven through ten are in iambic pentameter. The entire poem is built around a series of overstatements or hyperboles. For instance, the speaker believes that his love affair is so important to the universe and kings and princes imitate it. To him the world is contracted and contained within the two lovers' bedroom which he claims to be the center of the universe and the sun's orbit has contracted to the bedroom of the two lovers.

All these hyperbolic assertions are not true and metaphorically reflect the wakeful lover's subjective feelings. The man claims that all the riches and beauties of the world are all in his bed and he needs nothing more from life. The speaker's displacement of the macrocosm or the outside world in favour of the two lovers' microcosm reveals the main theme of the poem: the centrality of love amidst the physical world. To the two lovers their microcosm of love is self-contained; larger and more important than the macrocosm or the external world which is now contained within the walls of their bedroom. When the poet says that the two lovers seem to form the core of the universe around which all heavenly bodies rotate, he argues for the strength of mutual or reciprocal love which transcends all boundaries of time and place.

"The sun Rising"

Test your understanding:

1- What does the persona mean by the word "busy" with which the poet
begins the poem   and appears in the three lines quoted underneath?

> Busy old fool, unruly Sun,
> Why dost thou thus,
> Through windows, and through curtains, call on us ?

A) The two lovers are busy making love in bed.

B) The sun is busy ogling the two lover's naked bodies through the
curtains of the bedroom.

C)The two lovers are busy looking at the sun while it is rising and
stealthily entering their bedroom to look to look at their naked
bodies.

D) (A&B)

2- In the lines quoted underneath why does the speaker rebuke the sun and
give it an order to leave the bedroom and go somewhere else?

> Saucy pedantic wretch, go chide
> Late school-boys and sour prentices,
> Go tell court-huntsmen that the king will ride,
> Call country ants to harvest offices;
> Love, all alike, no season knows nor clime,
> Nor hours, days, months, which are the rags of time.

A) He believes that the sun rays will hurt the eyes of his mistress.

B) He believes that love making is a sin and a crime and that he and his
beloved feel sorry for doing that in front of the gazing sun.

C) He believes that the sun should rebuke wrong doers such as late
school boys, unskillful workers, and lazy farmers rather than
scolding two lovers making love in bed.

D) He asserts that love making can be done only in the bedroom not in
the open air.

3-What does the speaker mean by the two Indias in the lines quoted below?

> Whether both th' Indias of spice and mine
> Be where thou left'st them, or lie here with me.

A) The speaker metaphorically compares his mistress to India; a hot country rich in spices, because she is hot and spicy like India and is burning with sexual desire.

B) The male lover reveals that the woman sleeping in bed with him is Indian.

C) The speaker addresses the sun and asks it to go and shine on India.

D) (B&C)

4-What do the lines quoted below reveal about the speaker's intention toward the woman lying in his bed?

> She's all states, and all princes I;
> Nothing else is;
> Princes do but play us; compared to this,

A) He regards her as his territory and he is the prince and owner of that territory.

B) To him she is merely a sex object; an embodiment of all the beauties of the world.

C) He believes that he is a real prince because he is making love with his mistress and all the other princes are fake princes who imitate what he does.

D) (A, B &C)

5- What does the speaker mean when he says "All honour's mimic, all wealth alchemy"?

A) He claims that love making is a kind of honour for him; the best honour one can wish to have. Other honours are imitations of this honour.

B) To him the woman sleeping with him is more valuable than any wealth in the world. She is real wealth. Money and treasures are merely fake imitations of this wealth.

C) To please his mistress he will practice alchemy to change cheap metals into gold and give it all to her.

D) (A, B &C)

6- In the line quoted below, what does the speaker mean by the concept of "contraction in love"?

"In that the world's contracted thus"

A) When caught in love trance and sexual ecstasy the two lovers feel that the world around them has contracted to the place where they are thus they become unaware of time and place.

B) While making love the bodies of the two lovers have contracted.

C) The two lovers' microcosm contracts to their bedroom.

D) (B&C)

Elements of Poetry

Chapter Sixteen

Metaphysical Poetry: Religious Poetry

John Donne

Death, Be Not Proud

Death be not proud, though some have called thee
Mighty and dreadful, for, thou art not so,
For, those, whom thou think'st, thou dost overthrow,
Die not, poor death, nor yet canst thou kill me.
From rest and sleep, which but thy pictures be,
Much pleasure, then from thee, much more must flow,
And soonest our best men with thee do go,
Rest of their bones, and souls delivery.
Thou art slave to Fate, Chance, kings, and desperate men,
And dost with poison, war, and sickness dwell,
And poppy, or charms can make us sleep as well,
And better then thy stroke; why swell'st thou then?
One short sleep past, we wake eternally,
And death shall be no more; death, thou shalt die.

"Death, Be Not Proud"

Summary:
"Death, Be Not Proud" is John Donne's best divine or holy sonnet in which he rhetorically mocks and rebukes mighty death. The poem explores one of the most fundamental mysteries of human life: death, the leveler and the conqueror. The poet personifies death as a tyrant without real power and disarms it of its fake power "some have called thee / Mighty and dreadful, for, thou art not so". The poet wages a verbal war against death and continues to dismantle it from something mysterious and formidable, to something weak and irrelevant. The poet begins his religious sonnet with repeating the title of the poem "Death , be not proud " and then releases many arguments to refute the assumption that death constitutes man's greatest fear and conqueror and to assert his claim that death exercises no power and no control over him because he is a pious and devout Christian. The whole poem is an apostrophe which the poet uses to anthropomorphize death. Death is something abstract, but is given human attributes. The poet addresses death as an embodiment of fake pride.

The poet plays the role of a preacher and a clergyman who advises devout Christians not to fear death as long as they stick to their creed and faith. Several of the poet's arguments are aimed at humbling death. The first argument the poet makes is that death is not formidable or dreadful, but is rather a kind of rest and sleep "From rest and sleep, which but thy pictures be, Much pleasure, then from thee, much more must flow". If people find joy and pleasure in rest and sleep, then death must be more enjoyable than them both. The second argument the poet makes to assert his claim that death is not horrible or dreadful is that the best human beings including prophets, messengers, pious men, great emperors and kings died, then why should ordinary people fear death? For him death is not something to be feared, but rather is something pleasant and should be met with a smile. For the poet, death is inescapable and unavoidable and therefore, should not be feared. Some of the best men such as prophets and kings died and soon other good men will die "soonest our best men with thee do go". The poet says he can not understand why people fear death as long as their great predecessors and ancestors faced the same end.

The poem takes a twist when Donne mocks death and refutes people's claim that it is "mighty and dreadful". The poet believes that death is merely a slave who takes orders from God. It is also a slave to kings who wage wars against other countries in which many people die in the war. It is also a slave to fate for people are destined to die at a certain age. Death is also a slave to chance for some people die in accidents. Death is also a slave to desperate and depressed men and women who commit suicide and thus put an end to their lives at any moment they wish "Thou art slave to Fate, Chance, kings, and desperate men". The poet then despises death and calls it a dweller of disgusting places such as poison, war and sickness "And dost with poison, war, and sickness dwell". The poet's diction becomes grandiose and even more aggressive when he calls death "poor" and inquires with bewilderment; "why then does death boast of being dreadful and formidable? "why swell'st thou then?". For the poet, it is not so.

The poet believes that pious men whom death boasts of having killed are still alive in Heaven and they are happy living eternal life there "For, those, whom thou think'st, thou dost overthrow, Die not, poor death, nor yet canst thou kill me". The poet challenges death and claims that it will not kill him as long as he is a devout and pious believer in God. Being a devout Christian and a pious man will certainly take him to Heaven where he will enjoy eternal happiness. The poet humbles death further when he asserts that drugs and magic can also make us sleep just like death. Such sleeping magnets are even stronger and more powerful than death itself "And poppy or charms can make us sleep as well, And better then thy stroke". Then, why is death so proud of its power? "why swell'st thou then? In this context , the poem has a biblical reference and reflects the Christian belief that those who believe in Christ will never die but live eternally, "That whosoever believeth in him should not perish, but have eternal life" (John. 3.15 . The Bible: King James Version).

Commentary:
"Death, Be Not Proud" is one of John Donne's nineteen "holy sonnets" which discuss themes that pertain to *Christian philosophy*. The whole poem is a reflection on Christian philosophy and Christians' perception of death. For devout Christians death is the end of strife and difficult life, but the beginning of eternal life. For pious Christians, who are true believers in God, death is merely a short sleep, a transitory stage between mundane life and eternal life "one short sleep past" and then they wake to live eternally, "we wake eternally". In Christian faith death is ephemeral and insignificant compared to eternal life in Heaven. The poet ends the poem with

a paradoxical statement "And death shall be no more; death, thou shalt die". Upon first reading, the statement seems contradictory, but when one contemplates it, it appears true for there will be no death in Heaven and people will live eternally.

The poet does not fear death and considers it a liberation from the hardships of life. He believes that death is fake and illusory; a false concept. According to Christian faith, when people die their earthly perishable bodies are discarded in the graves while their souls descend to Heaven to live eternally thereby escaping death "rest of their bones, and soul's delivery". The poet, who is himself a devout Christian and a preacher, believes in the continuation of life after death "One short sleep past, we wake eternally". For all devout Christians death is a short transitory stage between mundane life and eternal life. Death is merely a breath taken for a while then released once again. So what separates mundane life from eternal life is merely a breath. The body is discarded and the soul goes to Heaven to live eternally.

Death is a natural phenomenon; something inescapable and unavoidable. It exists everywhere and attacks us at any moment without any prior notification. It kills our families, friends and beloved ones, and then kills us. It fills people's hearts with fears and sorrows. Devout Christians believe that death is powerless for it can not prevent their resurrection and redemption that Jesus Christ has granted them. The whole sonnet is centered around one major metaphor which is death is a short sleep after which people wake up on the Day of Judgment to lead a better eternal life.

"Death, Be Not Proud"

Test your understanding:

1- John Donne's "Death, Be Not Proud" belongs to a collection of nineteen sonnets known as ……….
   A) The Religious Sonnets
   B) The Metaphysical Sonnets
   C) The Holy Sonnets
   D) The Confessional Sonnets

2- In the two lines quoted below from John Donne's sonnet "Death, Be Not Proud", the poet ……………
   "Death be not proud, though some have called thee
   Mighty and dreadful, for, thou art not so"
   A) Personifies death as an undefeatable tyrant with unquestionable power.
   B) Asserts the fact that death is the leveler for it treats people equally the same without bias and prejudice
   C) Refutes the assumption that death constitutes man's greatest fear and conqueror and claims that death exercises no power and no control over since it is not formidable as people think.
   D) Fears death because it is mighty and formidable.

3- In the two lines quoted below from John Donne's sonnet "Death, Be Not Proud", the poet ……………
   "For, those, whom thou think'st, thou dost overthrow,
   Die not, poor death, nor yet canst thou kill me."
   A) Humbles death and asserts the fact that devout Christians who died are not indeed dead because they now lead eternal life in Heaven.
   B) Challenges death and claims that it can not take his life forever because as a pious Christian he will live eternally in Heaven.
   C) Submits to death and acknowledges defeat because he is powerless in front the mighty conqueror.
   D) (A&B)

4- What is the poet's idea in the two lines quoted below from John Donne's sonnet "Death, Be Not Proud"?

"From rest and sleep, which but thy pictures be,
Much pleasure, then from thee, much more must flow"

A) Death is not formidable or dreadful, but is rather a kind of rest and sleep

B) If people find joy and pleasure in rest and sleep, then death must be more enjoyable than them both.

C) (A&B)

D) Death is less pleasurable than rest and sleep

5- What Christian belief do the two lines quoted below from John Donne's sonnet "Death, Be Not Proud" echo ?

"And soonest our best men with thee do go,
Rest of their bones, and souls delivery"

A) Those who believe in Jesus Christ will never die but live eternally, "That whosoever believeth in him should not perish, but have eternal life" (The Bible: King James Version 3:15).

B) Eternal life is much better than this mundane and hard life

C) The human soul does not perish after death but rather descends to Heaven, whereas the body in which it was imprisoned is discarded in the grave to be rotten and dismantled.

D) Death is man's detestable enemy.

6- What Christian belief do the two lines quoted below from John Donne's sonnet "Death, Be Not Proud" stress?

"One short sleep past, we wake eternally,
And death shall be no more; death, thou shalt die"

A) The human soul does not perish after death but rather descends to Heaven, whereas the body in which it was imprisoned is discarded in the grave.

B) As long as the best human beings including prophets, messengers, pious men, great emperors and kings died, then ordinary people should not fear death.

C) Death is undefeatable and unbeatable.

D) Those who believe in Jesus Christ will never die but live eternally, "That whosoever believeth in him should not perish, but have eternal life" (The Bible: King James Version 3:15).

7- In the line quoted below from John Donne's sonnet "Death, Be Not Proud", ...

"And dost with poison, war, and sickness dwell"

A) The poet detests death because its natural habitat is ugly and disgusting places such as poison, sickness and in wars.

B) The poet praises death for being the only leveler in the world as it treats people equally the same.

C) Poison, sickness and wars have killed more people than natural death has.

D) Poison, sickness and death have killed less people than natural death has.

8- In the line quoted below from John Donne's sonnet "Death, Be Not Proud" , why does the poet describe death as a slave?

"Thou art slave to Fate, Chance, kings, and desperate men"

A) It can be summoned by a king when he orders the execution of a traitor.

B) Some people accidentally die in horrible accidents such as a plane crash or a car accident or any   other accident.

C) Desperate men and women who suffer from cute depression can commit suicide any time they wish and it is people's fate to die.

D) (A,B &C)

9- In the two lines quoted below from John Donne's sonnet "Death, Be Not Proud" , the expression which the poet uses to address death "why swell'st thou then? literally means...............

And poppy, or charms can make us sleep as well,

And better then thy stroke; why swell'st thou then?

A) Why are you afraid?

B) Why are proud of yourself?

C) Why are you mercilessly killing people?

D) Why are you happy?

Elements of Poetry

Chapter Seventeen

Narrative Poetry

Narrative poetry is poetry that narrates a story. The story is told in the form of a poem to make it more concentrated, more emotionally appealing and more memorable to the reader. This is the oldest form of poetry and the oldest narrative poems were known to almost all civilizations such as the epic of *Gilgamesh, the Iliad* and *Odyssey*. A narrative poem can be too long and complex in the form of an epic like *Gilgamesh*, or it can be short and simple like Arlington Robinson's poem "Richard Cory". Narrative poems include epics, ballads, and idylls.

Epic is a lengthy, narrative poem that tackles a serious subject of high importance to a nation. The epic describes heroic deeds and events significant to the culture of that nation. The first original epics are called primary epics, whereas, epics that imitated the original epics like Virgil's *The Aeneid* and John Milton's *Paradise Lost* are known as literary or secondary epics.

Idyll is a short narrative poem that describes the rustic life of shepherds in the countryside. An idyll narrates the story of shepherds and how they live happily with their cattle in the countryside. Shepherds and animals are portrayed in a natural rural setting living harmoniously. An idyll portrays the serenity of the shepherds' lives, and the naivety of their thinking. Although the shepherds' life is simple, it is happy and cheerful. Idylls are highly emotional and sometimes sentimental. **Ballad** is a short narrative poem set to music in the form of a song. It usually has foreshortened, alternating four-stress lines and simple repeating rhymes, often with a refrain. If the subject matter or the theme of a ballad is religious, a ballad is then called a hymn.

Narrative Poetry
Richard Cory
by Edwin Arlington Robinson, 1869-1935

Whenever Richard Cory went down town,
We people on the pavement looked at him;
He was a gentleman from sole to crown,
Clean favored, and imperially slim.

And he was always quietly arrayed,
And he was always human when he talked;
But still he fluttered pulses when he said,
"Good-morning," and he glittered when he walked.

And he was rich—yes, richer than a king—
And admirably schooled in every grace:
In fine, we thought that he was everything
To make us wish that we were in his place.

So on we worked, and waited for the light,
And went without the meat, and cursed the bread;
And Richard Cory, one calm summer night,
Went home and put a bullet through his head.

Summary:

"Richard Cory" is a narrative poem which tells the story of how a rich man in a calm Summer night mysteriously and shockingly commits suicide without any apparent reason. It is an open ended story which leaves the reader with an open mouth and a frowning face. Richard Cory is portrayed as an elegant man of mystery; a successful and impressive rich gentleman. He is cultured, educated and well-mannered. He talks gently and behaves calmly like a king. The poem is told from the viewpoint of a narrator and Richard Cory does not say a single word in the poem. In the first three stanzas of the poem the narrator praises Richard Cory and shows how the other people in the town admired his personality and envied him for being so rich and so cultured. They thought he was richer than a king and lived without having to worry about anything in life, while they had to work hard in order to earn their daily bread and meat. Richard Cory, the narrator says was "a gentleman from sole to crown", always clean-shaven "Clean favored, and had a nice slim figure "imperially slim". He was always dressed smartly "always quietly arrayed" and he talked properly and tenderly "And he was always human when he talked", and he was cultured and educated "schooled in every grace". Richard Cory is a true gentleman. He behaves like a gentleman, dresses like a gentleman and talks like a gentleman. Because he was rich, decent and proper all his town fellow men used to envy him and look at him with admiration. He was an object of attention for all the people in the town. "we people on the pavement looked at him". Though Richard Cory does not speak so much to his town fellow men, and seems completely detached from his society, he used to say "Good morning" to his admirers sitting on the pavement.

The poet's diction is regal and his description of Richard Cory does not fit an ordinary man, but is well-suited for a king. For instance, the word crown is highly poetic and well-suited to a king not an ordinary man "He was a gentleman from sole to crown", then he explicitly compares him to a man better and richer than a king "And he was rich—yes, richer than a king" and finally compares him to an emperor when he says that he was "imperially slim".

Critical Analysis

The narrator perfectly describes Richard Cory's external appearance, but seems ignorant of his internal reality. For the narrator Richard Cory was a polite and rich gentleman with decent manners and proper language, but he failed to notice the man's subjective state which might have been completely different from his outward glittering appearance. The narrator, like all the people of the town, was deceived by the man's appearance and failed to notice his sad internal reality. The narrator failed to understand the fact that appearances are sometimes deceptive and they do not reflect man's inner self. The people sitting on the pavement including the narrator envied Richard Cory and wished to be as rich as he was and as decent and schooled as he was. They thought that the man had achieved all his ambitions in life and needed nothing more in life "we thought that he was everything" and they envied him and wanted to be as rich and successful as he was "To make us wish that we were in his place".

However, the end of the story is quite shocking to both the people sitting on the pavement and to readers. The final stanza of the poem takes a dark, ominous and sudden twist. Richard Cory commits suicide by shooting himself with a pistol. His death is so violent. He put the pistol's barrel inside his wide open mouth and pushed the trigger thus exploding the back of his head. The man took his own life for no apparent reason. Neither the narrator nor the people sitting on the pavement nor even the readers know why such an impressive, successful and rich man suddenly committed suicide. It is an open ended story indeed that leaves the readers with much time to contemplate the violent and shocking death of such a bizarre person. The poem ends here, but many questions are raised. Why did the man commit suicide? Does he suffer from any chronic illness? Does he suffer from depression or any hidden agony or sin? Does he suffer from loneliness and spiritual emptiness? The poet intentionally leaves these questions and more for readers to contemplate and answer.

The narrator and all the townspeople mainly those sitting on the pavement are all poor and for that reason they envied Richard Cory and spoke highly of him. The narrator says, "So on we worked, and waited for the light" "And went without meat and cursed the bread". They thought that while Richard Cory lived in luxury, they lived in poverty without having anything to eat. They could do nothing, but hopefully waited for a sudden change in their fortune in life which would make them as rich as Richard Cory.

The last stanza of the poem has a biblical reference. Bread in the bible has several meanings and one of them seems to be applicable to this poem. In the Bible Jesus said "Man shall not live by bread alone, but by every word that proceedeth out of the mouth of God" (Matthew 4:4). This verse from the Bible means that physical nourishment is not sufficient for a healthy life; man also has spiritual needs. Although Richard Cory portrayed in the poem was rich and successful, his life was spiritually empty and lacked meaning. Although he had everything he wanted in life, he could not give meaning to his life. He was fed up with the luxuries of life which could not give him happiness. Having got fed up with luxurious living and having failed to give meaning to his life, and having failed to achieve spiritual richness the man committed suicide. It becomes apparent that it is ironical that the people sitting on the pavement and the narrator himself wished to be in the rich man's place. Their wish to be in Richard Cory's place "wish that we were in his place" gradually diminishes and they lose interest in that wish when they heard that the man committed suicide. The poet uses the words bread, meat and light symbolically. Unlike meat and bread which are used as symbols of physical nourishment and material values, light represents spiritual richness and true faith. Richard Cory lacked the spiritual light that the other townspeople seemed to have.

The narrator in the poem blasphemously curses the bread. He is not content with what God has given him. He says he has to eat bread without meat every day while Richard Cory lived luxuriously. Being poor, like all the people sitting on the pavement, the narrator could not afford to buy meat for dinner and he had to eat cheap bread every day. Therefore, he began cursing the bread. The poet seems to say that for every Richard Cory living in the world, there are less fortunate people who envy him and look upon him in awe. In fact, the narrator in the poem and all the people sitting on the pavement are not only jealous and envious of Richard Cory, but they are also spiteful and hateful of such a successful and rich man.

The poet positions Richard Cory above ordinary folk in terms of material success and proper and decent manners. Although he was very wealthy, the man was not self-conceited and spoke calmly and affectionately to his townspeople. Ironically, Richard Cory's suicide brings about a complete reversal of roles in the poem. As Cory is dethroned and his life ends sadly, the poor people sitting on the pavement are elevated and they continue living.

Richard Cory made several attempts to communicate with his townspeople, but they seemed nonresponsive. His social detachment, spiritual emptiness and loneliness might have driven the man to commit suicide. Ironically enough, instead of making him happy, wealth made Richard Cory socially detached and spiritually barren and finally drove him to commit suicide. However, the motive for his suicide remains a mystery.

Themes:
- Appearances are sometimes deceptive.
- We never know everything about other people even the ones we are quite familiar with.
- We do not have access to the inner reality and subjective life of other people.
- External reality is sometimes deceptive and does not by any means reflect inner reality.
- Wealth and power are not sufficient to make one happy.
- Inward happiness is more important than success and wealth.
- Spiritual and materialistic values together make people happy
- The poem seems to refute the popular belief that rich people are necessarily happy and poor people are necessarily unhappy.

Structure of the Poem:
The structure of "Richard Cory" is simple and classic. The poem consists of four classical quatrains written in iambic pentameter. Every line of the poem contains five feet each of which contains an unaccented or unstressed syllable followed by a stressed or accented syllable. The scansion of the first quatrain looks like this:

u — u — u — u — u —
WhenEV /er RICH /ard COR /y WENT /down TOWN,

u — u — u — u — u —
We PE /ople ON /the PAVE /ment LOOKED /at HIM:

u — u — u — u — u —
He WAS /a GEN /tleMAN /from SOLE /to CROWN,

u — u — u — u—u—
Clean FAV /ored AND /imPER/iAL/ly SLIM

Richard Cory:

Test your understanding:
1-"Richard Cory" by Edwin Robinson is a representative specimen of ....
  A) Pastoral Poetry
  B) Narrative Poetry
  C) Confessional Poetry
  D) Narrative Poetry

2- In the two lines quoted below, the poet diction is regal and his description of Richard Cory does not fit an ordinary man, but is well-suited for a king. What royal word or words does the poet use when he compares the successful gentleman to a king?
"He was a gentleman from sole to crown,
Clean favored, and imperially slim"
  A) gentleman
  B) clean favoured
  C) sole
  D) crown and imperially slim

3- In the second stanza quoted below, what perception does the narrator seem to have of Richard Cory?
"And he was always quietly arrayed,
 And he was always human when he talked;
 But still he fluttered pulses when he said,
"Good-morning," and he glittered when he walked"
  A) He knows nothing about Richard Cory except for his external appearance.
  B) The narrator like all the town fellow men mistakenly believes that Richard Cory is rich and happy because he is always seen smartly dressed and he shines when he walks.
  C) The narrator knew for sure that Richard Cory was not happy though he was rich
  D) (A&B)

4- The two lines quoted underneath from Edwin Robinson's "Richard Cory" are highly thematic. What theme or themes can be abstracted from these lines?

"In fine, we thought that he was everything
To make us wish that we were in his place"

 A) Appearances are sometimes deceptive and do not faithfully reflect people's internal reality.

 B) Success and wealth are more important than inward happiness because materialistic values rather than spiritual values make people happy.

 C) People's internal reality is quite subjective and personal and they might not reveal it even to their closest companions.

 D) (A &C)

5- Who narrates the events in the poem ?

 A) Richard Cory himself

 B) The town fellow men sitting on the pavement and keep looking at Richard Cory

 C) An omniscient narrator who knows every thing about Richard Cory's internal and external reality.

 D) A narrator who seems , like all the town fellow men, ignorant of Richard Cory's internal feelings and his social and psychological dilemmas.

Questions for Contemplation:

1- The poet describes Richard Cory as the peak of human accomplishment, but then, in one stanza reveals to the reader the true tragedy behind his existence? What does the poet want to say about man's existence? What themes can be abstracted from Richard Cory's story?

2- What perception of inward happiness and outward appearance does the poet have? Which does he believe is more important?

3 - Having read the poem, what is the poet's perception of success and inward happiness?

4- The poem is replete with many examples of irony working on multiple levels. Cite some of these specific uses of irony and examine how they enrich the meaning of the poem?

References

Abrams, M. H. *A Glossary of Literary Terms*. Sixth Edition. Fort Worth, Texas: Harcourt Brace College Publishers, 1993.

Alfred, Lord Tennyson. "The Eagle". In *Literature, Structure, Sound, And Sense*. Fifth Edition. Laurence Perrine. Florida: Harcourt Brace Jovanovich, Inc., 1988. 511

Annas, Pamela. *A Disturbance in Mirrors: The Poetry of Sylvia Plath. Contributions in Women's Studies, No. 89*. New York: Greenwood Press, 1988

Aristotle. *Poetics*. Trans. Gerald F. Else. Ann Arbor: University of Michigan Press, 1967.

Baer, William. *Writing Metrical Poetry: Contemporary Lessons for Mastering Traditional Forms*. New York: Writers Digest Books, 2006.

Bennett, Andrew . *Romantic Poets and the Culture of Posterity*. Cambridge: Cambridge University Press, 1999.

Blake, William. "The Chimney Sweeper". In *Literature: Structure, Sound, And Sense*. Fifth Edition. Laurence Perrine. Florida: Harcourt Brace Jovanovich, Inc., 1988. 612

Bloom, Harold, and William Golding, Eds. *Graham Greene: Modern Critical Views Series*. New York: Chelsea House, 1992.

Bloom, Harold. "Introduction" *Modern Critical Interpretations: William Shakespeare's Hamlet*. Ed. By Harold Bloom. New York: Chelsea House, 1986. 1-10

Bloom, Harold. Ed. *Modern Critical Views: John Donne and the Seventeenth-Century Metaphysical Poets*. New York: Chelsea House Publishers, 1986.

Bowers, Fredson. *Hamlet as Minister and Scourge and Other Studies in Shakespeare and Milton*. Charlottesville, VA: University Press of Virginia, 1989.

Bradley, A.C. *Shakespearean Tragedy*. New York: St. Martin's Press, 1966.

Bullinger, E. W. *Figures of Speech Used in the Bible: Explained and Illustrated*. USA: Baker Books, 2003.

Burnett, Mark, Ed. *New Essays on Hamlet*. New York: AMS Press, 1994.

Butscher, Edward. *Sylvia Plath: Method and Madness: A Biography*. Second Edition. Schaffner Press, 2004.

Campion, Thomas. "There is a Garden in Her Face". In *Literature: Structure, Sound, And Sense*. Fifth Edition. Laurence Perrine. Florida: Harcourt Brace Jovanovich, Inc, 1988. 575

Card, Orson. *Elements of Writing Fiction: Characters & Viewpoint*. Cincinnati: Writers Digest Books, 1999.

Carper, Thomas and Derek Attridge. *Meter and Meaning: An Introduction to Rhythm in Poetry*. New York: Routledge, 2003.

Cartwright, Kent. *Shakespearean Tragedy and its Double: The Rhythms of Audience Response*. Pennsylvania State University Press, 1987.

Clark, W. and William Wright, Eds. "The Tragedy of Hamlet" .In *The Complete Works of William Shakespeare*. Volume Two. New York: Nelson Doubleday INC., 1985. 598-634

Cornford, Frances. "The Guitarist Tunes Up". In *Literature: Structure, Sound, And Sense*. Fifth Edition. Laurence Perrine. Florida: Harcourt Brace Jovanovich, Inc, 1988. 565

Corcoran, Neil. *The Cambridge Companion to Twentieth-Century English Poetry*. Cambridge: Cambridge University Press, 2008.

Cuddon, J. A. *The Penguin Dictionary of Literary Terms and Literary Theory*. London: Penguin Books, 1991.

Danson, Lawrence. "Tragic Alphabet." *Modern Critical Interpretations: William Shakespeare's Hamlet*. Ed. by Harold Bloom. New York: Chelsea House, 1986. 65-86.

Dibell, Ansen. *The Elements of Fiction Writing: Plot*. Cincinnati: Writer's Digest Books, 1988.

Dickinson, Emily. *"There Is No Frigate Like A Book"*. In *Literature: Structure, Sound, And Sense*. Fifth Edition. Laurence Perrine. Florida: Harcourt Brace Jovanovich, Inc, 1988. 540

Donne, John. "The Sun Rising". In *Literature: Structure, Sound, And Sense*. Fifth Edition. Laurence Perrine. Florida: Harcourt Brace Jovanovich, Inc, 1988. 606

Donne, John. "Death, Be Not Proud". In *Literature: Structure, Sound, And Sense*. Fifth Edition. Laurence Perrine. Florida: Harcourt Brace Jovanovich, Inc, 1988. 723

Emily Dickinson. "There is No Frigate Like a Book" In *Literature: Structure, Sound, And Sense*. Fifth Edition. Laurence Perrine. Florida: Harcourt Brace Jovanovich, Inc, 1988. 540

Evans, Gareth. *Shakespeare IV*. London: Oxford University Press, 1967.

Feldman, Hans. "The Idea of History in Graham Greene's 'The Destructors". *Studies in Short Fiction*. 19:3. 1982. 241-45.

Fenton, James. *An Introduction to English Poetry*. New York: Farrar, Straus and Giroux Publishers, 2002.

Francis Cornford. "The Guitarist Tunes Up". In *Literature: Structure, Sound, And Sense*. Fifth Edition. Laurence Perrine. Florida: Harcourt Brace Jovanovich, Inc, 1988. 565

Frankovich, Nicholas, ed. *The Columbia Granger's Index to Poetry in Collected and Selected Works*. New York: Columbia University Press, 1996.

Gardner, Helen. *The Metaphysical Poets*. London: Penguin Classics, 1972.

Gill, Stephen. Ed. *William Wordsworth-The Major Works: including The Prelude*. USA: Oxford University Press, 2008.

Glucksberg, Sam. *Understanding Figurative Language: From Metaphor to Idioms*. USA: Oxford University Press, 2001.

Graham Greene. "The Destructors" In *Literature: Structure, Sound, And Sense*. Fifth Edition. Laurence Perrine. Florida: Harcourt Brace Jovanovich, Inc, 1988. 49-61

Granville-Barker, Henry. *Prefaces to Shakespeare*. New York: Hill and Wang, 1970.

Greg, Walter. *Pastoral Poetry and Pastoral Drama*. Indy Publish, 2007.

Grennen, Joseph. *The Poetry of John Donne and the Metaphysical Poets: Monarch Literary Notes*. New York : Monarch Press, 1982.

Harmon, William and Hugh Holman. *A Handbook to Literature*. Seventh Edition. New Jersey: Prentice Hall, 1996.

Hobsbaum, P. *Metre, Rhythm and Verse Form: The New Critical Idiom.* London: Routledge, 1995.

Joseph, C. and Sitterson Jr. *Romantic Poems, Poets, and Narrators.* Kent, Ohio: Kent State University Press, 2000.

Lancashire, Ian. (2002) . *Glossary of Poetic Terms.* Version 3.0 . Department of English, University of Toronto. Internet Document: http://rpo.library.utoronto.ca/display_rpo/poetterm.cfm. Retrieved15/1/2008

Lanham, Richard. *A Handlist of Rhetorical Terms.* Second Edition. Berkeley: University of California Press, 1991.

Lathem, Edward . Ed. "After Apple Picking". In *The Poetry of Robert Frost.* New York: Holt, Rinehart and Winston, 1969.

Lathem, Edward . Ed. "Out, Out-". In *The Poetry of Robert Frost.* New York: Holt, Rinehart and Winston, 1969.

Lathem, Edward . Ed. "The Road Not Taken". In *The Poetry of Robert Frost.* New York: Holt, Rinehart and Winston, 1969.

Marlowe, Christopher. "The Passionate Shepherd to His Love". In *The Golden Treasury of the Best Songs and Lyrical Poems in the English Language.* Francis Palgrave. London: Macmillan, 1875.Internet Document: Bartleby.com, 1999. www.bartleby.com/106/. Retrieved12/1/2008

Morley, John. Ed. *The Complete Poetical Works of William Wordsworth* V1. Whitefish, *Montana,* USA: Kessinger Publishing, LLC, 2007.

Noble, William. *Elements of Writing Fiction: Conflict, Action and Suspense.* Cincinnati: Writers Digest Books, 1999.

Opie, Iona and Opie, Peter. Eds. *The Oxford Book of Narrative Verse.* USA: Oxford University Press, 2004.

Peake, Mervyn. *Figures of Speech.* London: Walker Books Ltd , 2003.

Perrine, Laurence. *Literature: Structure, Sound, And Sense.* Fifth Edition. Florida: Harcourt Brace Jovanovich, Inc., 1988.

Plath, Sylvia . *"Mirror".* In *Literature: Structure, Sound, And Sense.* Fifth Edition. Laurence Perrine. Florida: Harcourt Brace Jovanovich, Inc, 1988. 537

Quinn, Arthur and Barney Quinn. *Figures of Speech: 60 Ways To Turn a Phrase*. London: Lawrence Erlbaum Publishers, 1995.

Rae, Gail. *Guide to Literary Terms*. New York: Research and Educational Association, 1998.

Reuben, Paul . "PAL: Appendix G: Elements of Fiction." *PAL: Perspectives in American Literature: A Research and Reference Guide.* URL:http://web.csustan.edu/english/reuben/pal/append/axg.html Retrieved15/2/2008

Reuben, Paul P. "PAL: Appendix F: Elements of Poetry." *PAL: Perspectives in American Literature: A Research and Reference Guide.* URL:http://www.csustan.edu/english/reuben/pal/append/axf.html Retrieved16/2/2008

Roberts, Edgar and Henry Jacobs. "Glossary of Literary Terms." In *Literature: An Introduction to Reading and Writing*. Sixth Edition. New Jersey: Prentice Hall, 2001. 2028-50.

Roche, Mark. *Tragedy and Comedy: A Systematic Study and a Critique of Hegel*. New York: State University of New York Press, 1997.

Robinson, Arlington. "Richard Cory". In *Literature: Structure, Sound, And Sense*. Fifth Edition. Laurence Perrine. Florida: Harcourt Brace Jovanovich, Inc, 1988. 545

Scholes, Robert. *Elements of Poetry*. USA: Oxford University Press, 1969.

Scholes, Robert, Carl Klaus, Nancy Comley and Michael Silverman. Eds. *Elements of Literature: Essay, Fiction, Poetry, Drama, Film*. New York: Oxford University Press, 1991.

Shakespeare, William. Sonnet 18 "Shall I compare thee to a summer's day?" In *The Complete Works of William Shakespeare*. Volume Two. New York: Nelson Doubleday INC., 1985. 1095

Shakespeare, William. Sonnet 138 "When My Love Swears that She is Made of Truth". In *The Complete Works of William Shakespeare*. Volume Two. New York: Nelson Doubleday INC., 1985. 1111

Shelley, Percy Bysshe. "Ozymandias". In *Literature: Structure, Sound, And Sense*. Fifth Edition. Laurence Perrine. Florida: Harcourt Brace Jovanovich, Inc, 1988. 612

Smith, Kirby. *The Celestial Twins: Poetry and Music Through the Ages*. Amherst :University of Massachusetts Press, 2000.

Stanton, Kay. "Hamlet's Whores". *New Essays on Hamlet*. New York: AMS Press, 1994. 176-181.

Styan, J. L. *Elements of Drama*. England: Cambridge University Press, 1960.

Swain, Dwight. The Elements of Fiction Writing: *Creating Characters*. Cincinnati: Writer's Digest Books, 1990.

Triggs, Jeffery. "A Mirror for Mankind: The Pose of Hamlet with the Skull of Yorick". *The New Orleans Review,* 17(3), Fall 1990, 71-79.

Yeats, William Butler. "Sailing to Byzantium". In *Literature: Structure, Sound, And Sense*. Fifth Edition. Laurence Perrine. Florida: Harcourt Brace Jovanovich, Inc, 1988. *819*

Wainwright, J. *Poetry: The Basics*. London: Routledge, 2004.

A Glossary of Literary Terms

Act: A major division in a play. Each act may have one or more scenes. Greek plays were performed as continuous wholes, without act or scene divisions but were interrupted with comment from the Chorus. Horace appears to have been the first to insist on a five-act structure. Shakespeare's plays are usually divided into five acts, and these acts are themselves divided into individual numbered scenes. The first act sets the scene and provides background information, the second and third acts move the action forward, the fourth act provides the turning point in the action, and the fifth act concludes the story with a fierce climax and provides the *dénouement*.

الفصل في مسرحية : ويشتمل الفصل في المسرحية عادة على خمسة مشاهد وقد يكون العدد اقل او أكثر من ذلك

Action: Two basic meanings may be distinguished: (1) the main story (in cinematic jargon 'story-line') of a play, novel, short story, narrative poem, etc.: (2) the main series of events that together constitute the plot. Action is fundamental to drama, and implies motion forward. Much action is achieved without physical movement on stage, or even without anything being said. An essential part of action is the unfolding of character and plot.

أحداث القصة أو المسرحية

Allegory is a narrative or description having a second meaning beneath the surface one. Although the surface description or narrative is applicable and has its own interest, the poet's main interest is in the second or hidden meaning. Allegory is applicable to all genres of literature: poetry, fiction and drama. Allegory is often used to disguise the meaning of a poem from certain people and reveal it to others. Fables like George Orwell's *Animal Farm* is an allegory

القصة الرمزية هي قصة لها معنى ضمني رمزي بالإضافة إلى المعنى الصريح. و رغم أهمية المعنى الصريح للقصة الظاهر للقارئ فان المعنى الرمزي غير الصريح هو ما يريد كاتب القصة إيصاله للقراء من خلال الرمز وليست أحداث القصة كما يرونها. وتعتبر الخرافات التي تجري على السنة الحيوانات مثل رواية حيوانات المزرعة للروائي جورج اورويل من القصص الرمزية الشهيرة.

Alliteration is the repetition at close intervals of the initial consonant sounds of accented syllables or important words (for example cat- camel, man-moon). Important words and accented syllables beginning with vowels can also alliterate with each other when they all lack the initial consonant sound.

الجناس الإستهلالي هو تكرار نطق الصوت الصحيح consonant في بداية كلمتين أو أكثر في بيت الشعر الواحد

Allusion is a reference, explicit or implicit, to something in previous literature or history.

التلميح هو إشارة الكاتب أو الشاعر في عمله إلى عمل أدبي أو تاريخي آخر. و قد يكون التلميح صريحا بذكر عبارة أو عنوان من العمل الأدبي أو التاريخي الآخر. وقد يكون التلميح مأخوذا من الكتاب المقدس أو الأساطير اليونانية القديمة.

Anapest is a metrical foot consisting of two unaccented syllables followed by one accented syllable (for example understand ﮮ ﮮ —)
Anapestic Meter is a meter in which the majority of feet are anapests

بحر الأنبسط : يشتمل على تفعيلات كل تفعيلة تحتوي على مقطعين قصيرين غير مشددين ومقطعا طويلا مشددا

Antagonist is any force in a story that is in conflict with the protagonist. An antagonist maybe another wicked person or it maybe the whole society. The antagonist can also be any aspect of the physical or social environment, or even a destructive element in the protagonist's own nature. All the forces arrayed against the protagonist whether persons, things, conventions of society or even traits of his own character such as anger, rash or excessive ambition and pride all can act as antagonists.

الخصم : شخصية في صراع دائم مع الشخصية الرئسة في العمل الأدبي . وقد يكون الخصم المجتمع بأكمله، أو قد يكون خصما من داخل الشخصية متمثلا فيه قوى داخلية

Apostrophe (المناجاة) is a figure of speech in which someone absent or dead or something nonhuman is addressed as if it were alive and present and could reply.

المناجاة هي صورة بلاغية يتم فيها مخاطبة شخص غائب أو ميت كما لو كان موجودا بجسده وروحه ومشاعره . كما تعني مخاطبة الجماد أو الحيوان كما لو كان حاضرا يستطيع الحديث مع الشاعر.

Aside is a brief speech in which a character turns from the person he is addressing to speak directly to the audience, a dramatic technique of letting the audience know what a character is really thinking and feeling as opposed to what he pretends to think or feel.(Characters speaking in soliloquies and asides are always telling the truth). **Aside:** a device in common use in drama whereby a character addresses the audience whilst other characters are still on stage. (It contrasts with soliloquy when a character on stage alone addresses the audience.) It is normally the playwright's intention that what is said is said sincerely. An aside is a common dramatic convention in which a character speaks in such a way that some of the characters on stage do not hear what is said, while others do. It may also be a direct address to the audience, revealing the character's views, thoughts, motives and intentions.

الحديث الأحادي الجانبي

Assonance (السجع) is the repetition at close intervals of the vowel sounds of accented syllables or important words (for example hat- ran- cat- , vein – made).

السجع: هو تكرار صوت العلة في الموقع ذاته في كلمتين أو أكثر في بيت الشعر الواحد

Auditory imagery: (Associated with hearing) An image that represents a sound that can be heard.

الصورة الشعرية السمعية هي صورة شعرية تمثل صوتا يمكن سماعه في القصيدة

Ballad is a narrative poem usually set to music; thus, it is a story told in the form of a song. Myths and fairy tales in verse form can be sung as ballads.

قصيدة قصصية غنائية: قصة شعرية مغناه . يمكن لبعض الأساطير والخرافات المكتوبة بلغة الشعر أن تغنى على اعتبار أنها قصائد قصصية غنائية.

Blank Verse: Verse that does not employ a rhyme scheme. Blank verse, however, is not the same as free verse because it employs a meter e.g. *Paradise Lost* by John Milton is written in iambic pentameter, but does not have a fixed rhyme scheme.

الشعر المرسل: شعر غير مقفى إلا انه يلتزم ببحور الشعر المتعارف عليها في الشعر الإنجليزي مثل بحر العنبر و بحر الأنبسط وبحر الداكتيل وبحر التروتشيه وبحر السبوندي.

Characterization

The means by which writers present and reveal character. Although techniques of characterization are complex, writers typically reveal characters through their speech, dress, manner, and actions. Readers come to understand the character Miss Emily in Faulkner's story "A Rose for Emily" through what she says, how she lives, and what she does.

تصوير الشخصيات في العمل الأدبي

Chorus in Greek tragedy:

In Greek tragedy a group of actors speaking or chanting in unison, often in a chant, often while dancing with highly formalized steps. The chorus is an unrealistic theatrical device the function of which is to reveal the tragic hero's inner thoughts and feelings and to comment on the course of action he has taken or is supposed to take.

الكورس أو الخورس : مجموعة من المنشدين والراقصين في مسرحية إغريقية كلاسيكية يقفون جانبا على خشبة المسرح حيث لا ينظر إليهم على أنهم شخصيات في المسرحية. يكمن دور الخورس في التعليق على أحداث المسرحية والإفصاح عن بعض المعلومات التي تتعلق بالأحداث خاصة تلك التي يقوم فيها البطل التراجيدي . كما استخدم الخورس لإظهار انفعالات البطل التراجيدي و أفكاره و الطريق الذي سيسلكه لتحقيق أهدافه. كما يعلق الخورس على أخطاء البطل التراجيدي والقدر الذي يجهله.

Climax

The turning point of the action in the plot of a play or story. The climax represents the point of greatest tension in the work. It includes that part of a story or play at which a crisis is reached and resolution achieved.

ذروة الأحداث في القصة أو المسرحية: النقطة الأكثر أهمية في أحداث القصة أو المسرحية التي تمثل النقطة الأكثر إثارة للقارئ أو المشاهد في المسرح. وهي النقطة التي تصل فيها الأحداث ذروتها وتحل عندها العقدة .

Comedy: a drama which ends in happiness for its characters after a period of trouble. Comedy has its origins in the Greece of the fifth century BC. In modern usage the term now means something that makes an audience or reader laugh; in its original form, it simply meant a play or other work with a happy ending. It is tempting and very wrong, to see comedy as very lightweight. A comic work, with either or both of the above meanings, can make extremely serious points.

الكوميديا أو الملهاة

Conflict is a clash of actions, desires, ideas, or goals in the plot of a story. Conflicts in fiction can either be external or internal. **External conflict** may exist between the main character in the story whom we consider as the hero or protagonist and some other person or persons (man against man); or between the main character and some external force mainly nature, society or malignant fate (man against environment). **Internal conflict** exists within the main character's psyche. It is a conflict between the main character and some destructive element in his own nature (man against himself). Conflict maybe physical, mental, emotional or moral.

الصراع في القصة أو المسرحية : الصراع بين الشخصيات والصراعات الداخلية . يكون الصراع الخارجي بين الشخصية الرئيسة الذي يطلق عليه اسم البطل the hero or protagonist وشخصية أخرى في العمل الأدبي ذاته تسمى الخصم antagonist . أما الصراع الداخلي فيكون داخل الشخصية الرئيسة ، صراع بين الشخصية والقوى والرغبات الداخلية .

Connotation is what a word suggests beyond its denotative meaning. Connotations of a word are its shades of meanings and overtones of meaning.

دلالات الكلمة والمعاني المجازية للكلمة وتشمل الإيحاءات والاستخدامات المجازية والبيانية للكلمة

Consonance (انسجام، تتناغم صوتي) is the repetition at close intervals of the final consonant sounds of accented syllables or important words (for example book-back-block- thick)

الانسجام أو التناغم الصوتي: هو تكرار نطق الصوت الصحيح consonant في نهاية كلمتين أو أكثر في بيت الشعر الواحد

Couplet – two successive lines, usually in the same meter, linked by rhyme and usually situated at the end of a sonnet.

الدوبيت : مقطع شعري يتكون من بيتين من الشعر في نهاية السونيتة الانجليزية

Dactyl is a metrical foot consisting of one accented syllable followed by two unaccented syllables (for example merrily — ᴗ ᴗ)

بحر الداكتيل : يشتمل على تفعيلات كل تفعيلة تحتوي على مقطع طويل مشدد و مقطعين قصيرين غير مشددين

Dactylic Meter is a meter in which the majority of feet are dactyls

Denotation is the basic meaning or dictionary meaning or meanings of a word.

المعنى المعجمي للكلمة أو المعنى الحرفي للكلمة

Developing or dynamic character is a character who undergoes a drastic and permanent change in some aspect of personality or outlook. The change might be slight or major; it may be a change for better or for worse, but it is a significant change noticeable to all readers. There are more static characters in fiction than developing characters. People in real life do not usually change drastically and fiction is supposed to be a mirror of society in this respect. To be convincing to readers the change that occurs within a developing or dynamic character should be sensible and should meet these conditions. First, the change should be within the possibilities of the character who makes it. Second, the change should be sufficiently motivated by the circumstances in which the character is placed. Third, the change must be given sufficient time to take place.

الشخصية النامية أو المتغيرة : شخصية يطرأ عليها تغيير أثناء تنامي أحداث القصة ، وقد تكون التغيرات جسـدية أو نفسـية أو كلاهما معا . وقد يكون التغيير نحو الأفضل أو نحو ا لأسوأ لكنه ظاهر للقارئ

Dialogue

The conversation of characters in a literary work. In fiction, dialogue is typically enclosed within quotation marks. In plays, characters' speech is preceded by their names.   الحوار

Dramatization of Characters:

Dramatization is the presentation of character; his feelings and thoughts merely through speech and action rather than through exposition, analysis, or description by the writer. A story becomes more artistic and interesting when characters are **dramatized**- shown speaking and acting for themselves, as in a play. Readers will not be convinced that a certain character is greedy until they see him behave in such a way that shows his greediness. Great writers rely entirely on indirect presentation in portraying their characters and use direct presentation occasionally.

التعريف الدرامي بالشخصيات في القصة أو المسرحية: ويتم ذلك دون تدخل الكاتب أي من خلال الحوار بين الشخصيات و أفعالهم التي تظهر فيها انفعالاتهم وسماتهم الشخصية

○Elegy:

A lyrical poem of mourning in which the poet laments and mourns the death of someone dear to him (beloved or esteemed person).   An elegy is a reflection on the death of someone. In addition, an elegy may be a type of musical work, usually in a sad and somber attitude.

الرثاء : قصيدة غنائية حزينة يرثي فيها الشاعر شخصا عزيزا عليه . و قد يكون الرثاء عبارة عن مقطوعة موسيقية حزينة ترثي الميت.

Epic:

Poetry written on a grand scale and usually narrative in nature e.g. *The Odyssey* by Homer or *Paradise Lost* by John Milton. The epic celebrates the victories of a nation, the beauty of a country and the major love stories of that nation.   ملحمة شعرية

Eulogy is a speech or writing in praise of a person or thing. Eulogies praise people who are successful and great or very dear to us .Eulogies are said at birthdays, weddings, graduation ceremonies and other happy occasions. However, the term "eulogy" may refer to a funeral oration given in tribute to a person or people who have recently died. Eulogies may be given as part of funeral services.

المديح أو التأبين : كلام قد يكون شعرا أو نثرا ، مكتوبا أو منطوقا في مديح شخص معروف أو قريب من الكاتب . يكثر استخدام المديح في المناسبات السعيدة .و قد يكون المديح لشخص ميت يذكر فيه مناقب الميت وحسناته وأعماله الخيرة في الجنازة أثناء دفنه.

Fable is a story, in prose or verse with animals, plants, inanimate objects, or forces of nature as the dominant characters. In a fable inanimate objects mainly animals are anthropomorphized or given human attributes. All fables illustrate a moral lesson. A good example of a fable is George Orwell's *Animal Farm*.

الفيبل (خرافة الحيوانات) : قصة خرافية ذات مغزى تجري على ألسنة الحيوانات و الجمادات وقوى الطبيعة. مثال : " مزرعة الحيوانات" للكاتب الإنجليزي جورج أورويل

Farce is a very funny comedy based on funny situations and improbable events. A farce aims to entertain the audience by means of unlikely, extravagant, and improbable situations. A farce makes use of verbal and physical humour , absurdity or nonsense and word play. The plot of a farce is usually fast and increases rapidly culminating in an ending which often involves an elaborate chase scene. The characters' performances are highly stylized.

كوميديا الفارس (مسرحية هزلية ساخرة): مسرحية هزلية ساخرة هدفها إضحاك الجمهور وتسليتهم من خلال عرض مواقف طريفة غريبة مبالغ فيها . حيث توضع الشخصيات في مواقف مضحكة مبالغ فيها يغلب عليها طابع التهريج المسرحي.

Figure of Speech is any way of saying something other than the ordinary way. It is a way of saying one thing and meaning another. Through figures of speech the poet can say less or more than what he means, he can say the opposite of what he means, and he can say something other than what he means. There are many figures of speech in English poetry mainly metaphor, simile, personification, apostrophe, synecdoche, metonymy, overstatement, understatement and paradox. الصورة البلاغية

Figurative language is poetic language that employs figures of speech such as metaphor, simile or any other figure of speech. Figurative language is not to be taken literally but should be understood figuratively in the context of the poem. اللغة المجازية (لغة البلاغة)

Flashback (also called **analepsis**) is an interjected scene that takes the narrative back in time from the current point the story has reached. Flashbacks are often used to recount events that happened prior to the story's primary sequence of events or to fill in crucial backstory. The character remembers events that happened in the past and retrieves them in the present.

فلاش باك (الارتجاع الفني) : قطع تسلسل الأحداث الحالية في عمل أدبي لسرد أحداث ماضية .
و يتم ذلك عندما تتذكر شخصية في العمل الأدبي أحداثا ماضية.

Flash-forward (or prolepsis) reveals events that will occur in the future. The technique is used to create suspense in a story, or develop a character.

فلاش فورورد (التنبؤ الفني) : التنبؤ بأحداث القصة و ما سيحدث في النهاية

Flat character is a character who is characterized by one or two traits which can be summed up in a sentence.

الشخصية المسطحة : شخصية بسيطة لها سمة واحدة أو سمتين يمكن تلخيصهما في جملة

Foil character is a minor character whose situation or actions parallel those of a major character, and thus by contrast illuminates the major character.

الشخصية المغايرة : شخصية ثانوية في القصة بعض سماتها و أفعالها توازي أعمال شخصية البطل و من خلال المقارنة تسلط الضوء على العديد من جوانب شخصية البطل

Foreshadowing is a literary technique in which the writer gives hints about plot developments to come later in the story. An example of foreshadowing might be when a character cleans a gun or knife early in the story. Cleaning the deadly weapon might suggest terrible consequences later on (also known as Chekhov's gun).

النذير أو التنبؤ القصصي: أسلوب روائي مسرحي يساهم في التنبؤ بما سيحدث لاحقا في القصة أو المسرحية. كأن تقوم شخصية بجلخ سكين حاد أو تنظيف بندقية . يعتبر هذا العمل نذيرا لارتكاب جريمة . ويعرف هذا الأسلوب المسرحي أيضا ببندقية تشخوف Chekhov's gun نسبة للكاتب الروسي الشهير أنتون تشيخوف.

Free Verse: Verse without formal meter or rhyme patterns. Free verse, instead, relies on the natural rhythms of everyday speech and musical devices. The American poets T.S. Eliot and Ezra Pound are generally regarded as the major poets of English free verse. Free verse is particularly associated with both the imagist and modernist movements.

الشعر الحر: شعر يتحرر من الوزن و بحور الشعر و القافية.

Gustatory imagery: (Associated with tasting) An image that represents a taste of something.

الصورة الشعرية الذوقية هي صورة شعرية لها علاقة بحاسة التذوق. مثل الطعام والشراب والفواكه

Happy ending is an ending in which events turn out well for the sympathetic protagonist at the end of a story or a play. In a story with a happy ending the central character whom readers like and admire fulfills his dreams, achieves his goals and solves all his problems. In a story with a happy ending, the protagonist defeats the villain and good triumphs over evil.

النهاية السعيدة في القصة أو المسرحية

Hubris: This shortcoming or defect in the Greek tragic hero leads him to ignore the warnings of the gods and to transgress their laws and commands. Eventually hubris brings about downfall and nemesis.

الغرور المرضي : خلل سيكولوجي في شخصية البطل التراجيدي تؤدي إلى تدميره .

Iamb is a metrical foot consisting of one unaccented syllable followed by one accented syllable. (for example, the sun ᴗ — **and** refer ᴗ —)

بحر العمبق: يشتمل على تفعيلات كل تفعيلة تحتوي على مقطع غير مشدد قصير يتبعه مقطع قوي مشدد طويل

Iambic Meter is a meter in which the majority of feet are iambs. This is the most frequently used meter in English poetry. بحر العمبق

Imagery is the personification of some experience through language.

الصورة الشعرية

Irony is a literary or rhetorical device which involves a sort of discrepancy or discordance between what is said and what is meant or is generally understood. e.g. Saying: " He's a pretty sight" to a mud-splattered child is an illustration of irony. سخرية أو تهكم

Interior Monologue:

A narrative technique in which characters' thoughts are revealed in a way that appears to be uncontrolled by the author. The interior monologue typically aims to reveal the inner self of a character. It portrays emotional experiences as they occur at both a conscious and unconscious level.

الحوار الداخلي

Kinesthetic imagery:

(Associated with movement or tension in the muscles or joints)
An image that represents movement of people, animals and objects through poetic imagery.

الصورة الحركية هي صورة شعرية تمثل حركة الناس والحيوانات والأشياء في القصيدة. كما تمثل حركة أطراف الإنسان.

Lampoon: (Spoof) A poem that mocks and ridicules a person using satire.

الهجاء: قصيدة يهجو فيها الشاعر شخصا ما بطريقة تهكمية

Literal language

A form of language in which writers and speakers mean exactly what their words denote

المعنى اللغوي الحرفي الذي يخلو من المجاز والصور البلاغية

Litotes is a figure of speech employing ironic understatement which affirms something by denying or negating its opposite e.g. "She is not a bad actress" to mean she is a good or even excellent actress.

العبارة التهكمية المنفية: صيغة بلاغية يعبر فيها عن الموجب بضده النفي.

Lyric is a form of poetry that expresses a subjective, personal point of view. The Greek word lyric means a song sung with a lyre .

قصيدة غنائية : قصيدة غنائية تعبر عن أحاسيس الشاعر وانفعالاته و رؤيته للحياة . و في اللغة اليونانية تعني كلمة lyric القصيدة الغنائية التي تغنى مع ألحان القيثارة.

Major characters—those characters whom we see and learn about the most mainly the protagonist and the other characters with major parts in the play or story.

الشخصيات الرئيسة في القصة أو المسرحية

Melodrama is a kind of tragedy that features sensational incidents, emphasizing plot at the expense of characterization, relying on cruder conflicts. A melodrama often has a happy ending mainly the protagonist triumphs over the antagonist and good triumphs over evil.

الميلودراما أو المشجاة : مسرحية تراجيدية عاطفية تعتمد على الأحداث والعقدة أكثر مما تعتمد على تصوير الشخصيات و
تكثر فيها الصراعات و تنتهي غالبا بنهاية سعيدة

Metaphor is a figure of speech in which an implicit comparison is made between two things essentially unlike. There are four forms of metaphor. (1) A metaphor in which the literal term and the figurative term are named; (2) A metaphor in which the literal term is named and the figurative term is implied; (3) A metaphor in which the literal term is implied and the figurative term is named; (4) A metaphor in which both the literal term and the figurative term are implied. For example: She is an angel.

الاستعارة المجازية تتضمن مقارنة بين شيئين غير متشابهين. ومن أشهر أنواع الاستعارة المجازية الاستعارة التصريحية التي
يكون فيها المشبه والمشبه به مذكورين بشكل صريح.

Metaphorical language is a form of language in which writers and speakers use figurative language to intensify their language.

لغة المجاز هي اللغة التي تستعمل الصور البلاغية

Meter is regularized rhythm, an arrangement of the poetic language in which the accents occur at apparently equal intervals in time. بحر الشعر

Metonymy is a figure of speech in which some significant aspect or detail of an experience is used to represent the whole experience. Metonymy (the use of something closely related for the thing actually meant) is to be distinguished from synecdoche (the use of the part for the whole).

الكناية هي صورة بلاغية تتمثل في الإشارة إلى صفة من صفات الشيء للإشارة إلى الشيء كله .

E.g. We often speak of a king as "the crown" which is closely associated with kingship . e.g Sweat is a metonymy for hard labour

مثال : "ليلى فتاة ناعمة الكفين" كناية عن الأنوثة والرقة والجمال والعيش الرغيد والرفاهية

Minor characters—those figures who fill out the story but who do not figure prominently in it. The characters we see and learn about the least in a story or a play.

الشخصيات الثانوية في القصة أو المسرحية مثل ساعي البريد أو السائق أو النادل

Monologue: A term used in a number of senses, with the basic meaning of a single person speaking alone - with or without an audience. Most prayers, much lyric verse and all laments are monologues, but, apart from these, four main kinds can be distinguished: a) monodrama, (b) soliloquy, (c) solo addresses to an audience in a play, d) dramatic monologue - a poem in which there is one imaginary speaker addressing an imaginary audience

المونولوج : مناجاة المرء نفسه على خشبة المسرح . مشهد مسرحي يؤديه ممثل واحد

Multiple conflict is a multilayered and complex conflict in which the protagonist finds himself in conflict with other many people, with society or nature, and with himself, all at the same time. Sometimes he is aware of these conflicts, but in most cases he seems to be ignorant and unaware of them.

الصراعات المعقدة : يكون فيها البطل في صراع مع مجموعة من الأطراف معا . فيكون في صراع مع شخصية أو شخصيات أخرى في العمل الأدبي، وفي نفس الوقت في صراع مع المجتمع والقدر والظروف المحيطة به تتكالب عليه لتدميره.

Ode is a kind of stately and elaborate poetry in the form of a song that can be sung by a chorus. *Ode to a Nightingale* by John Keats and *Ode to a Skylark* by Shelley are both examples of Odes.

قصيدة من الشعر الغنائي: قصيدة غنائية تغنى من قبل خورس أو مجموعة مغنيين.

Olfactory imagery: (Associated with smelling) An image that represents a smell that can be sniffed or smelt.

الصورة الشعرية الشمية هي صورة شعرية تمثل رائحة يمكن شمها أثناء قراءة القصيدة مثل رائحة زهرة.

Organic imagery: (Associated with internal sensation) An image that represents an internal organic sensation such as hunger, thirst, fatigue, or nausea.

الصورة الشعرية العضوية هي صورة شعرية تمثل إحساسا داخليا كالجوع والعطش والتعب والغثيان

Overstatement (Also known as hyperbole) is a figure of speech in which exaggeration is used in the service of truth.

المبالغة : صورة بلاغية تتمثل في المبالغة في الوصف

Oxymoron -(antithesis) is a figure of speech that combines two normally contradictory terms. It is used intentionally, for rhetorical effect, and the contradiction is only apparent, as the combination of terms provides a strange expression of some concept, such as "cruel to be kind". The most common form of oxymoron involves an adjective-noun combination. For example, the following line from Tennyson's *Idylls of the King* contains two oxymorons: "And faith unfaithful kept him falsely true" and a cheerful pessimist.

الطباق أو الإرداف الخلفي : كلمتين متناقضتين .كقول أحدهم : " المتشائم المبتهج"

Paradox is a statement or situation containing apparently contradictory elements.   التناقض الوهمي

Paradoxical statement is a figure of speech in which an apparently self-contradictory statement is nevertheless found to be true and does indeed make sense.

عبارة التناقض الوهمي هو صورة بلاغية أو عبارة تتضمن تناقضا وهميا في ظاهرها لكنها
في واقع الأمر صحيحة.

Parody is a literary work created to mock, comment on, or poke fun at an original literary work, its subject, or author, by means of humorous or satiric imitation.

(البارودي)المحاكاة الساخرة: عمل أدبي يحاكي عمل أدبي آخر بطريقة ساخرة مثيرة للضحك والهزل

Personification is a figure of speech in which human attributes are given to an animal, an object, or a concept. e.g. His religion tells him he can't drink wine.

التشخيص صورة بلاغية تتمثل فيه مخاطبة الحيوان والجماد والأشياء كما لو كانوا بشرا يتكلمون ويشعرون. كما يتضمن
التشخيص منح الحيوانات والجماد والأشياء بعض صفات البشر وانفعالاتهم.

Play: A dramatic work designed to be presented on a stage (or in a television studio) and performed by actor and actress.   المسرحية

Plot: Sequence of events in a play, poem or work of fiction; and, further, the organization of incident and character in such a way as to induce curiosity and suspense in the spectator or reader.

الحبكة : أحداث القصة أو المسرحية التي تشكل القصة. وتشمل الحبكة على كل ما يقوله أو تقوم به الشخصيات في القصة
أو المسرحية

Protagonist is the central character in the story. He can be either sympathetic or unsympathetic. The protagonist is the main character in a story whom we follow with interest and share his dreams, ambitions, fears and we even share him his conflicts and the way he struggles to deal with them.

البطل أو الشخصية الرئيسة في العمل الأدبي أسواء كانت مسرحية أو رواية أو قصة قصيرة

Pun (or **paronomasia**) is a phrase that deliberately exploits confusion between similar-sounding words for humorous or rhetorical effect. A pun is a play on word for rhetorical effects. E. g "son" and "sun", "I" and "eye", "skip" and "escape"

التورية: تلاعب لفظي بكلمات متشابهة بالأصوات

Rhyme is the repetition of the accented vowel sound and all succeeding sounds in important words (for example old-cold- fold-hold, cat-fat-sat)

القافية: تكرار أصوات العلة المنبرة والأصوات التالية لهذه الأصوات في نهاية أبيات القصيدة الشعرية المتتالية

Round character is a character with complex and many-sided traits.

الشخصية المركبة : شخصية معقدة التركيب ذات سمات عديدة يصعب فهمها وتحتاج إلى تحليل دقيق

Scansion is the process of measuring verse, that is, of marking accented and unaccented syllables, dividing the lines into feet, identifying the metrical pattern of a poem, and noting significant variations from that metrical pattern.

تقطيع الشعر و وزنه بالموازين العروضية لمعرفة بحر الشعر والتفعيلات التي تتكون منها القصيدة

Scene: A sub-division of an act in a play or an opera or other theatrical entertainment. مشهد في مسرحية

Setting is the time and place of a literary work that establish its context. The stories of James Joyce are set in Dublin, Ireland in the early 20th century.

مكان وزمان المشهد المسرحي أو الروائي: المكان والزمان اللذان تجري فيهما أحداث القصة أو المسرحية والسياق التاريخي والاجتماعي والثقافي المحيط بأحداث القصة

Simile is a figure of speech in which an explicit comparison is made between two things essentially unlike. The comparison is made explicit by the use of some word or phrase as *like, as, than, similar to, resembles,* or *seems.* **e.g.** He is brave like a lion

التشبيه صورة بلاغية صريحة يتم فيها مقارنة أو تشبيه شيئين مختلفين باستخدام أداة تشبيه صريحة.

Simple conflict is single conflict that can be identified easily even by immature readers. The protagonist is in conflict with one antagonist at a time. However, the protagonist may be in conflict with one person or he might be in conflict with the society where he lives or he might be in conflict with environment and fate or he might be in conflict with a destructive flaw un his psyche which he seems unable to control or live with.

الصراع البسيط في المسرحية أو الرواية : صراع واحد يمكن للقراء معرفته بسهولة . حيث يكون البطل في صراع واحد مع شخصية واحدة فقط في   العمل الأدبي . فقد يكون الخصم شخصية أخرى أو المجتمع أو القدر أو سمة مدمرة في شخصيته لا يمكنه السيطرة عليها.

Soliloquy "thinking out aloud" is a speech, often of some length, in which a character, alone on the stage, expresses his thoughts and feelings. In this way the audience is given information in a form of dramatic irony not revealed to the other characters in the play. Its advantages are inestimable because it enables a dramatist to convey direct to an audience important information about a particular character: his state of mind and heart, his most intimate thoughts and feelings, his motives and intentions.

السوليلوكوي : مناجاة المرء نفسه على خشبة المسرح من خلال خطاب طويل وهو يقف وحده على خشبة المسرح يلقيـه على الجمهور يعبر فيه عن أفكاره وانفعالاته و رؤيته للحياة والطبيعة البشرية . وهو أسلوب درامي قديم يمكن المشاهدين في المسرح من معرفة مكنونات الشخصية الرئيسة و انفعالاته وطريقة تفكيره.

Sonnet is a poem with a fixed form of fourteen lines, normally iambic pentameter, with a rhyme scheme conforming to or approximating one of the two main types –the Italian sonnet or the Shakespearean or English sonnet.

السونيتة : قصيدة تتكون من أربعة عشر بيتا . حيث تتكون السونيتة من ثلاثة مقاطع شعرية في كل مقطع شعري أربعة أبيات وبيتين شعريين في النهاية يسميان couplet

Spondee is a metrical foot consisting of two equally accented syllables (for example true blue — —)

بحر السبوندي : يشتمل على تفعيلات تحتوي كل تفعيلة على مقطعين طويلين مشددين

Spondaic Meter is a meter in which the majority of feet are spondees

Stanza is a group of lines in a poem. The metrical pattern of a stanza or its rhyme scheme is repeated throughout the poem.

المقطع الشعري : مجموعة من الأبيات الشعرية تقع في مجموعة واحدة من القصيدة و تتردد في جميع القصيدة .

Static character is the same sort of person at the end of the story as at the beginning. A static character does not change throughout the course of action.

الشخصية الثابتة غير المتغيرة: شخصية لا يطرأ عليها تغيير خلال القصة منذ البداية حتى النهاية حيث تحتفظ بسماتها دون تغيير .

Stock character is a stereotyped figure who has appeared so often in a large number of stories that his character is well known and fully understood by all readers. The brilliant detective with bizarre and eccentric habits i.e. Sherlock Holmes, the handsome international spy of mysterious background, the smart courageous hero, the seductive coquettish woman , the comic English man with a monocle and an exaggerated oxford accent and the sinister wicked villain who wants to destroy the hero; all these characters are stock characters who are quite recognizable to all readers because they have read about or have seen such prototypes in various previous works of literature.

الشخصية النمطية : شخصية مسطحة معروفة للكثير من القراء لكثرة تكرارها في الأعمال الأدبية مثل شخصية المحقق في القصص البوليسية .

Stream of consciousness: **(Train of thoughts)** is a literary technique used by many modernist novelists and dramatists to portray the character's thought processes and subjective feelings in the form of interior monologue and flashbacks. The stream of consciousness technique is used to show what goes on inside the character's mind and what feelings roam his heart.

تيار الوعي: أسلوب روائي مسرحي ظهر في الأدب الحديث نتيجة للتأثر بعلم النفس، يستخدمه الروائيون وكتاب المسرح في إظهار عمليات التفكير التي تدور في عقل الشخصية و الأحاسيس والمشاعر التي تختلج قلبه.

Suspense is a quality of a literary work that makes the reader eager to know what happens next and how it will end. Suspense becomes quite interesting when the readers' curiosity is combined with anxiety about the fate of the central character whom they find sympathetic. Suspense is often linked with certain types of fiction that rely heavily on such an element of fiction mainly murder mysteries or detective stories in which the reader goes on reading the story to find out who committed the crime.

التشويق : عنصر من عناصر القصة تدفع القارئ لقراءة العمل الأدبي بأكمله حتى النهاية لمعرفة ما سيحصل في نهايته. يكثر استخدام عنصر التشويق في القصص البوليسية لمعرفة القاتل الذي ارتكب الجريمة.

Symbol can be defined as something that means more than what it is. Besides its literal meaning, an object has a figurative or symbolical meaning. Thus, a symbol is a figure of speech which may be read both literally and figuratively.

الرمز هو نوع من أنواع المجاز الأدبي له معنيين : معنى حرفي صريح ومعنى رمزي خفي. و يعبر العديد من الشعراء والكتاب عن أفكارهم وعواطفهم من خلال الرموز والإيحاءات. و يستخدم هؤلاء الكتاب والشعراء الشخصيات والأماكن والأشياء بطريقة رمزية

Synecdoche is a figure of speech in which a part is used for the whole.

الكناية أو المجاز المرسل هي الإشارة إلى الجزء بدلا من الكل

e.g. hands for manual workers   الأيدي العاملة

The enemy's eyes   عيون العدو يقصد بها الجواسيس

Tactile imagery:

(Associated with touching) An image that represents touching such as hardness, softness, wetness, or heat or cold.

الصورة الشعرية اللمسية هي صورة شعرية تمثل شيئا يمكن لمسه أو مسكه مثل لمس شيء صلب أو ناعم أو شيء رطب أو حار أو بارد.

Theme is simply the central idea in a literary work. The theme in a work of fiction is its dominant idea and central insight. The theme represents the writer's perception of life and human nature.

المغزى : الفكرة الرئيسة من القصة أو المسرحية و تمثل رؤية الكاتب للحياة والطبيعة البشرية و تكون في الغالب ضمنية وليست صريحة.

Tragedy is usually a play with an unhappy ending, though both poetry and novels can contain strong elements of tragedy.   التراجيديا أو المأساة

Tragic flaw: Traditionally that defect in a tragic hero or heroine which leads to their downfall. To all intents and purposes a synonym for the Greek *hamartia* .

الخطأ التراجيدي : خلل سيكولوجي في شخصية البطل التراجيدي يؤدي إلى تدميره ، وفي غالب الأحيان يكون خطأ سيكولوجي في شخصيته يصعب السيطرة عليه مثل الغرور والتسرع في إصدار ا لأحكام. وفي التراجيديا الإغريقية يطلق عليه hamartia

Tragicomedy: A play which mingles tragic and comic elements in its plot and characterization   الدراما التراجيديا الكوميدية

Trochaic Meter is a meter in which the majority of feet are trochees (— ᴗ one accented syllable followed by one unaccented syllable)
Trochee is a metrical foot consisting of one accented syllable followed by one unaccented syllable (for example doctor — ᴗ)

بحر التروشيه: يشتمل على تفعيلات كل تفعيلة تحتوي على مقطع قوي مشدد طويل يتبعه مقطع غير مشدد قصير

Trope is a figure of speech that involves changing the sense of a word from its literal meaning to its metaphorical meaning or meanings. Trope involves using the word metaphorically rather than literally. Figures of speech such as similes, metaphors, paradoxes, and ironies are examples of tropes.

البيان : لغة المجاز والتشبيه في لغة الشعر

Understatement is a figure of speech that consists of saying less than one means, or saying what one means with less force than the occasion warrants

التصريح المكبوت هو صورة بلاغية تتمثل في أن يقول الشاعر أقل مما يعنيه أو أن يصف الشاعر شيئا مستخدما وصفا اقل شأنا من الموصوف.

Unhappy ending, on the other hand, is an ending in which events turn out unhappily for the sympathetic protagonist at the end of a story or a play. In stories with unhappy endings, the protagonist dies at the end of the story or loses his mistress or something bad happens to him.

النهاية غير السعيدة أو الحزينة في العمل الأدبي

Visual imagery: (Associated with seeing)
Images or poetic mental pictures seen in the mind's eye. The reader of poetry can discern such visual images through seeing or forming an imaginary mental picture of the poetic experience. Most images in poetry belong to this kind of imagery for it occurs most frequently and heavily in most poetry.

الصورة الشعرية المرئية هي صورة شعرية عقلية يمكن رؤيتها أو تخيلها أو تشكيلها في العقل أثناء قراءة القصيدة. وهي أكثر أنواع الصور الشعرية استخداما في الشعر.

Printed in the United States
By Bookmasters